IMAGES OF ENGLAND

MIDDLESBROUGH
A CENTURY OF CHANGE

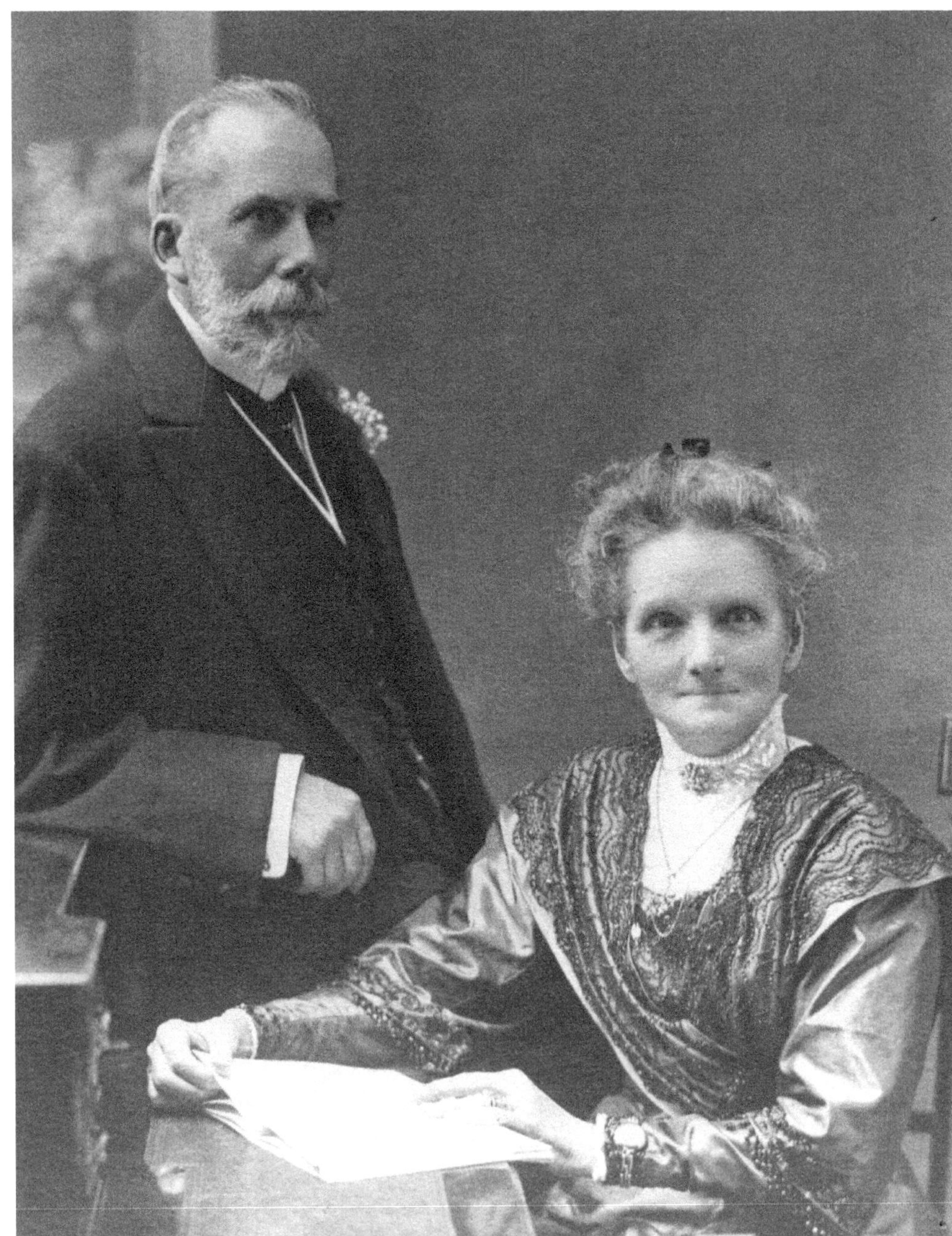

IMAGES OF ENGLAND

MIDDLESBROUGH
A CENTURY OF CHANGE

IAN STUBBS AND JENNY PARKER

TEMPUS

Frontispiece: Mr and Mrs Amos Hinton.

First published 2006
Reprinted 2008, 2013

The History Press
The Mill, Brimscombe Port,
Stroud, Gloucestershire, GL5 2QG
www.thehistorypress.co.uk

© Ian Stubbs and Jennifer Parker, 2006

The right of Ian Stubbs and Jennifer Parker to be identified as the Authors
of this work has been asserted in accordance with the
Copyrights, Designs and Patents Act 1988.

British Library Cataloguing in Publication Data.
A catalogue record for this book is available from the British Library.

ISBN 978 0 7524 3720 0

Typesetting and origination by
The History Press.
Printed in Great Britain.

Contents

Acknowledgements

This volume of photographs is but the latest in a long tradition of publications about the history of Middlesbrough supported by Middlesbrough Council. Former librarians and curators have contributed hugely over the past century to the historical heritage of Middlesbrough by delving into the abundant and priceless resources of the town's library and museum local history collections, and it is trusted that this work may add to that legacy.

When Ian suggested to me that we take up Tempus' offer to produce a volume in their successful series *Images of England* about old Middlesbrough, utilising the photographic collections of our respective institutions, I was initially somewhat sceptical. I was convinced that previous authors had made free with the contents of our collections to the extent of leaving very few images that were not already widely known and recognised. How wrong I was! The process of producing and editing this book has been a wonderful journey of exploration and discovery, uncovering unconsidered treasures from familiar sources.

The title of this book, *Middlesbrough: A Century of Change*, takes as its central theme the town's history and development from the date of the granting of its county borough status in 1889 to date. The townscape has naturally altered considerably over that length of time and many familiar landmarks have disappeared. We have therefore taken the opportunity to indicate where artefacts and documents associated with vanished parts of the townscape may now be discovered. The pictures published in the book are taken almost exclusively from the collections at the Dorman Museum and the central Reference Library. We have been at pains to select illustrations that reflect not only that century of change but also the important contribution that Middlesbrough's cultural institutions – the museum and library services – have made to the town in that period.

Exceptions to that rule are fully acknowledged in the text. Recognition is due to the Bodleian Library for the copy of the Buck drawing of the Middlesbrough Priory buildings. Over the years many individuals have donated images to our collections, which it would be impossible to acknowledge individually but without whom this book could never have been made.

We are grateful to our respective heads of service, Godfrey Worsdale and Chrys Mellor, for allowing the prosecution of this venture, to Larry Bruce, Ken Sedman and Phil Philo for releasing us from other duties to work on this project and to all our colleagues in the museum and library for their support. Particular thanks are due to Ken Sedman for his patience in what proved to be a lengthy process when at times the end seemed to be perpetually just out of sight.

We have tried our best to research all these images thoroughly before allowing them to appear in the book. To all those who have helped with that process much gratitude is due. We would like to thank especially Paul Stephenson for the use of a number of photographs, and also to thank Jenny and Geoff Braddy and other members of the Cleveland and Teesside Local History Society for their inspiration, expertise and encouragement.

We the authors, however, remain solely responsible for any errors of identification which may have crept in.

Jenny Parker
Reference Department
Central Library
Victoria Square
Middlesbrough

www.middlesbrough.gov.uk

Ian Stubbs
Assistant Curator
Dorman Museum
Linthorpe Road
Middlesbrough

www.dormanmuseum.co.uk

Introduction

Middlesbrough is entirely a product of Victorian enterprise. When Gladstone visited Middlesbrough in 1862 he famously described the town as an 'infant Hercules'. At that time settlement was still largely confined to the area now known as St Hilda's and a small area beyond the railway. Yet by 1889, when Middlesbrough became a county borough, the infant had reached maturity. Its foundations were firmly resting on the economic prosperity brought by the industries of iron and steelmaking, shipbuilding and the railways. Over the next hundred or so years, although the area covered by settlement expanded and infilled, the nature of that settlement remained largely stable. Middlesbrough rapidly developed a sense of civic pride, perhaps best displayed in corporate expressions of self-commemoration such as the jubilee in 1881 and the centenary celebrations in 1931, and through hosting royal visits. There is a great affection for the surviving townscape features even though few very old buildings remain.

The land on which the early streets of Middlesbrough were laid out originally formed part of the lordship of Acklam, belonging to the Boynton and then later the Hustler families of Acklam Hall. During the medieval period the monks of Whitby Abbey had maintained a property there which, after the Dissolution, had been allowed to fall into disrepair. The Middlesbrough part of the estate was sold to William Chilton in 1807 and he, in turn, sold 500 acres in 1829 to a group of enterprising Quaker businessmen associated with the Stockton & Darlington Railway Co., under the chairmanship and guidance of Joseph Pease, with the express purpose of developing the land at what was then called Port Darlington on the south bank of the river into coal-shipping staithes. The intention was to export coal from the Durham coalfield and to develop a port that would rival Sunderland or Newcastle.

Pease quickly realised the potential of the site for further development. A subsidiary company was set up, known as the Owners of the Middlesbrough Estate, to develop the land. The Owners commissioned the laying out of a purpose-built town, to be called Middlesbrough, under their land surveyor, Richard Otley. Otley's plan was based on a roman fort, with a gridiron pattern. It had a civic space at its centre, with room for a small town hall and church, and four main radiating arterial streets: North, South, East and West. The land was parcelled out in plots for private development. The first house was built in West Street in April 1830.

Development was rapid but piecemeal. By 1853, when Middlesbrough was granted its charter, the population was estimated at 9,332 and 1,359 houses had already been erected, according to the census of 1851. Settlement was largely confined to the area north of the present railway line until the 1880s, with a few notable exceptions such as Albert Park and the Royal Exchange building, built in 1868, and the railway station and Middlesbrough High School, built in 1877.

The building of the new municipal buildings and town hall, which was officially opened by the Prince and Princess of Wales in the year in which Middlesbrough became designated a county borough, marks a convenient watershed in the history and development of the town. By this date there were over 13,000 inhabited houses forming the community of Middlesbrough.

A revival in civic pride is embodied in G.G. Hoskins' design for the town hall building, with its gothic flamboyance and a clock tower 170 feet high. The project took over five years to bring to fruition and cost an astonishing £130,000 to erect. It was designed from the outset to act as a focus for the expression of municipal social and cultural activity within the town, a function which it continues to promote to this day. Speaking at the opening ceremony on 23 January 1889, the Prince of Wales echoed Gladstone's sentiment when he alluded to the town's rapid rise from its origins as a decaying farming community in a little over fifty years: 'your borough is young in years but the great increase in its population since 1841, and the wonderful development of its commerce are most remarkable and have given it already a position usually reserved for age'. He continued, 'It may be truly said that at the present moment Middlesbrough ranks amongst the highest reputations – not of England only but of the World for the importance of her great and varied inductors, especially her vast iron trade.'

Middlesbrough's prosperity is founded on the twin pillars of commerce and industry. Its spectacular early growth owed its success to the ironworks set up by Bolckow and Vaughan in 1841. Within ten years over forty blast furnaces lined the Tees marshes, producing over 84,000 tons by 1855, rising to 640,000 tons in 1872. During the 1870s there was a slump, and iron production gave way to steel production. A total of 1,213,544 tons of steel were manufactured in the north-east by 1918. Coal shipped from the riverside staithes rose from just 281 tons in 1831-32 to a staggering 1,500,374 tons by 1840.

There were also other industries. An earthenware company, the Middlesbrough Pottery Co., was founded in 1834 in Commercial Street, with the first kiln fired in April of that year. Exporting to Gibraltar, it was in production until 1857. The Linthorpe Pottery also proved a short-lived success in the 1880s. The flourishing of the iron and steel trades also fed other industries. Shipyards sprang up: Harkness, Dixon's, Rake Kimber, J.G. Holmes and the Cleveland Dockyard dominated the scene along with the ancillary industries of the coal fitters, mast makers, millers, sailcloth makers, wire works, breweries, shipping companies and printers. Later on salt works and chemical production developed.

The modern world is still stamped with the name of the town. Girders make up bridges throughout Africa, Asia, and Australia, and steel structured buildings around the globe bear the legend 'Dorman Long & Co. Ltd, Middlesbrough, England'. Landor Praed, the Newcastle journalist, summed up the situation eloquently in 1860 when he wrote:

the iron of Eston has diffused itself all over the world. It furnishes railways to Europe; it runs past Neapolitan and Papal dungeons; it startles the bandit in his haunts in Cicilia; it crosses the wild jungles of Africa; it streaks the prairies of America; it stretches over the plains of India; it surprises the Belochees; it pursues the peggunus of Gangontri. It has crept out of the Cleveland Hills, where it has slept since the Roman days, and now, like a strong and invincible serpent, coils itself round the world; and every articulation in its burnished body bears throughout our remotest lands the stamp of the industrious and energetic hands of Middlesbrough.

Industrial growth fed commercial success. A number of food trade giants started trading in Middlesbrough: Amos Hinton and Joseph Winterschladen first operated within the town, feeding its growing population and contributing to the civic life of the young community.

An efficient transport network was vital to Middlesbrough's success. Both passengers and freight made use of the river, crossing by ferry until the building of the Transporter Bridge in 1911, and later the Newport Bridge in 1934. The railways which had brought industry to Middlesbrough in the first place were developed to transport iron ore to the plants and finished iron and steel to outside markets. Roads were less important and toll bars were in place on some of the major arteries until 1916. Public road transport for those living further outside the commercial centre was provided from 1873 by the Middlesbrough & Stockton Tramways Co., and later by a series of private bus and coach operators. Middlesbrough's first car owner took to the roads in 1896 but motor vehicles remained rare for non-commercial use until after the Second World War.

As a result of the Owner's limited original vision, Middlesbrough very early on displayed a social disparity between the densely packed and often poorly serviced dwellings of the industrial workforce, characterised by Lady Florence Bell as the 'little brown houses' of the St Hilda's area, and the more mixed suburban developments south of the railway line. Otley's original plan envisaged up to 123 spacious plots with twelve wide streets, and some attempt at building control through the drawing up of deeds of covenant which were to be adhered to. Yet by the mid-1850s the majority of plots had been built on and new streets added. Commercial properties sat cheek by jowl with tightly packed residential dwellings and industrial premises.

It was the boost given by the discovery of ironstone deposits in the Cleveland Hills in 1850 that stimulated a second rapid expansion of the town. Numerous small builders acquired plots both sides of the railway, which were developed in an entirely unstructured manner, principally following Albert Road and Commercial Road, and eventually running out along the main arterial routes of Newport, Linthorpe and Marton Roads. Building was entirely driven by the need to provide accommodation to house the huge influx of workers to the iron industry. Sanitary provision was rudimentary and, perhaps inevitably, disease flourished. It was not until the enactment of the Public Health Act of 1875 that housing bylaws were created to regulate building standards.

The extension of Middlesbrough's boundaries after 1890 was prompted by continued population growth and the resultant creeping encroachment into the middle-class suburban enclaves on the southern outskirts, particularly the areas round the park, Grove Hill and Linthorpe Village. By 1891 the population had reached over 73,000, and it continued to rise steeply until the First World War. As the possibility of suburban living came within the achievable aspirations of even the lower-middle classes, new Edwardian terraces were erected to cater for their requirements. The borough boundaries were

regularly extended from 1866 to 1933, and more recently with the creation of the
Teesside and Cleveland local authorities to include North Ormesby, and parts of Marton,
Eston, Stainton and Acklam parishes. Farms formerly isolated from the urban centre,
such as Old Gate, Linthorpe or Kensington, were swallowed up and today only street
names record their former existence. Those further out gave rise to modern housing
estates such as Berwick Hills, Brambles Farm or Hemlington.

Little or no provision for public amenities was envisaged in the original town plan
for Middlesbrough, with the exception of numerous beerhouses. Not surprisingly,
drunkenness and disorder became an early problem. The only public amenity in the early
years was the Mechanics' Institute in Durham Street. Most schools, churches and other
facilities were provided by religious and philanthropic organisations. The first hospital
– it claimed to be the first cottage hospital in the country – was opened in 1859. North
Ormesby Hospital, the North Riding Infirmary, Middlesbrough General, the Cleveland
Asylum, the Fever and Isolation Hospitals, St Luke's Mental Hospital and the South
Cleveland Hospital have followed since. The main period of public building was to be
after 1890. The Dorman Museum was opened in 1904, and the central public library
in 1912. The town also developed a thriving social life with theatres, music halls and
cinemas being built up until the 1930s.

Growth inevitably ceased during the Second World War, following the economic
slump of the 1930s. Revitalisation was brought to a townscape suffering from blitz
damage and the economic stagnation of the mid-twentieth century by the adoption
of the Max Lock Plan in 1946. Housing density was to be thinned, new suburbs
built, transport links improved, industrial blight ameliorated, industry diversified,
and new amenities provided. It is from the post-war period that so much of our
current townscape originates – our shopping centres, libraries, cinemas, educational
establishments and office blocks.

Today Middlesbrough is engaged in an attempt to re-invent itself for the twenty-
first century, following the decline of its traditional industries, as a commercial and
cultural centre for the North-East region. The government has changed. The town was
one of the first to opt for an elected mayor and cabinet and in 2001 former 'Robocop
policeman' Ray Mallon, an exponent of zero tolerance policing, was elected as mayor.
The town is now home to many landmark structures: world famous bridges, the
Riverside Premier League football ground, a new university housing leading digital
media facilities, the state-of-the-art James Cook University Hospital, which is the biggest
single-site hospital in Europe, MIMA, the new Middlesbrough Institute of Modern Art,
the award-winning Captain Cook Birthplace and Dorman Museums, public sculptures,
new schools, revitalised and internationally recognised shops and housing developments
and the transformed area around the former Middlesbrough Dock, part of the
Middlehaven redevelopment.

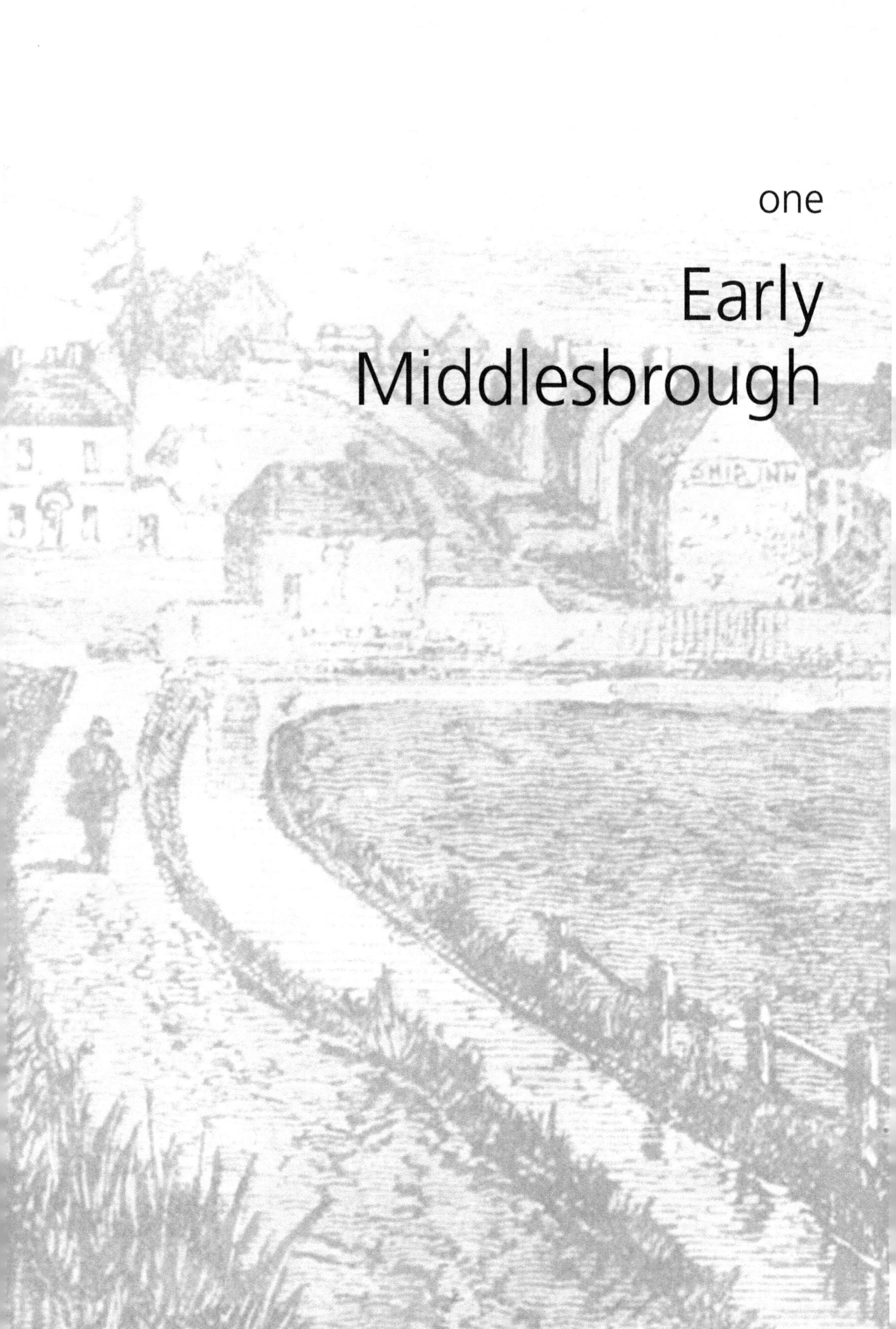

one

Early Middlesbrough

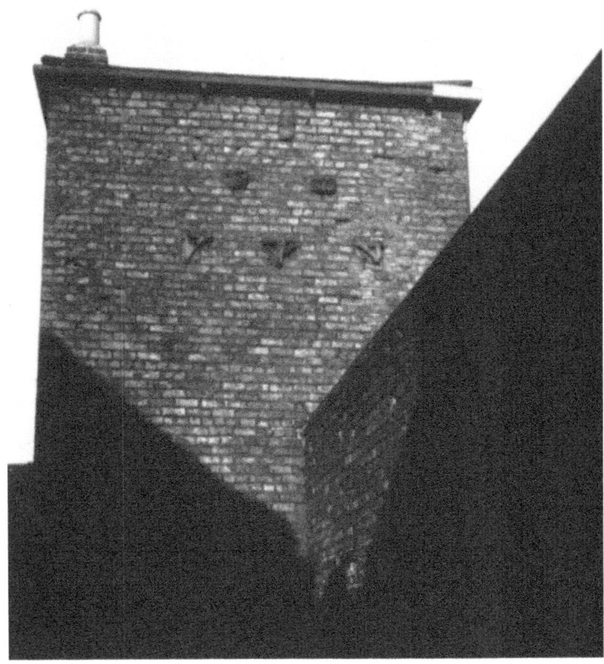

This unprepossessing wall once contained all that has survived of the medieval monastic buildings of early Middlesbrough, incorporated into the end wall of the Middlesbrough Hotel (built in 1846). It was demolished in 1963: the fragments were taken to the Dorman Museum where they are currently on display.

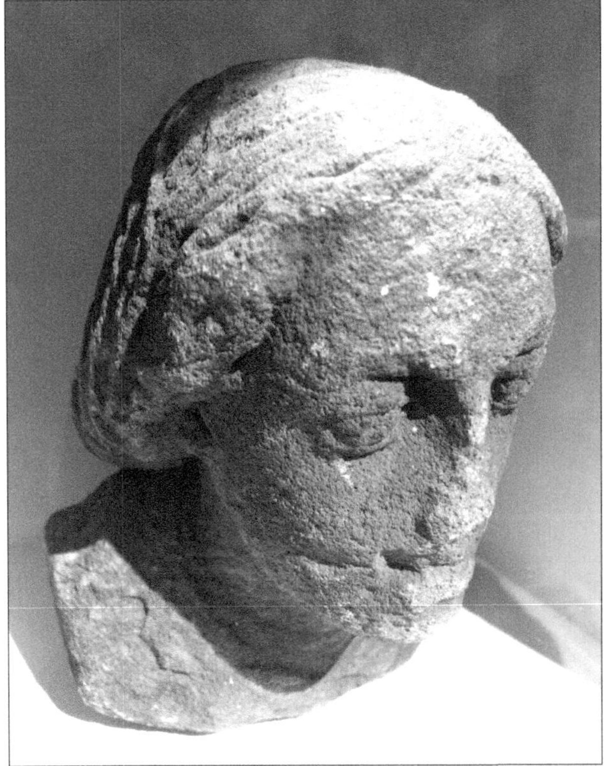

A carved stone head, also believed to have come from the medieval priory. It was reportedly built into the wall of a former brewery in 1889, which was demolished before 1911, and the stones transferred to a replica archway erected in Albert Park. In 1911 the stones were acquired for the west porch of St Hilda's church, where they remained until its demolition in 1969. It too is in the museum.

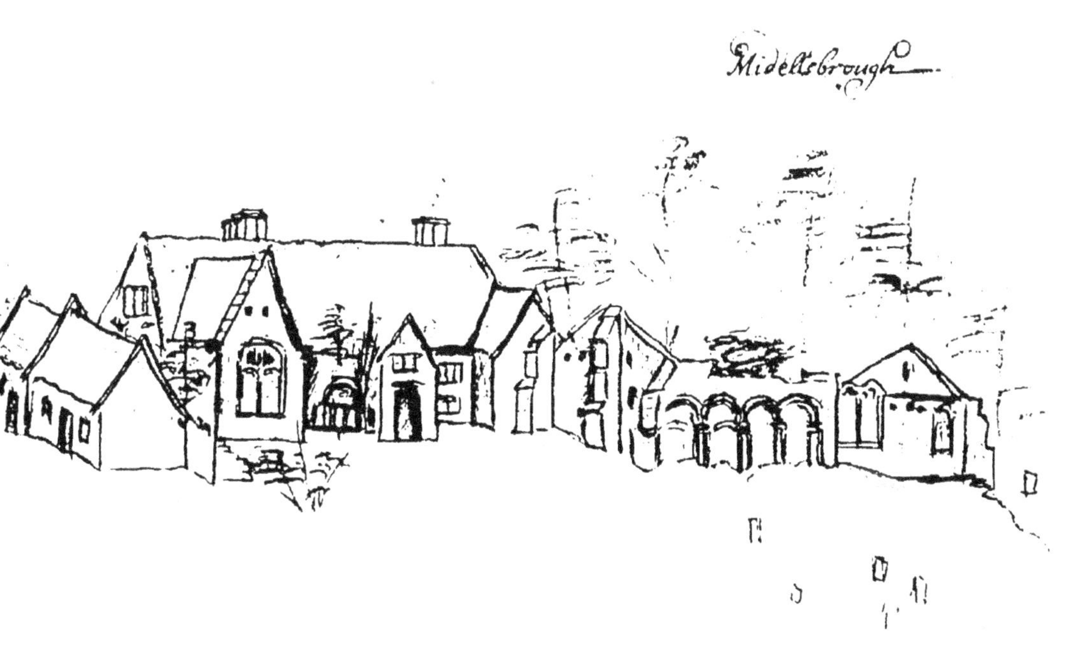

We have no clear impression of what the medieval priory buildings looked like, except for this sketch, drawn by Samuel Buck in 1718 from a manuscript at the Bodleian Library (fol. 325).

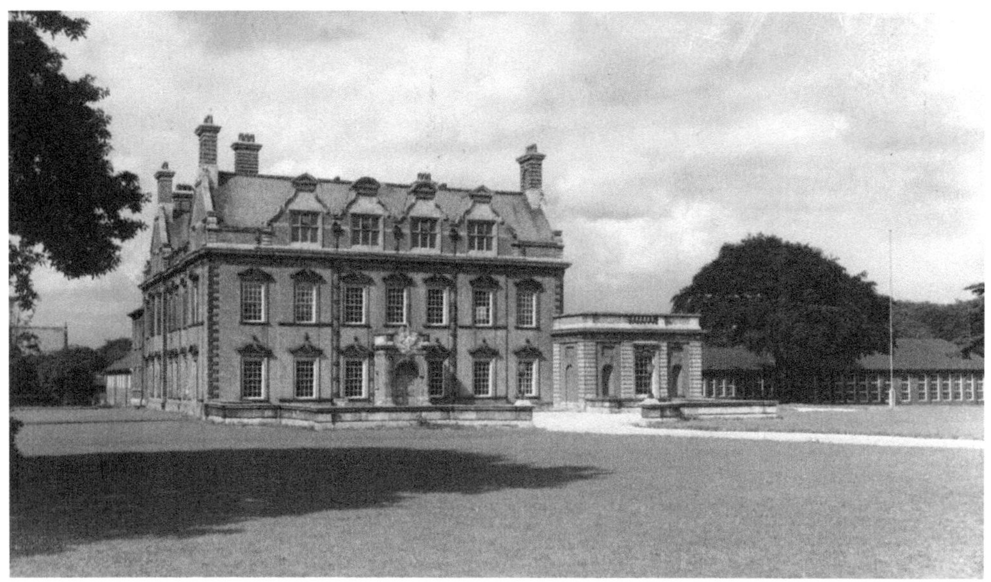

The focus of the parish in the eighteenth century was the gracious home of the lords of the manor, the Hustler family, at Acklam Hall, here shown after refurbishments in 1912 to alter the façade. It is Middlesbrough's only Grade 1-listed building.

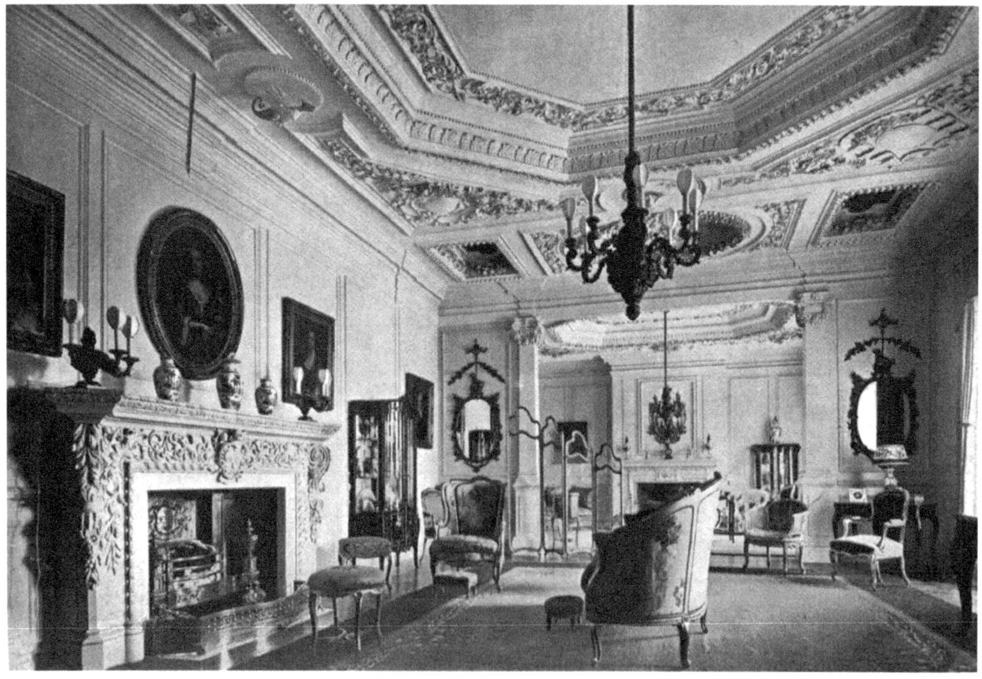

The large drawing room of Acklam Hall seen here at the time of its sale in 1928. It was converted into a grammar school for boys in 1935, and later became Middlesbrough College: its future use is currently a matter of debate.

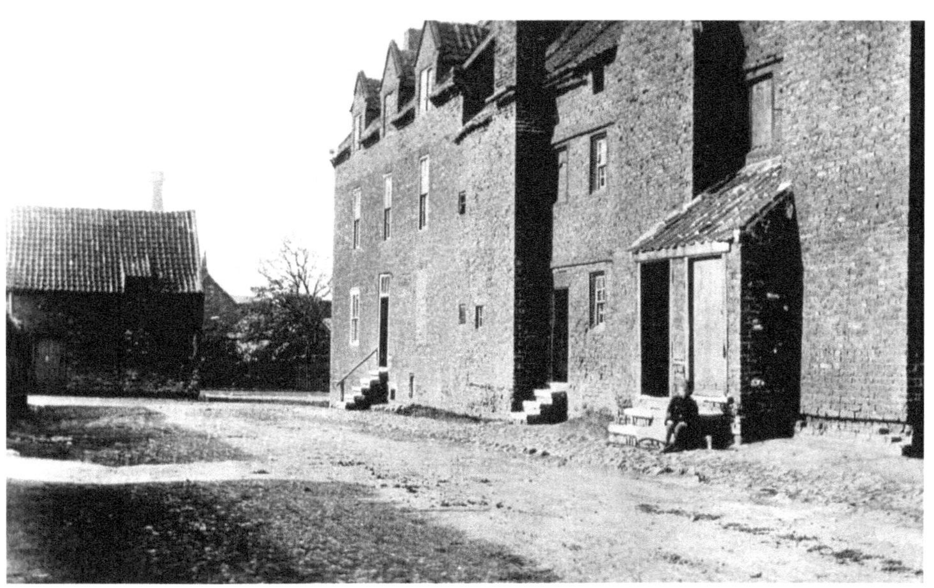

The commercial heart of the parish lay at Newport, where goods were loaded and unloaded from these granaries (now demolished) before ships proceeded upriver to the port of Stockton.

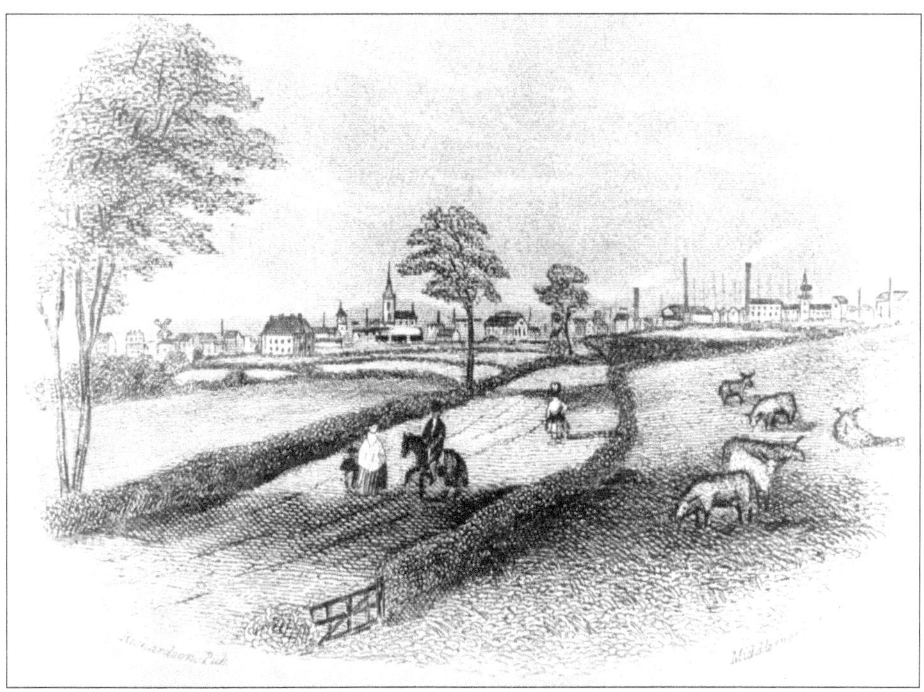

Middlesbrough from Marton Road in 1859. From left to right can be seen the windmill, St Hilda's church, Bolckow Vaughan's Ironworks and the dock tower.

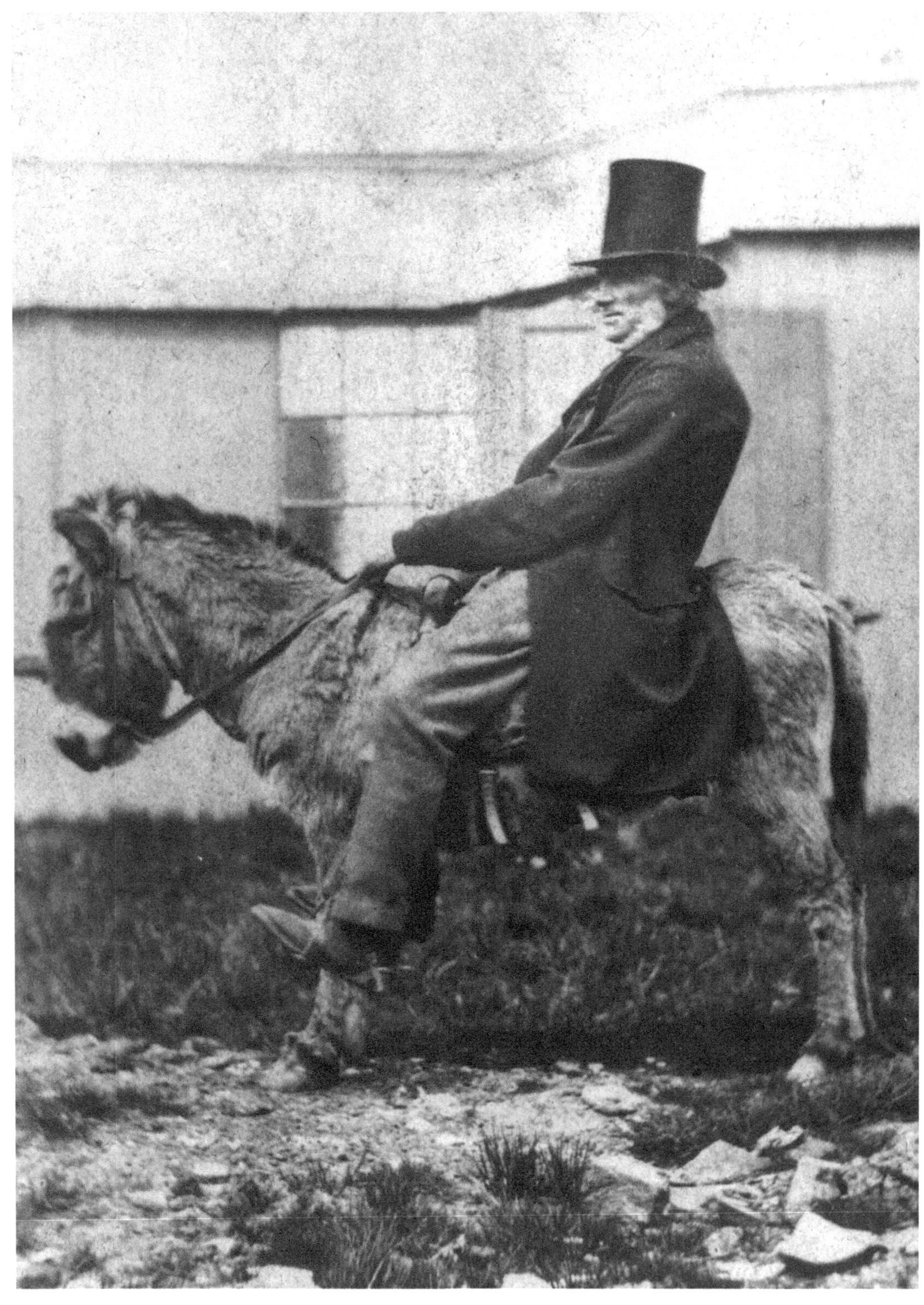

In the early days of the town of Middlesbrough, education and spiritual guidance were provided by the incumbent of Acklam church, the Revd Isaac Benson (1823-1864).

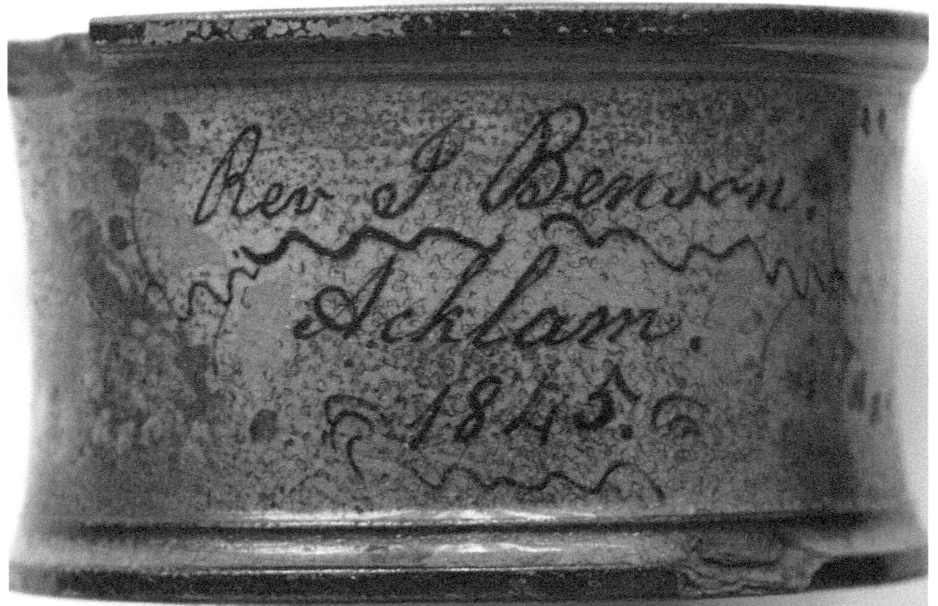

A presentation inkwell given by Isaac Benson: dated 1845, it is now in the Dorman Museum. Benson taught local boys in the days before schools were opened in Middlesbrough and was known to be a firm disciplinarian.

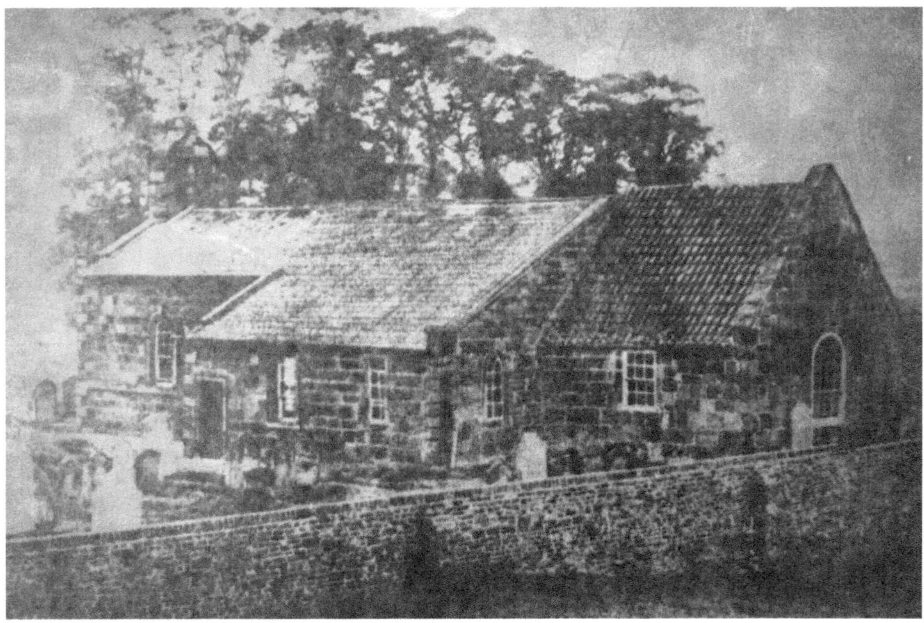

Acklam church as it would have appeared in the early nineteenth century. This building was demolished in or before 1874. The present St Mary's church was built in 1874 and enlarged in 1957. The boundary wall seen in this photograph has also been rebuilt and many of the gravestones resited.

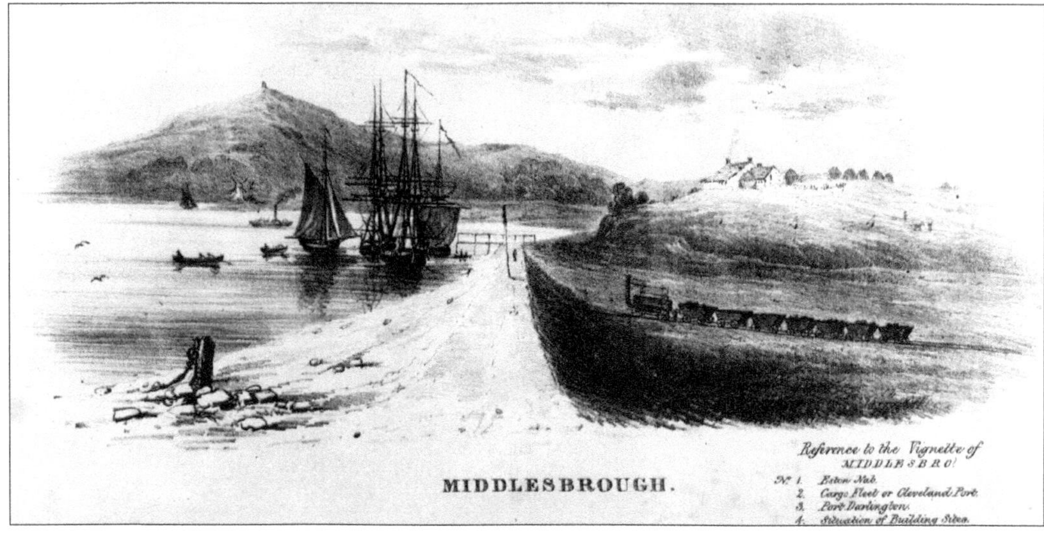

An artist's impression of Middlesbrough before the new town was developed in the later 1830s. It shows a locomotive pulling a string of coal trucks for loading into the vessel moored in the river. In the background can be seen the Napoleonic beacon on top of Eston Nab.

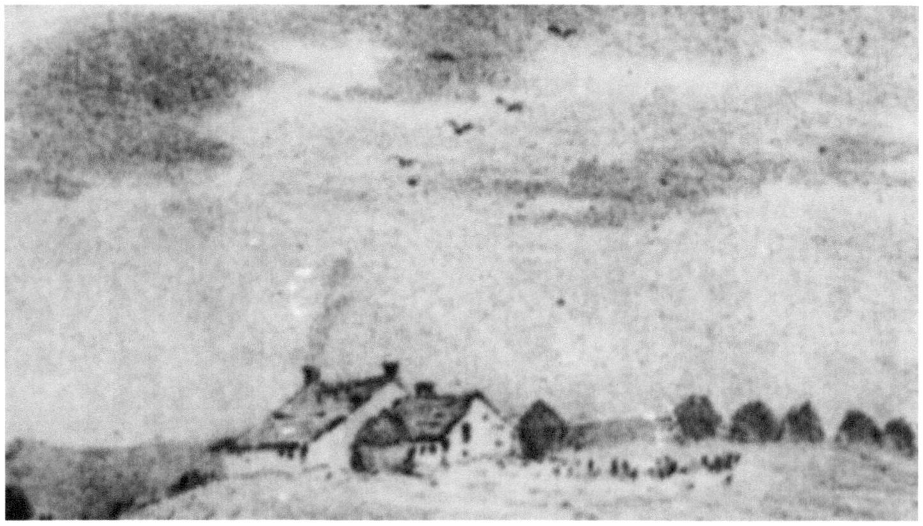

A detail of the Middlesbrough farmhouse. It was purchased in 1829 by the Owners of the Middlesbrough Estate and converted into a hotel. The building was demolished in 1846: a tile from the roof is preserved in the Dorman Museum.

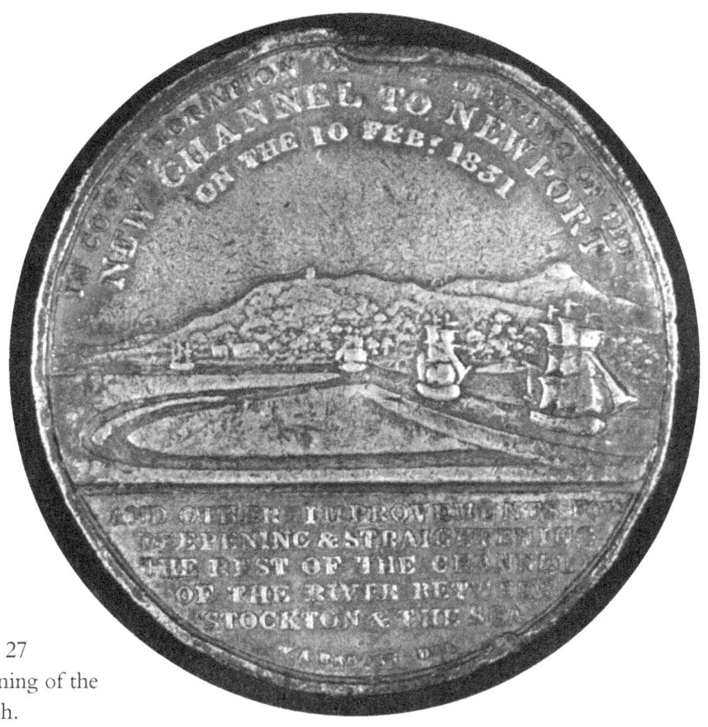

Right: Tees Navigation Co. medal to commemorate the cut in 1831 that shortened the tortuous journey up the Tees, and thus enabled the development of the port and town of Middlesbrough, formerly called Port Darlington.

Below: Coal trucks. The coal shipping staithes at Port Darlington were designed by Timothy Hackworth, and inaugurated by the Stockton & Darlington Railway Co. on 27 December 1830 with the opening of the Middlesbrough Railway branch.

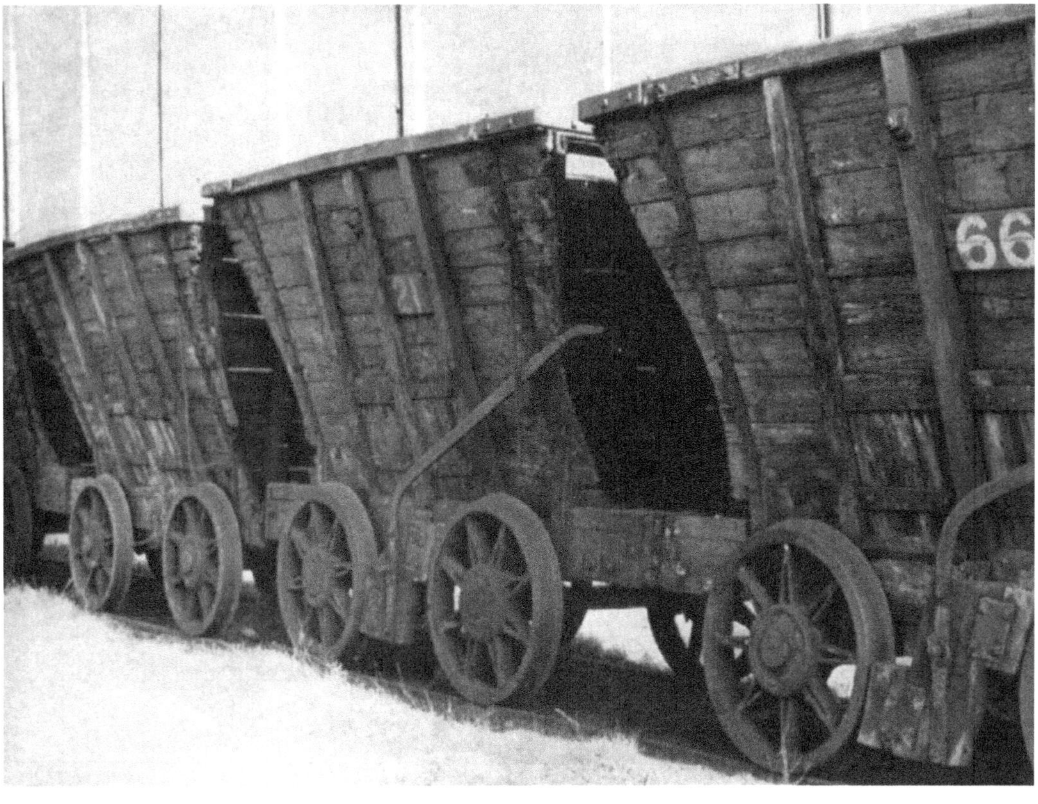

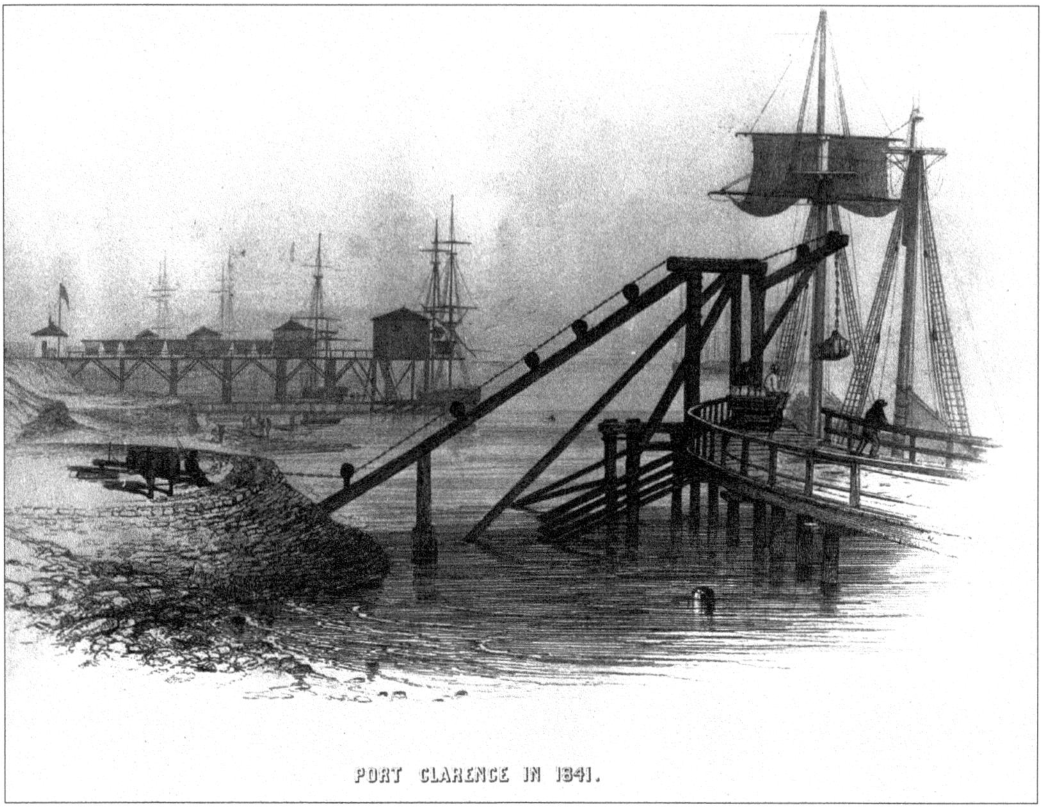

Coal staithes on the Tees at Port Clarence in 1841 (after the engraving by Thomas Hair).

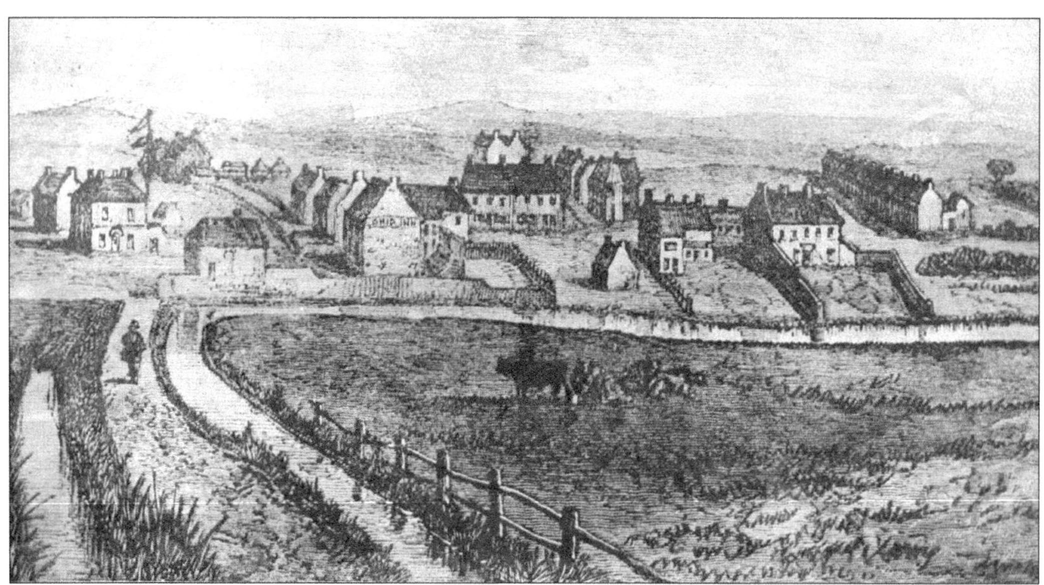

A view of Middlesbrough in 1832 from the south. It shows the Ship Inn, licensed in 1831, and some of the earliest houses to be built. The farmhouse is on the extreme left.

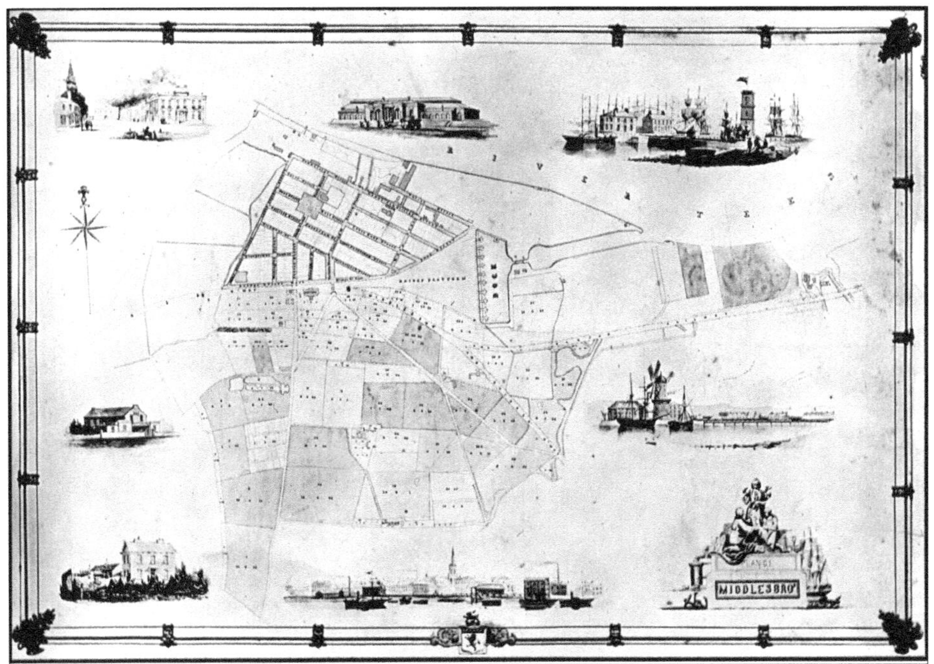

A map of Middlesbrough. The image centre right is significant in showing the windmill which stood in Sussex Street. (It can also be made out in a number of the other images of early Middlesbrough.)

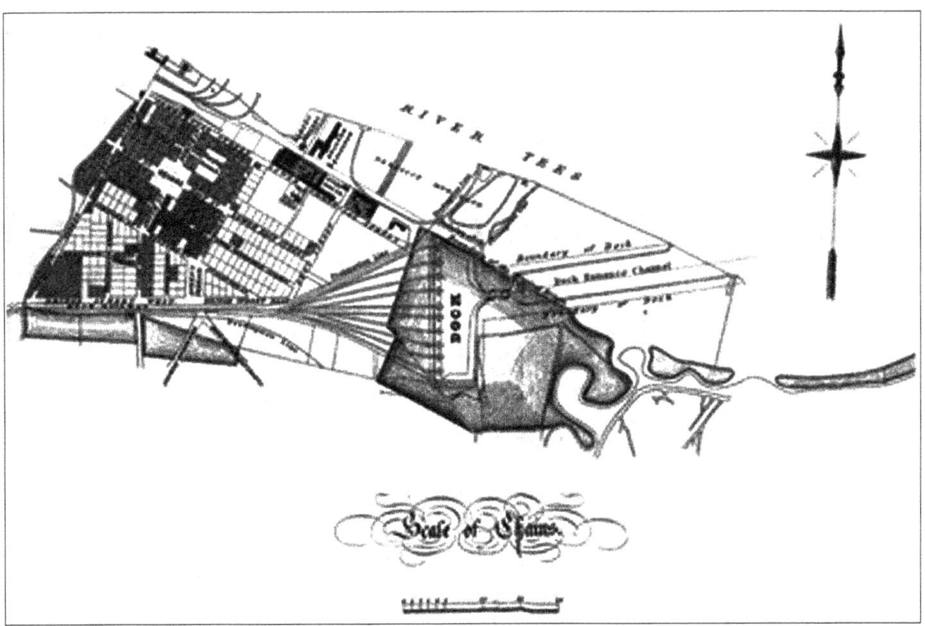

A plan of the town. The grid of streets radiating out from Market Square has already been infilled but the area to the east is still awaiting development. The first dock facility, built in 1842, already appears woefully inadequate.

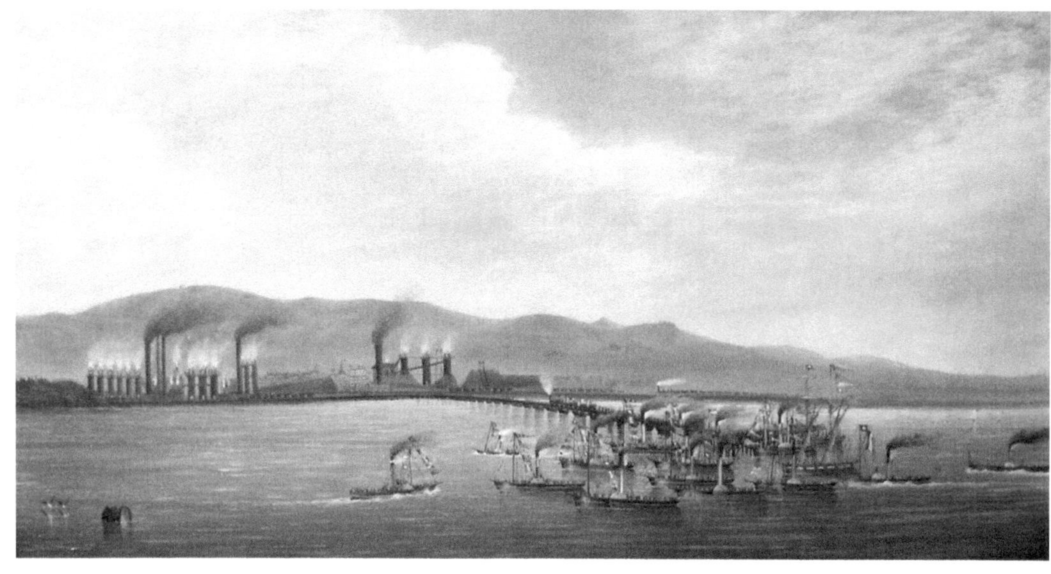

Gladstone's historic visit to Middlesbrough in 1862. The smoking chimneys of Bolckow Vaughan's Ironworks at Eston dominate the scene. In the foreground the flotilla that accompanied the statesman can be seen and, in the distance, the summit of Roseberry Topping.

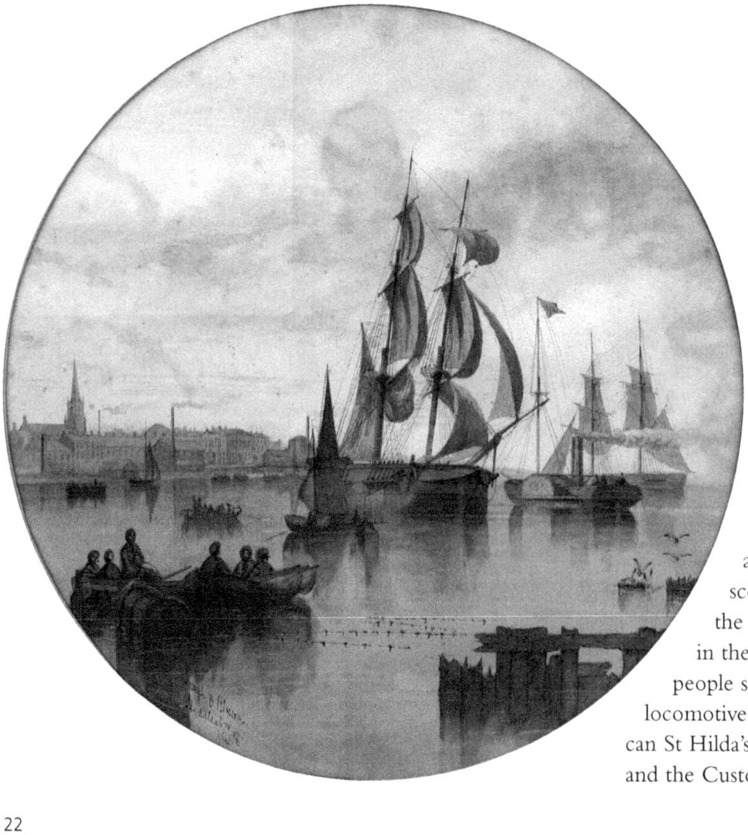

This painting by Joseph Blossom from the Dorman Museum collection, dated 1874, shows an altogether more tranquil scene, concentrating on the elegant masted ships in the river and a group of people salmon fishing. A railway locomotive can be made out, as can St Hilda's church, the windmill and the Custom House.

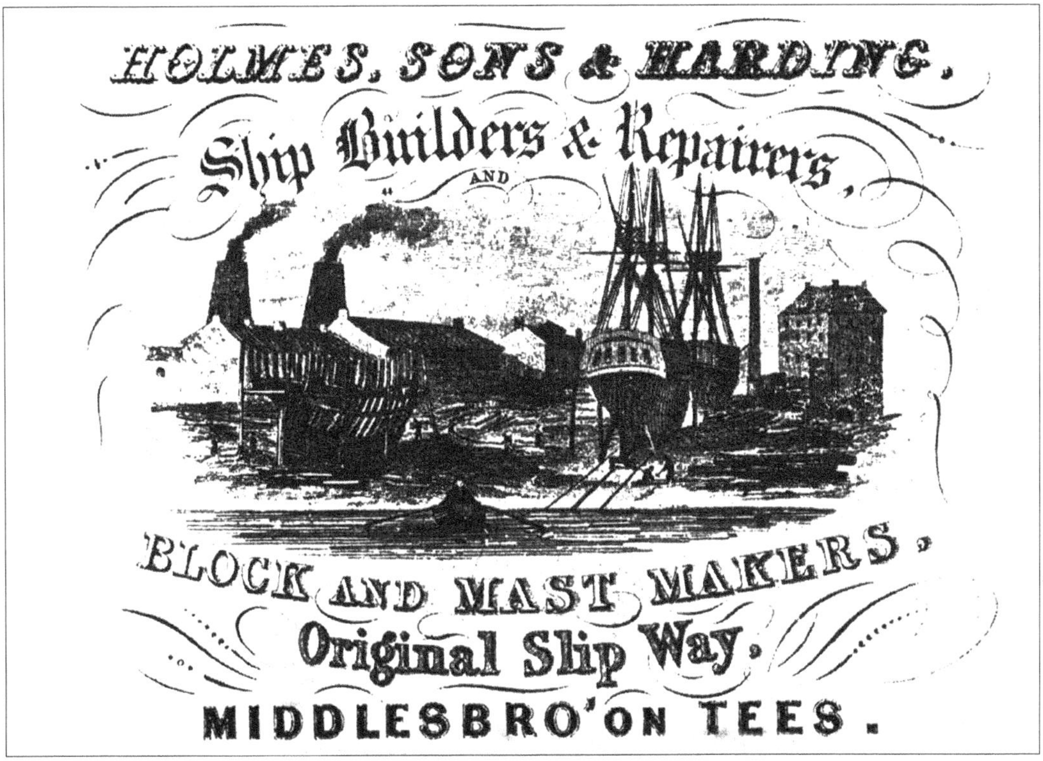

This advertising card for Holmes Sons & Harding brings together shipbuilding and the chimneys of the now forgotten Middlesbrough Pottery. The pottery was the town's first major employer and opened for business in Commercial Street in 1834.

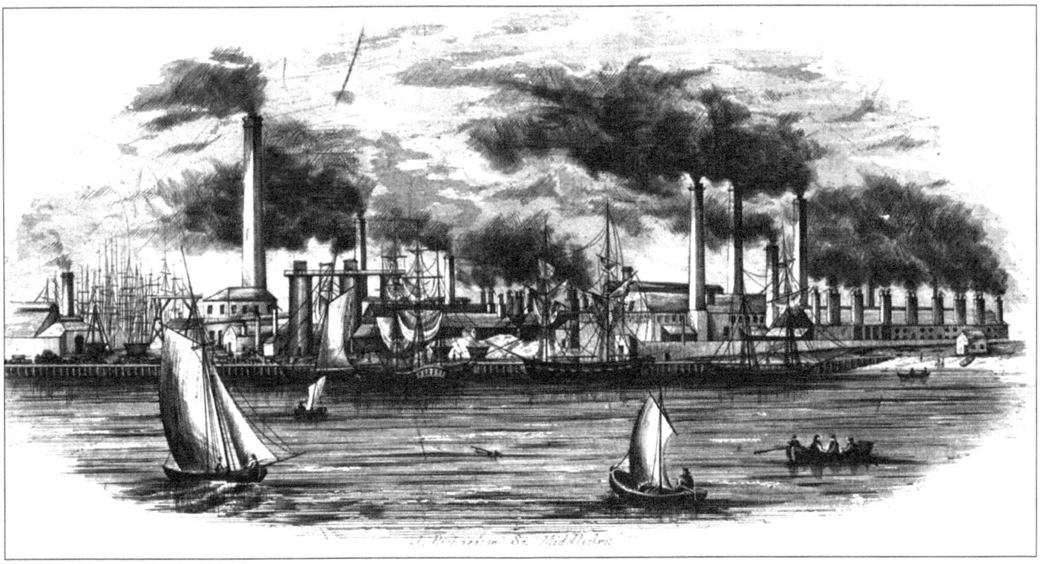

Bolckow & Vaughan's Ironworks in 1860. The works were opened on a site adjacent to Commercial Street in 1841, producing rails and bar iron.

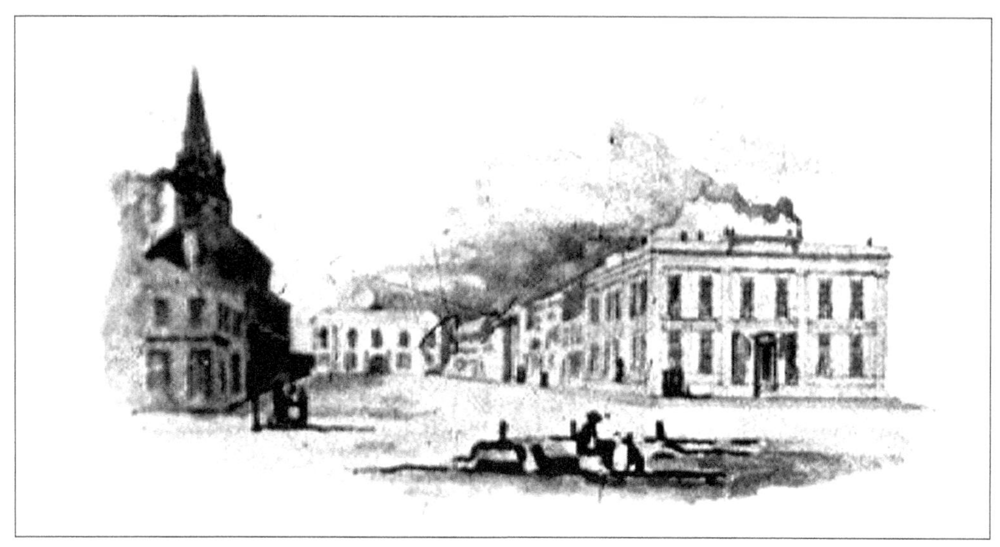

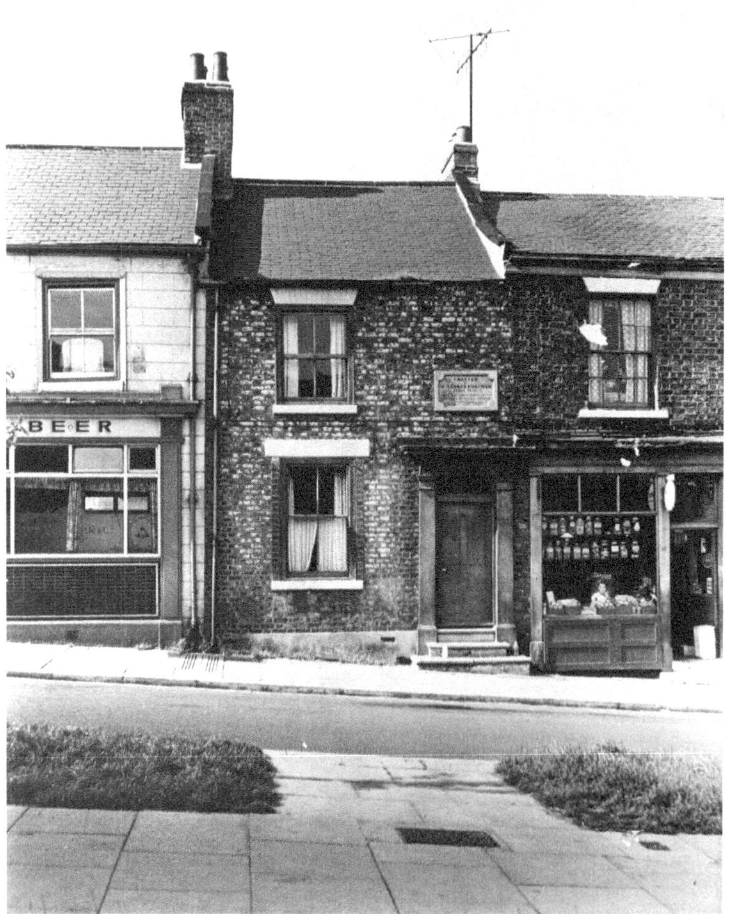

Above: The early town featured broad, elegant streets and some handsome public buildings. Here the Custom House of 1836, the only Greek revival style building in the town, is shown to advantage before the infilling development which later took place.

Left: The first house built in West Street: this photograph was taken shortly before its demolition in 1959. It belonged to George Chapman and was erected in April 1830. The plaque recording this historic event is now in the Dorman Museum.

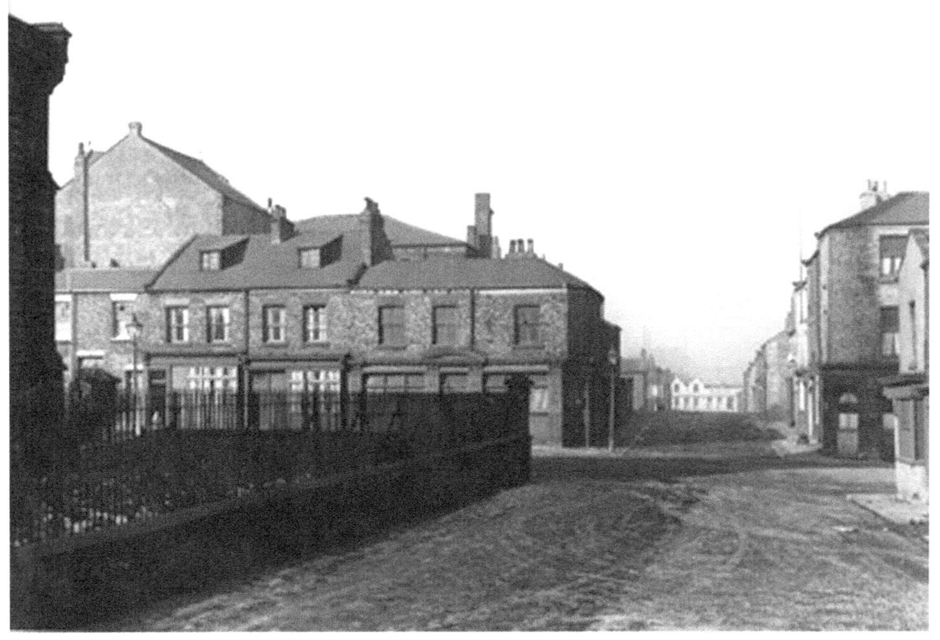

Dacre Street: a view taken from just outside the churchyard of St Hilda's, looking towards the river. In the distance a ship can just be made out.

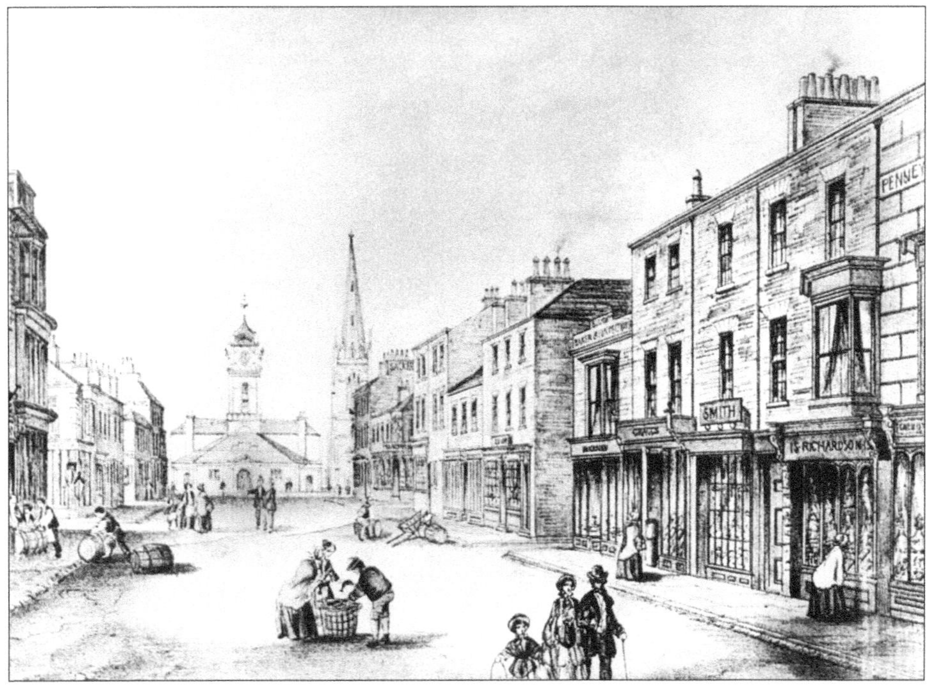

The town hall with St Hilda's church spire in the background; the building on the left is the Fleece Hotel.

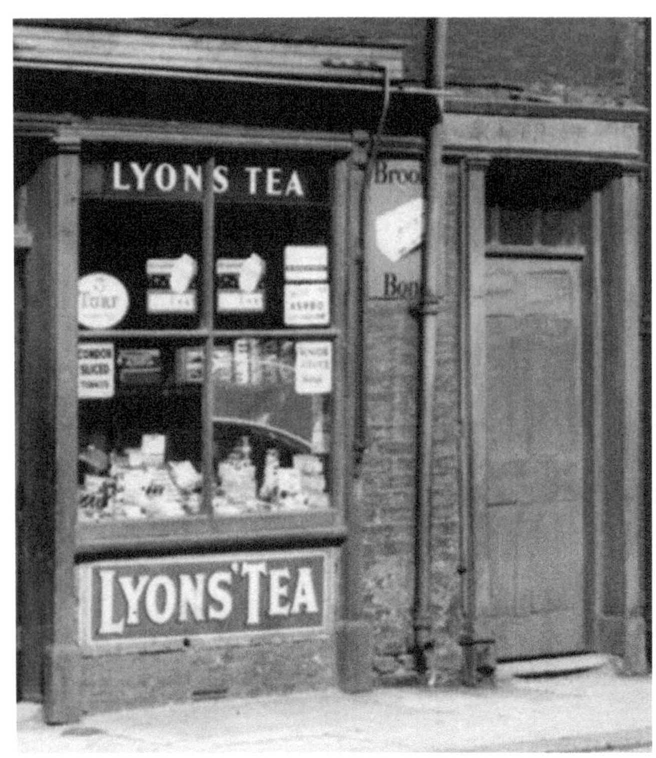

Opposite above: North Street looking north, showing the changes wrought on the townscape by twentieth-century development. The buildings at the end of the street are on the site formerly occupied by the office of the Tyne Tees Wharf. The custom house can also be seen covered in scaffolding.

Left: A shop in Durham Street in the 1950s.

Below: The Eagle Hotel in East Street. The impressive colonnaded frontage was a feature of its former use as a Congregational chapel.

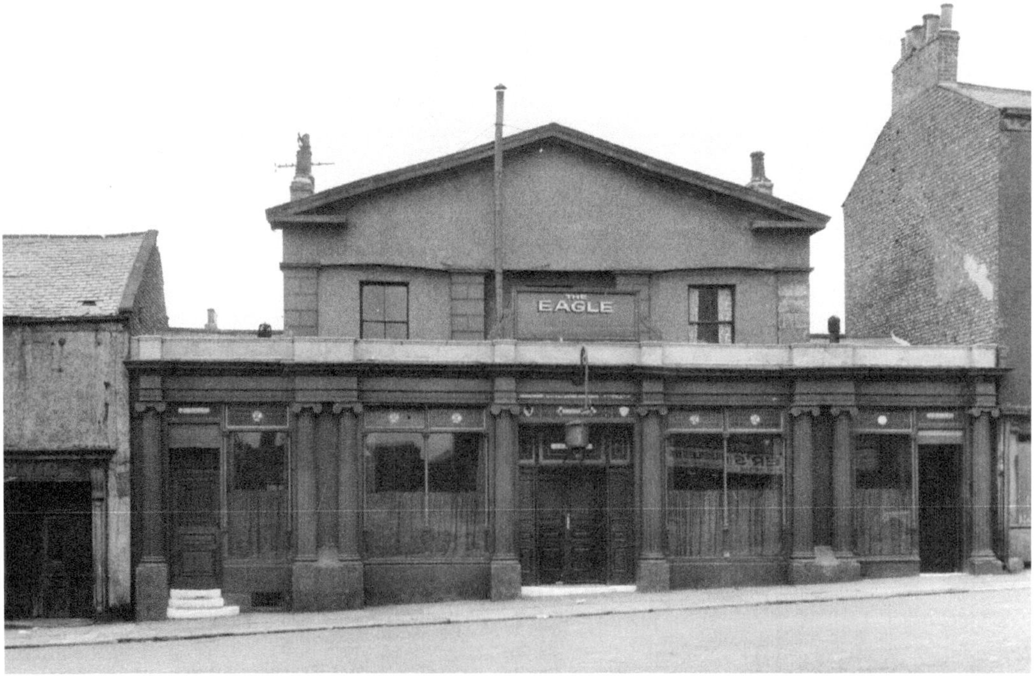

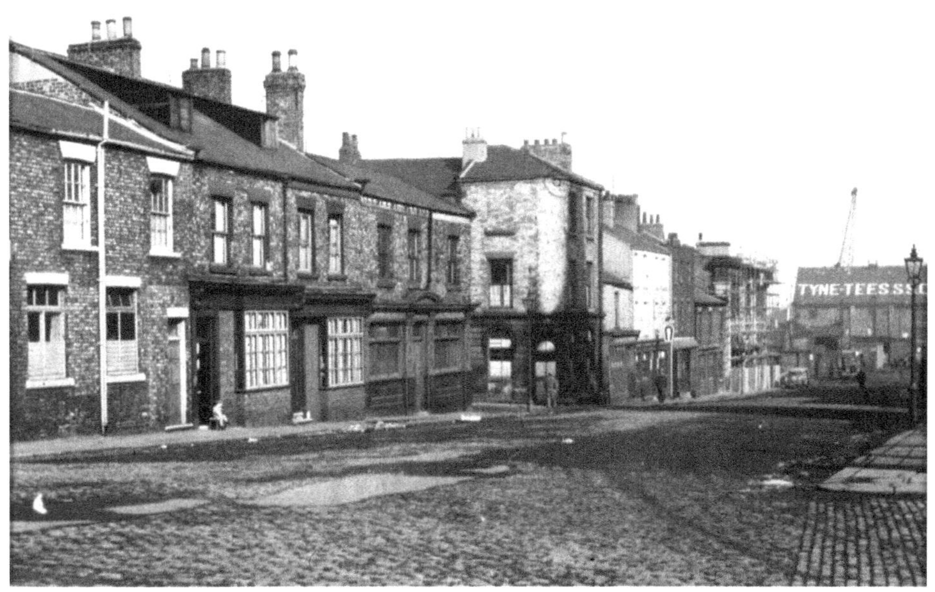

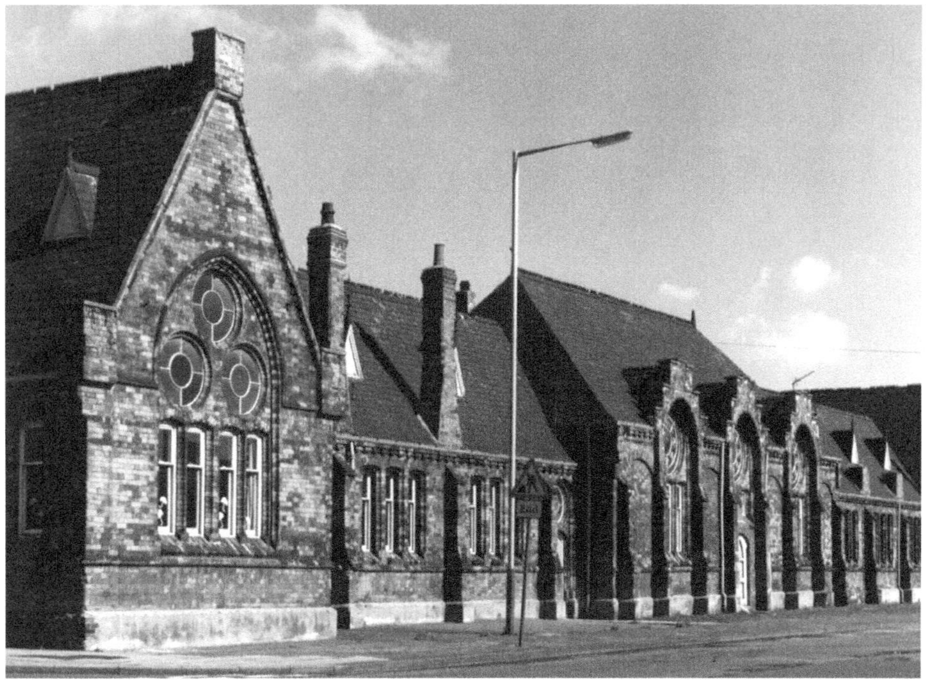

St Hilda's Church of England School, built in 1869 and closed in 1981. Built with money donated by Henry Bolckow, it was opened by His Grace the Duke of Devonshire. The author Naomi Jacob (1884 -1964) taught here briefly, where she came into conflict with the headmaster for wearing trousers. She wrote graphically of her experiences in her book *Me – again*. The school was later amalgamated with St Mary's Roman Catholic school in nearby Sussex Street and renamed St Christopher's.

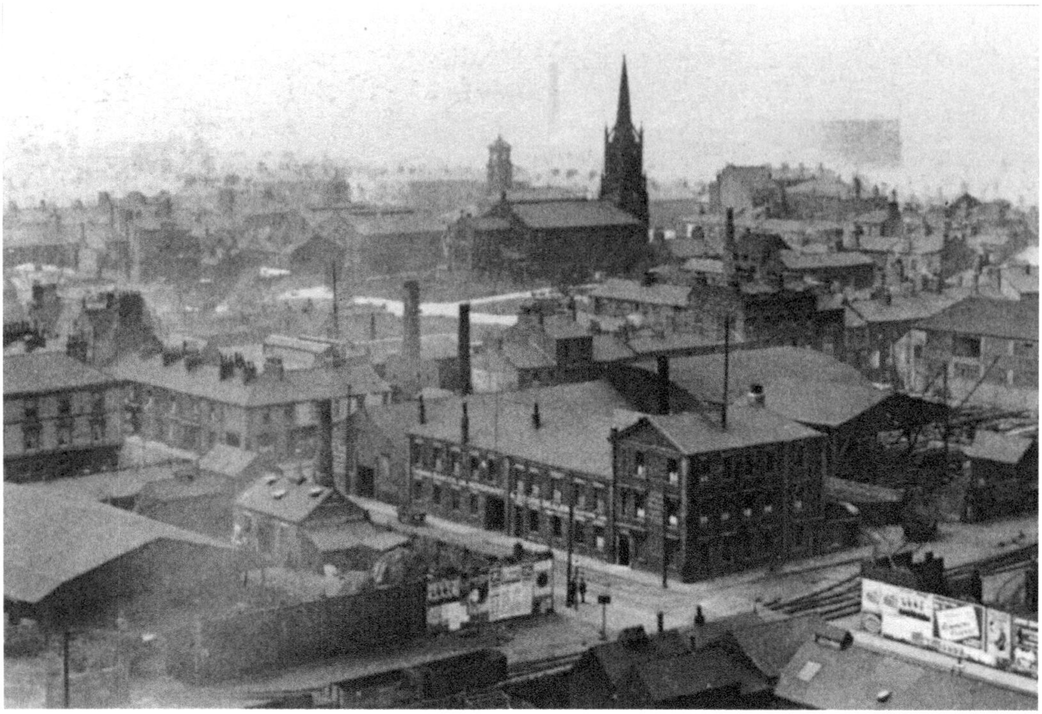

An aerial view of the town from the Transporter Bridge in the 1940s or 1950s. It gives an excellent impression of how far the town had developed by the time it was granted county borough status in 1889. The photograph shows St Hilda's parish church of 1840, and the old town hall of 1846 in the centre of the picture, and to the bottom left can be seen the Corporation Yard. (Note also, at the bottom of the photograph, the railway lines and sidings serving businesses and industry in what is now Vulcan Street.)

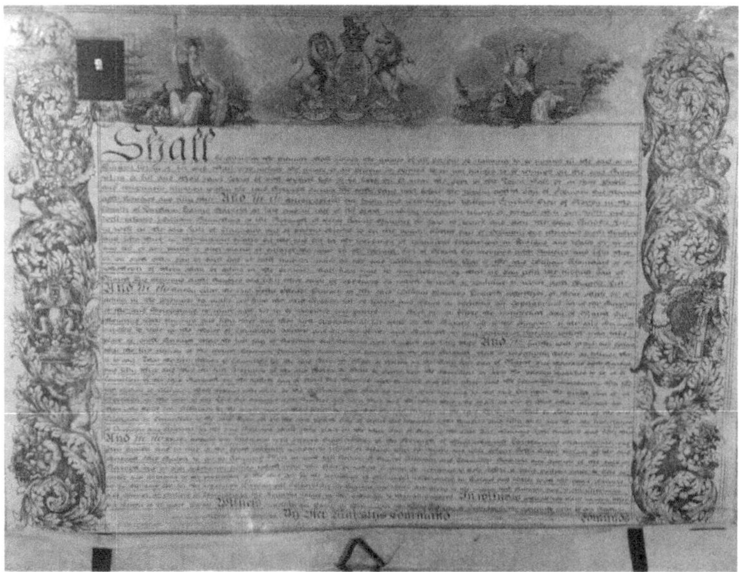

The elaborately decorated original charter of incorporation from 1853, which served the town during the first forty-six years of its corporate existence. Granted by her Majesty Queen Victoria, it was paid for by Bolckow and Vaughan. This was once on proud display in the town hall: it is now in the Dorman Museum.

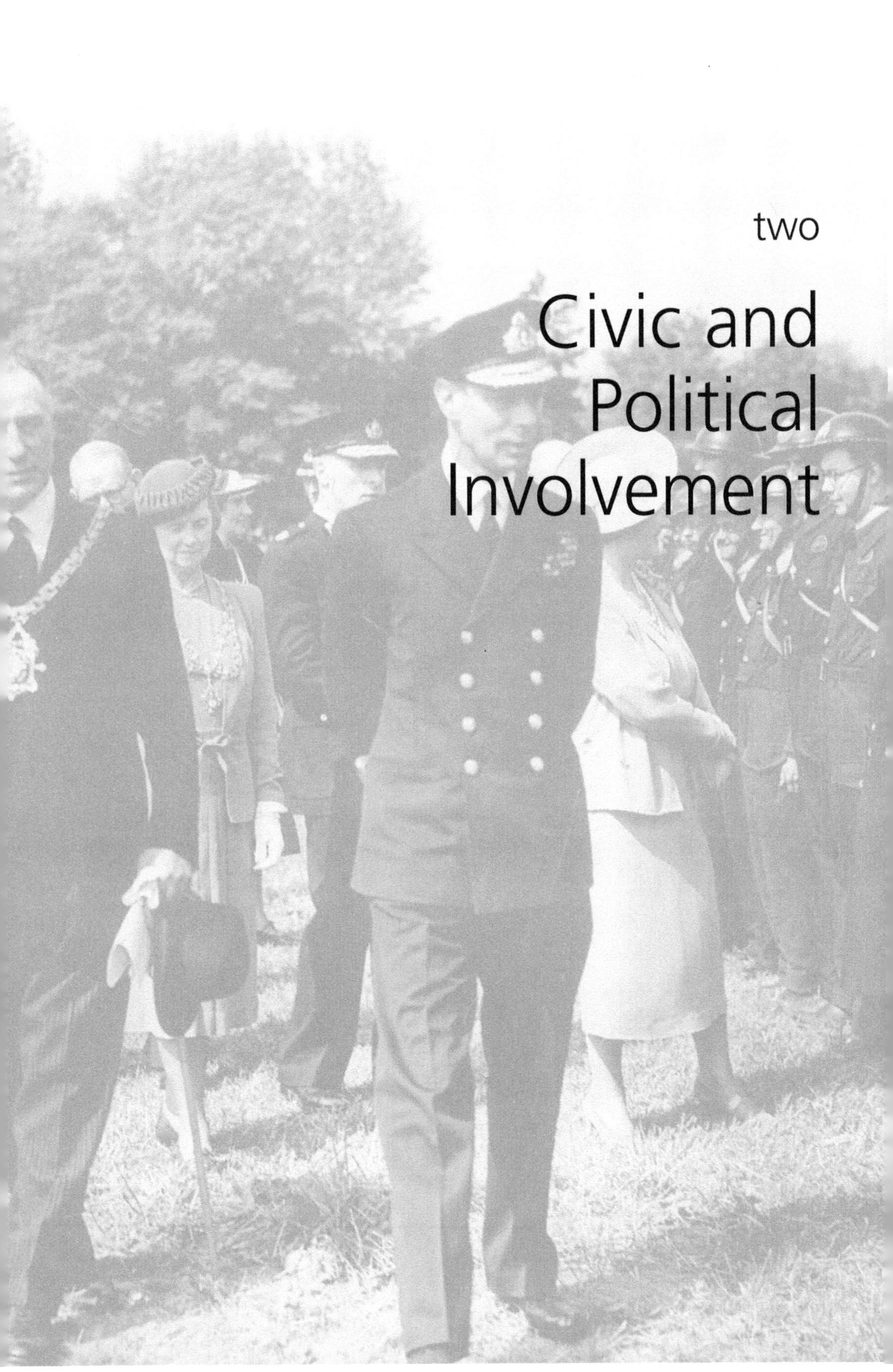

Civic and Political Involvement

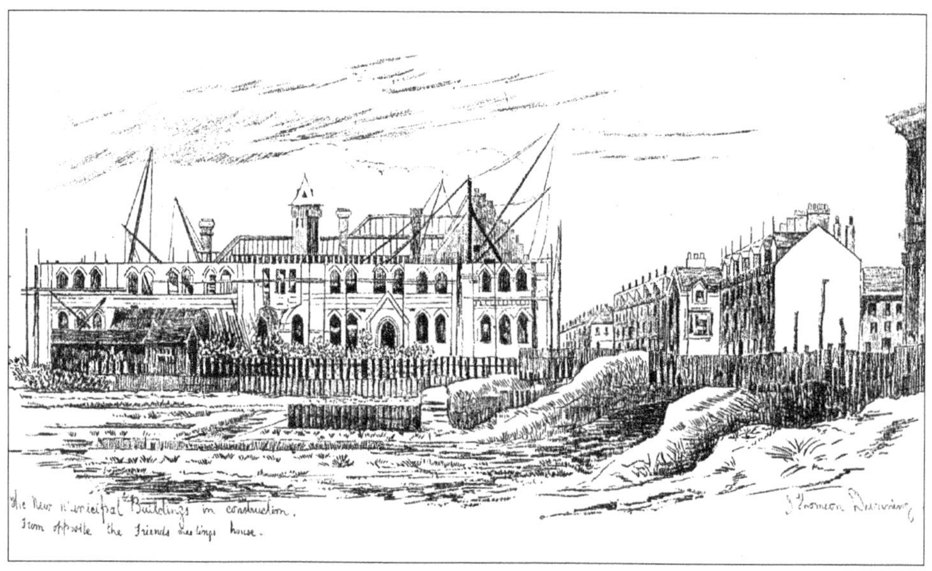

Building the new town hall: a line drawing made during the construction in the late 1880s by J. Thompson Dunning (born in 1850).

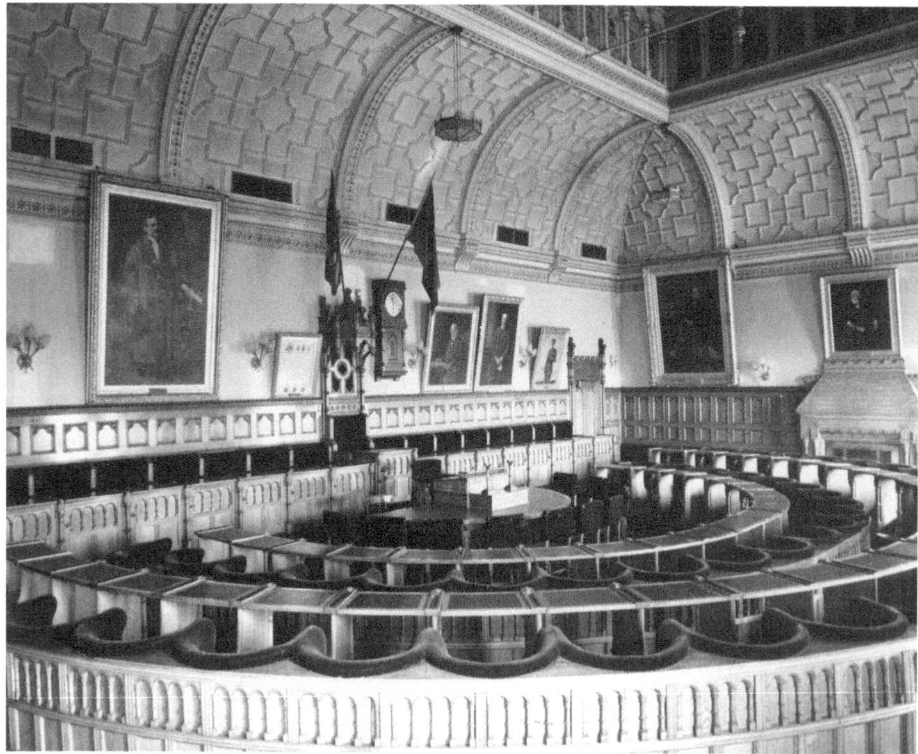

The council chamber of the town hall, the home of council meetings, seen here in the 1960s. The portraits of civic worthies can clearly be seen in this photograph. Left to right: Sir Samuel Sadler, Isaac Wilson, George Hutton Bowes Wilson, William Fallows and Isaac Lowthian Bell.

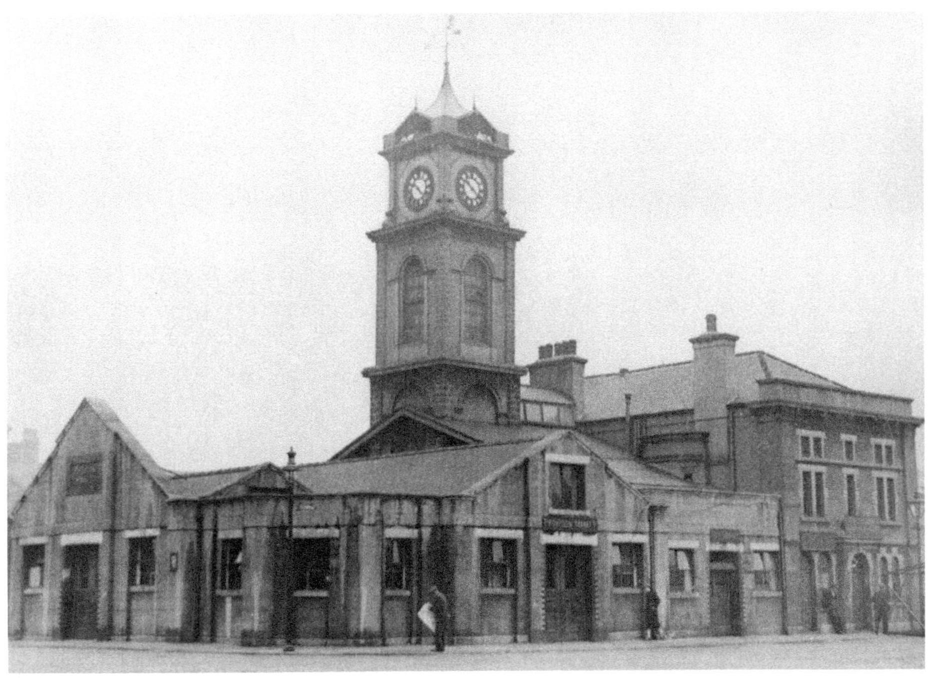

The old town hall stood in the centre of the Market Place, seen here in the 1950s. It was designed for the Middlesbrough Improvement Commissioners (the forerunners of the town council) in the Italianate style by William Lambie Moffatt of Doncaster in 1846.

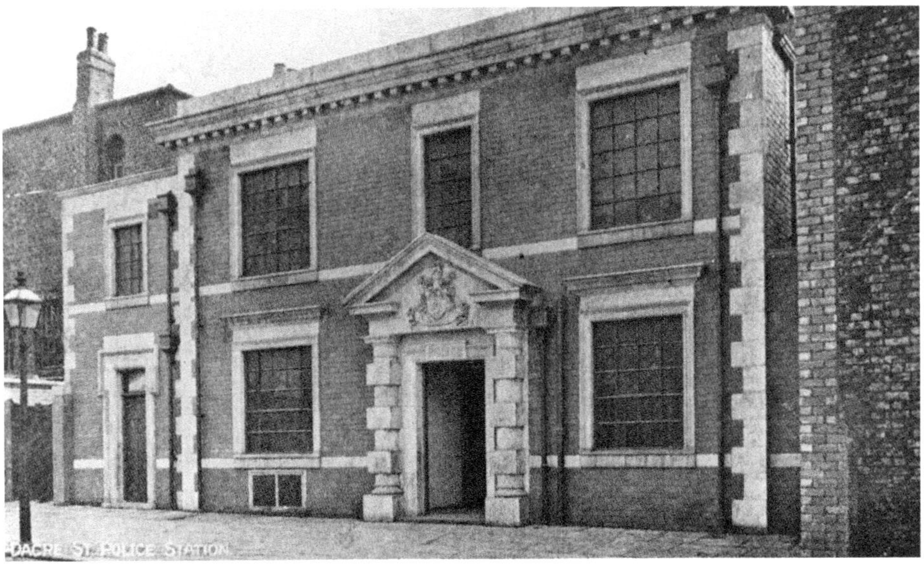

Dacre Street police station. After its use as a branch police station the building was used as a slipper baths (housing seventeen baths), a community wash house, and later as residential accommodation. The building was designed by S.E. Burgess, the borough engineer, and the whole façade was made using reconstituted stone patented by Bolckow and Vaughan, a by-product in the manufacture of iron and steel.

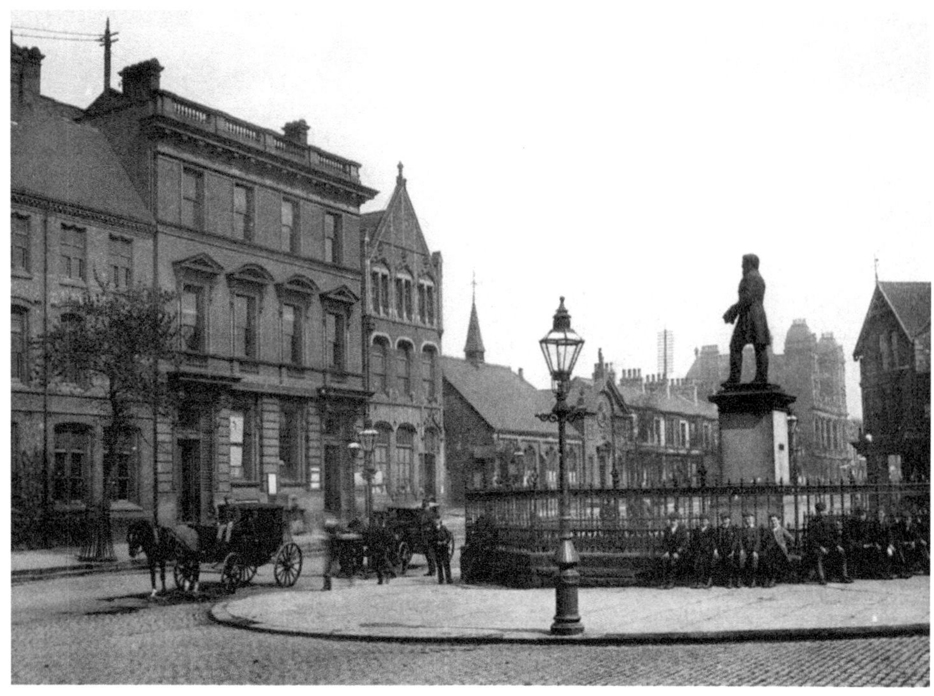

Marton Road near the railway station, seen here in the late 1880s. The building to the left was the main post office: it is now home to Teesside Archives. The building to the right of the lamp post is the Masonic Hall, and to the right of the statue of Henry Bolckow (1806 –1878) can be seen the twin towers of the Star and Garter public house (a close up of which can be seen on page 32).

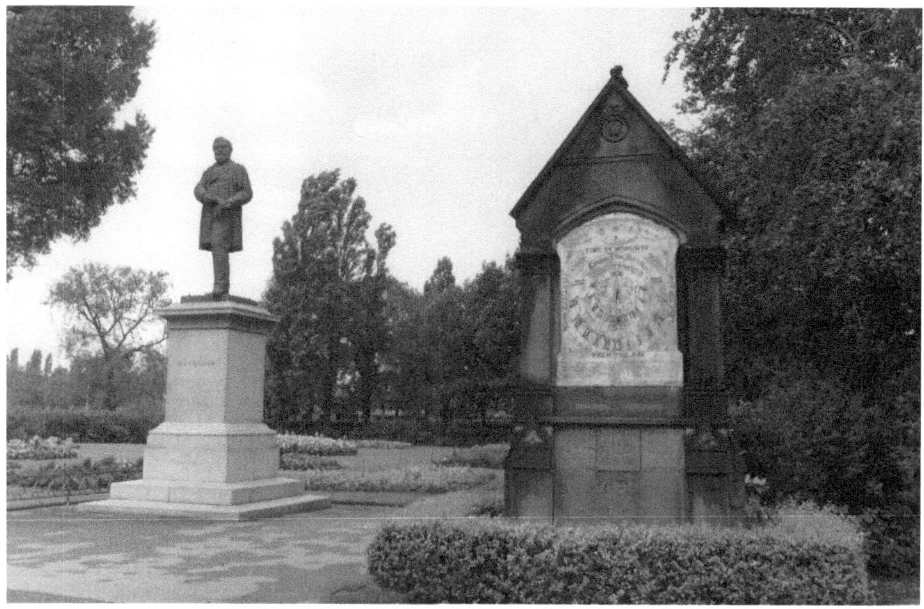

The Bolckow statue and sundial in Albert Park. This statue was in the park from 1925 and was moved back to (nearly) its original location only in the last twenty years.

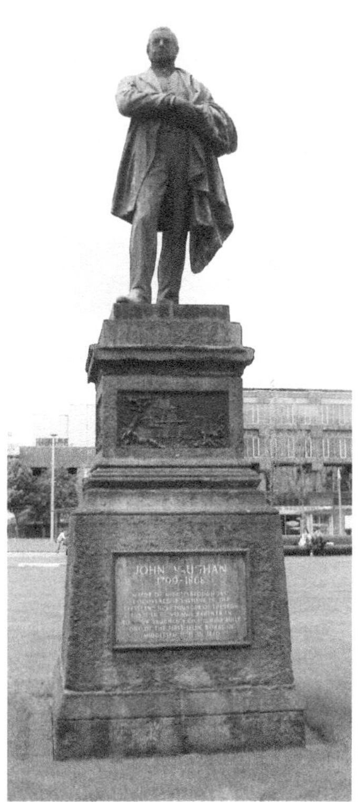

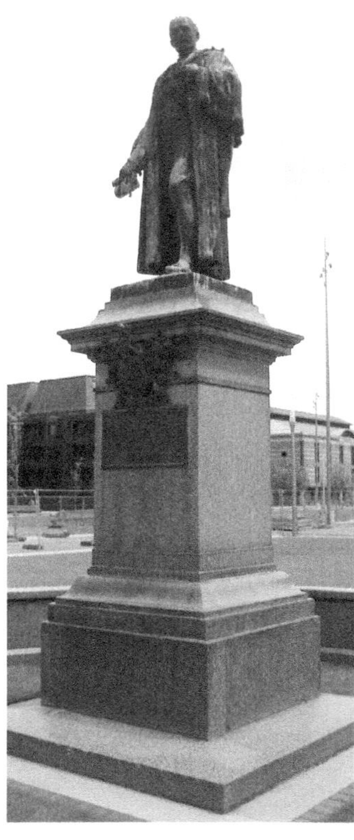

Right: Statue of John Vaughan (1799–1868) by George Lawson. Originally erected in 1884 opposite the railway station, it was removed to Victoria Square in 1914.

Far right: Statue of Sir Samuel Alexander Sadler (1842 –1911) by Professor Edouard Lanteri. It was paid for by a public appeal organised by the *Evening Gazette*, and unveiled in Victoria Square on 21 June 1913.

Below: Middlesbrough Central Library opened in 1912 and this image was used in the opening brochure. It was made possible by the generosity of the Scottish-American steel tycoon, Andrew Carnegie. The reading room can be seen on the right. It is now the site of the 1970s administration link block.

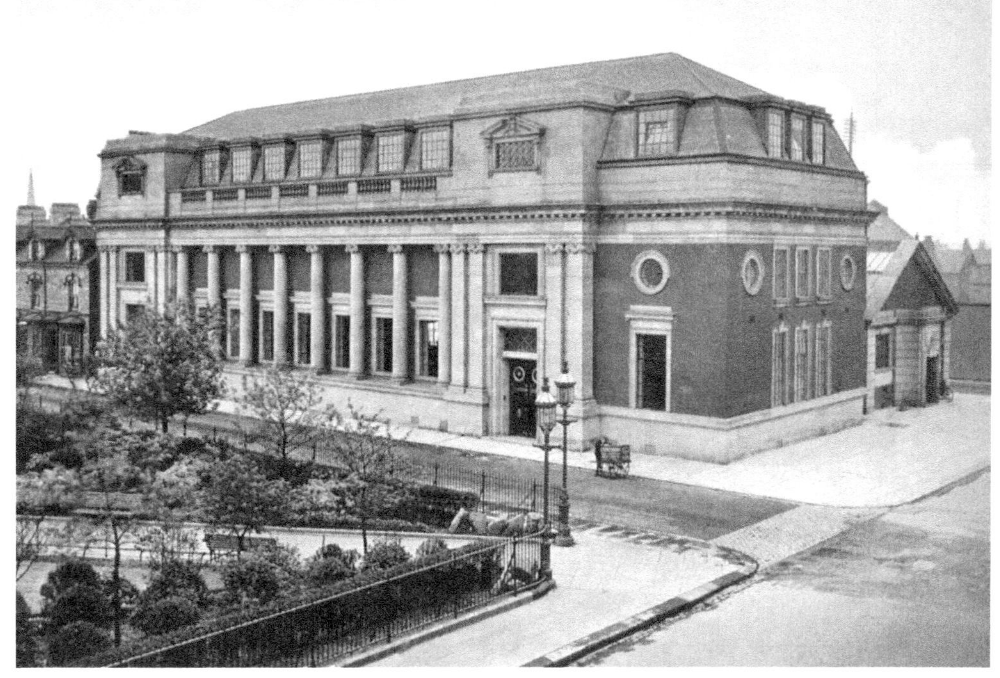

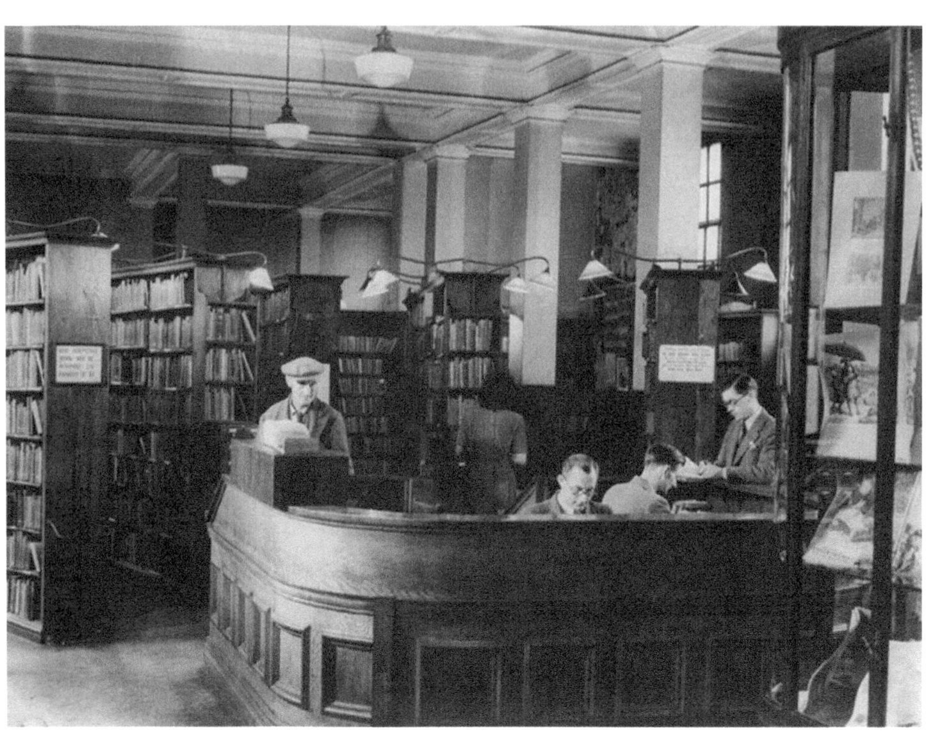

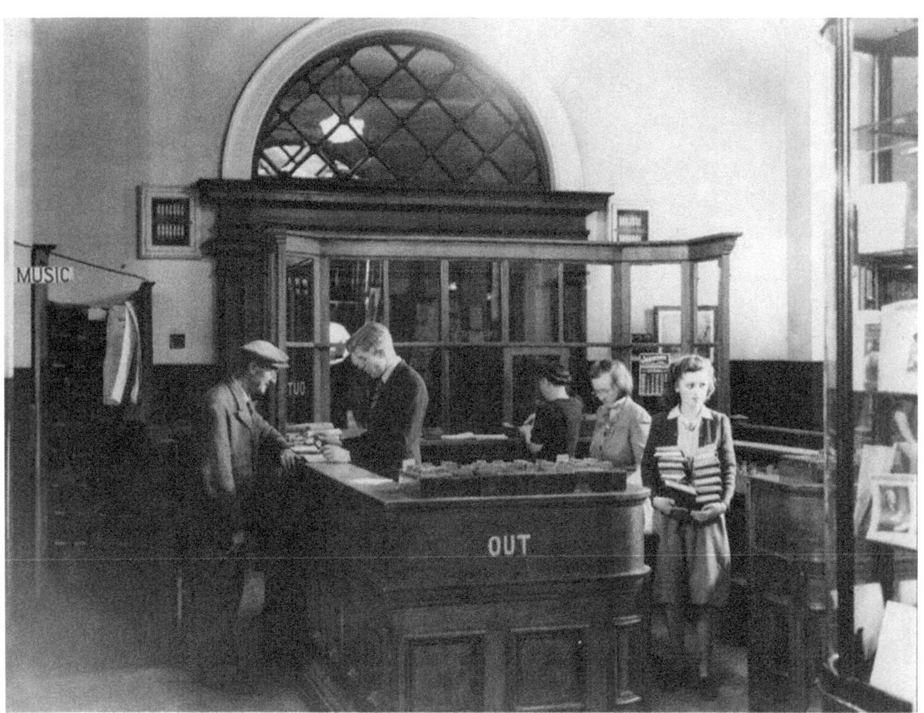
MUSIC
OUT
OUT

OFFICIAL OPENING — 10th MAY, 1967

Acklam Library, Middlesbrough's eighth branch library, opened on 10 May 1967 with a stock of 15,500 books and the innovation of easy chairs for adults. It was altered in 2004 to extend the front entrance.

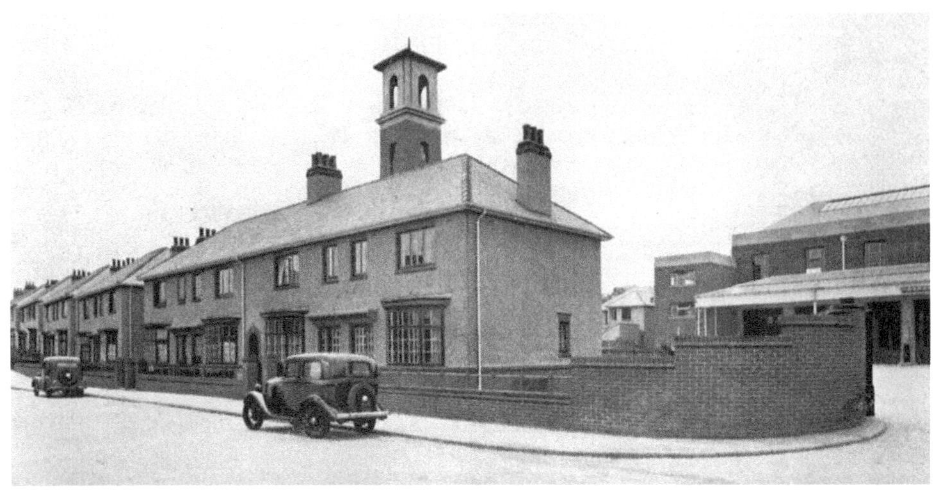

Middlesbrough fire station and fire brigade houses, built in 1939 in Park Road South, Cumberland Road and Westminster Road.

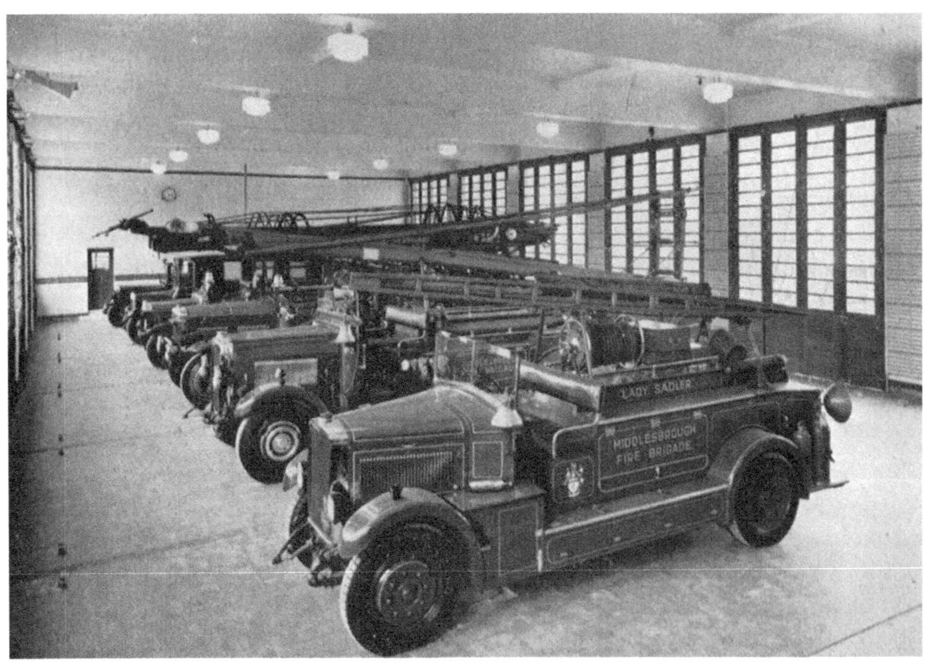

Fire engines inside the station – all ready for action on their assembly apron. The engine named after Lady Sadler can be clearly seen in the foreground.

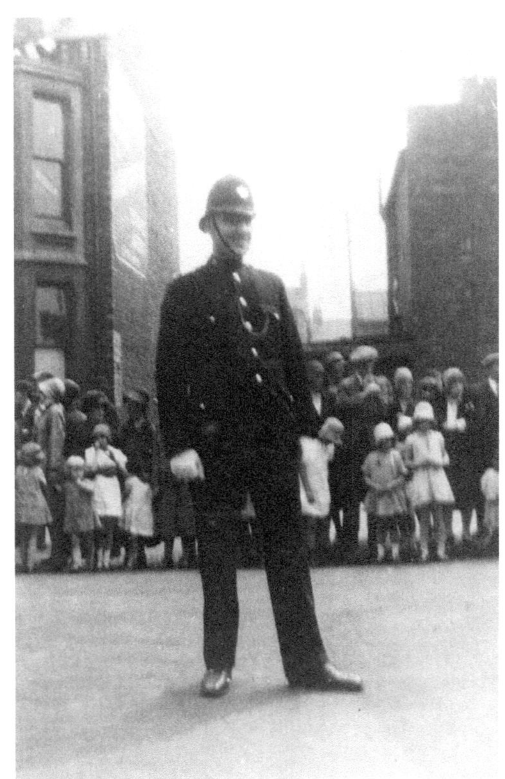

Right: A Middlesbrough policeman, wearing white gloves for a special occasion, keeps an eye on crowds gathered outside the town hall in the 1940s.

Below: Middlesbrough police force all assembled with the Chief Constable Mr Henry Riches (front row centre). Note the number of officers wearing medals and bravery decorations.

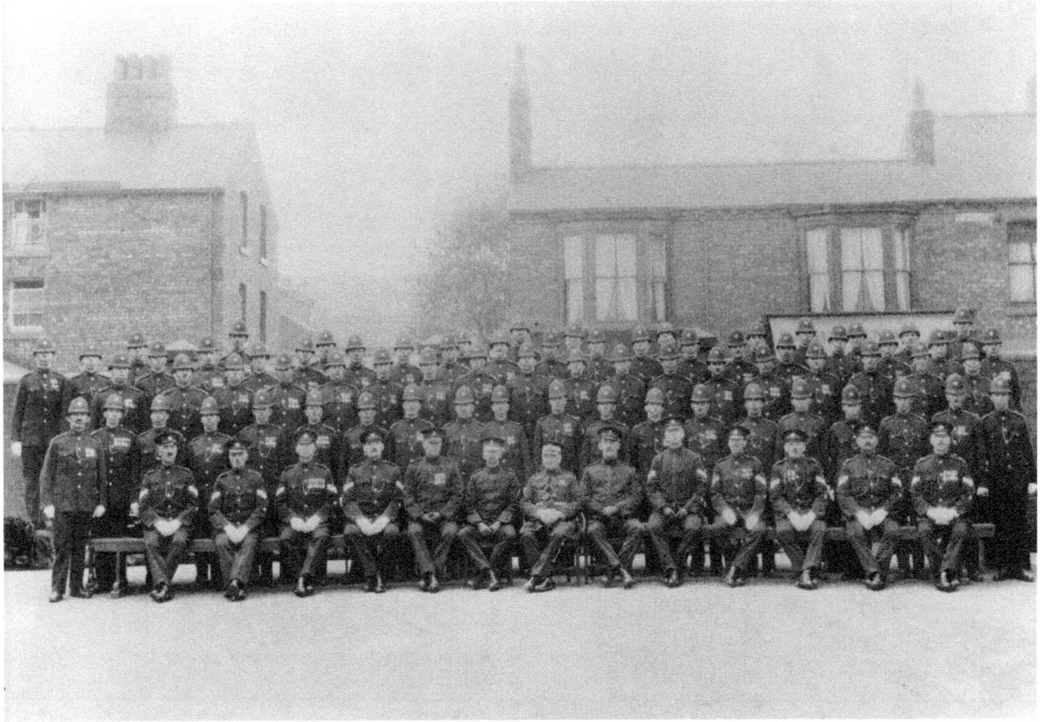

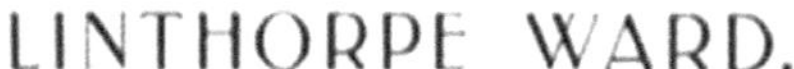
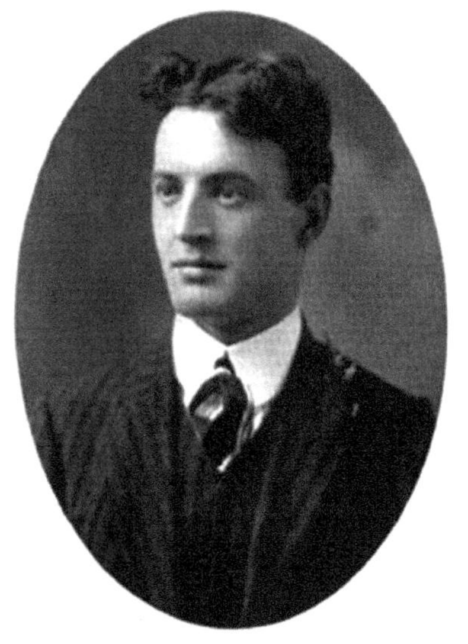

An election poster for Albert Edward Forbes (son of John Forbes, of Forbes' Bakery) from November 1910. Forbes was councillor for the Linthorpe Ward from 1910 until his death in 1920 (a result of wounds he received during the First World War).

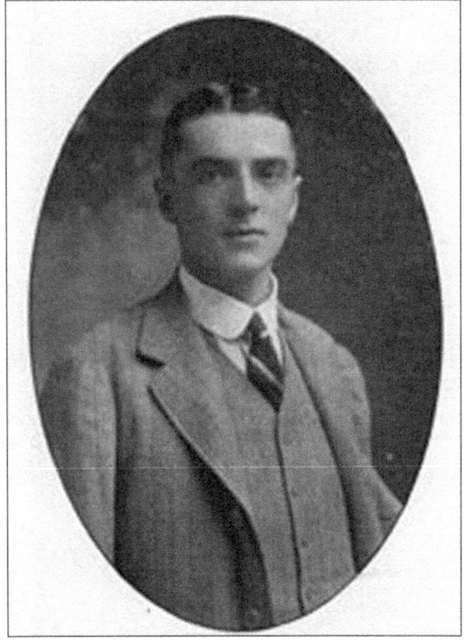

Photograph of George Hutton Bowes Wilson. Bowes Wilson was a solicitor from Hutton Rudby. He was councillor for the Exchange Ward from 1906-1916 and was the only member of the town council to be killed in action during the First World War. Captain Bowes Wilson was killed near Ypres in 1918, while serving with the 4th Battalion of the Yorkshire Regiment. His portrait, by George Kewley, was unveiled in the council chamber of the town hall on 12 July 1921.

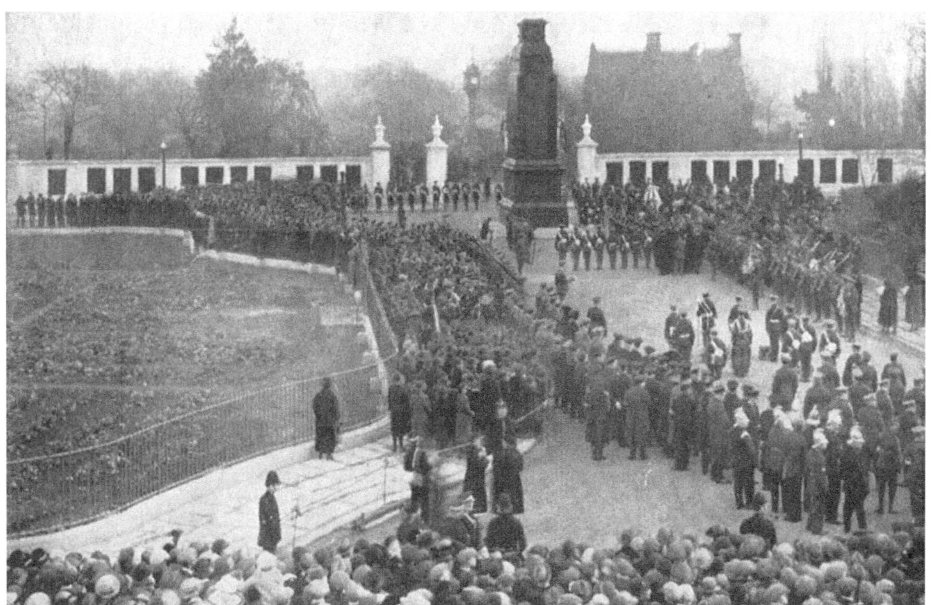

Unveiling the cenotaph and memorial walls on 11 November 1922. Paid for chiefly by public subscription, the thirty-four feet high cenotaph, made of Aberdeen granite, and the adjacent memorial walls record over 3,300 names.

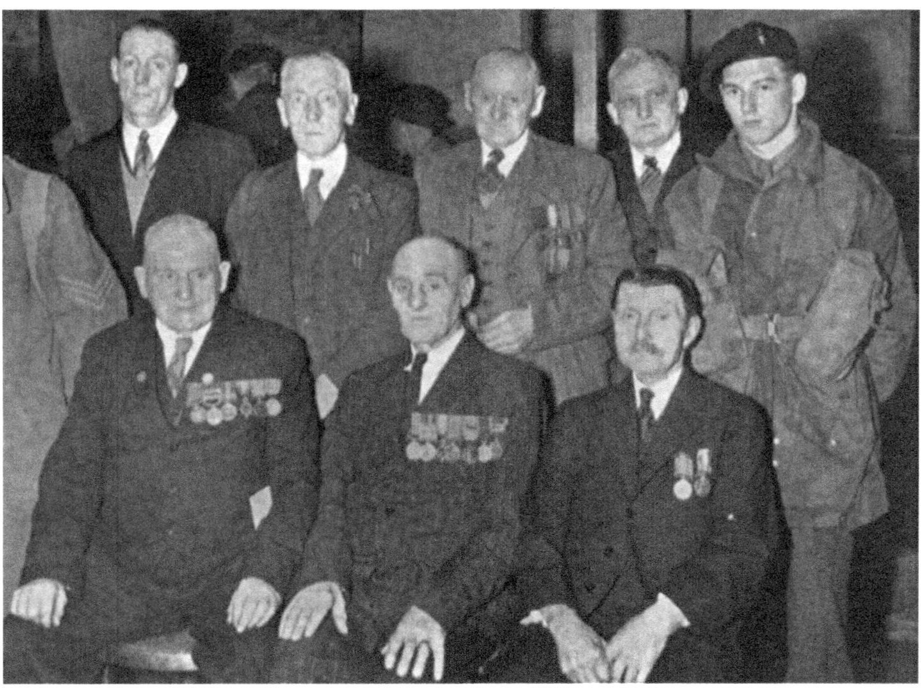

Middlesbrough's three Victoria Cross holders (Tom Dresser, Jim Smith and Stan Hollis), along with a soldier and Boer War veterans, photographed for the British Legion Festival of Remembrance programme for the 1961 gathering at the town hall.

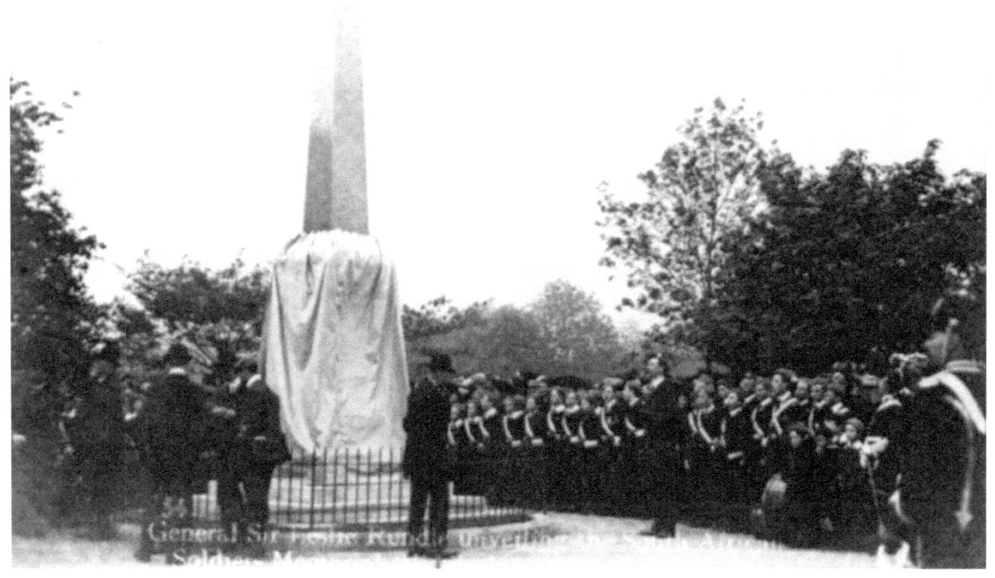

General Sir Leslie Rundle unveiling the South African (Boer) war memorial in Albert Park on 9 June 1905.

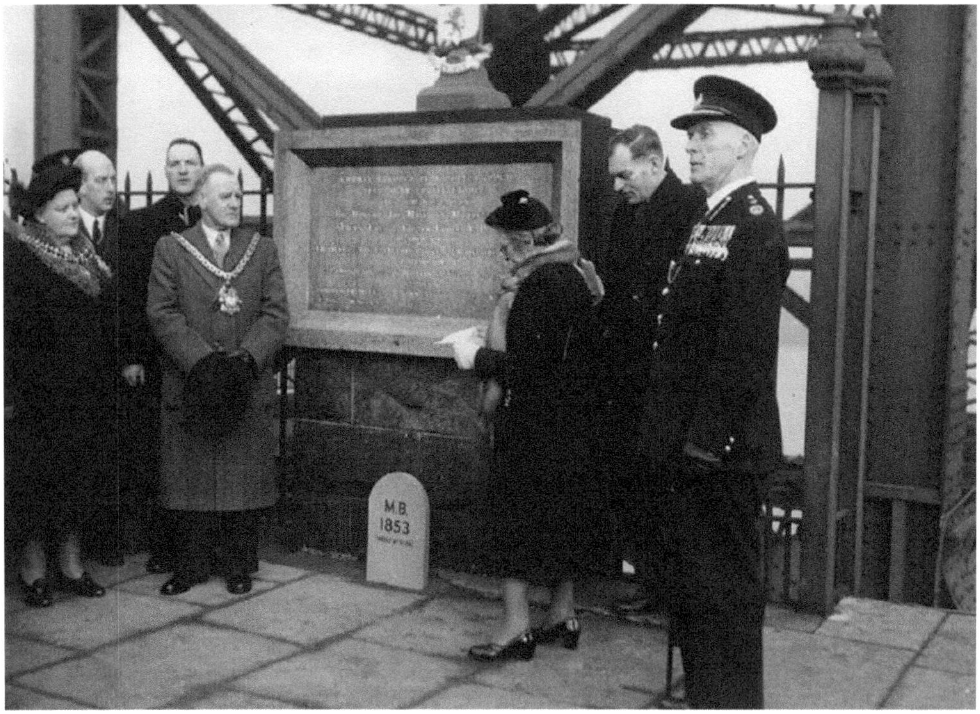

Beating the bounds at the Transporter Bridge: the stone shows that the boundary of the town in 1853 was in the centre of the river.

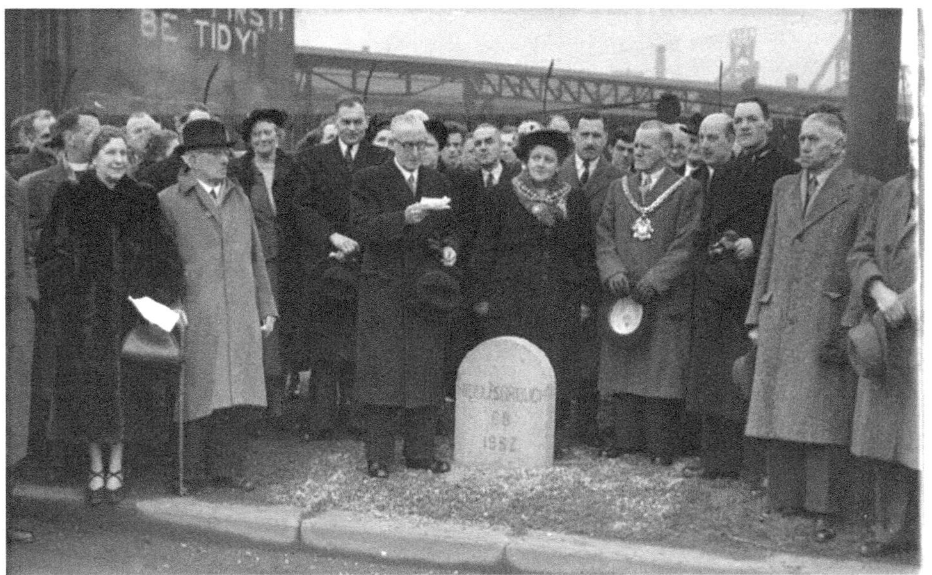

Beating the bounds at the 1932 boundary marker, in the industrial area of the town.

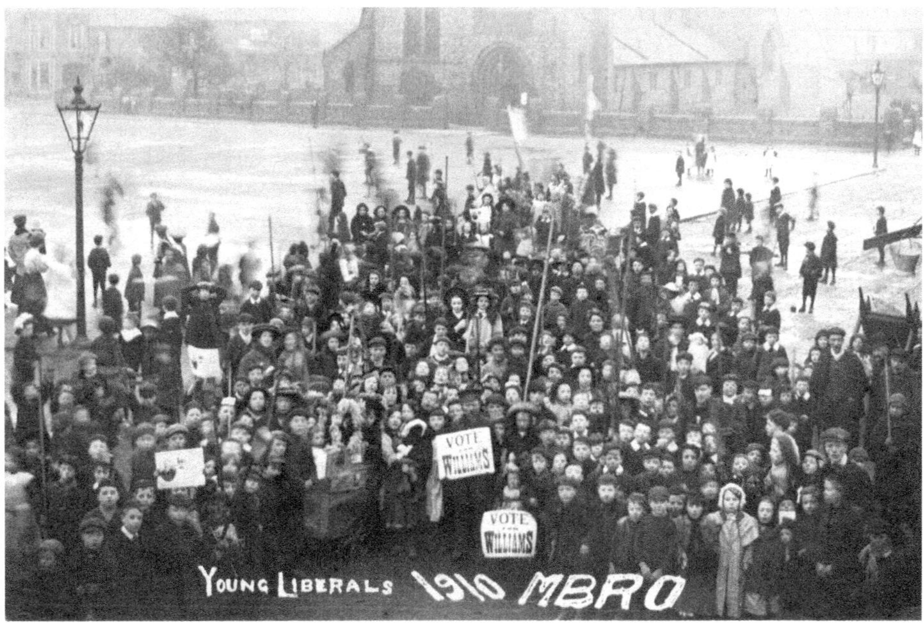

Young Liberals, seen in North Ormesby Market Place. They were campaigning for Penry Williams MP. Williams was the son of Edward Williams, manager of Bolckow and Vaughan. He was elected as a Liberal MP in 1910 with 9,670 votes, and re-elected again in 1911 with 10, 313 votes. In 1918, during Lloyd George's so called 'Khaki Election', he was re-elected with 8,470 votes. In 1922, however, he was returned at the bottom of the poll. He was elected again in the December of the following year, but 1924 saw the finish of Williams' political career when he was beaten into third place in an election that saw Ellen Wilkinson elected as Labour MP. She went on to be the first Labour woman MP to hold a cabinet seat when she became Minister for Education.

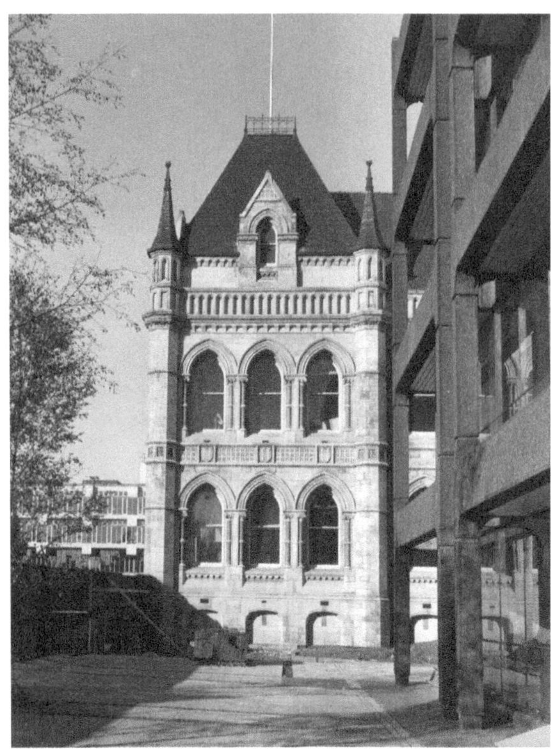

An unusual side view of the municipal buildings, showing the late twentieth-century civic centre extension to the building.

Robing the deputy mayor. Malcolm Pritchard JP (seen on the left) installs his deputy, the late Bryan Lonsborough, with his robes and chain of office.

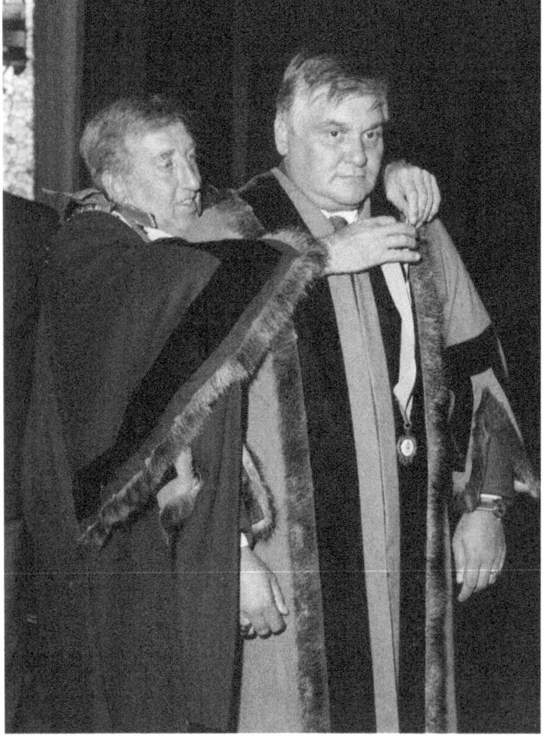

Opposite above: The town hall and municipal buildings, showing Victoria Square and the bandstand. Opened in January 1889 by the Prince and Princess of Wales, the Darlington architect G.G Hoskins was responsible for their design.

Opposite below: The Duke and Duchess of York opened the Tees (Newport) Bridge, the world's largest and heaviest vertical lift bridge then built, on 28 February 1934.

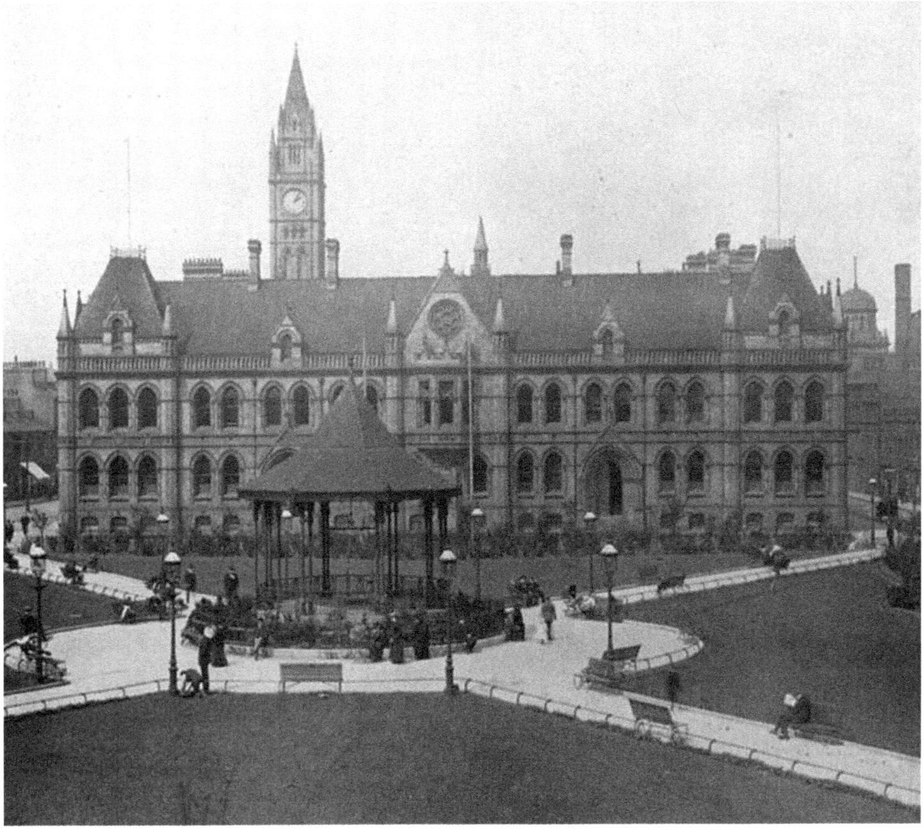

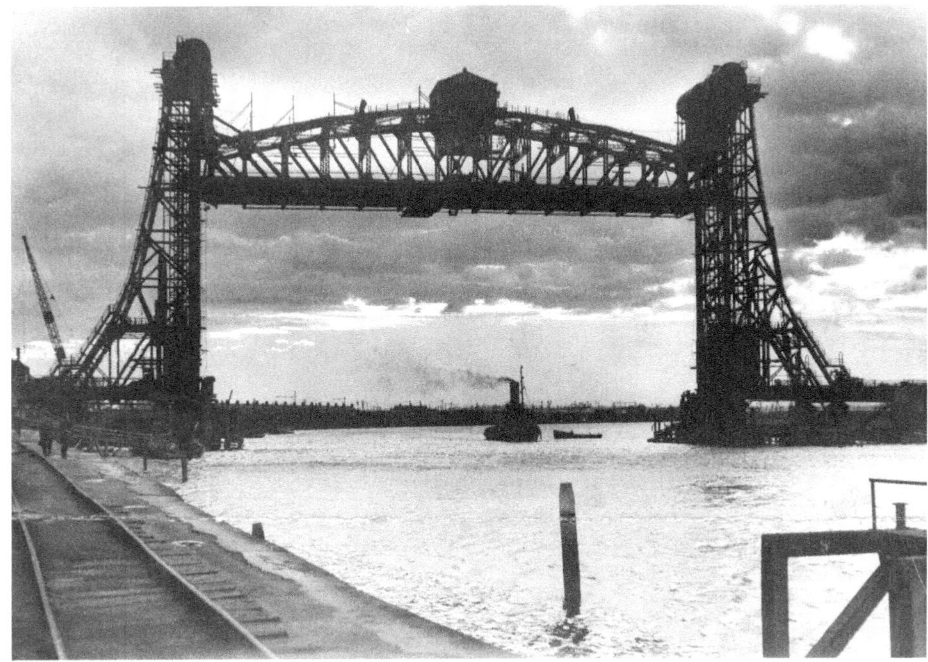

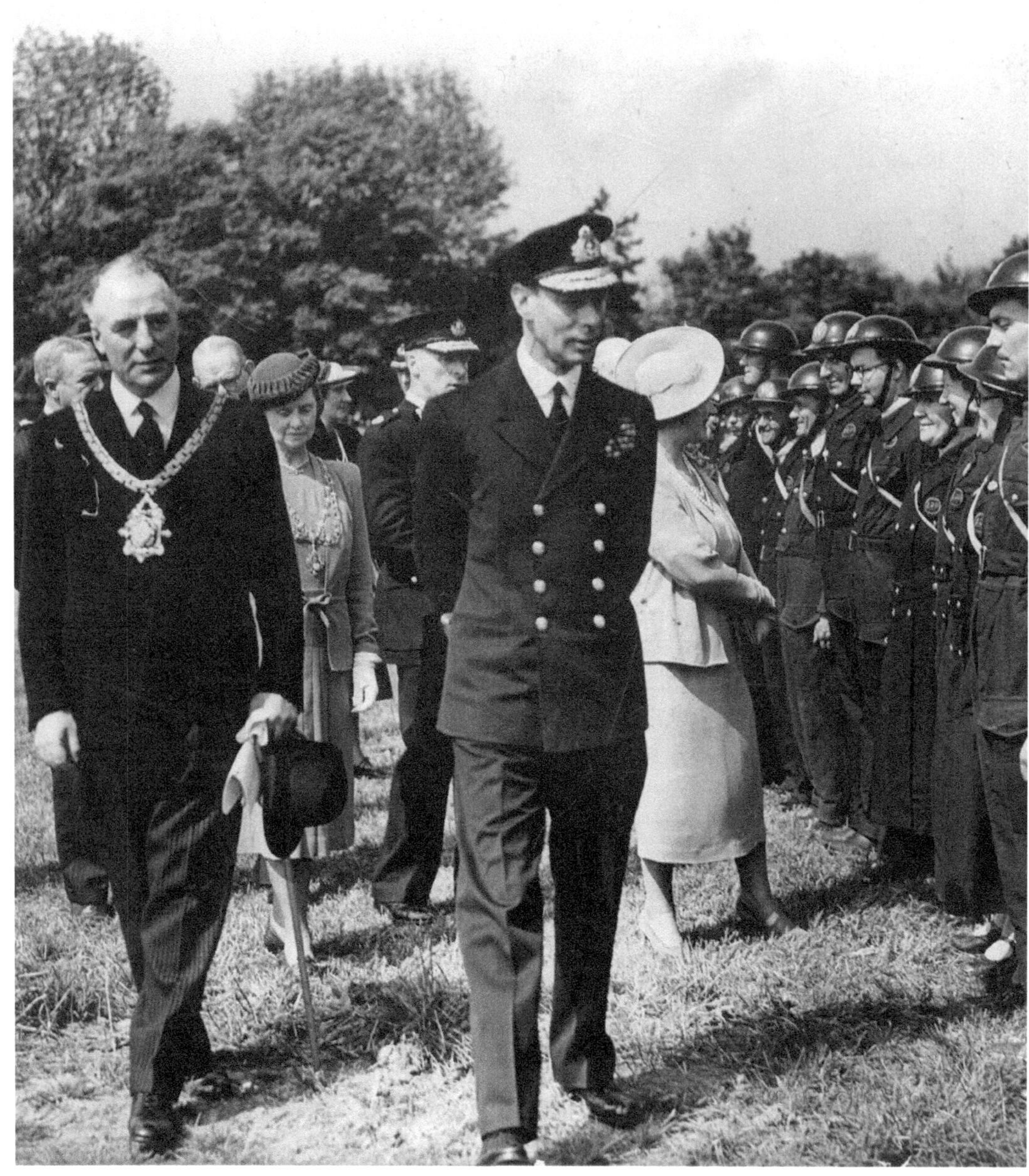

Scene in the Albert Park in 1942. Their Majesties King George VI and Queen Elizabeth, accompanied by the Mayor and Mayoress William and Mrs Crosthwaite and the town clerk, Preston Kitchen (seen in the background wearing glasses), reviewing Civil Defence volunteers.

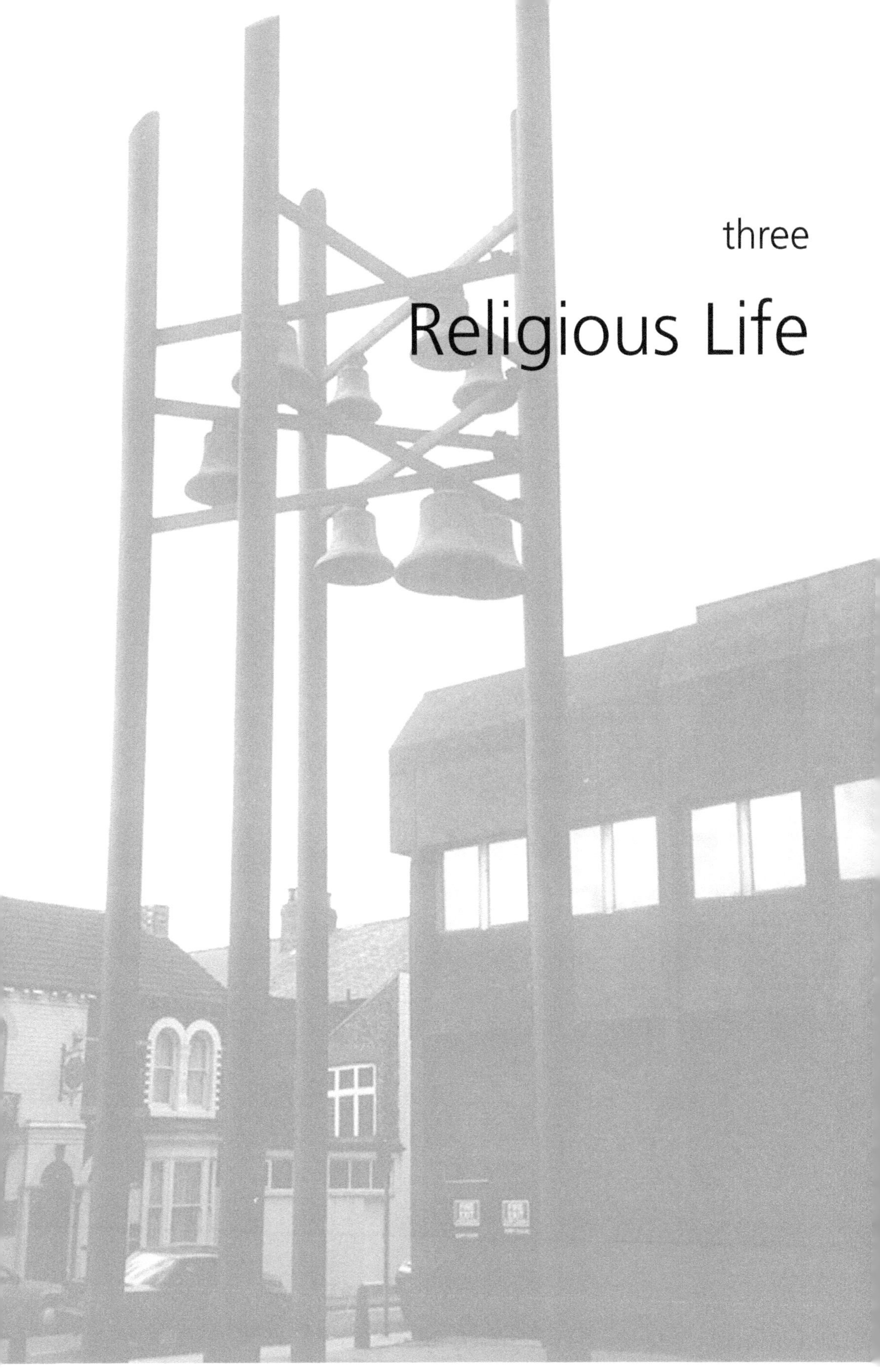
three
Religious Life

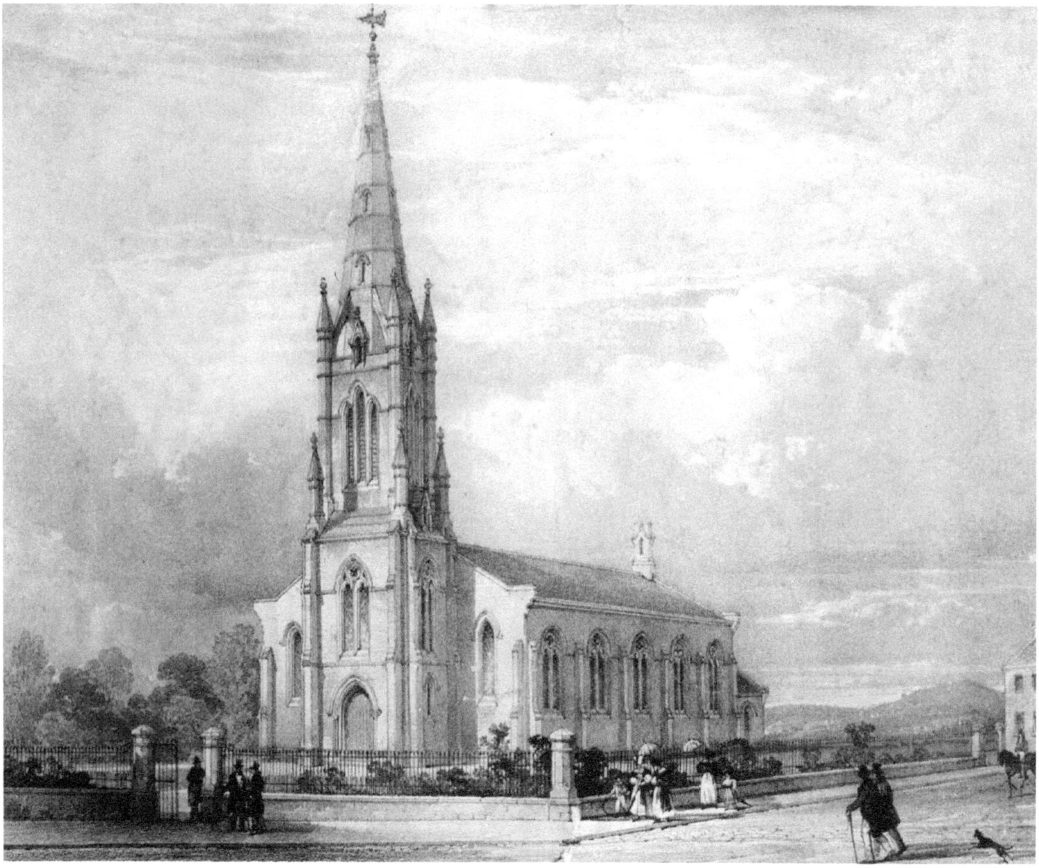

Above: St Hilda's, Middlesbrough's own parish church, as planned by the architect father and son team John and Benjamin Green of Newcastle. The building was opened in 1840, and consecrated by Dr Edward Maltby DD, FRS, the Bishop of Durham.

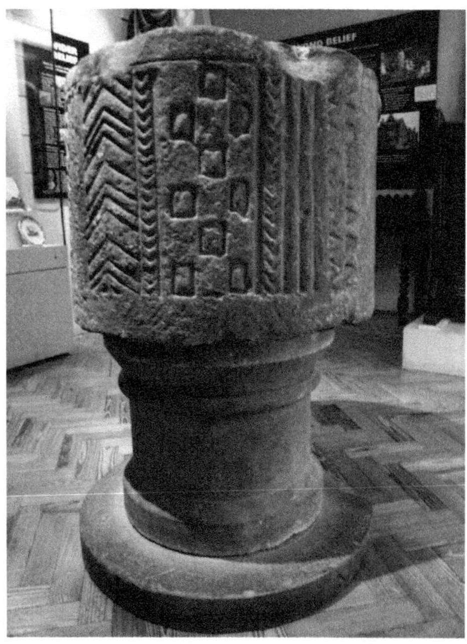

Left: The original font from the Middlesbrough priory was discovered, abandoned, by Joseph Pease in the 1820s: it was used by him as a plant pot at his home in Darlington, and after his death in 1879 it was left to St Hilda's church. When the church was demolished in 1969 the font became part of the Dorman Museum collection, where it is still on display.

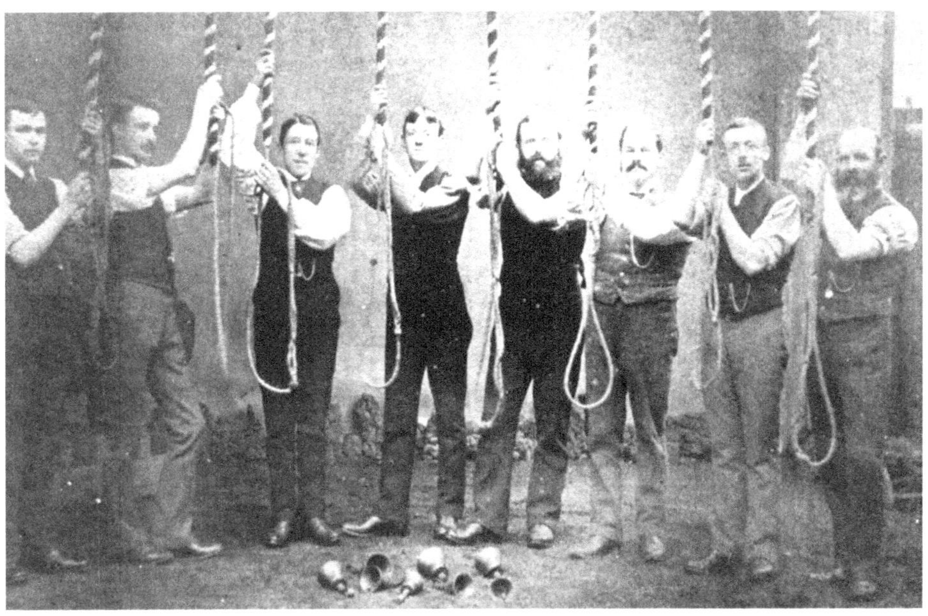

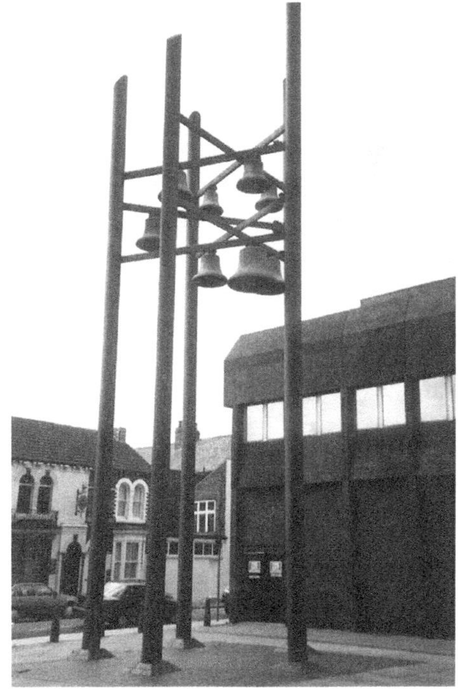

Above: St Hilda's church had a peal of bells in the tower. Here we see the proud campanologists posing with their bell ropes in the bell tower in the 1890s.

Right: The bells from St Hilda's church while they were outside All Saints church. They were installed in the tower of St Hilda's, and later removed to All Saints after the church was demolished in 1969. The bells are now on a campanile at the junction of Linthorpe and Grange Roads.

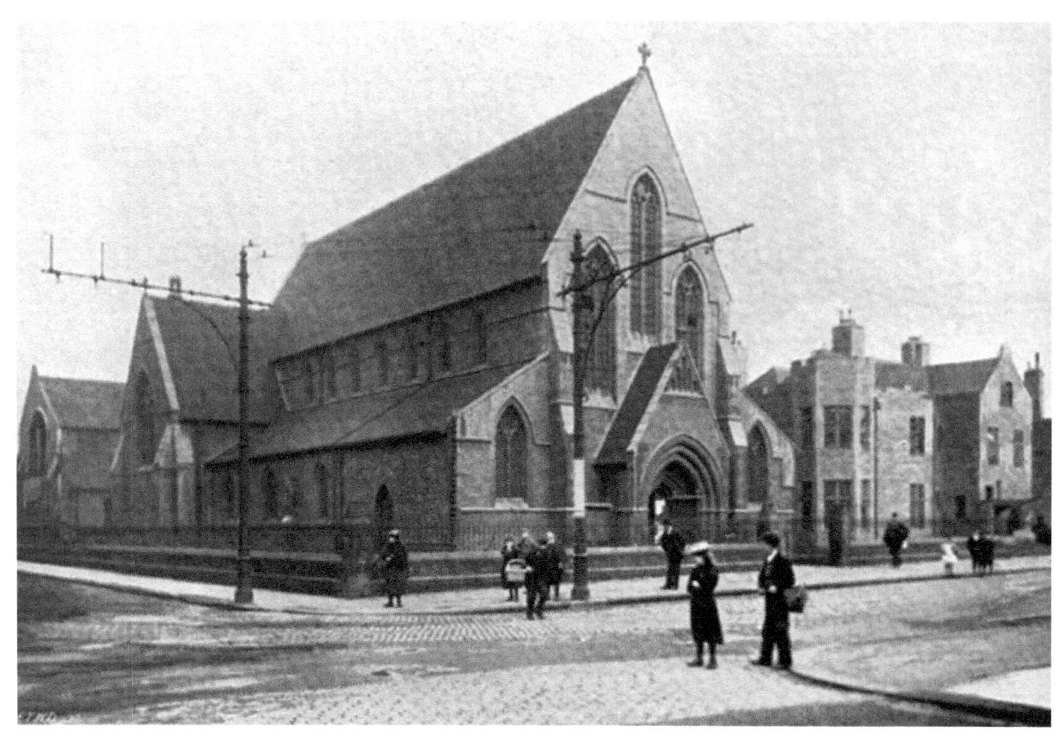

Above: All Saint's church at the corner of Grange Road and Linthorpe Road. Known as the ironmasters' church, it was designed by George Edmund Street in 1873 and its building and furnishing was funded by local industrialists such as W.R.I. Hopkins and John Gjers. Following a number of delays in building work, the church was consecrated in 1878.

Left: Father John Stote Lotherington Burn was the parish priest at All Saints for forty-one years. During the 1908 ironworks depression, Fr Burn helped to organise a Christian Social Union. He fed the hungry (he begged for scraps from the butcher's in order to make enough soup to feed 200 men, women and children every day), visited the sick and looked after the down-trodden, providing blankets for families and shoes for children. All this work earned him the title 'The Champion of the Poor'.

Opposite below: Father Burn died on Thursday 28 May 1925 at the age of seventy-one. The funeral took place shortly afterwards and brought the whole town to a standstill. Thousands turned out to show their respects and thronged the streets over six deep. The photograph is taken from a postcard produced as a reminder of the occasion.

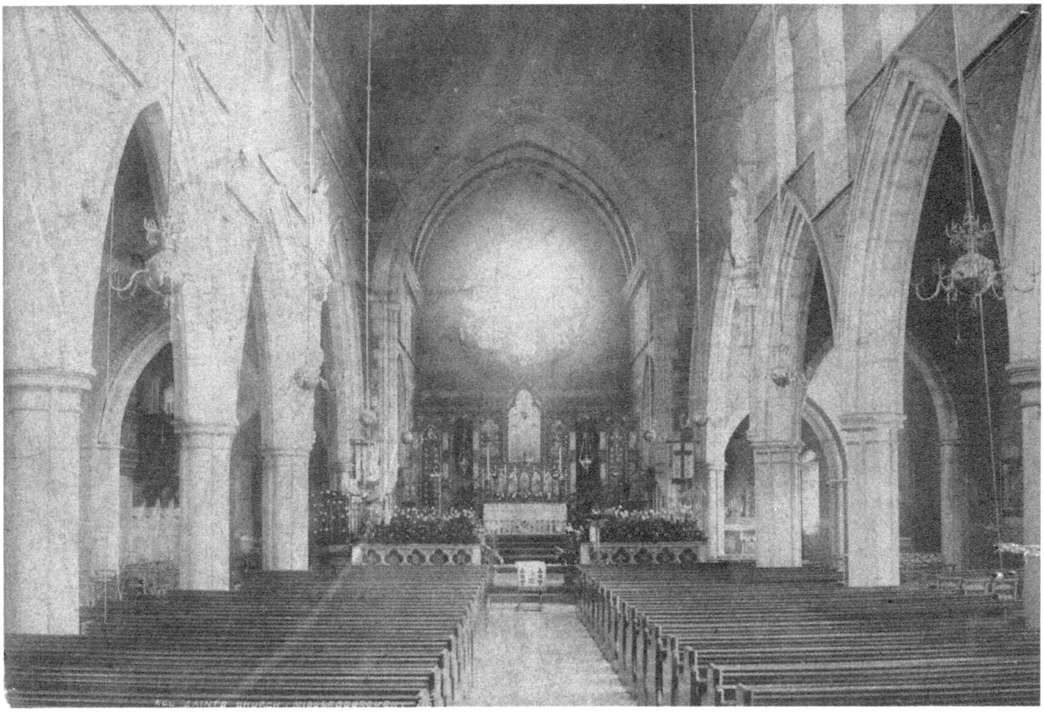

The interior of All Saint's church, showing the main aisle and the circular east window behind the altar. Its painted glass was designed by Burlison and Grylls and paid for by the ironmaster John Gjers in 1890.

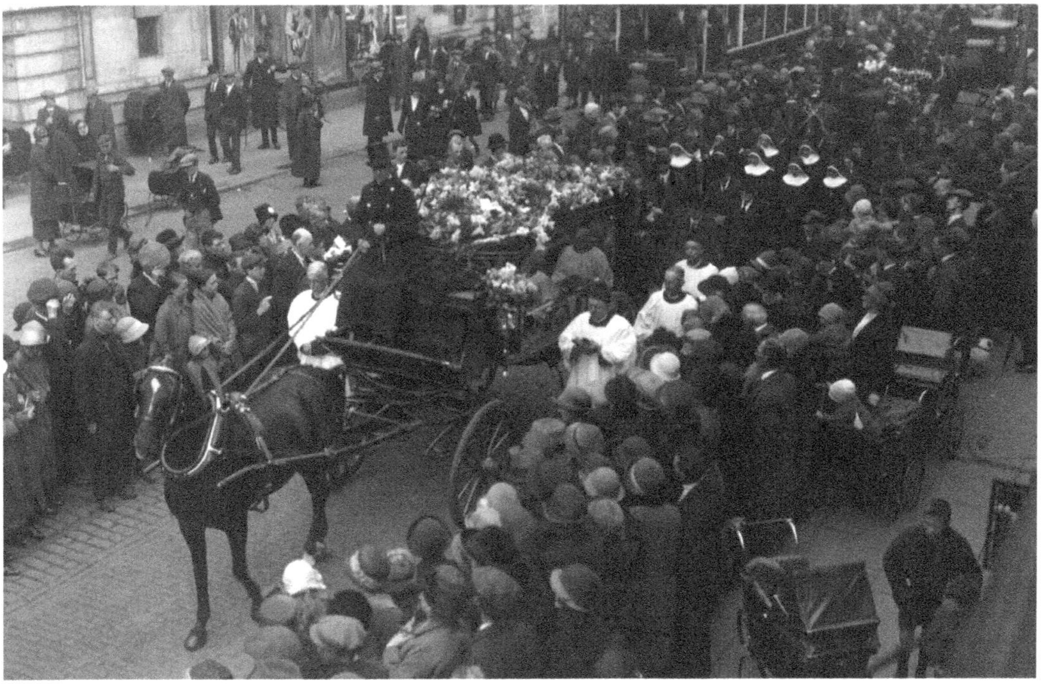

S. COLUMBA'S CHURCH
CANNON STREET

GRAND

BAZAAR

will be held in the

PARISH HALL, Boundary Road

on

SATURDAY, DEC. 7th, 1957

TO BE OPENED AT 2-30 P.M. BY

Lady Harrison - Nunthorpe.

Come and Buy your Xmas Gifts

PLENTY OF VARIETY · Toys, Fancy Goods, Household Linen, etc.

ADMISSION - - SIXPENCE (all ages)

Tea and Refreshments.

Kirby Bros. (Printers) Ltd., 67, Newport Road, Middlesbrough. Tel. 3306.

A poster for a fundraising bazaar at St Columba's church in Boundary Road. The church was designed by Temple Lushington Moore. Lady Harrison of Nunthorpe opened the bazaar on Saturday 5 December 1957.

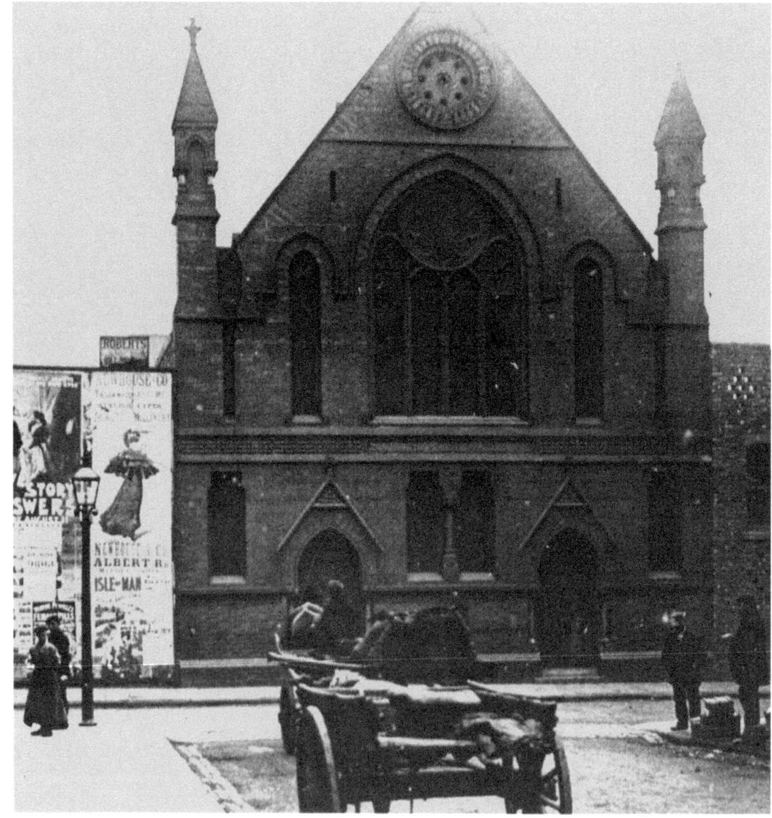

St Columba's church, Boundary Road. The church was designed in 1889 by Temple Moore.

Right: St John's church stands proudly on Marton Road. Here the tower and the west window are seen from Russell Street. Built in 1865 to the designs of John Norton and later extended, which was paid for by Sir Samuel Sader, it is the oldest place of worship still in use in the town centre today.

Below: St George's United Reformed church, Linthorpe Road. The church was built in 1894 and stood at the junction of Princes and Linthorpe Roads. The church closed for worship in May 1966, and was demolished in 1980.

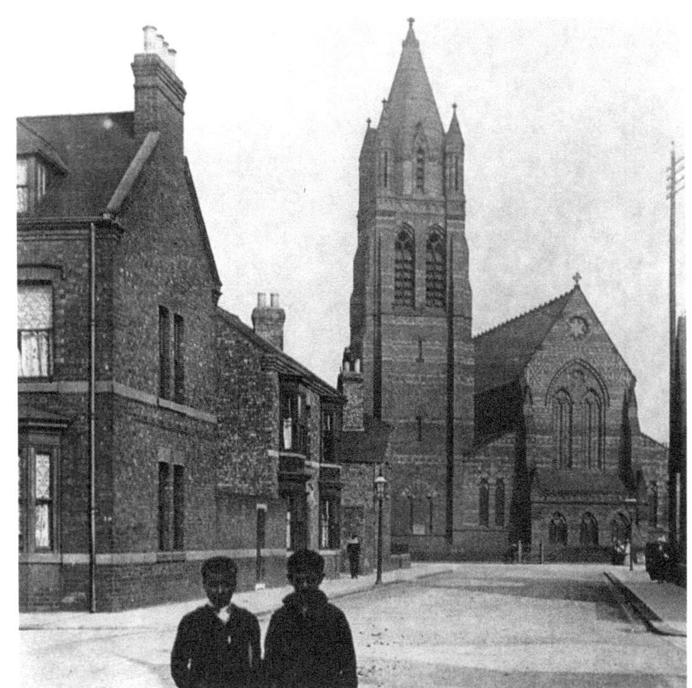

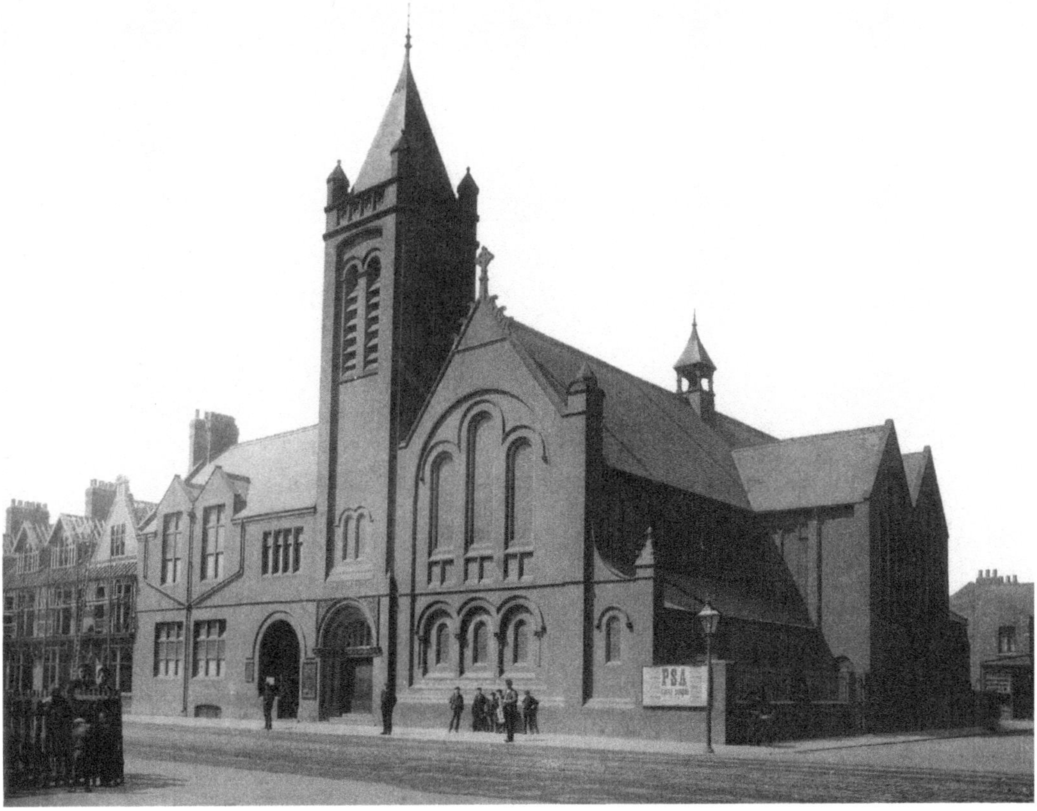

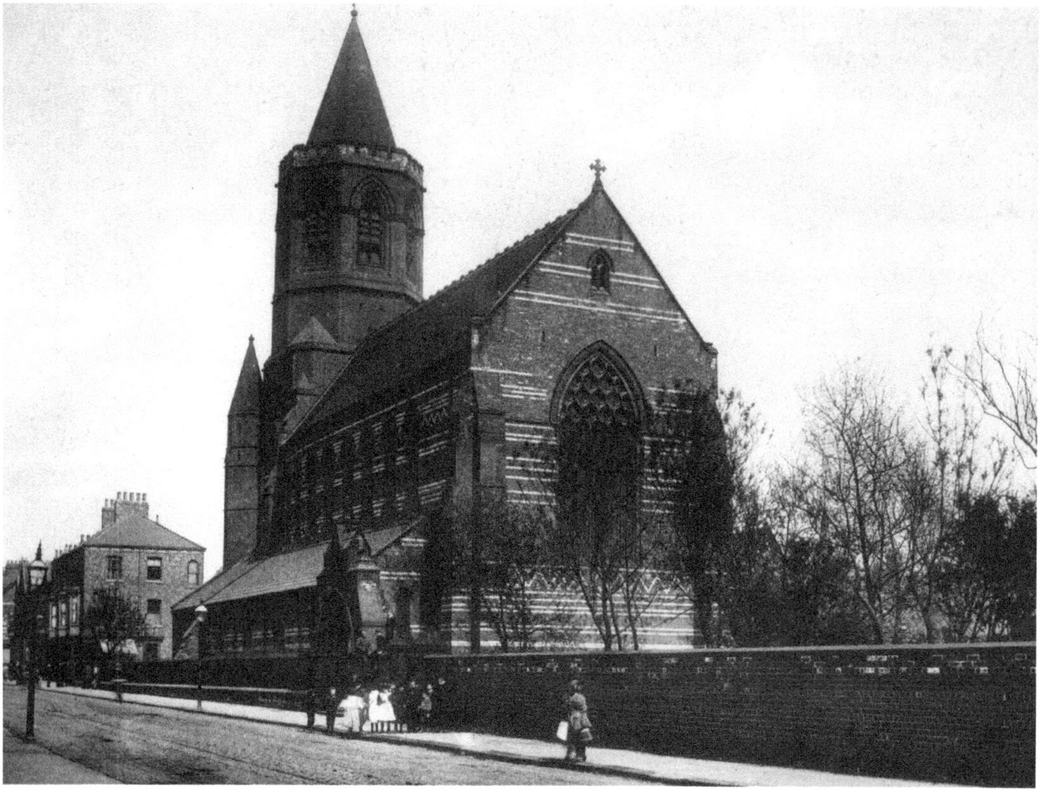

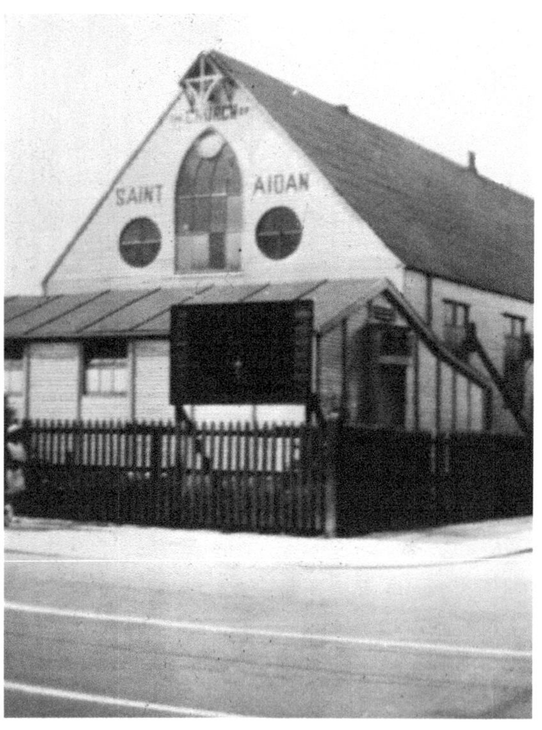

Above: St Paul's church, Newport. The church was designed by Thomas Austin and R.J. Johnson, the foundation stone was laid by Mrs Hustler of Acklam Hall on 25 June 1870, and the church consecrated on 14 December 1871. It closed in 1966 and was demolished in 1967, less than 100 years after it opened.

Left: St Aiden's church, Linthorpe Road. This temporary building was originally opened in 1898; it was dismantled and relocated to Clifton Street in the 1930s to make way for the Co-operative Stores Emporium. The site is now occupied by a supermarket.

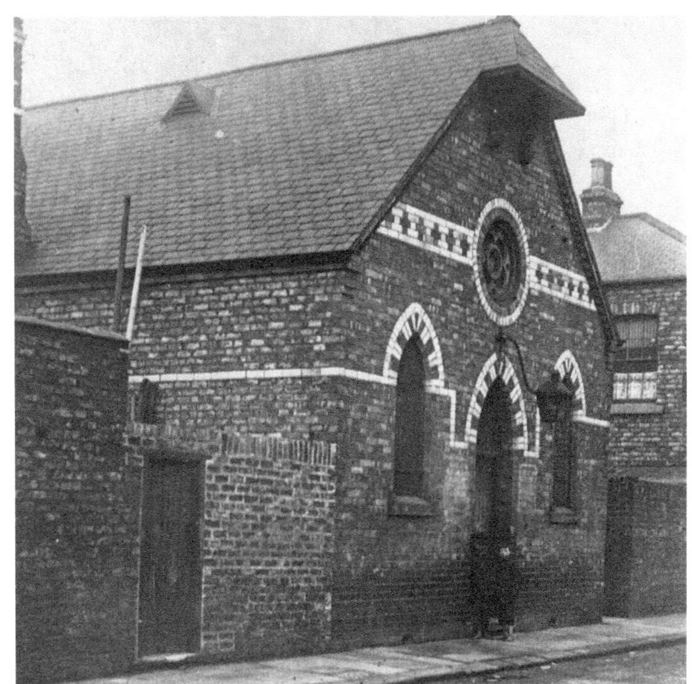

Right: St Lawrence's Mission church, Alfred Street. Opened in 1889.

Below: Wesley Central Mission, or 'Big Wesley' as it became affectionately known, stood at the junction of Linthorpe and Corporation Roads. It was opened on Sunday 20 September 1863. The last service took place on Sunday 28 March 1954 and the site is now occupied by British Home Stores. The town hall clock tower can be seen in the distance, and the building in between is the Athenaeum, which was the home of the Cleveland Literary and Philosophical Society, opened by Sir Stafford Northcote.

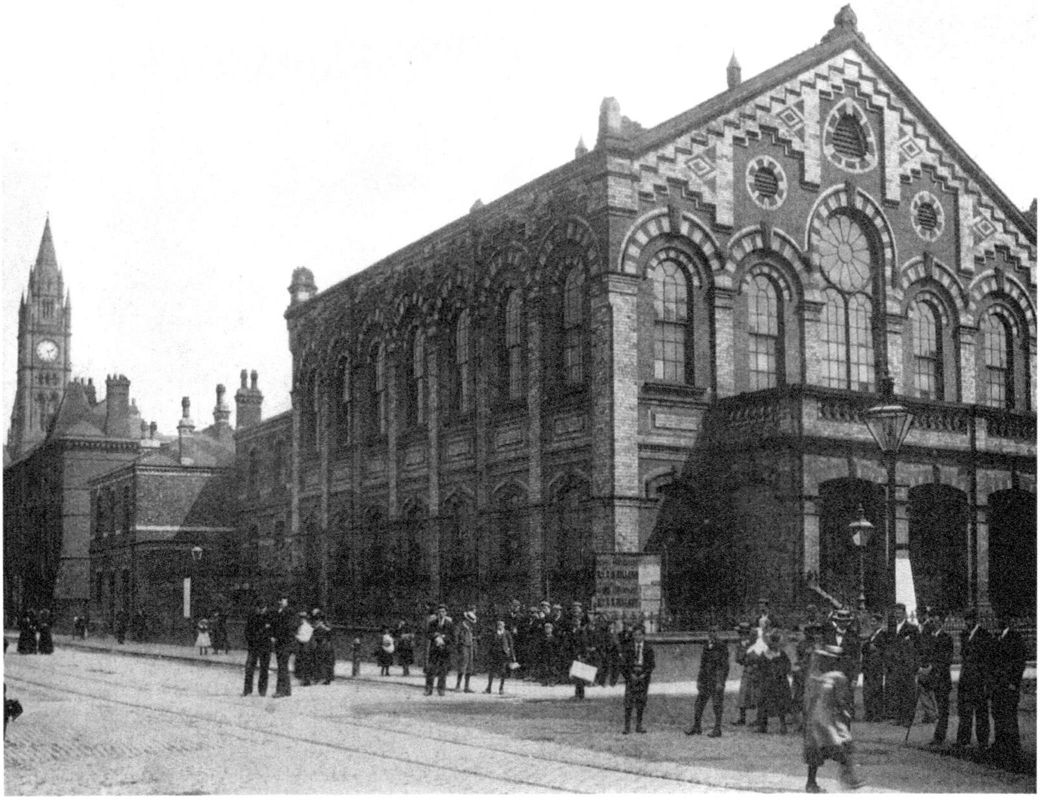

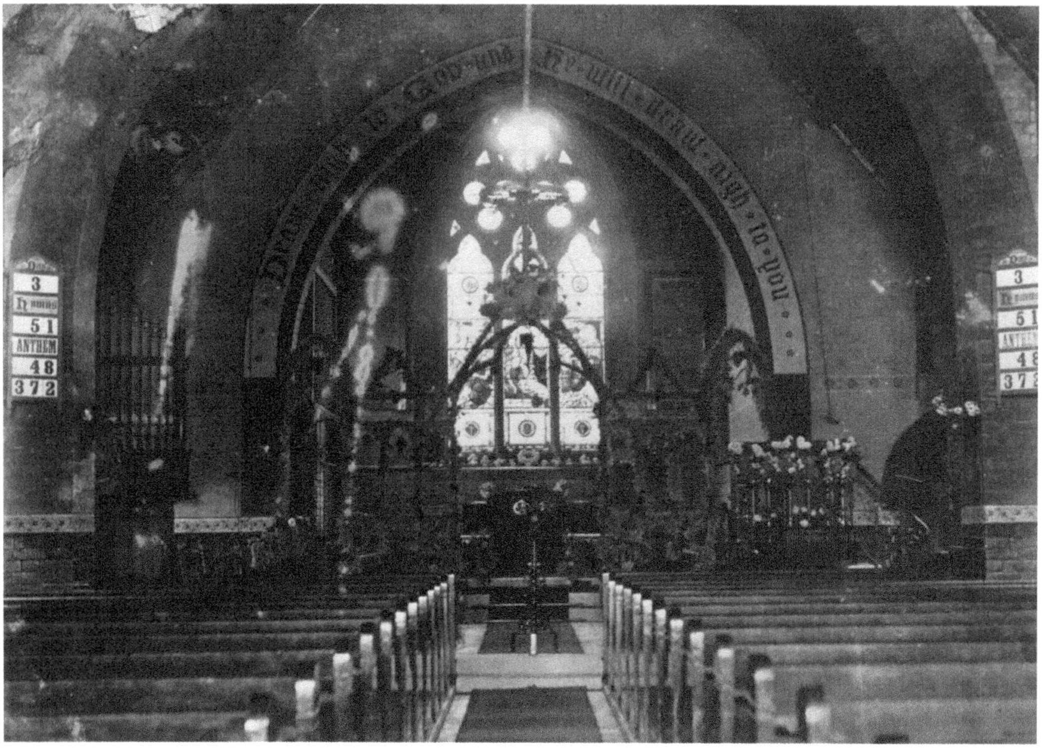

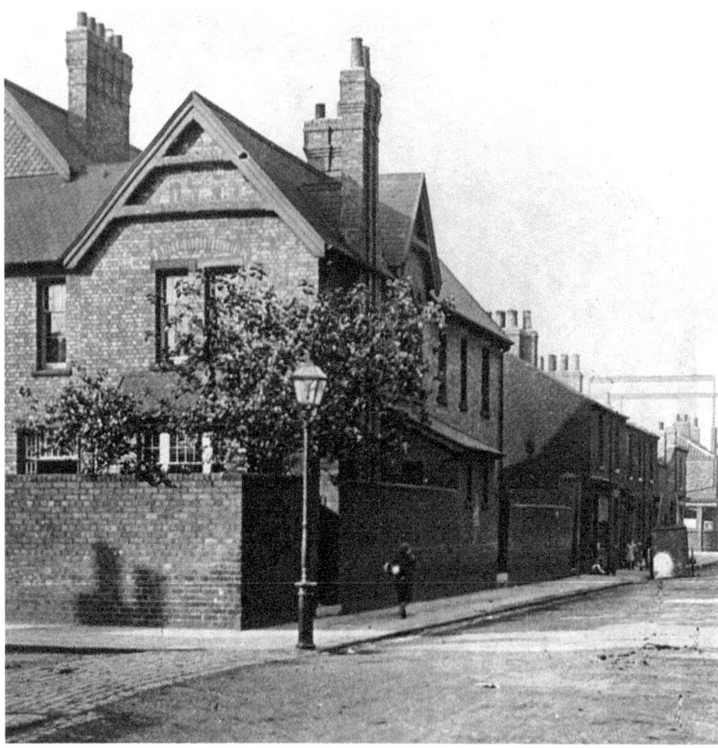

Above: St Peter's church, Lower Feversham Street. Paid for by Sir Raylton Dixon on land donated by Henry Bolckow, it was designed by the Middlesbrough architect William Blessley and opened in September 1873.

Left: St Peter's church became the first ecclesiastical casualty of the Second World War when it was damaged during an air raid in 1940; it was later demolished.

Grange Road Methodist church, at the corner of Dunning Road. It opened for worship in September 1877 but closed in July 1934, after which it was temporarily used as an art gallery by the council from October 1937. In the ten years as a gallery it held 105 exhibitions, and received over 307,000 visitors. It was later demolished to make way for the Middlesbrough police station.

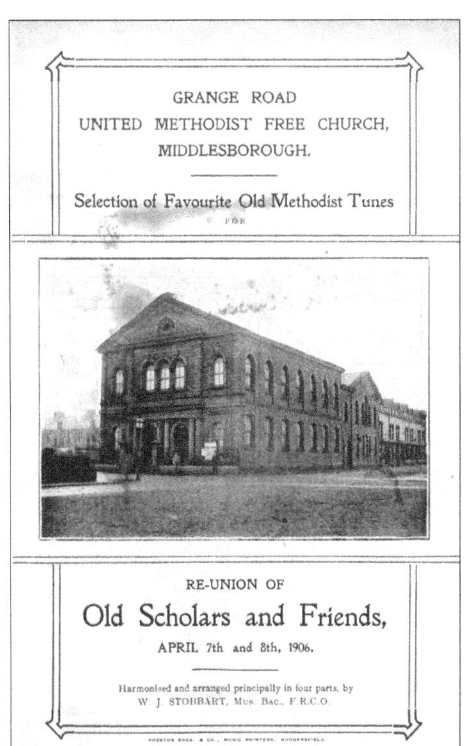

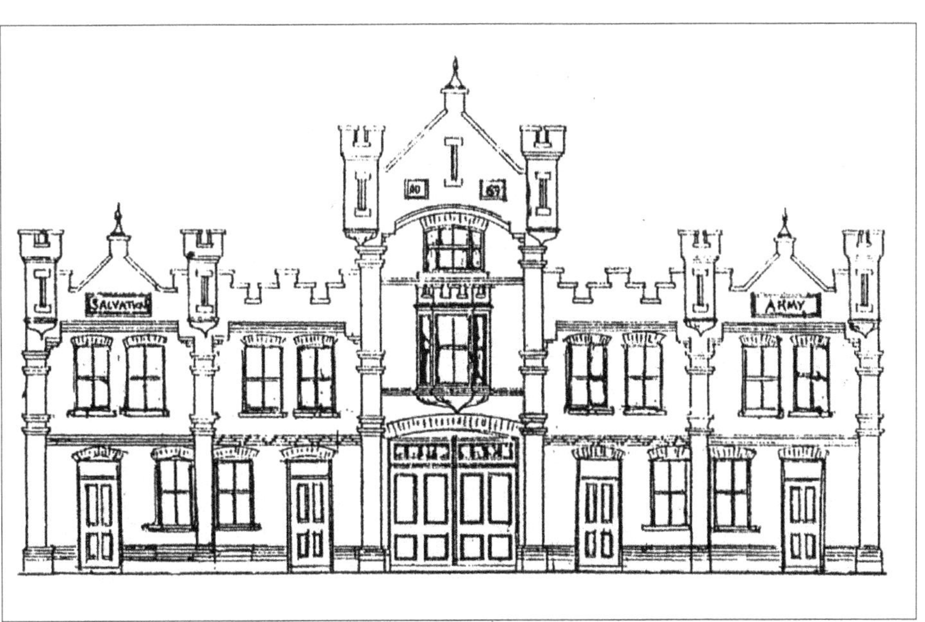

Salvation Army citadel, Richmond Street, St Hilda's. Known officially as the Middlesbrough No. 1 Corps, it was opened in 1892 and closed in February 1968.

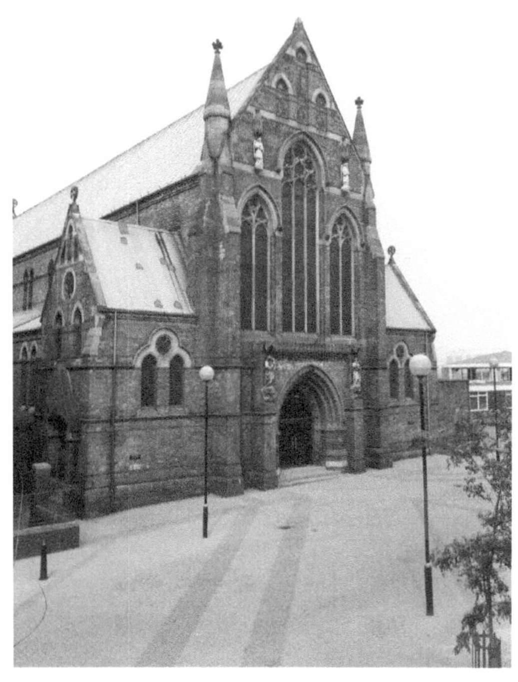

The Roman Catholic Cathedral of St Mary's in Sussex Street, St Hilda's. The building was opened in the 1870s on the site of the original 1857 church building. In 1879, His Eminence Cardinal Manning installed Richard Lacy, who was until then the parish priest, as the first Roman Catholic bishop of the newly created diocese of Middlesbrough in this building.

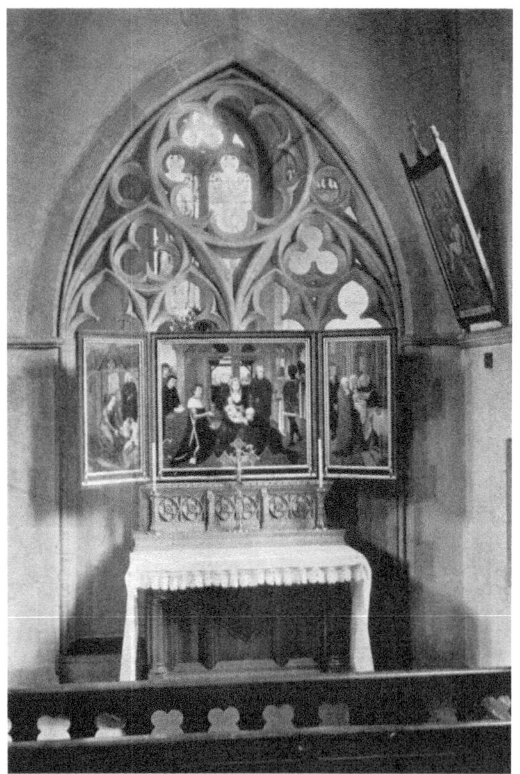

A Victorian copy of the famous triptych of Jan Floriens by Hans Memling, which was housed at the Magi Altar. The copy is painted on tin panels and has recently been extensively cleaned and restored, and along with a number of other objects from the former cathedral is housed in the Dorman Museum.

Right: St Patrick's Roman
Catholic church, Cannon Street.
At first, as was the case with
a number of Catholic mission
churches, the church services
were held in the school hall. St
Patrick's School stood in Lawson
Street and had been built in 1873.
The church was opened by the
Rt Revd Richard Lacy, Bishop
of Middlesbrough, on Thursday
25 July 1901. The last mass held
in the building was on Friday 11
October 2002. The building has
since been demolished.

Below: The former Roman
Catholic orphanage Nazareth
House, designed by George
Goldie. Formerly run by the
Sisters of Nazareth, it is now a
private care home.

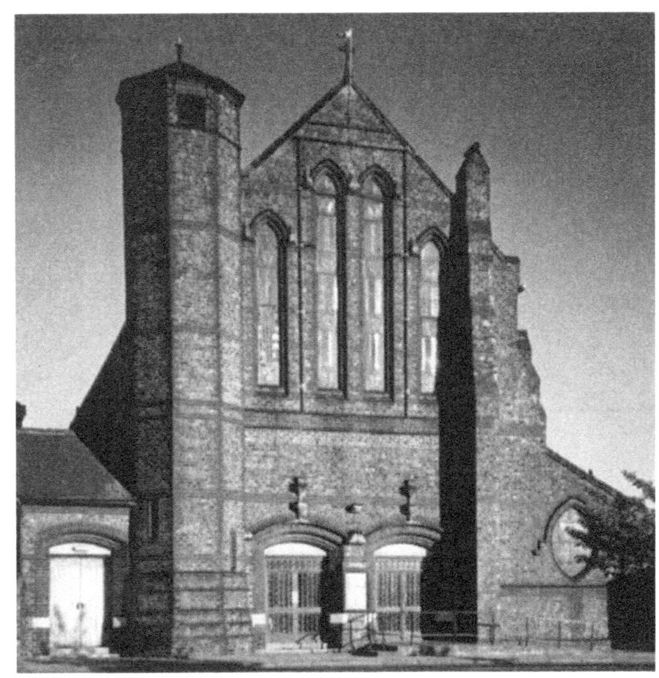

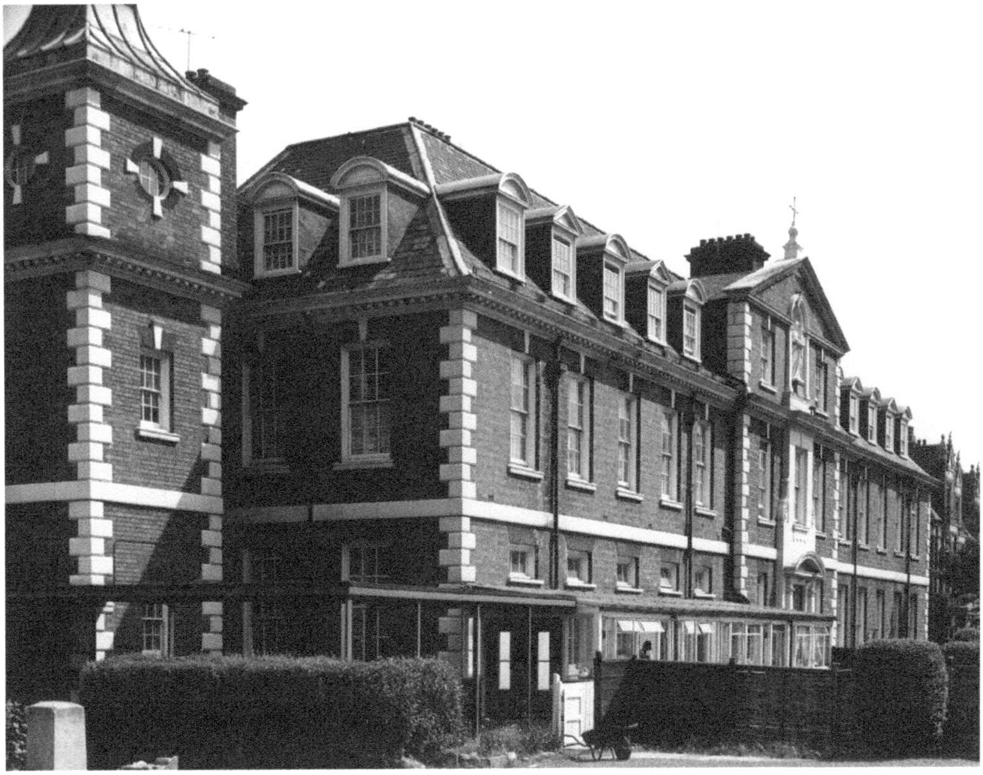

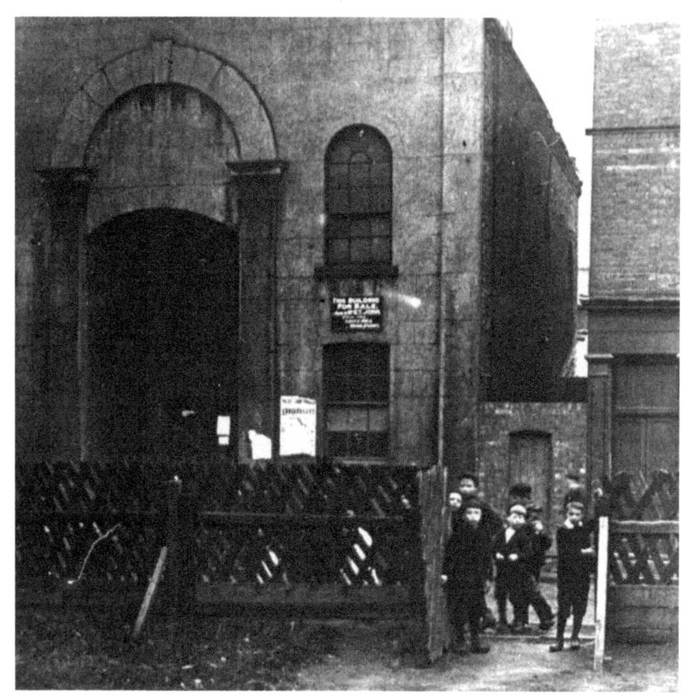

Left: Notice advertising the sale of the Centenary Methodist church, Market Place, St Hilda's.

Below: Centenary Methodist church during its demolition in 1959. The church had originally opened in 1838 and spent some time before its demolition in use as a shirt factory.

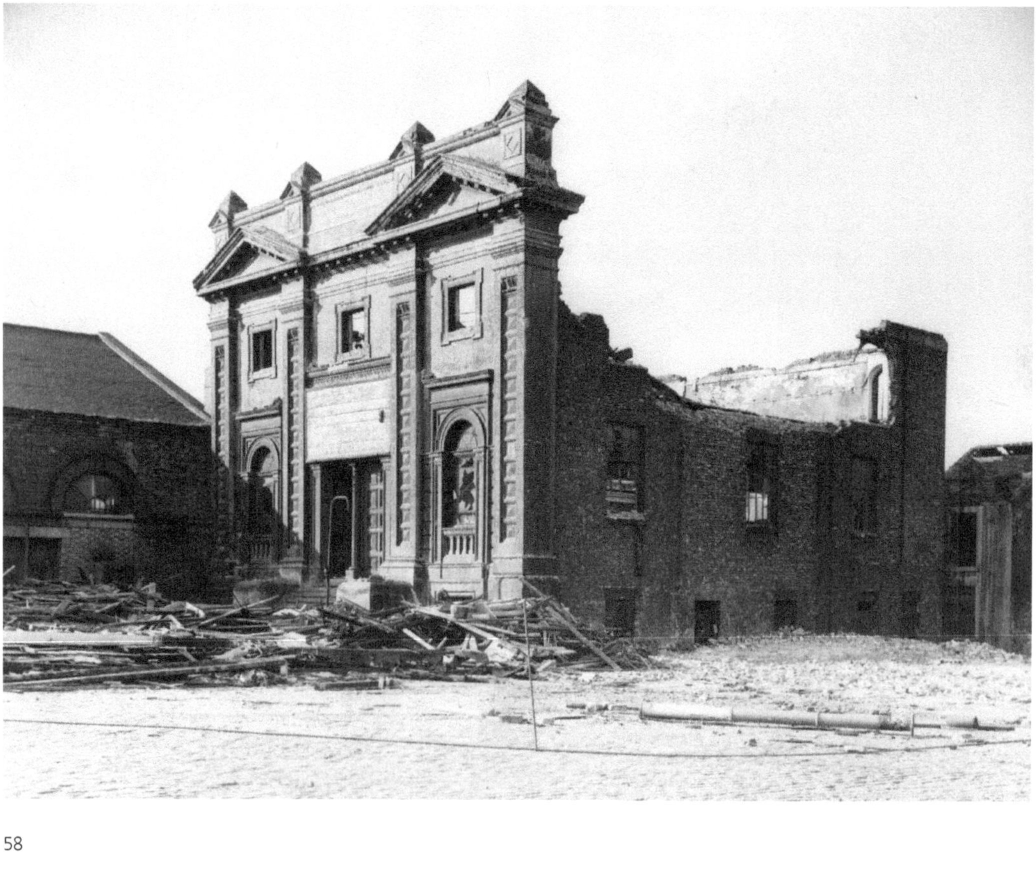

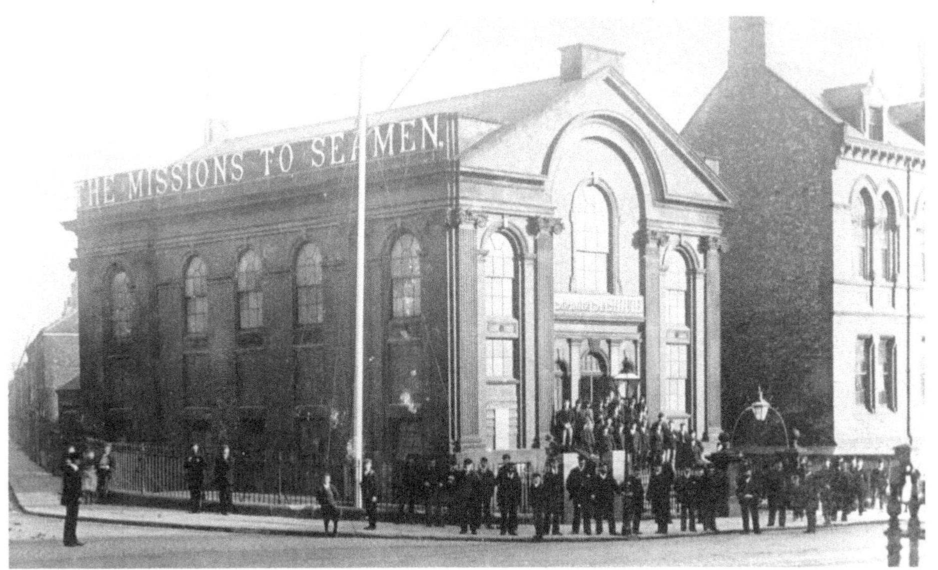

St Nicholas's Congregational chapel, Queen's Square, originally opened in 1857. It was later the home of the Missions to Seamen. It was opened as such on Wednesday 30 January 1895 by Lady Dixon, wife of the shipbuilding magnate Sir Raylton Dixon, on behalf of the Duchess of Northumberland. It closed in May 1964 when the Missions to Seamen moved to Flying Angel House at Wilton.

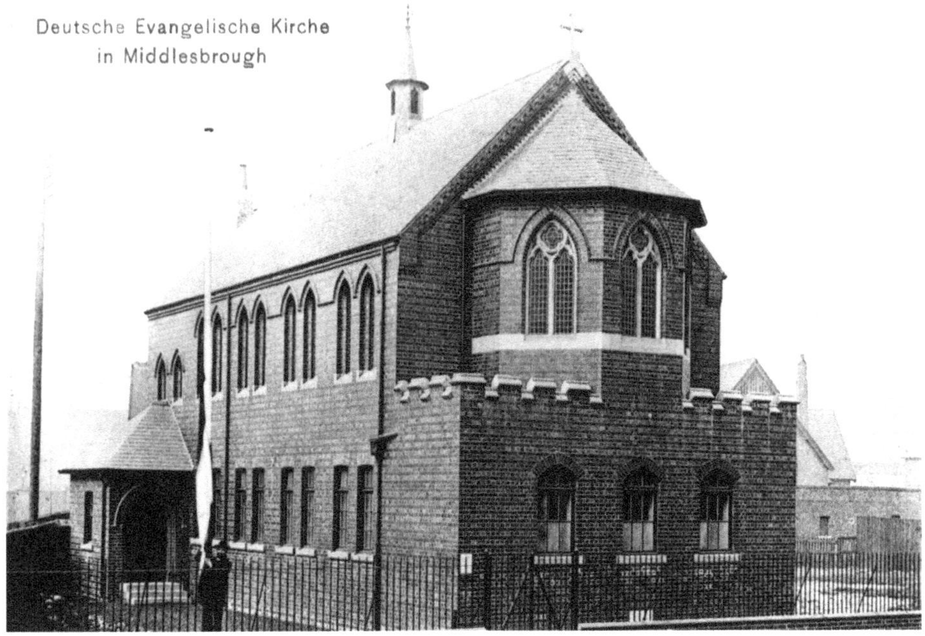

The German Lutheran church, Marton Road, Middlesbrough. The foundation stone of the building was laid on 27 November 1901. It closed in 1914, later being used as the Scandinavian Seaman's Mission, and a gospel hall. It is now the Cleveland Trade Unionists and Unemployed Workers Resource Centre. The German-speaking church community now worship at a converted house in Borough Road.

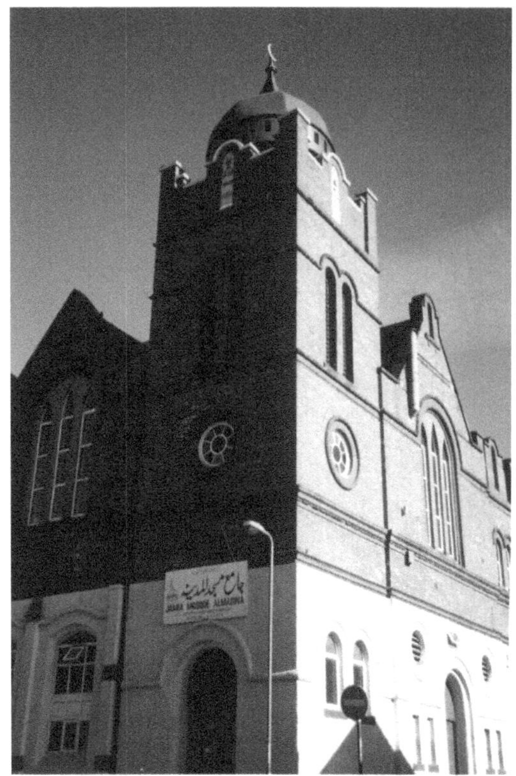

The former St Michael and All Angels' church, built in Waterloo Road in 1900. The last service was held in the church on Whit Sunday, 6 June 1976, and the church then became the Jamia Mosque Almadina.

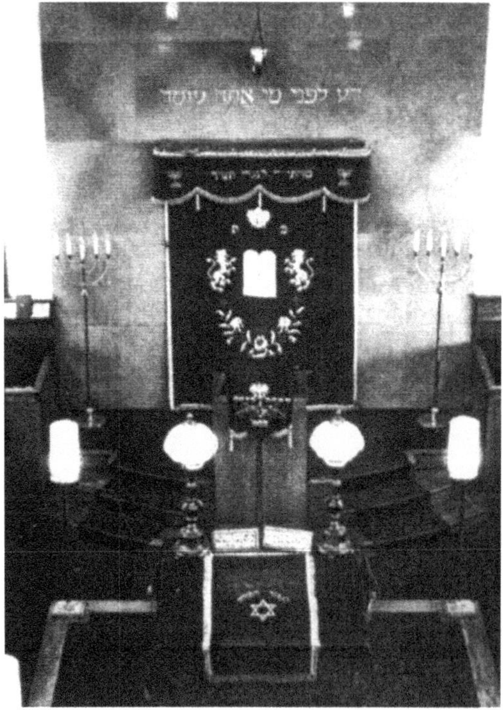

The Jewish Synagogue in Park Road South opened in 1938 and replaced an earlier building. The interior is seen here. When the building closed in 1998 the Hebrew Congregation gave a number of their archives and ritual objects to the Dorman Museum.

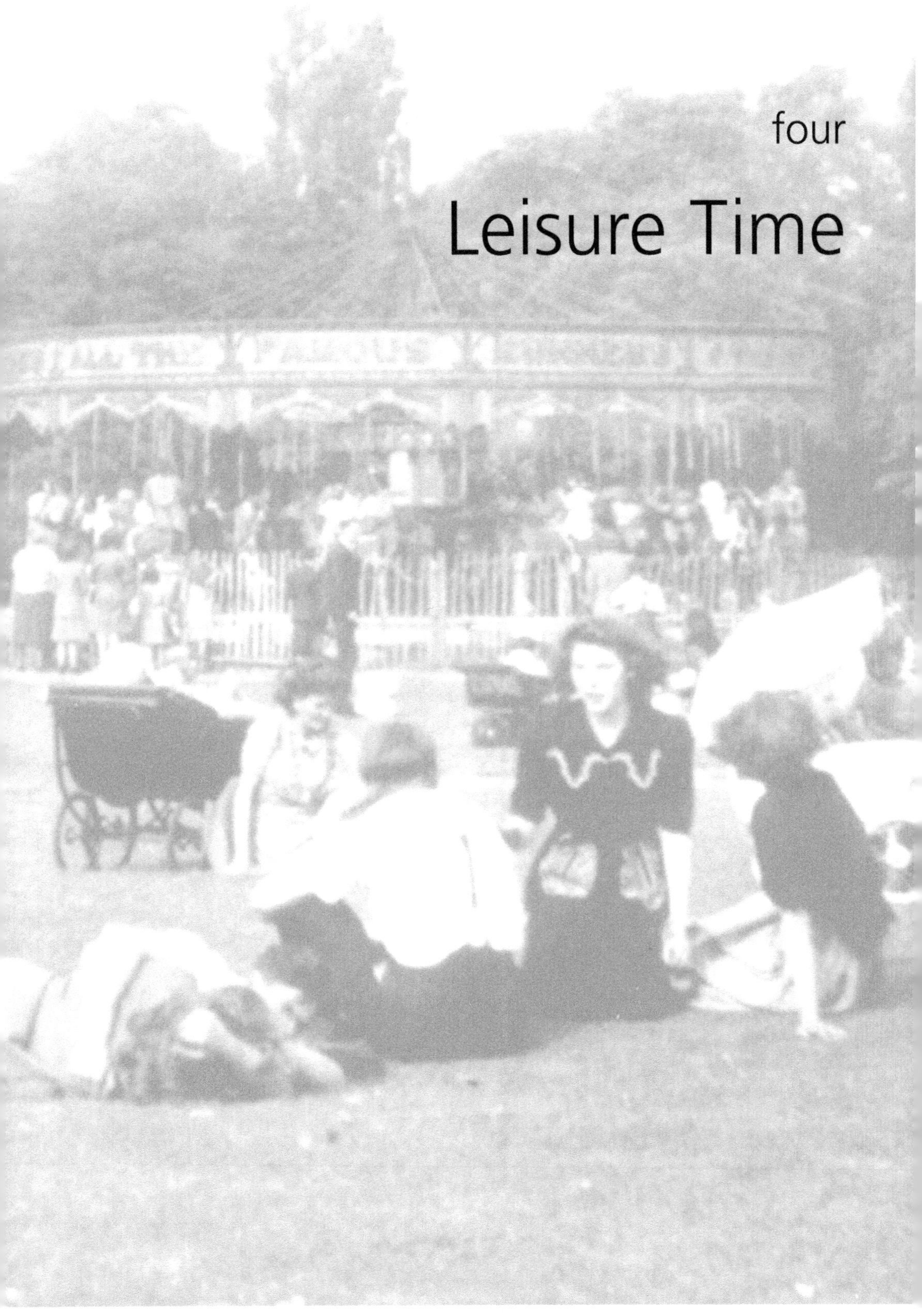

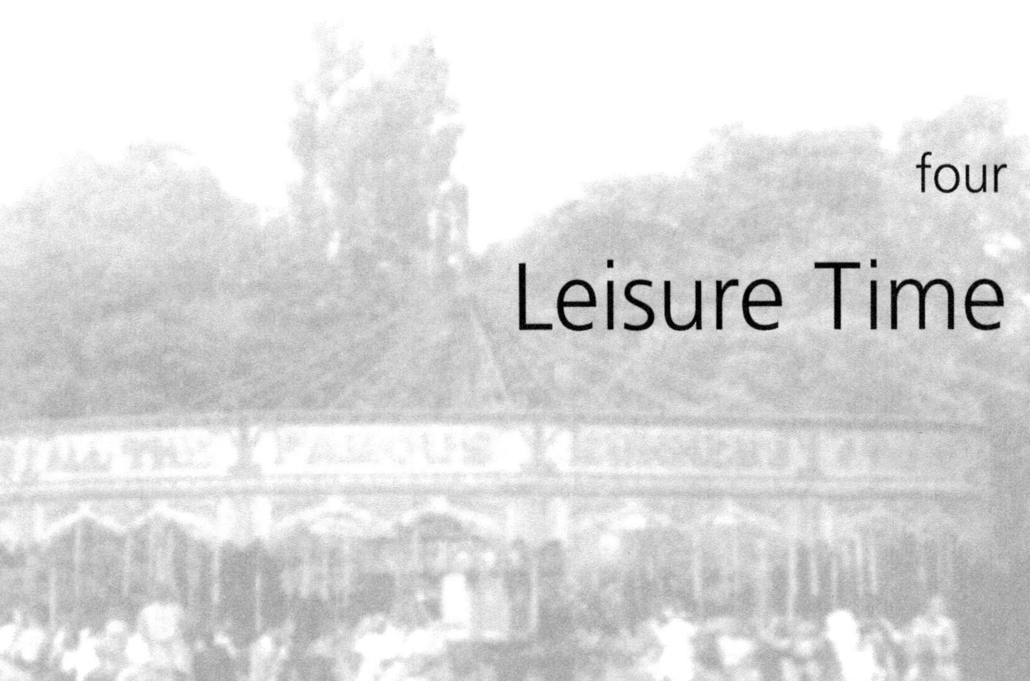

four

Leisure Time

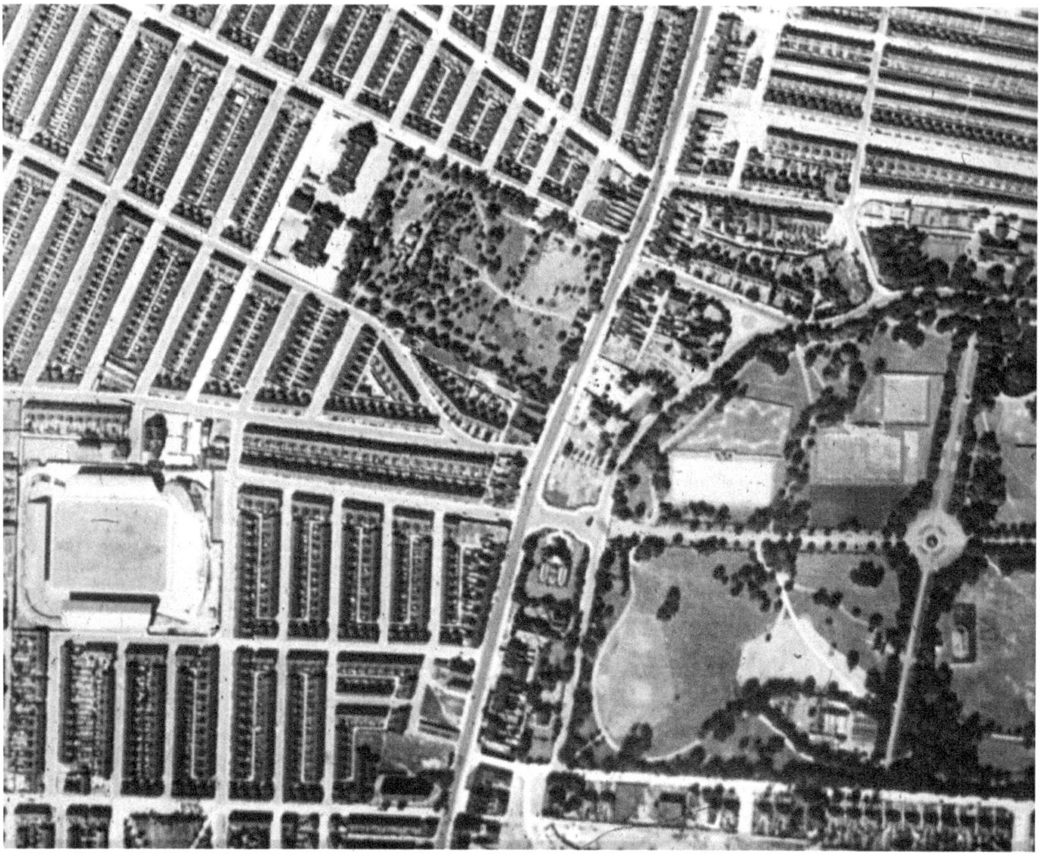

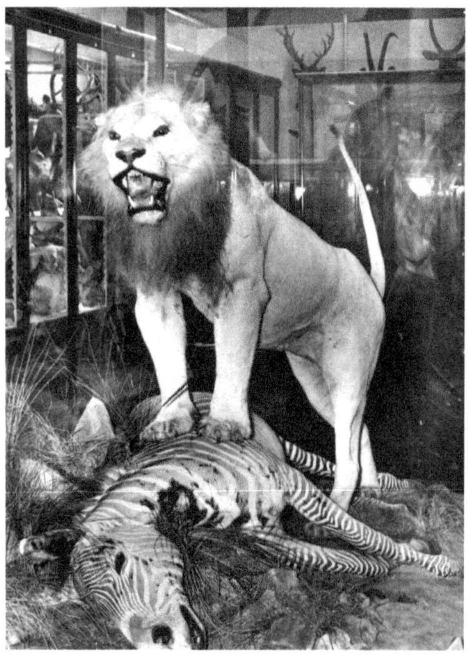

Above: This view shows Ayresome Park, the former home of Middlesbrough Football Club (extreme left), Ayresome Gardens, formerly the cemetery (top centre), the Dorman Memorial Museum (bottom centre), and Albert Park (far right), as seen from the air.

Left: Leo the Lion, symbol of the redeveloped Dorman Museum. Donated to the museum by Sir Alfred Pease, he was originally displayed surmounting a zebra when the museum opened in July 1904. The zebra no longer remains but Leo is still on display in the museum foyer.

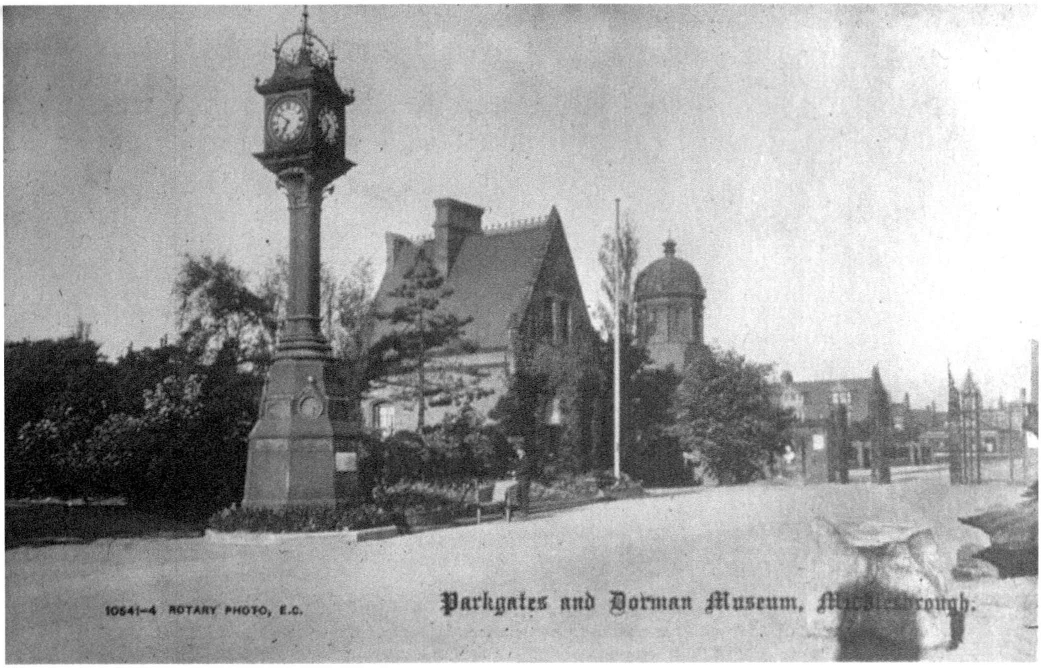

Above: West Lodge – formerly the park curator's house – and the cast-iron clock at the entrance to Albert Park. The clock was the gift from Alderman Thomas Sanderson JP. Prince Arthur opened the Albert Park, a gift from Henry Bolckow, on 11 August 1868.

Right: Prototype for the sundial in Albert Park, designed by John Smith of Stockton-on-Tees (now in the Dorman Museum). The dial itself has now been totally refurbished.

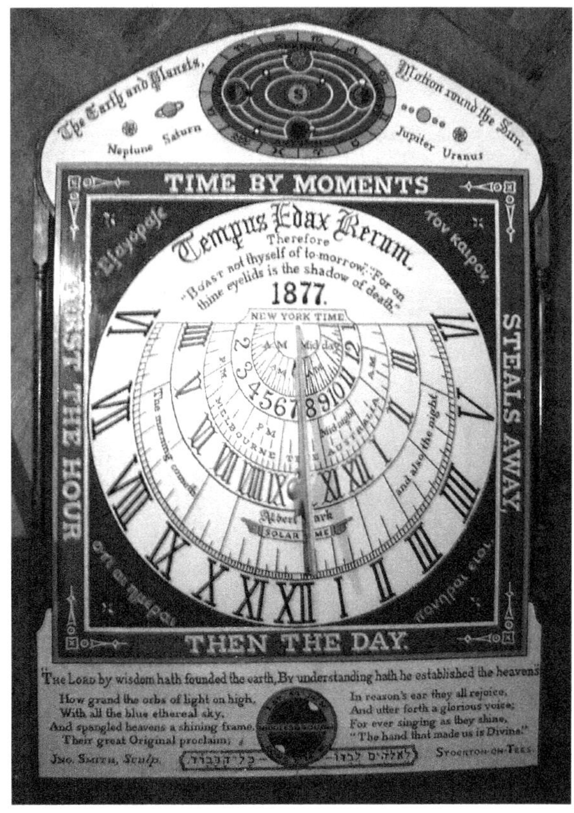

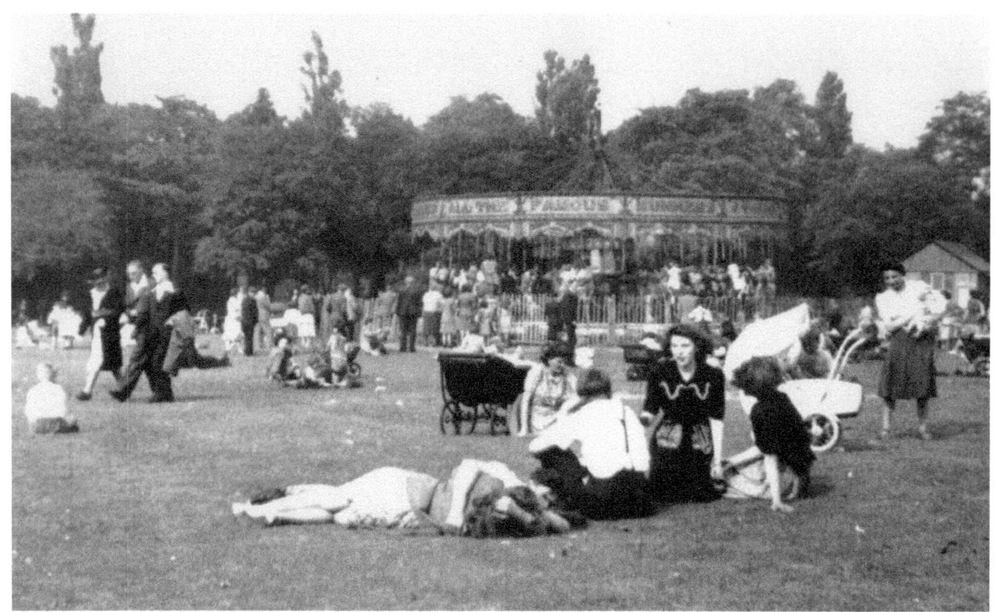

'Holidays at Home' in Albert Park were begun by the council during the Second World War to encourage people to stay at home and so conserve vital fuel supplies.

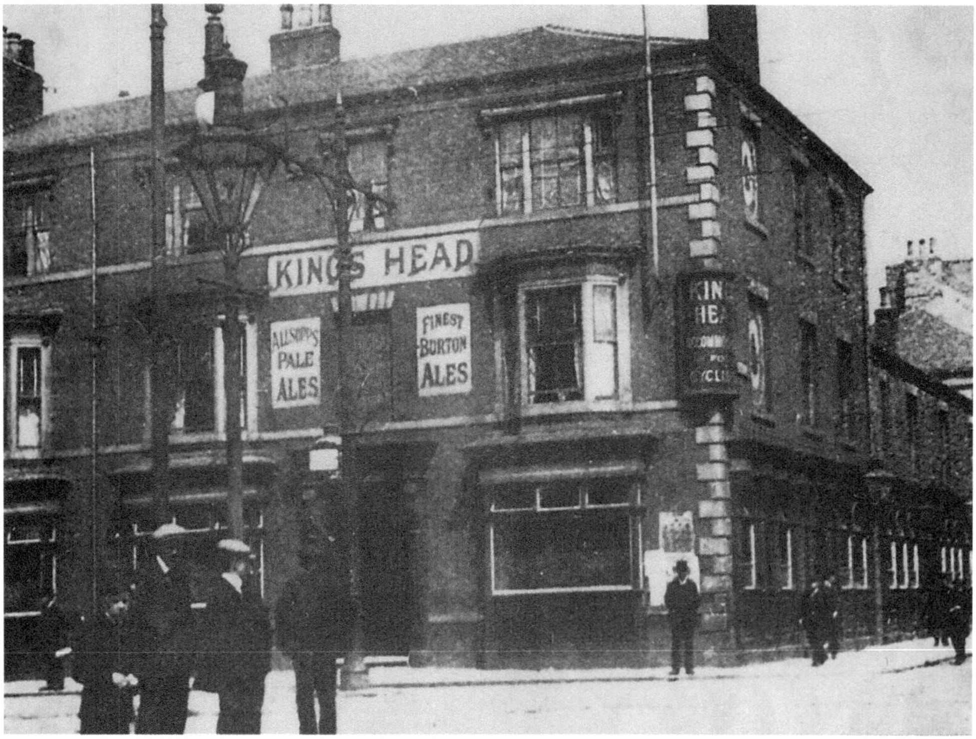

The King's Head public house, No. 1 Newport Road. It was opened originally in 1862 and was in use until 1910. The site is now occupied by Debenhams.

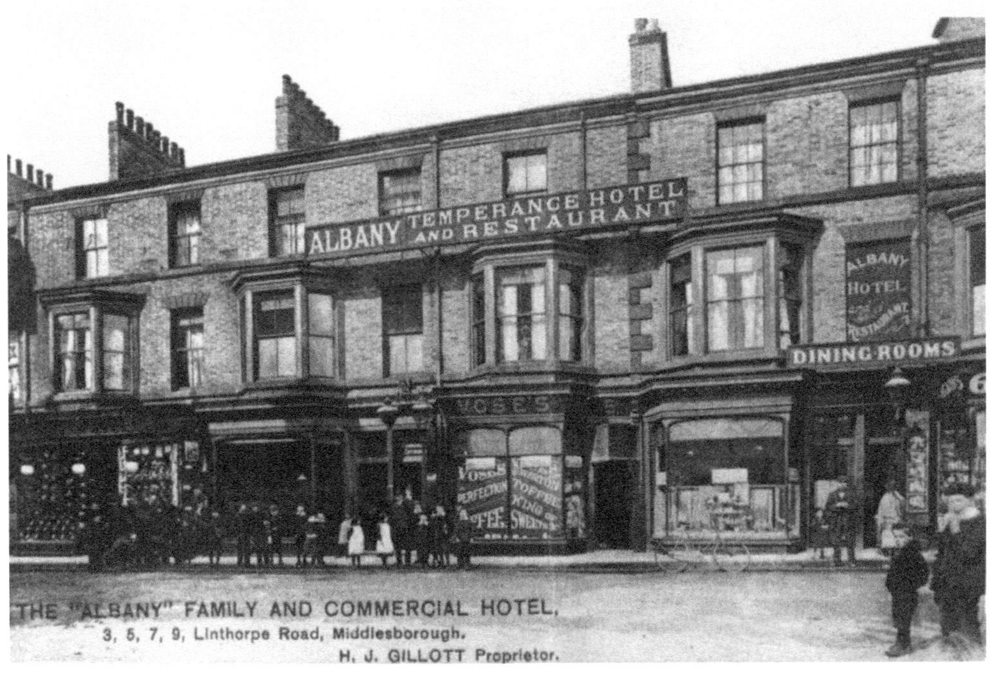

The Albany Family and Commercial Hotel, Linthorpe Road, Temperance Hotel and Dining Rooms, now the site of Crown House.

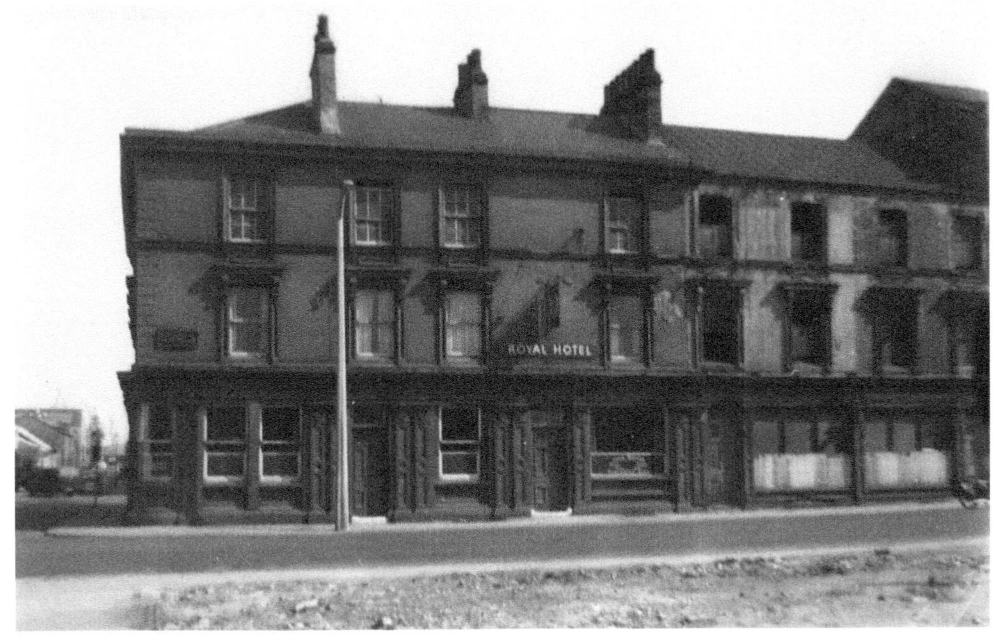

The Royal Hotel, Durham Street, St Hilda's, originally built in 1856. In 1859 it advertised 'families and shippers supplied', 'good stabling and coach house', 'Chaise, Gig- and Post-Horses', 'A Cab meets all the Trains' and also that 'Phillip Crannis late of Paragon Station, Hull' was the licensee.

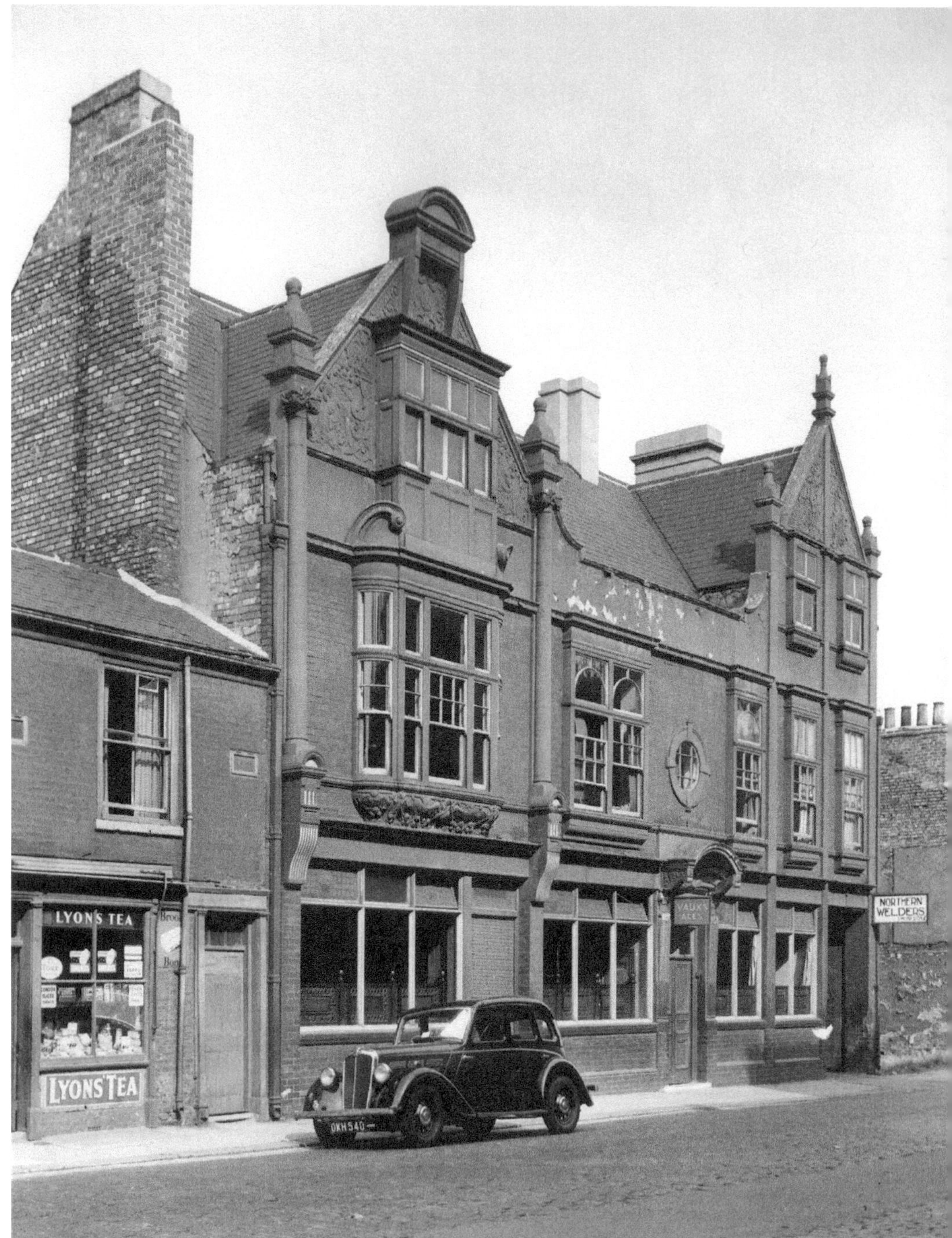

LYONS TEA
LYONS TEA
VAUX'S ALES
NORTHERN
WELDERS
DKH 540

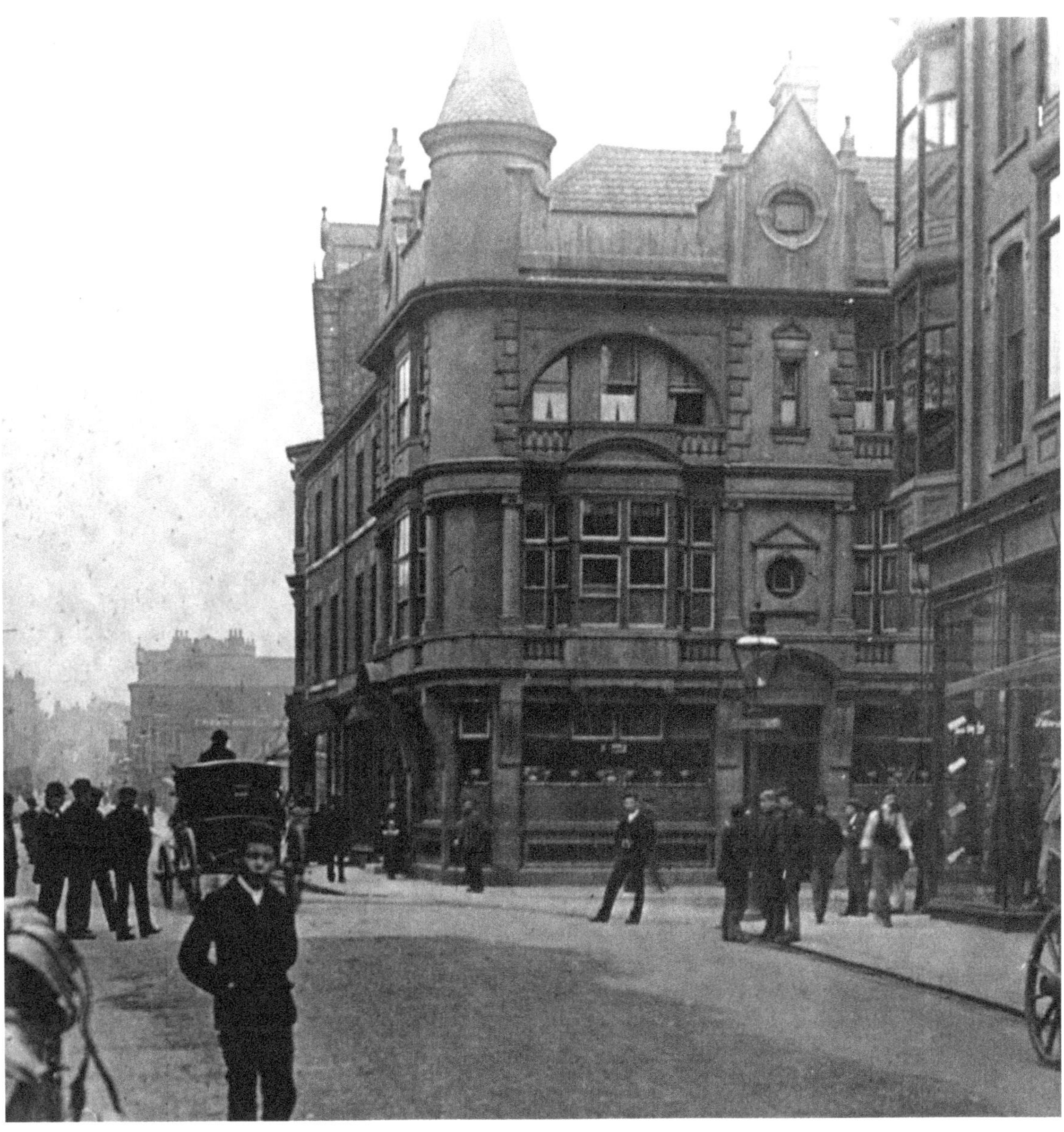

The Leeds Hotel. Originally opened in 1856, it was rebuilt in 1894 as seen here, and was destroyed during an air raid in August 1942.

Opposite: The Captain Cook public house, Durham Street, St Hilda's. Designed by Robert Moore in 1840 and named after the Marton-born explorer, it was extended in 1893 and it is still in use today.

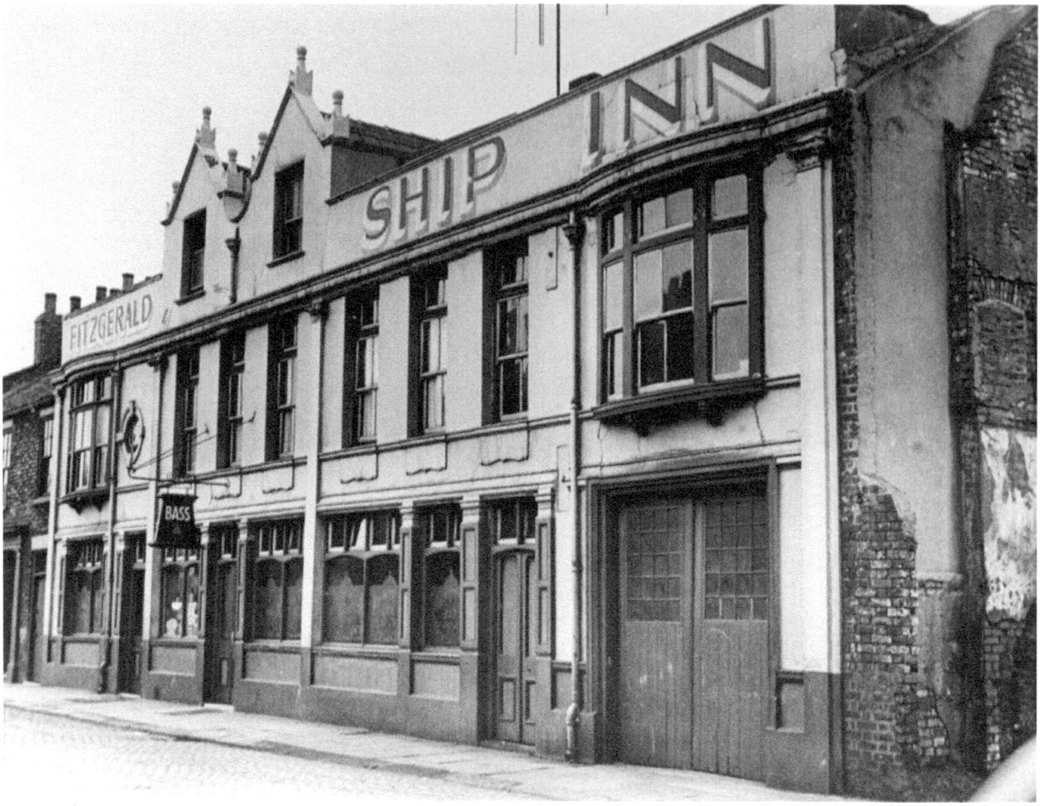

The Ship Inn, Stockton Street, St Hilda's. The Ship proudly boasts of being the oldest pub in the town: it was licensed in 1831 and is still in use today.

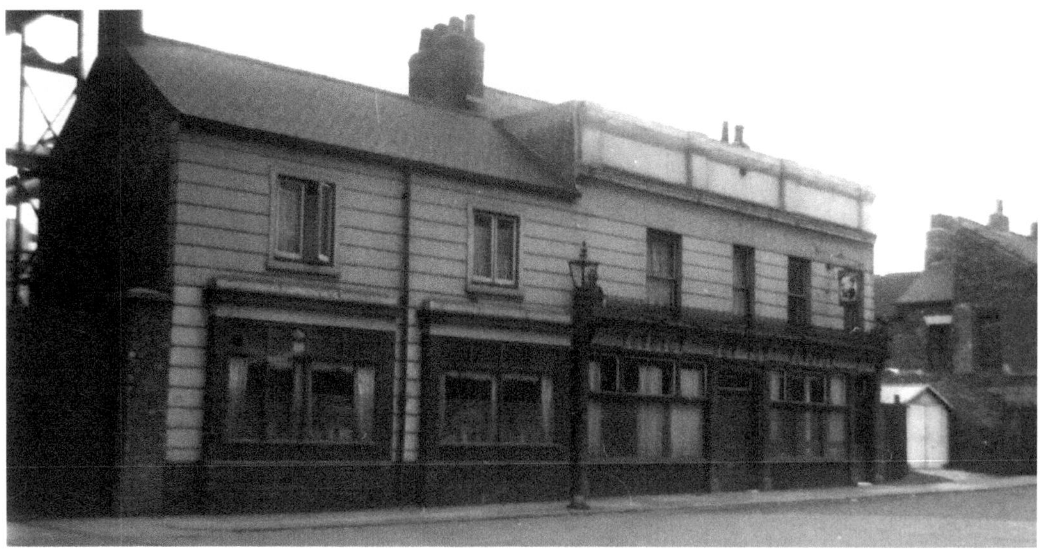

The Cross Keys, Lower East Street, St Hilda's. Opened originally in 1868, it was later used as a garage until 2005.

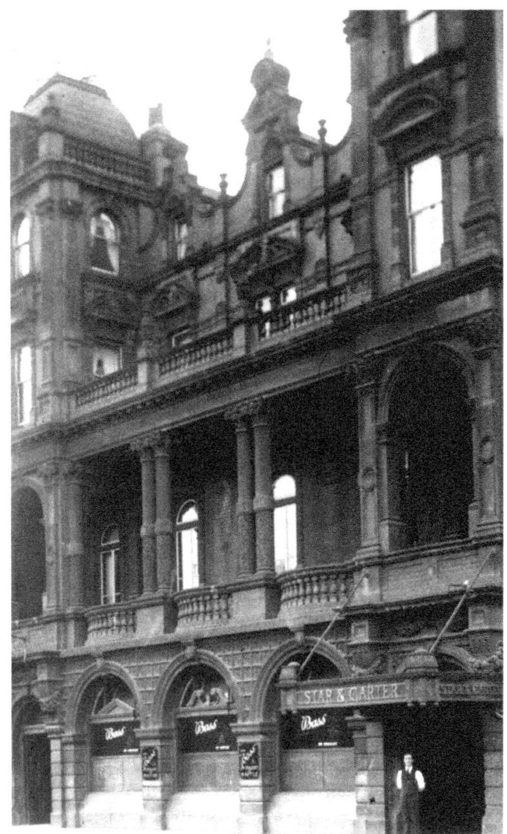

The Star and Garter, Nos 26 to 30 Marton Road, Middlesbrough. Opened in 1894, this highly ornate and exuberant-looking Victorian building was erected on the site of the former Welsh Congregational chapel. Sadly it was demolished to make way for the A66 in 1976.

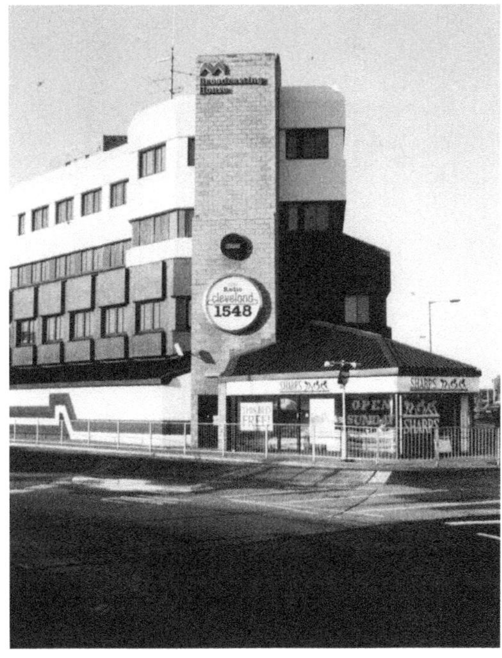

Broadcasting House, Newport Triangle. Developed by Middlesbrough Council, the building is the home of BBC Radio Cleveland, and office units based in the Vanguard Suite.

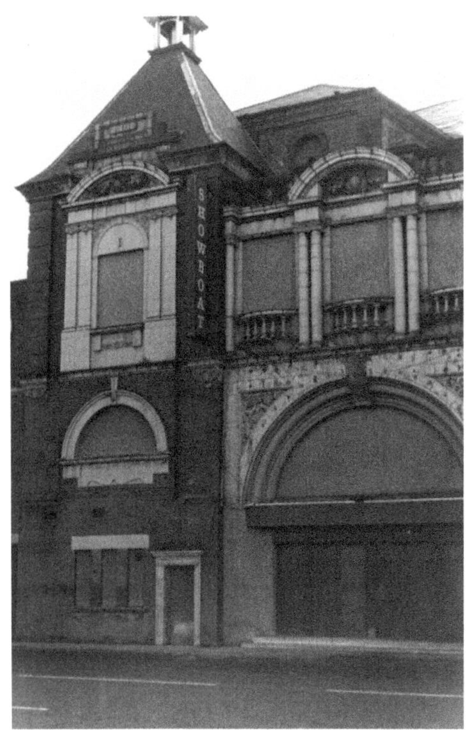

The Hippodrome, Wilson Street. Opened as a theatre on 17 August 1906 by Mayor Colonel Thomas Gibson Poole, it was built on the site of the Quaker burial ground. It closed less than two years later in February 1908, and was later converted into a cinema. It is now a pub and nightclub.

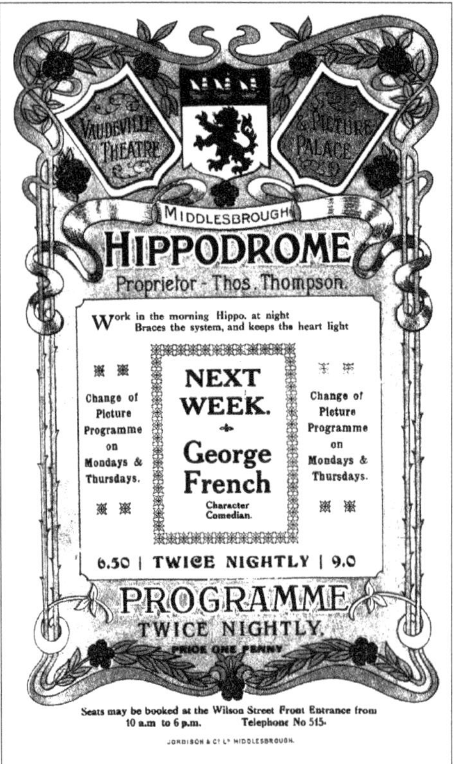

A programme for the Hippodrome Vaudeville Theatre and Picture Palace. George French, 'Character Comedian', was appearing. As a picture palace, the Hippodrome saw the first full talkie to be shown in the town when the legendary Al Jolson starred as *The Singing Fool* from 26 August 1929. From 1956, when it was closed as a cinema, it was then known as the Astoria Ballroom.

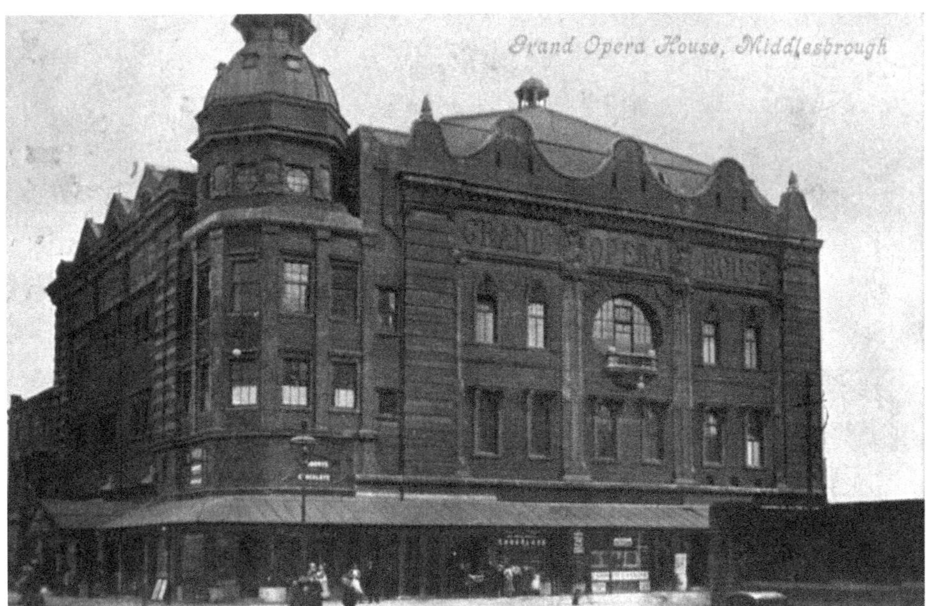

The Grand Opera House, later the Gaumont Cinema. Built on the site of Swatters Carr Farmhouse, the Opera House was opened on 7 December 1903 by Colonel Sir Samuel Sadler MP, and closed on 21 June 1930. It re-opened as the Gaumont Cinema on 31 March 1931 and finally closed its doors to the public on 29 February 1964. The site is now an office block on Southfield Road/Linthorpe Road corner.

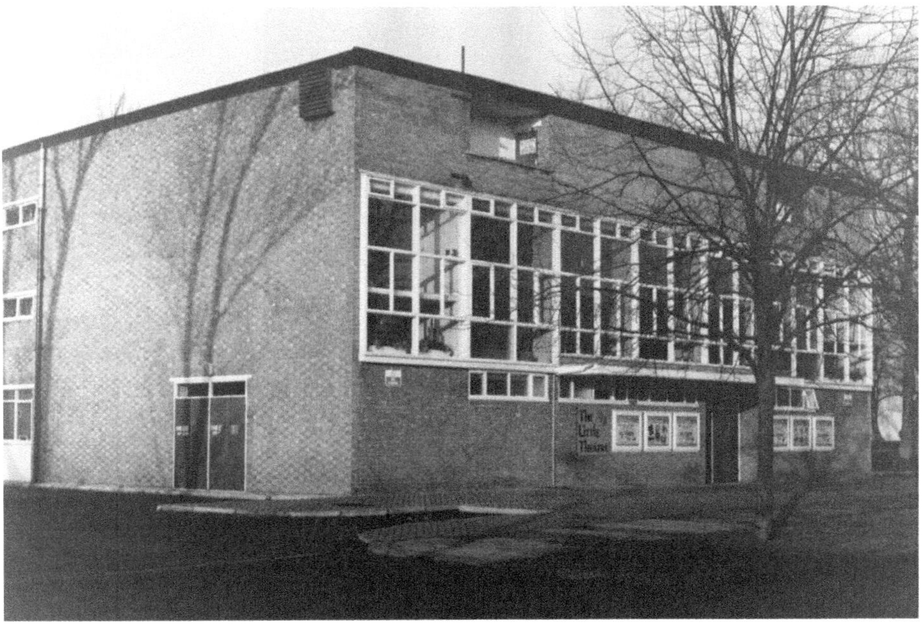

The Middlesbrough Theatre, formerly the Little Theatre. The building was only the second provincial theatre built after the Second World War and was opened by Sir John Gielgud on 21 October 1957.

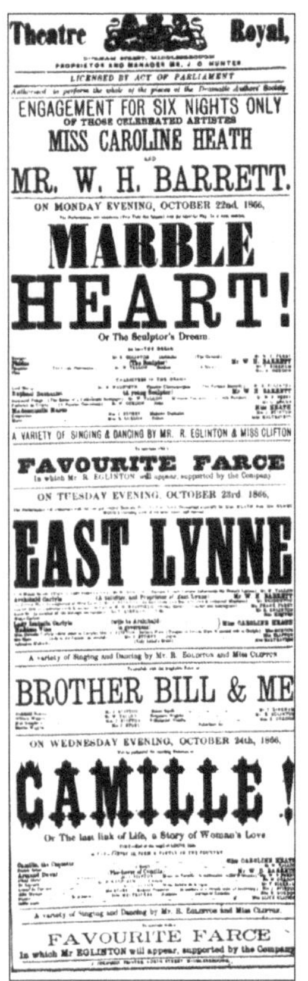

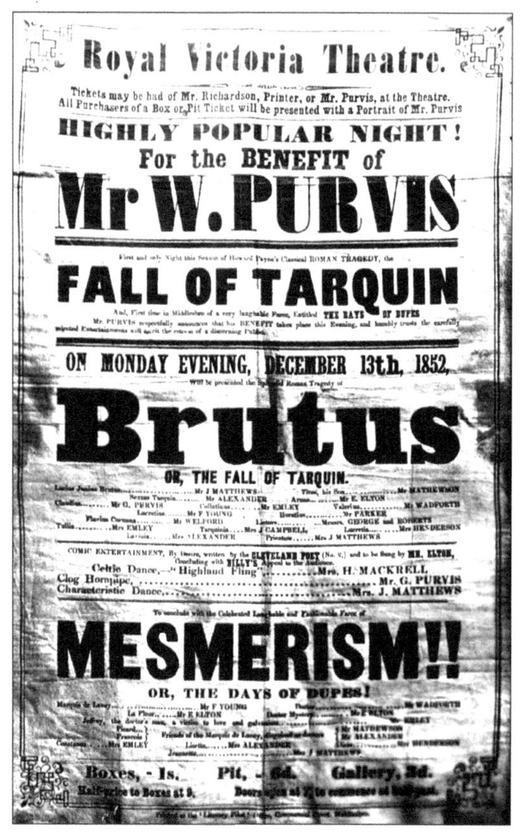

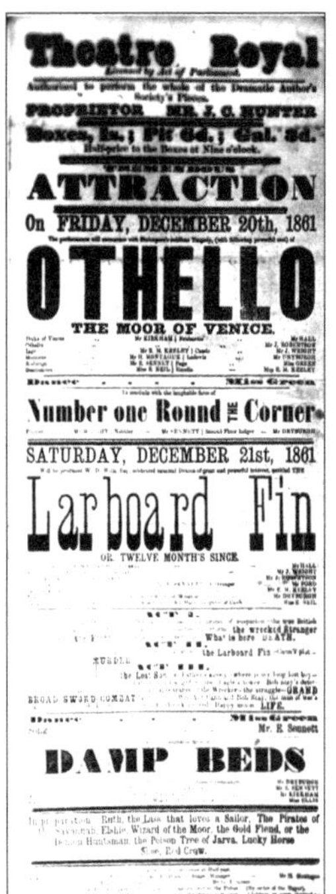

Above left: Poster for the Theatre Royal, Durham Street, St Hilda's in October 1866.

Above right: Poster for the Royal Victoria Theatre, December 1852.

Left: Poster for the Theatre Royal, Durham Street, St Hilda's, December 1861. The theatre had opened in March of that year.

Opposite above: Oxford Music Hall and Palace of Varieties. This building opened on 9 August 1867 in Rostock Terrace, Lower Feversham Street, St Hilda's, and seated over 1,800 persons. One of the original managers was Alderman Richard Weighell – who also bred racehorses and was the landlord of the Cleveland Bay Hotel. The Oxford played host to such stars as Dan Leno, Zena Dare, Vesta Tilley, Harry Lauder and Marie Lloyd, to name but a few.

Opposite below: Alvo's Empire, Corporation Road. This was a prefabricated building, used from 1893 until it was demolished (to make way for the Empire Palace of Varieties) to host circuses, fairs, zoos etc. Such famous names as Fossett's, Weldon's and Captain Tansfield's circus performed here. After its demolition Alvo built a new home at Belle Vue Grounds on the site of the old Linthorpe Pottery, charging sixpence admission.

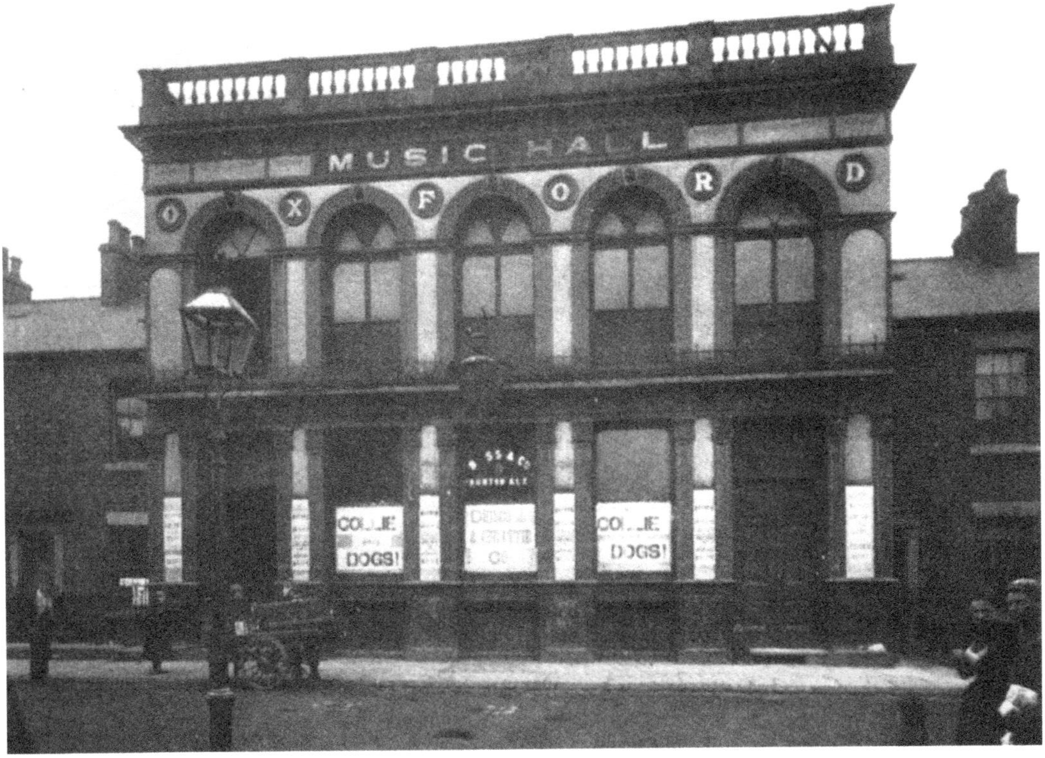

MUSIC HALL
OXFORD
COLLIE
DOGS!
COLLIE
DOGS!

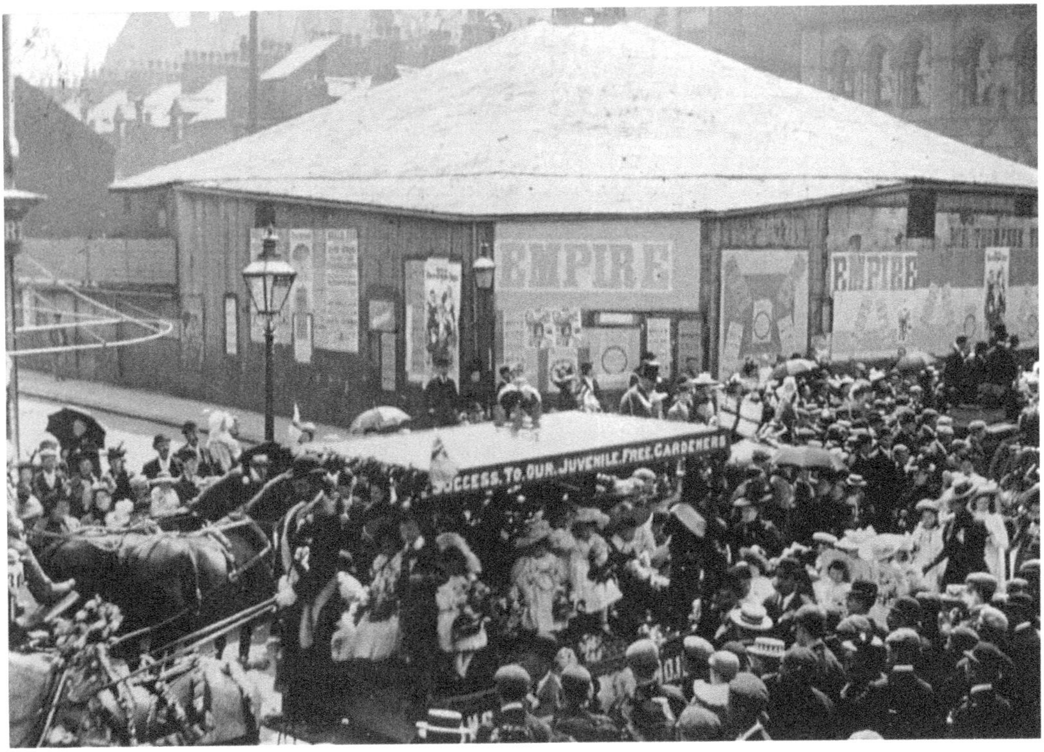

EMPIRE
EMPIRE
SUCCESS TO OUR JUVENILE FREE GARDENERS

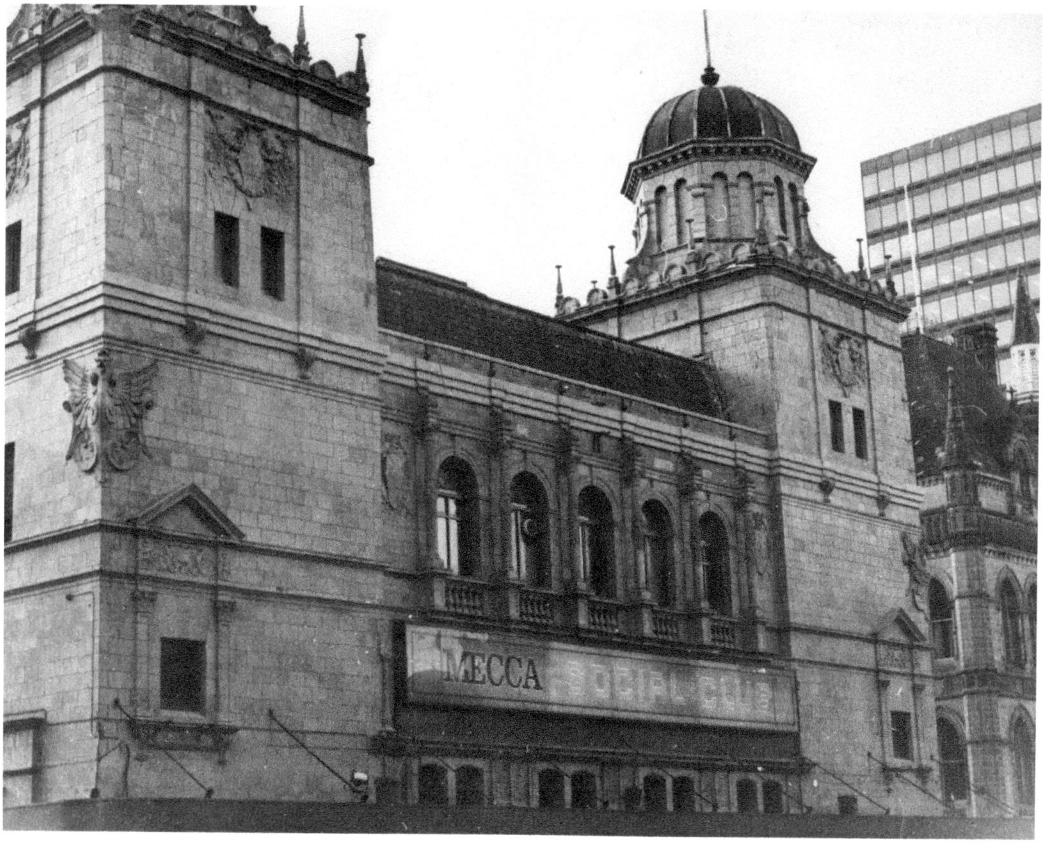

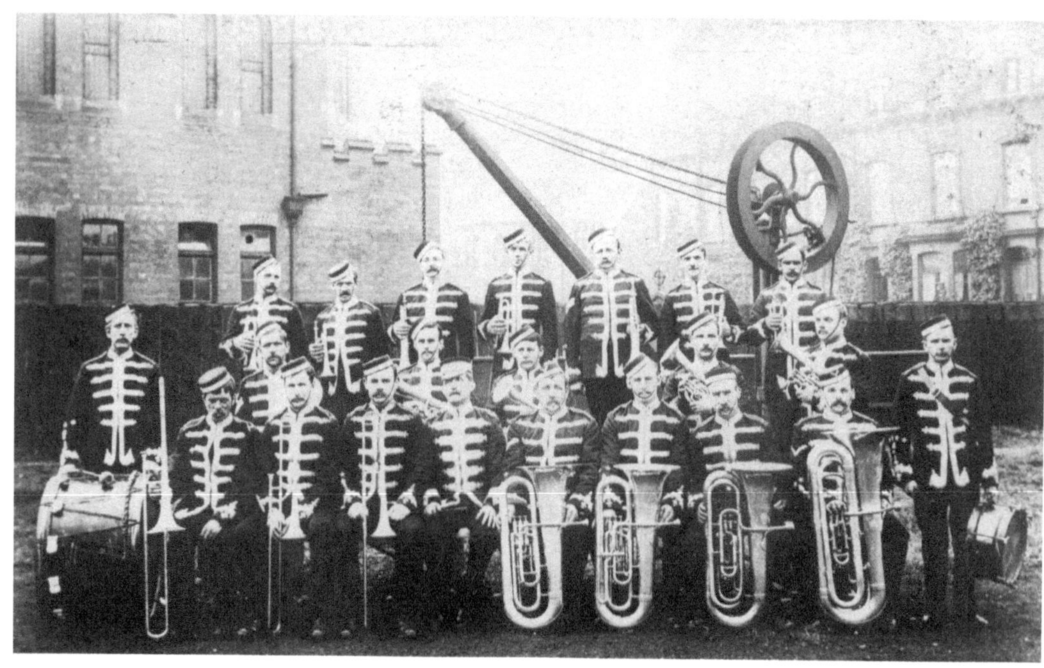

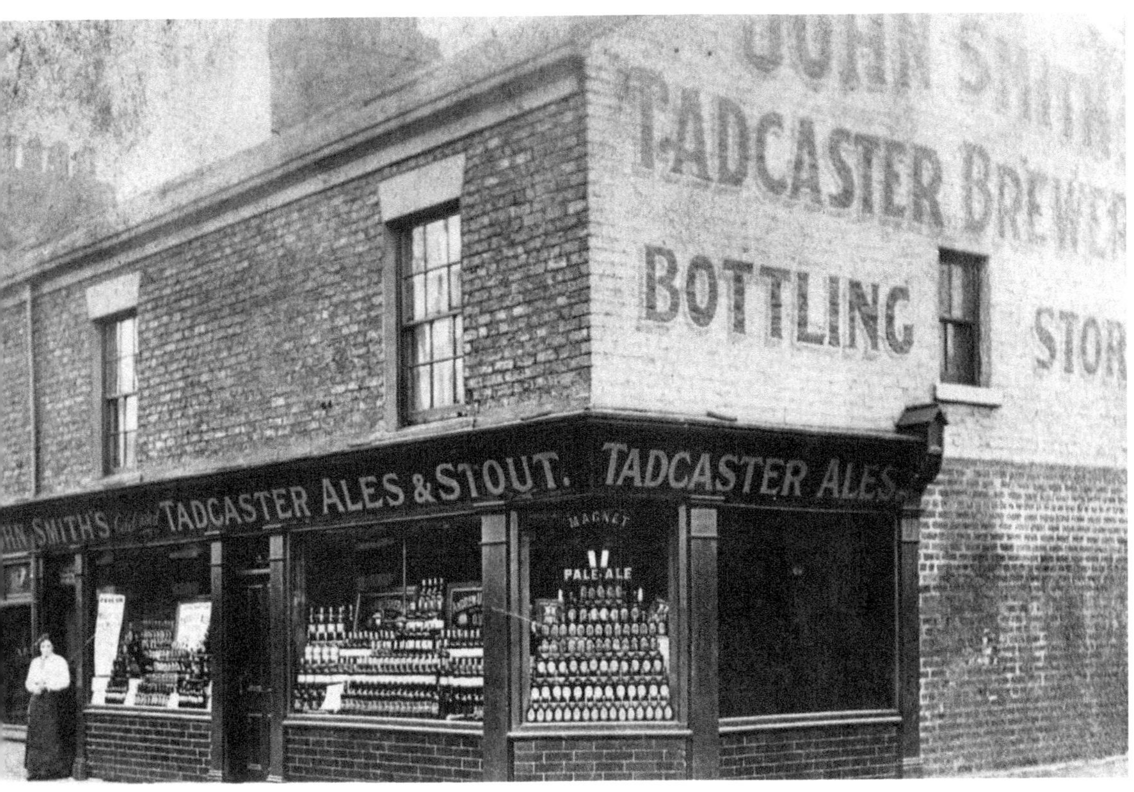

Off-licence in Station Street, St Hilda's, proudly announcing that it is supplied by John Smith's Tadcaster Brewery.

Opposite above: The Empire Palace of Varieties – built on the site of Alvo's Empire, the theatre played host to such names as Charlie Chaplin, Lillie Langtry, (who topped the bill on the opening night of 13 March 1889, appearing along with the Seven Savonas and the Elliott Troupe), Arthur Askey, Max Bygraves and many more. Now used as a nightclub it retains its original name.

Opposite below: Band of the Tees Division Submariners Royal Engineers, also known as Milburn's Model Band. They were photographed in the yard of their drill hall at the German church (see page 59).

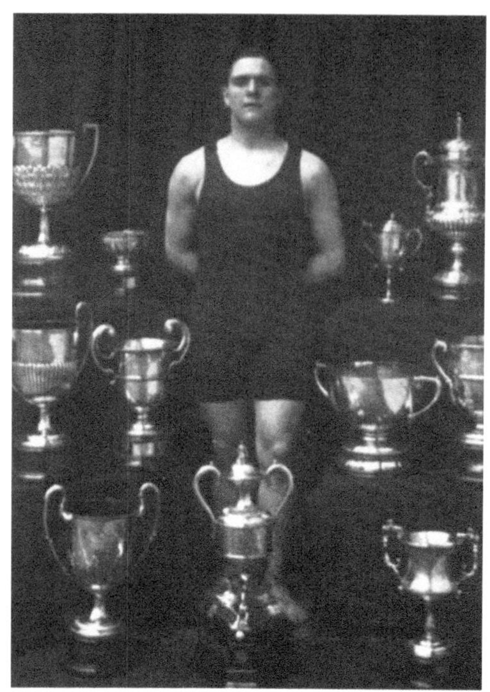

Left: Jack Hatfield (1893–1965), son of Tom Hatfield, the superintendent of Middlesbrough swimming baths. He became well known when he won two silvers and one bronze medal in the Olympic swimming events in Stockholm, Sweden, in 1912.

Below: Jack Hatfield & Sons sports shop, still in existence on Borough Road, Middlesbrough: although no longer in the family, it still retains its historic name.

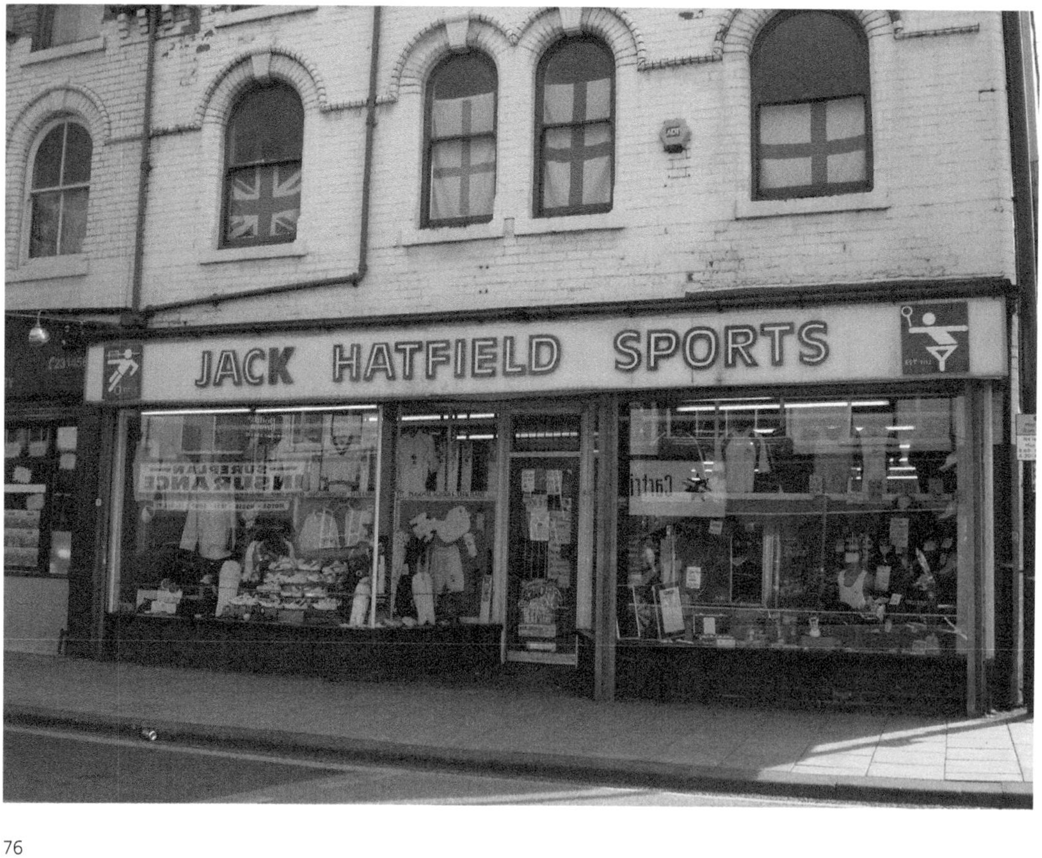

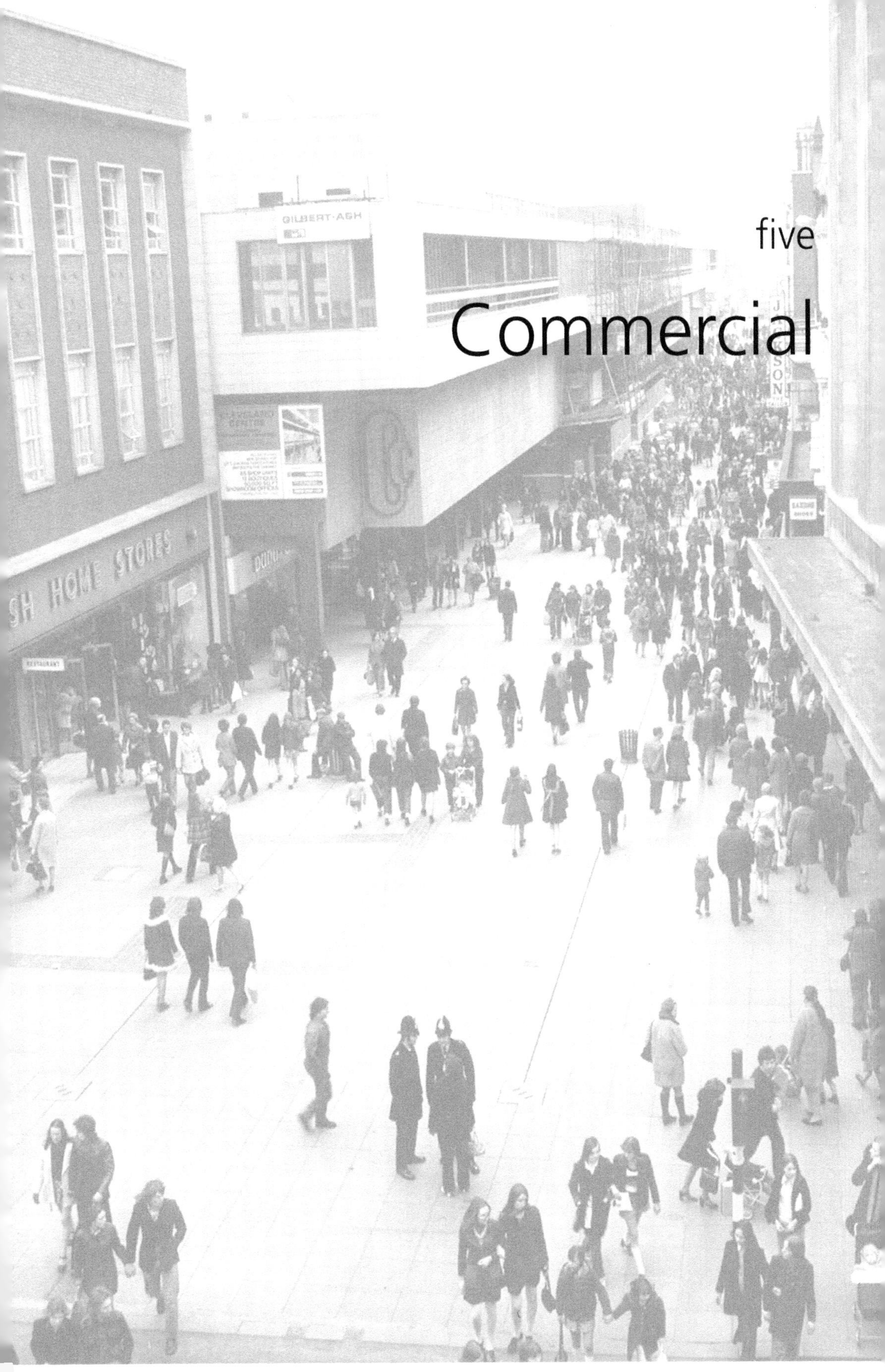

five

Commercial

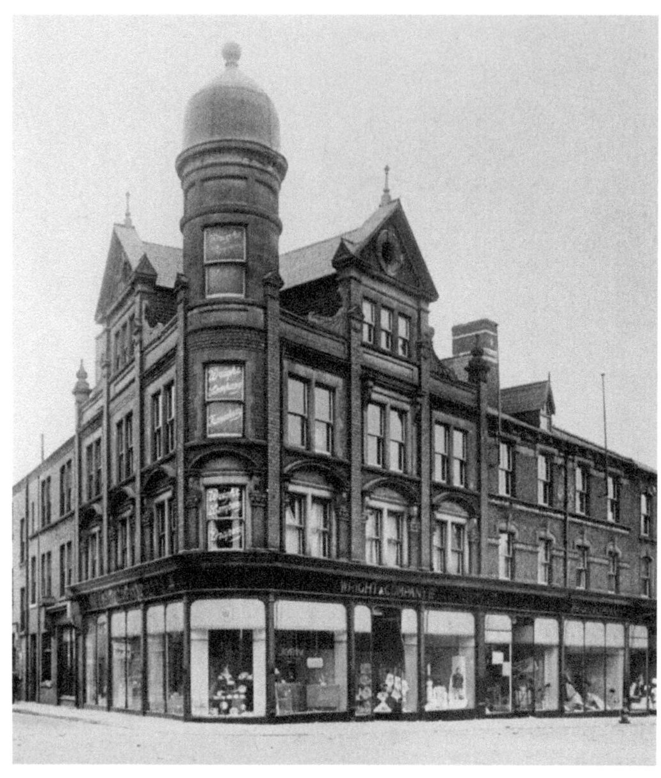

Wright's general store in Sussex Street. Founded originally in 1862 by Richard Archibald and Lawrence Wright on the west side of Sussex Street, they moved across the road to these magnificent premises in 1863.

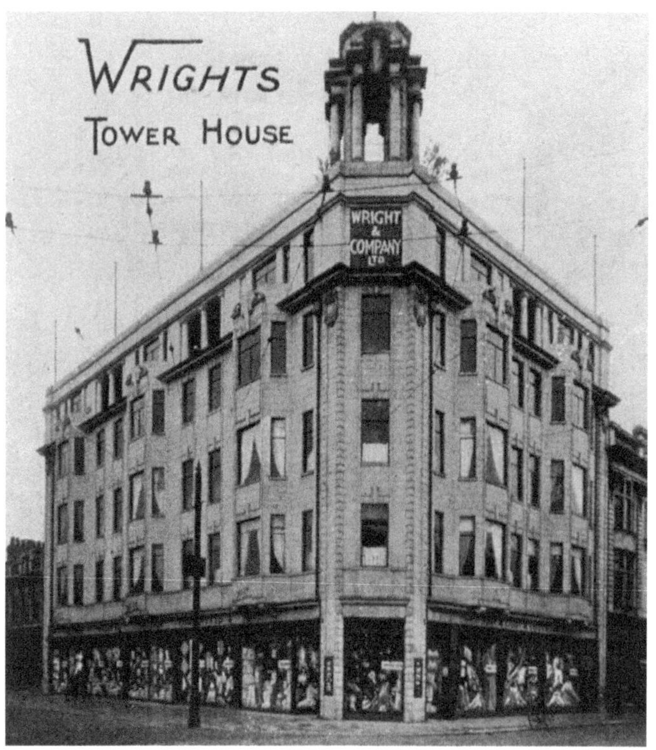

Wright's purchased the site on Linthorpe Road and Grange Road corner in 1910. Known as Wright's Tower House, it was only demolished in the 1980s and the site is now occupied by a fast-food restaurant.

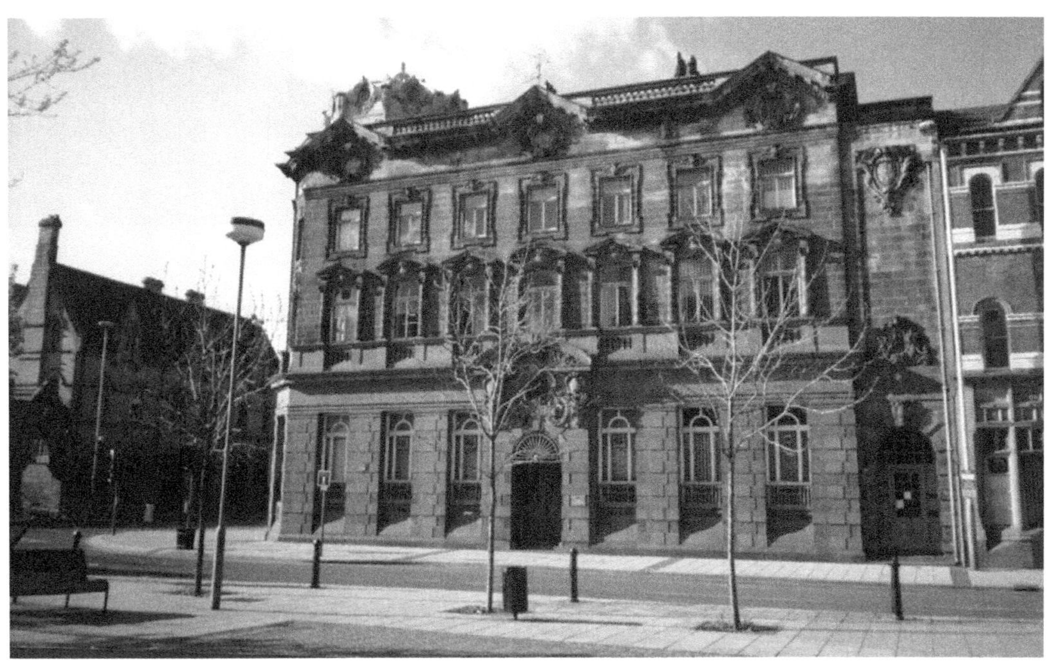

The former York City Banking Co. buildings in what was Marton Road. Designed by Barnes and Coates of West Hartlepool, the roof is said to be modelled on the Paris Opera House. It is now used as offices by the North-East Chamber of Commerce.

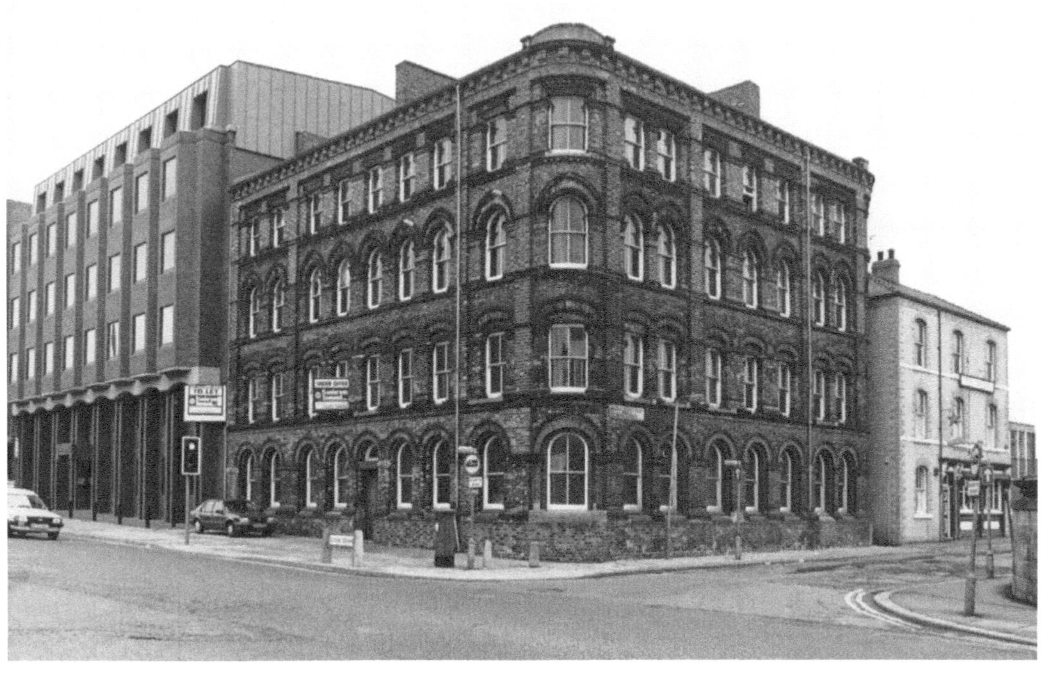

New Exchange Buildings, Queen's Square. Originally designed for use as offices in the Italian style by William Blessley, the building is still used as offices today.

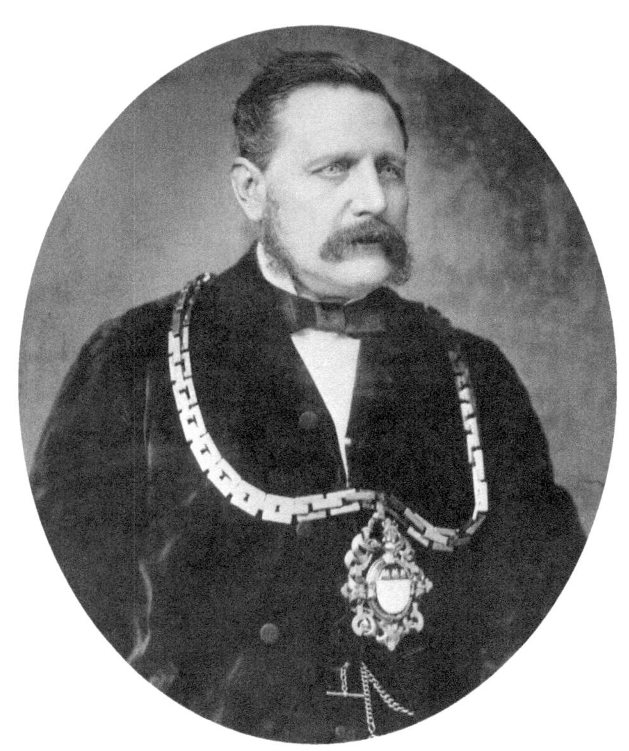

Left: Charles Willman, mayor in 1880. He died in 1894. He ran a successful auctioneers and valuers and was a land and estate agent.

Below: Willman's Auction House, Station Street, late nineteenth century.

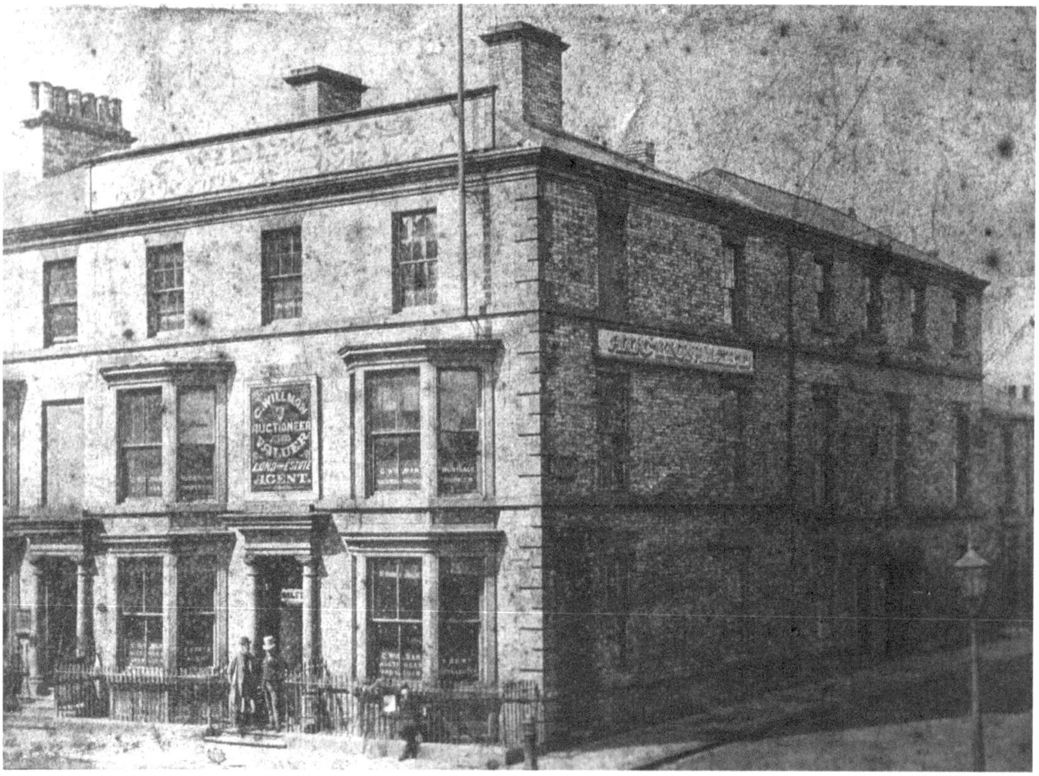

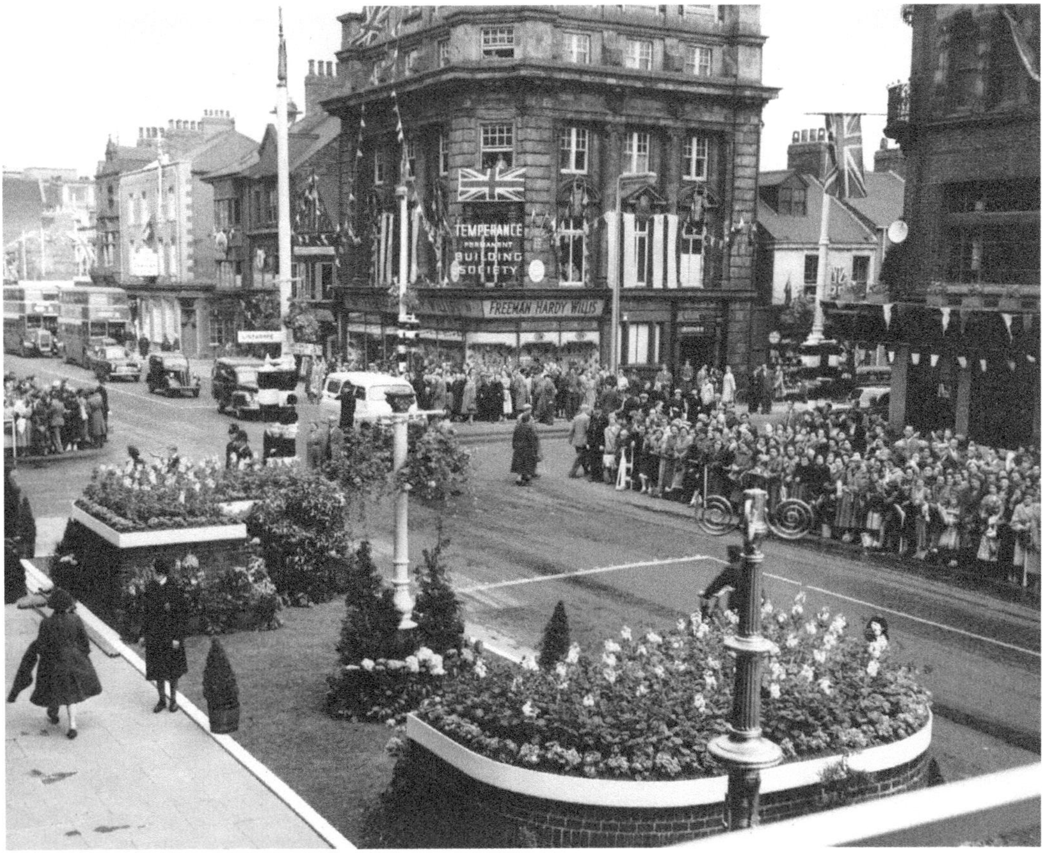

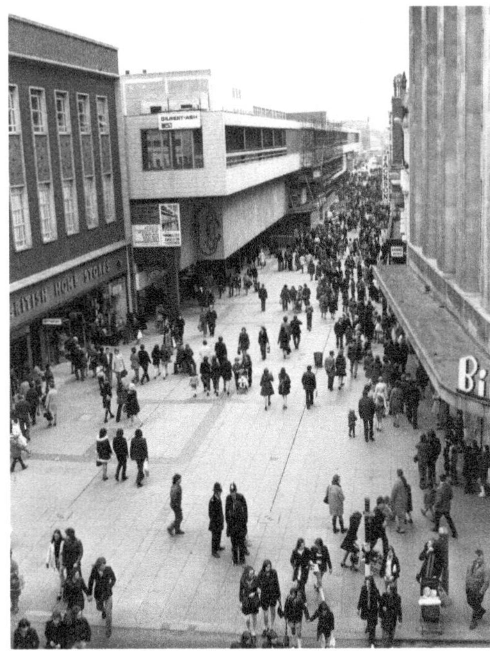

Above: The town hall and Corporation Road, decorated with flowers for a visit by the Queen and the Duke of Edinburgh in 1956.

Right: Linthorpe Road in the 1970s after pedestrianisation, looking south.

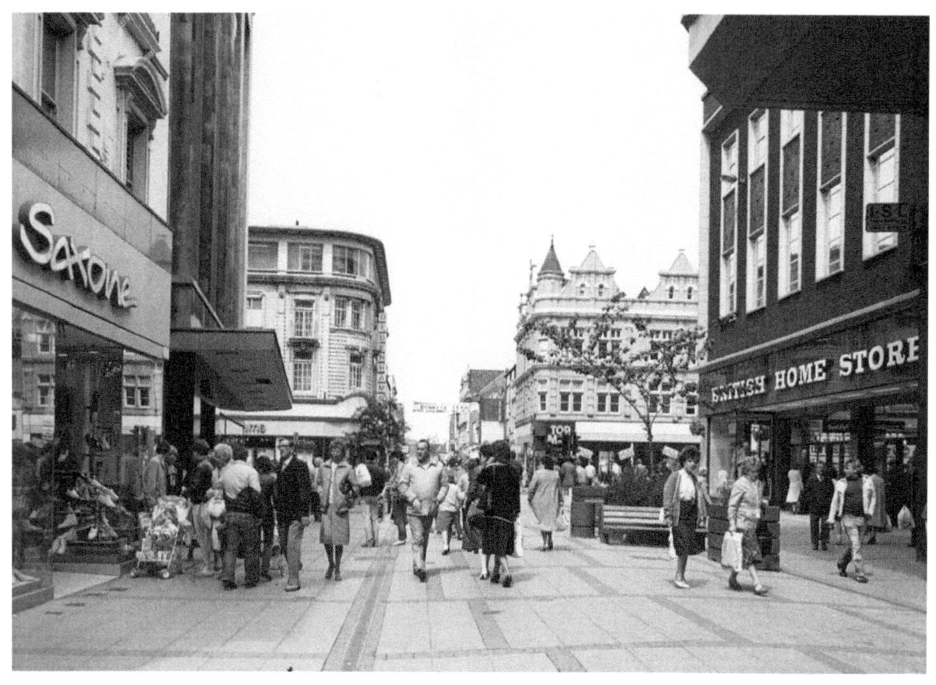

Linthorpe Road in the 1970s after pedestrianisation, looking north.

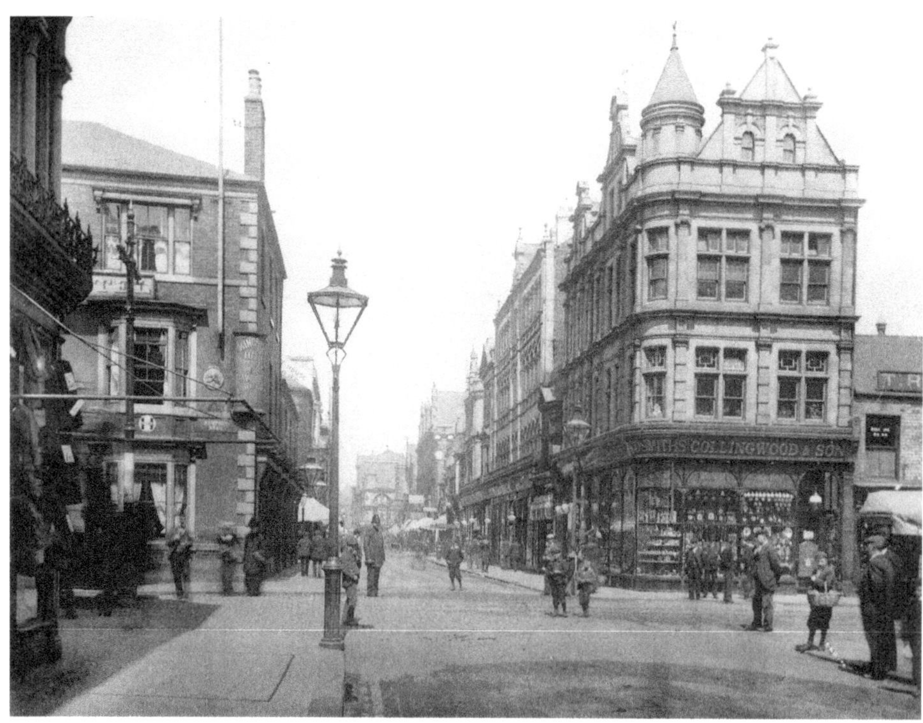

Newport Road and Corporation Road junction, showing Collingwood's the jewellers on the right, and the King's Head on the left, 1900s.

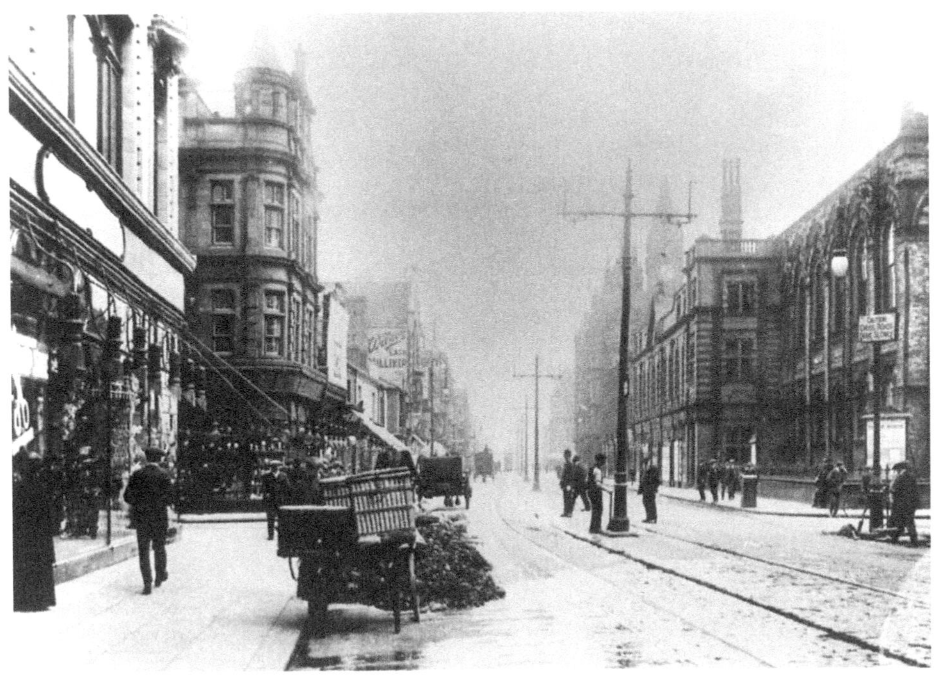

Corporation Road looking towards the town hall, *c.* 1900.

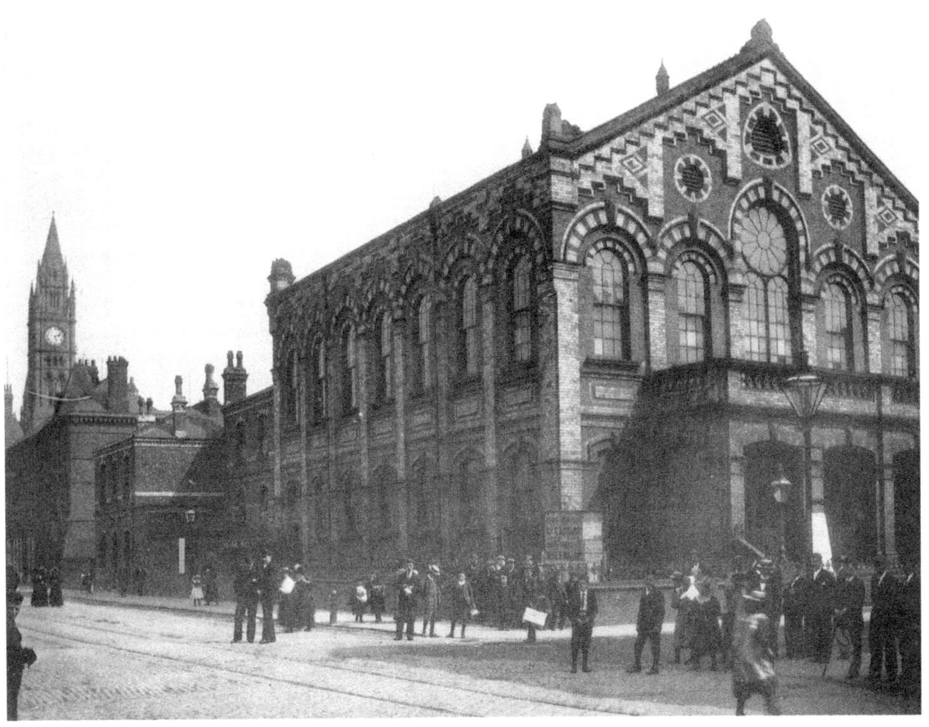

The same view, Corporation Road looking towards the town hall. On the right can be seen the Corporation Hotel, birthplace of Wendy Richard, star of *Eastenders.*

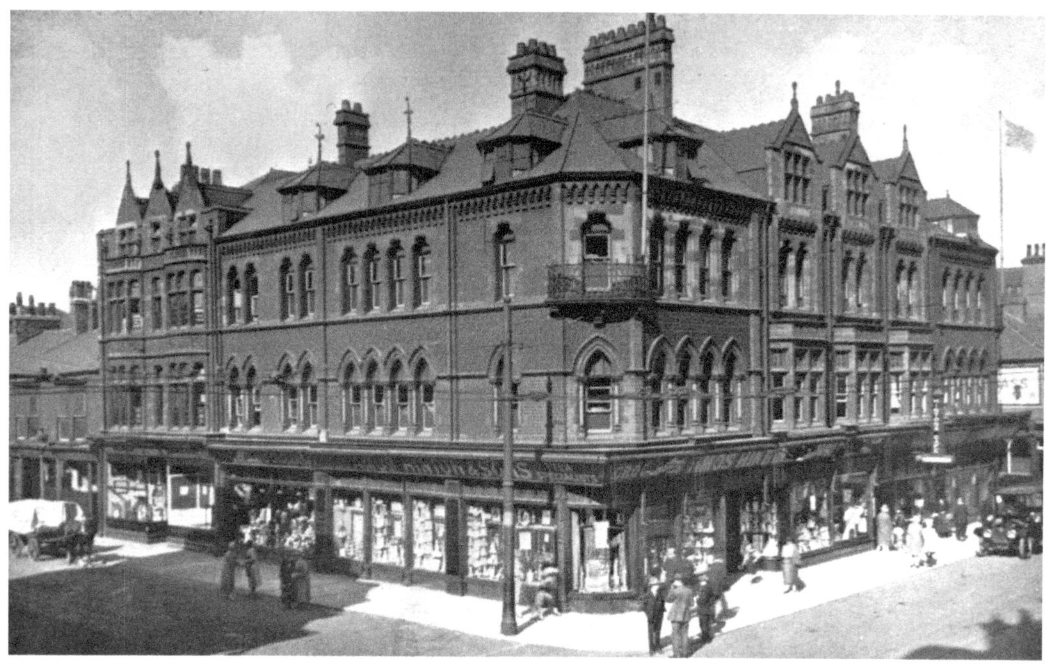

Amos Hinton's grocery shop at the junction of Albert Road and Corporation Road.

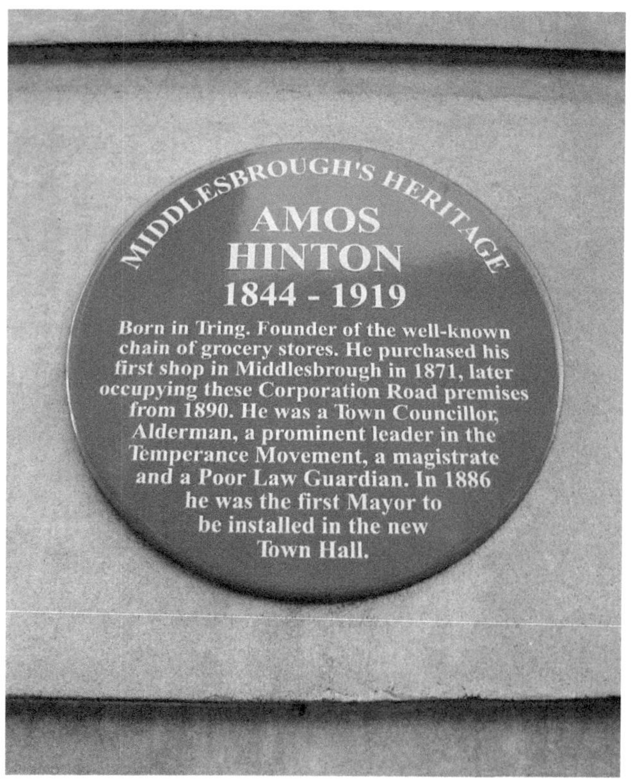

Left: The green plaque erected on the site of Hinton's store, sponsored by the founder's grandson, Patrick Hinton, in 2001. The site is now used by the HSBC Bank.

Opposite above: Hinton's staff assembled outside the original South Street premises, 1880s. Note the shop assistants' aprons and the obligatory bicycle-riding delivery boy.

Opposite below: Hinton's Oriental Café, built above the Corporation Road premises, *c.* 1900.

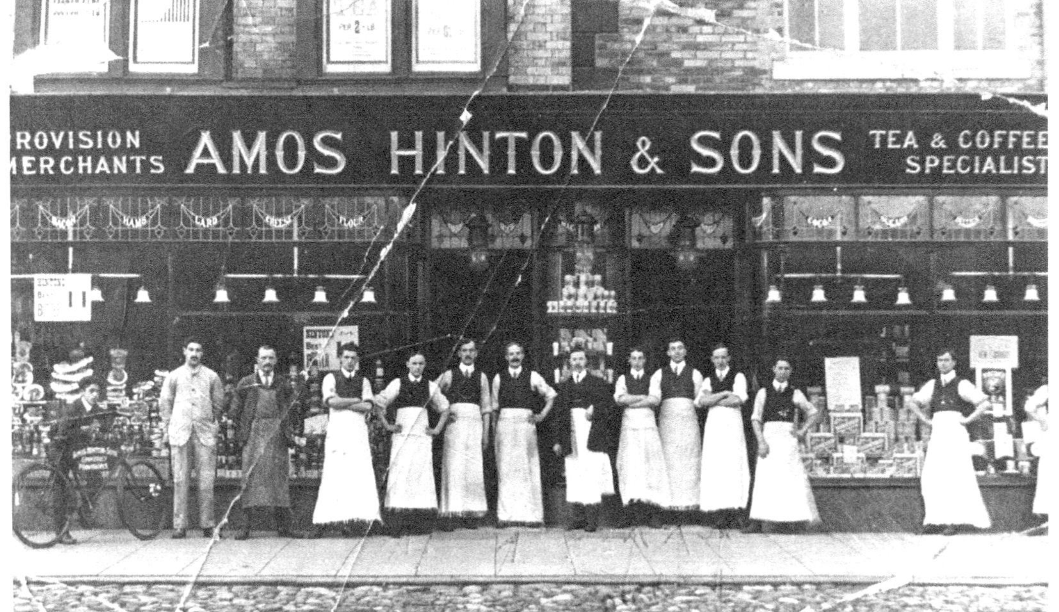

PROVISION
MERCHANTS
AMOS HINTON & SONS
TEA & COFFEE
SPECIALIST

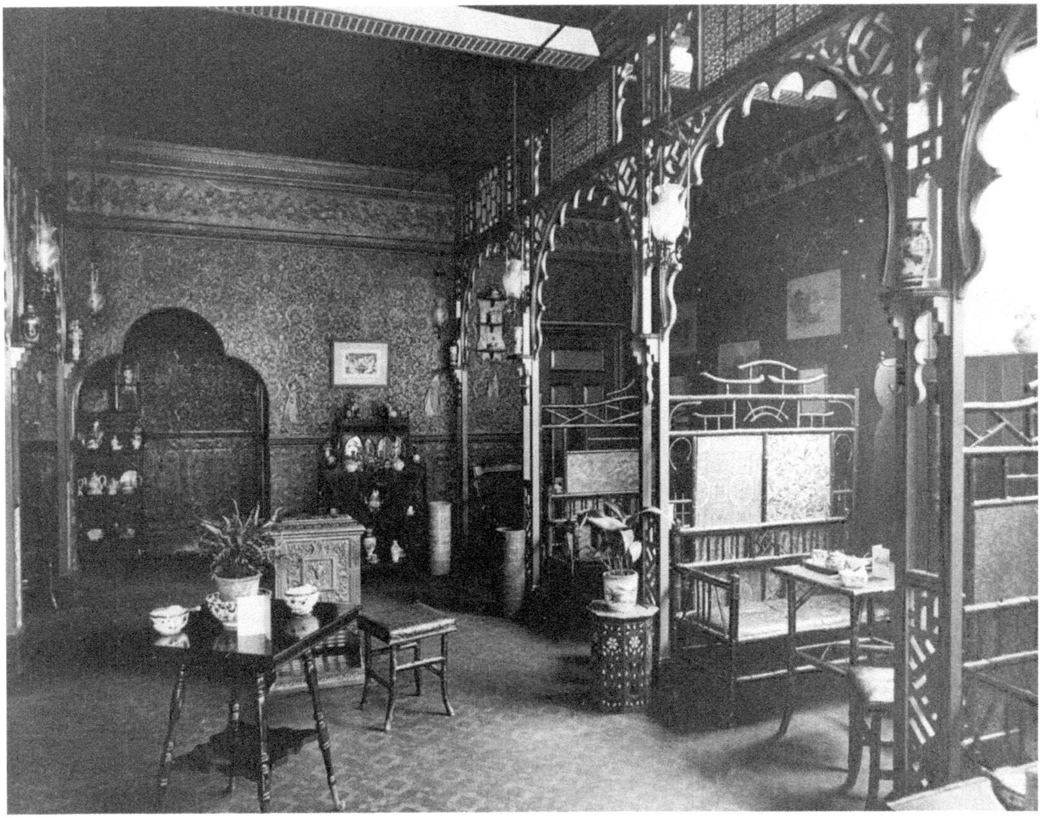

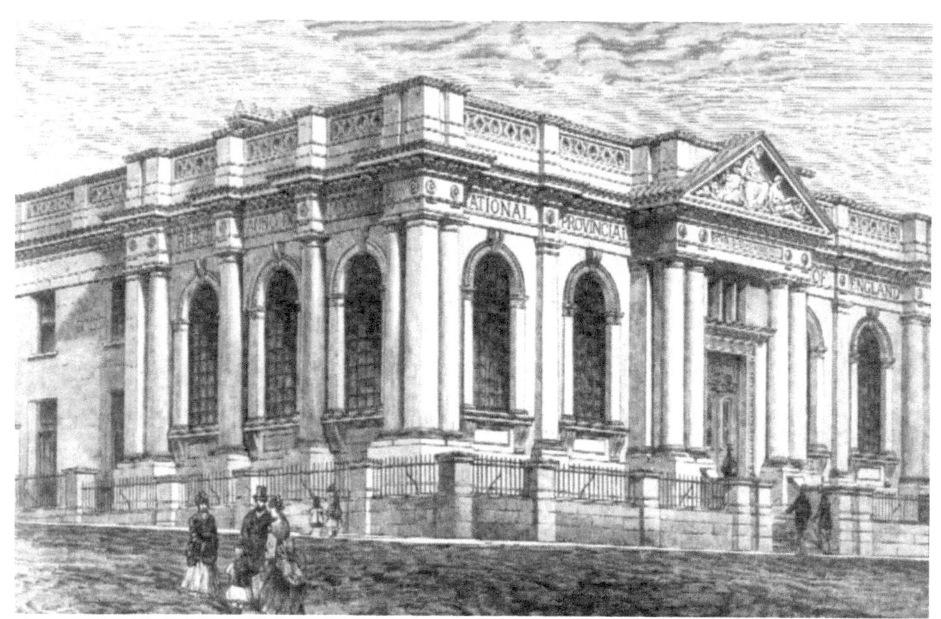

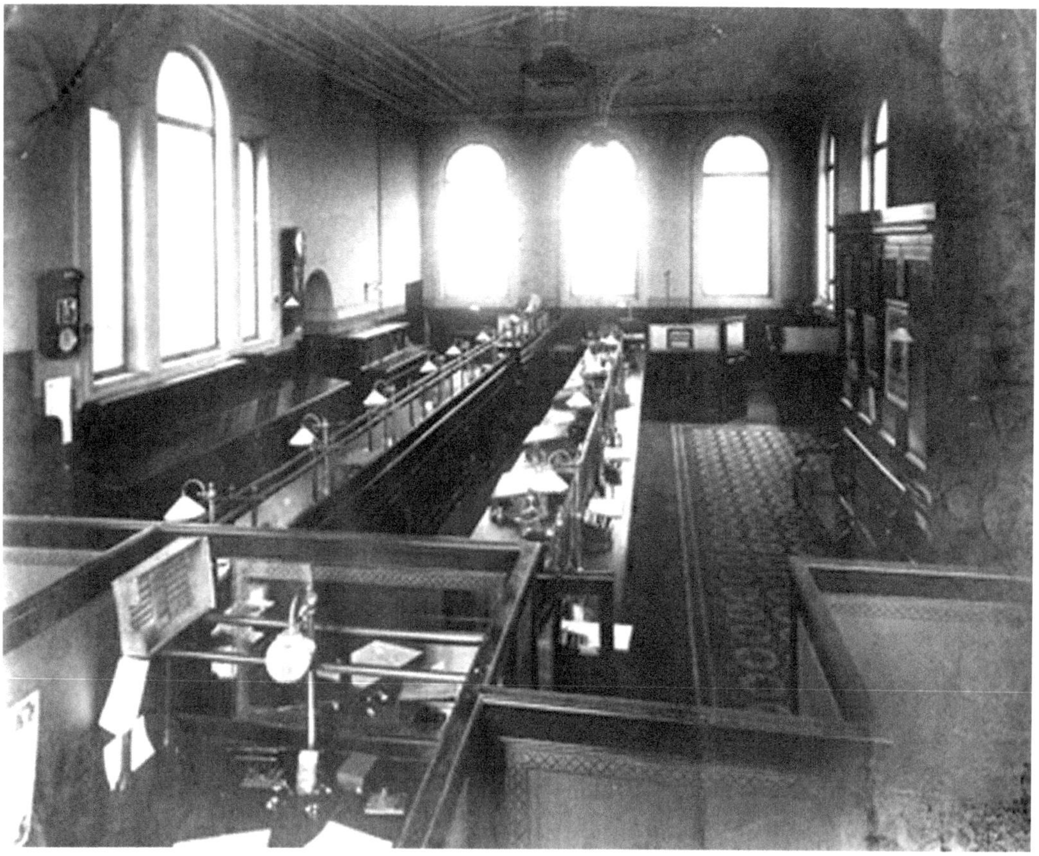

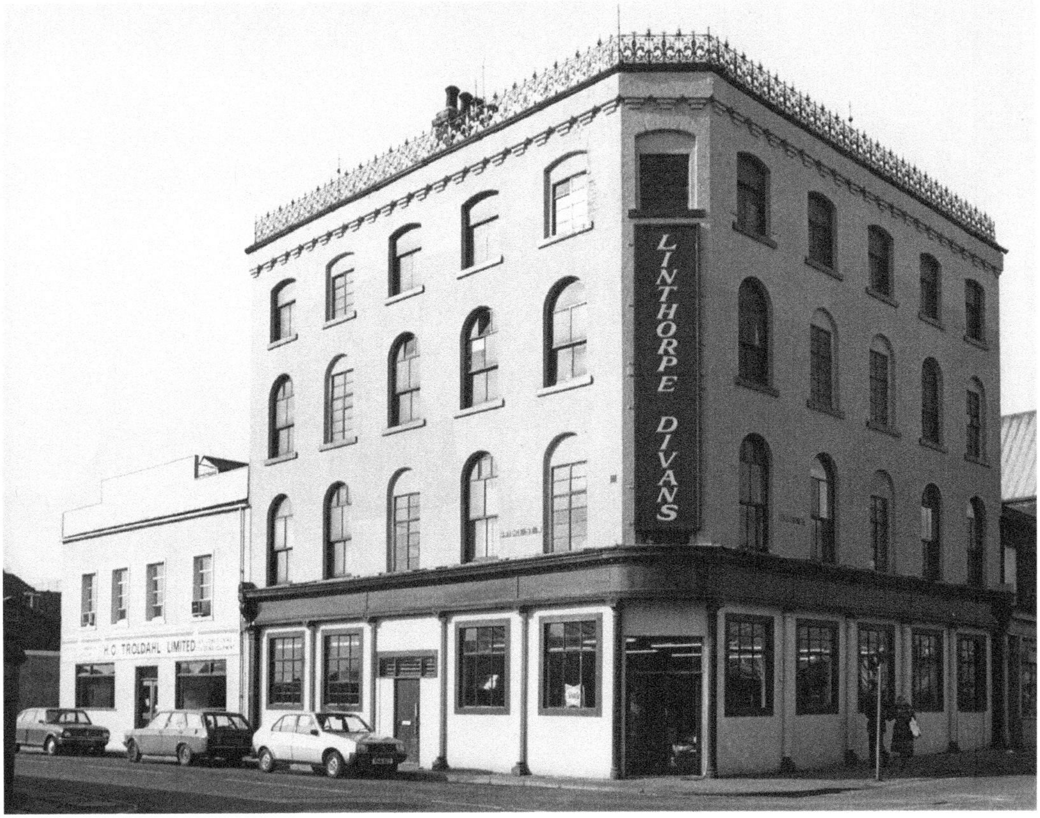

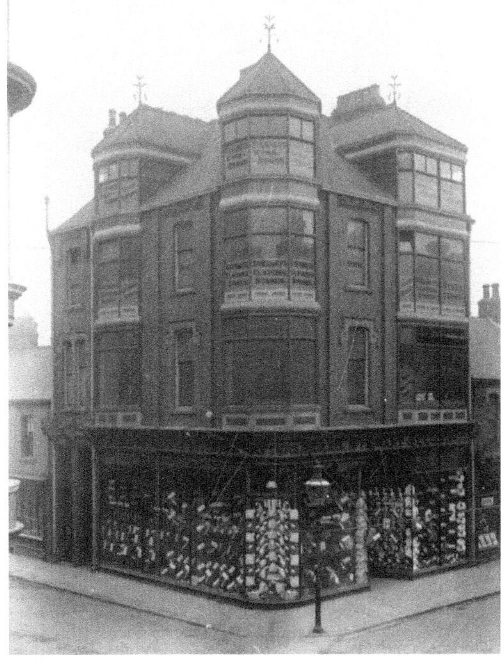

Above: Former shop building on the corner of Sussex Street and Bridge Street West, St Hilda's, when in use as 'Lock Stock and Barrel'.

Right: Stewart's Clothiers, Linthorpe Road, now the Halifax. Most Middlesbrough schoolchildren bought their uniform here in the 1960s and 1970s.

Opposite above: Former National Provincial Bank of England, Queen's Square, St Hilda's. It was opened in 1872 on the site of the home of the shipbuilder J.G. Holmes. The building was designed by John Gibson with a sculpture relief by Mabey, depicting Britannia, an iron worker and ironstone miner, symbols of the local industrial trade. It was later used as the home of the Cleveland Club, a meeting place for business gentlemen. It is now used for training purposes.

Opposite below: The banking hall's interior.

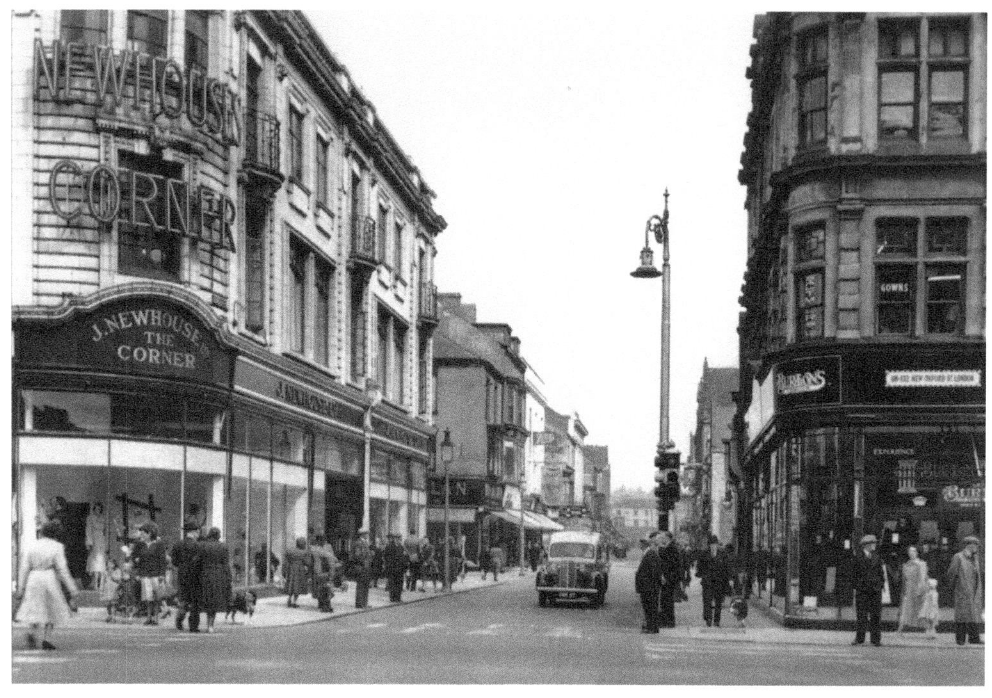

Newhouses Corner, Linthorpe Road, *c*. 1950. The shop was a drapers, tailors and general furnishers.

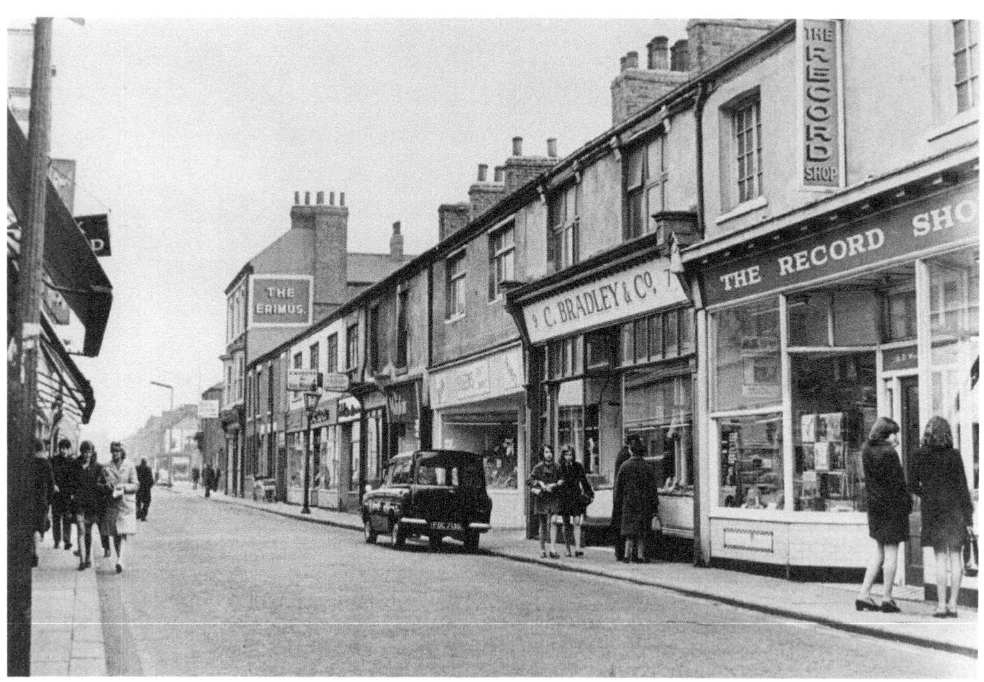

A disant view of the Erimus Hotel on the corner of Albert Road and Newton Street, named after the town's Latin motto, 'We Shall Be'. It was originally opened in 1880 and was in existence until 1971, when it was demolished to make way for the Cleveland Centre. This view is from the 1960s.

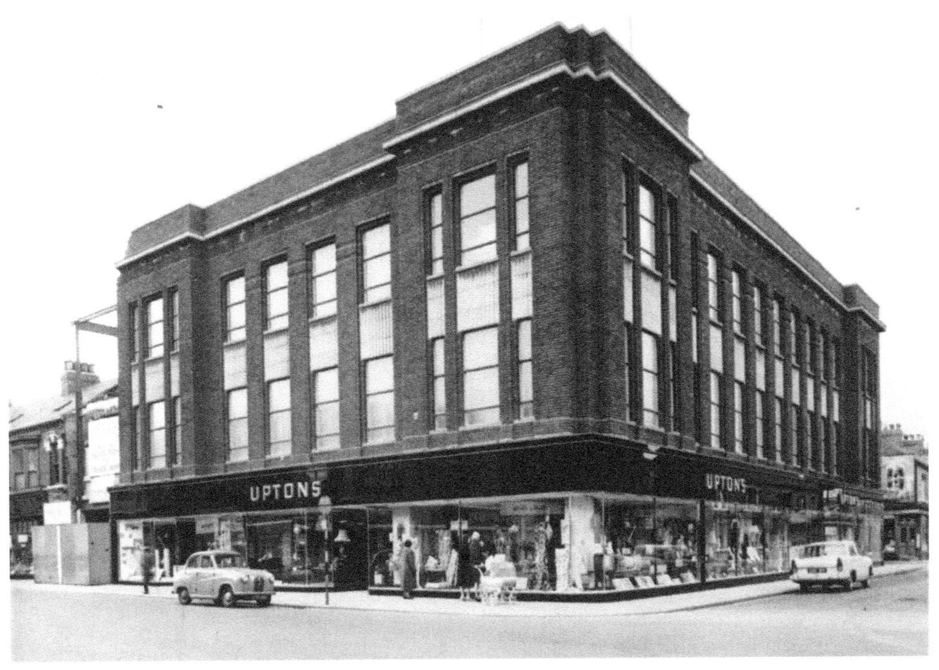

The former Upton's Department Store on Linthorpe Road, now the home to the award-winning fashion and design store Psyche. This view is from the 1960s.

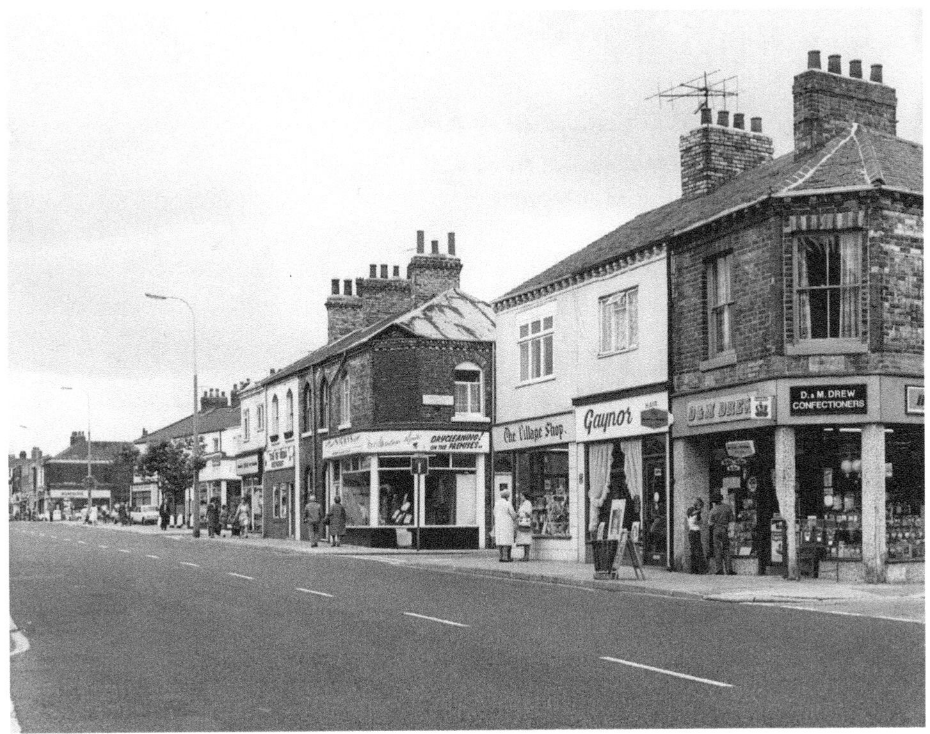

Linthorpe Road at the junction with St Barnabas Road, Linthorpe Village, in the 1980s.

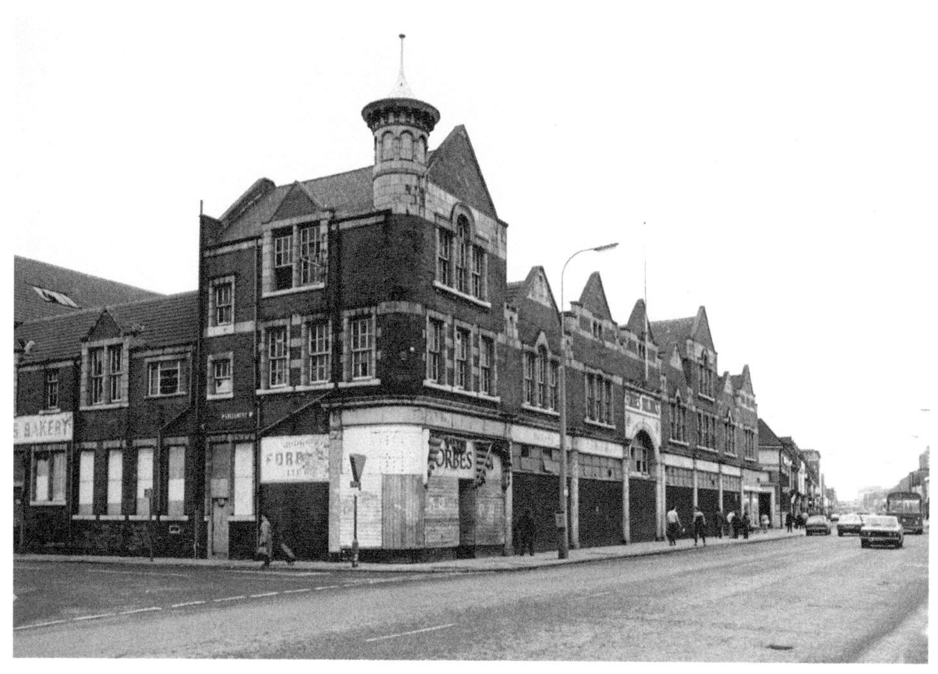

The former Forbes's bakery buildings on Linthorpe Road, closed and looking neglected.

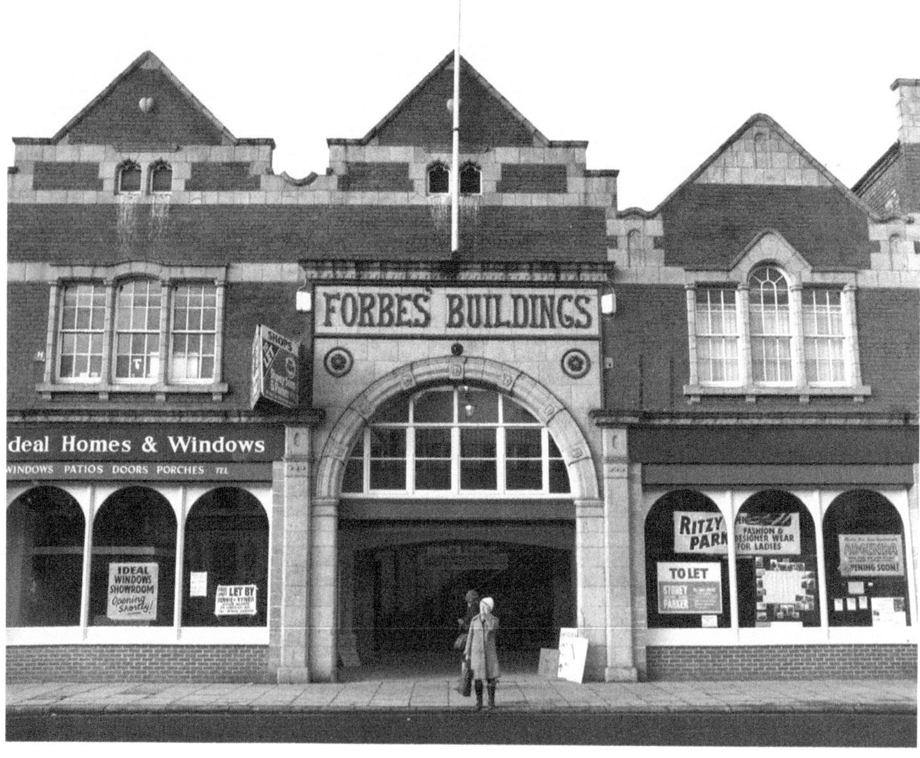

Another, more recent, view of the Forbes's buildings, showing signs of revitalisation.

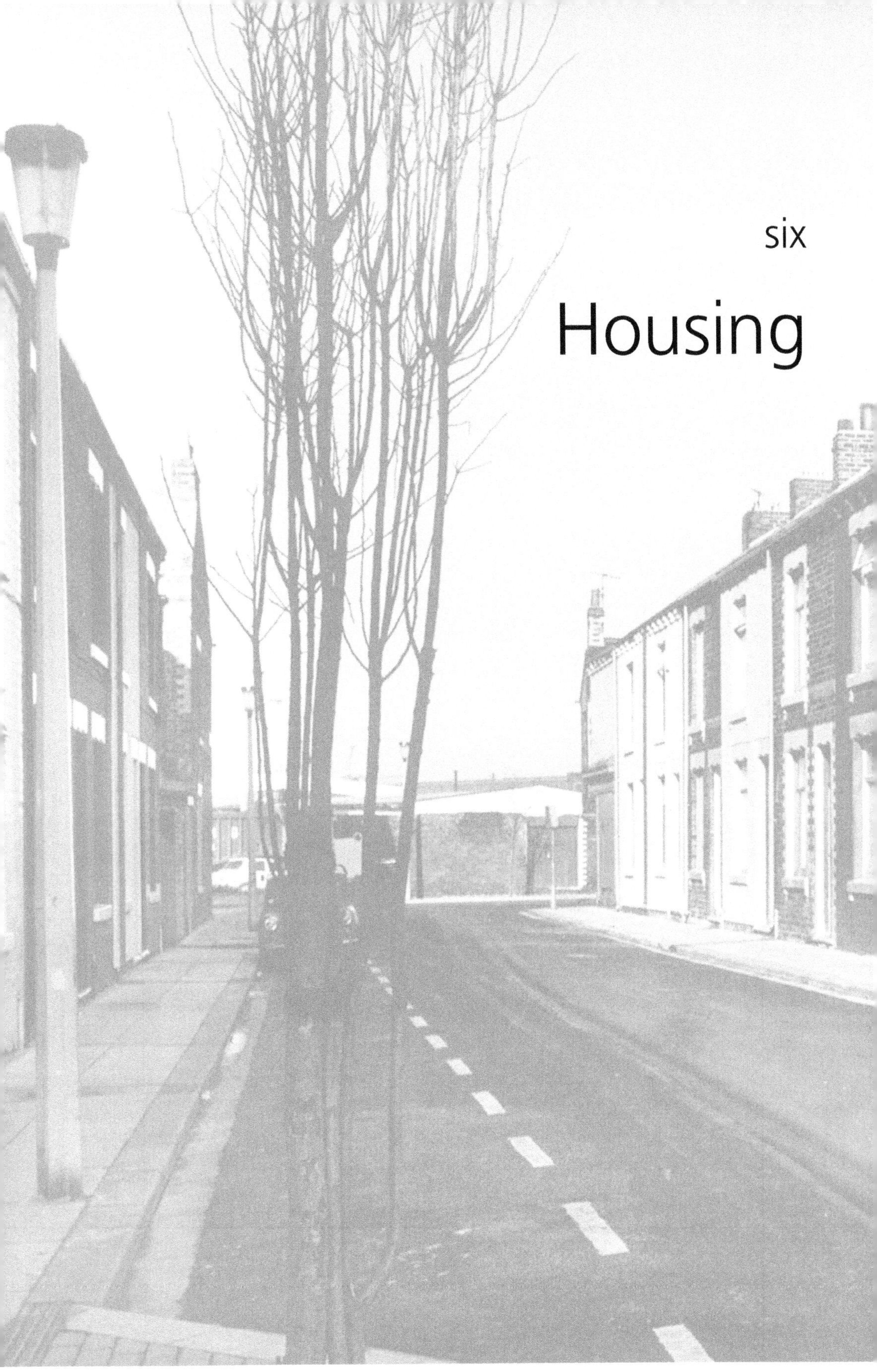
six
Housing

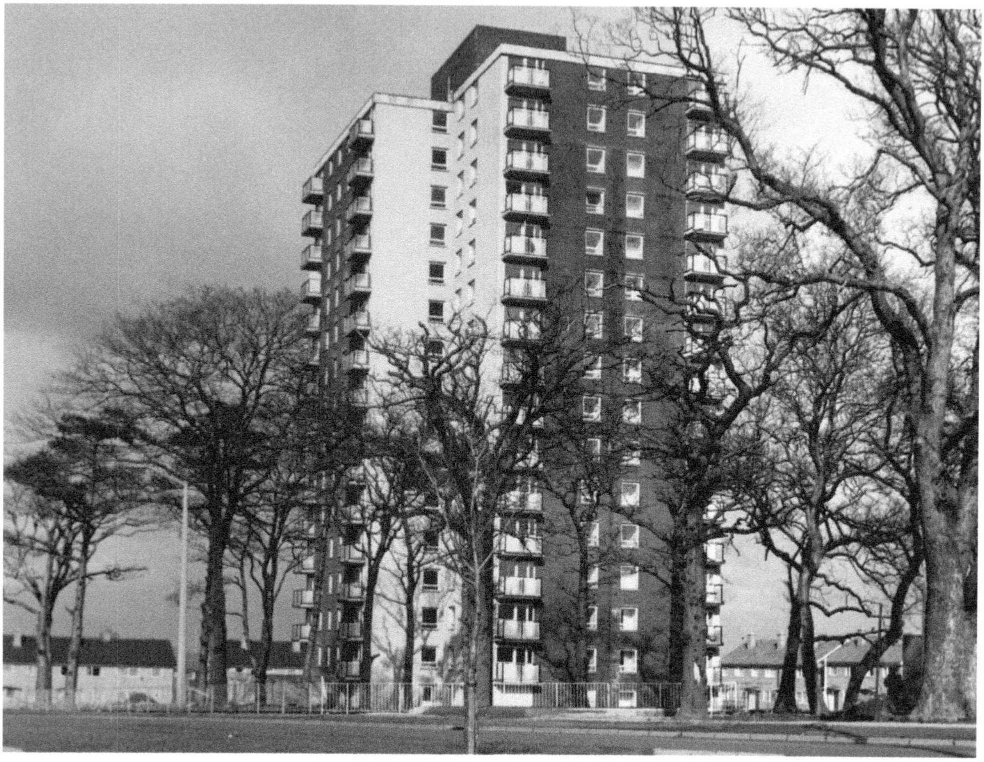

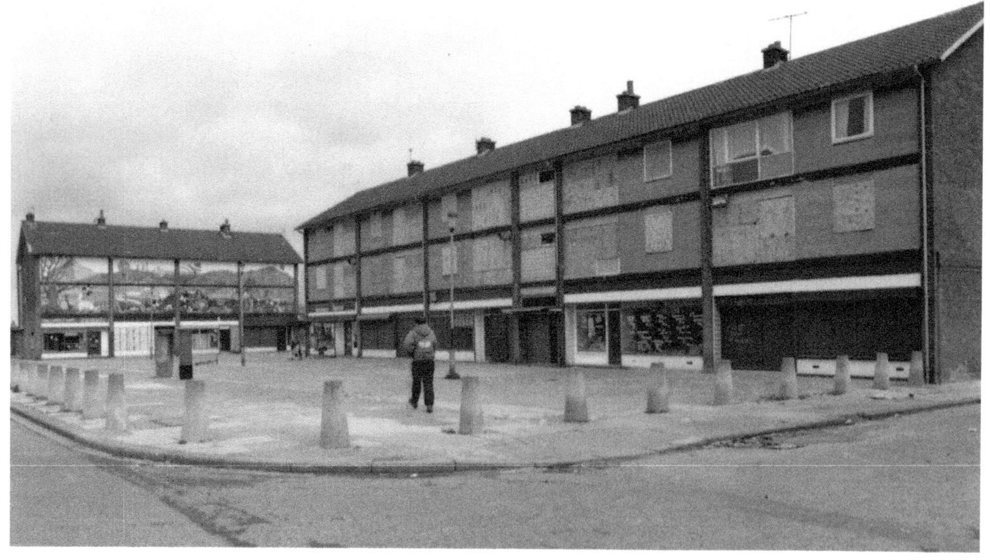

Glastonbury House, Ormesby Road, Priestfields Estate. The building was Middlesbrough's first residential tower block.

Langley Court, Park End Estate in the 1980s. It was originally a row of shops serving the estate, with flats above.

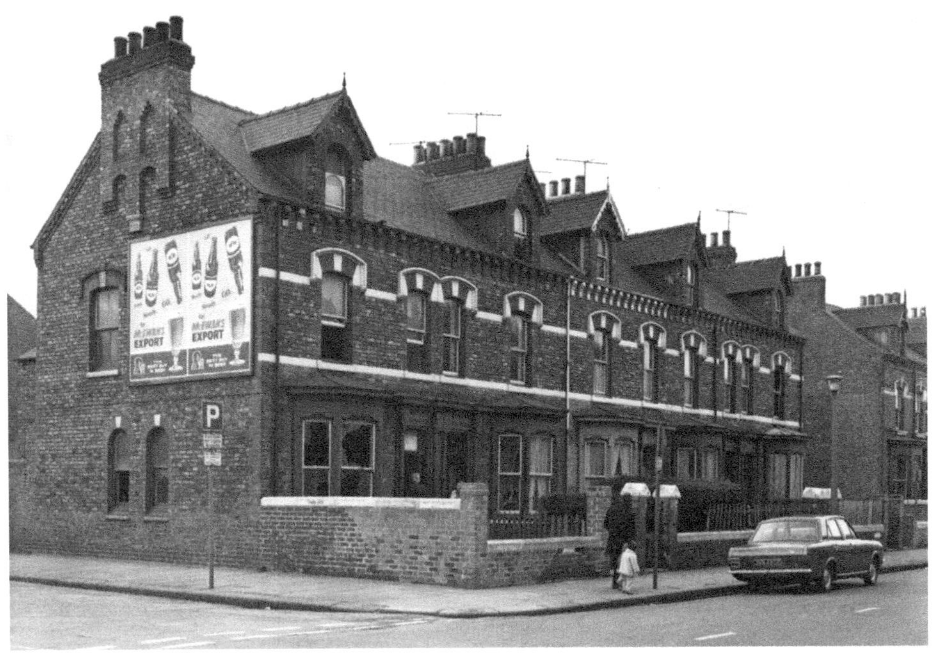

A view of one of the many Victorian terraces that once graced the town.

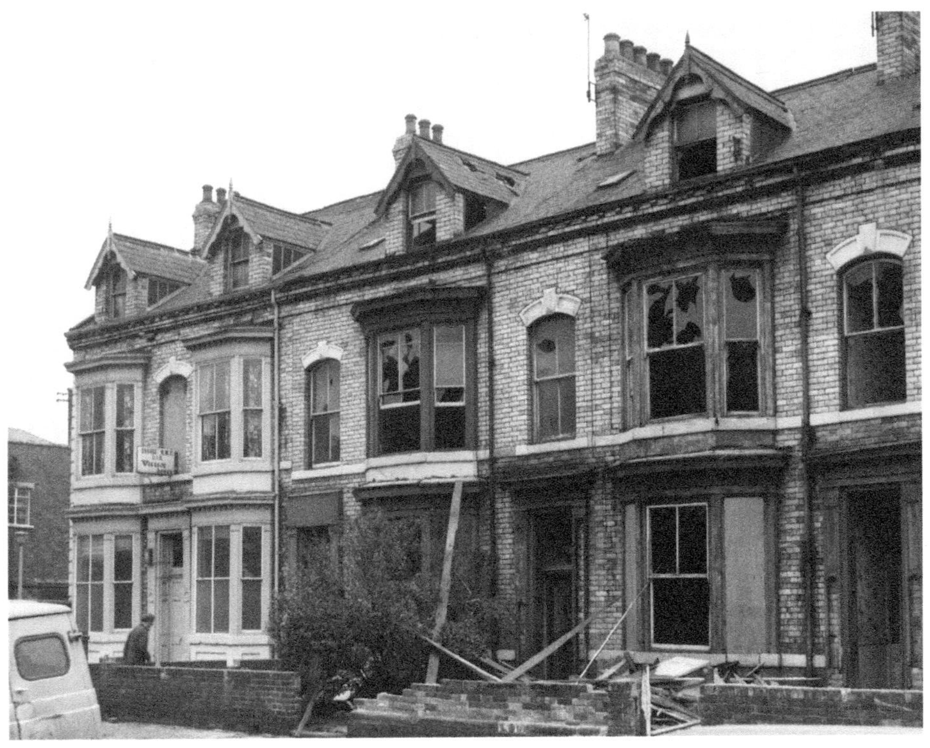

Town centre housing in Grange Road West, once an important residential address in the town but now awaiting demolition.

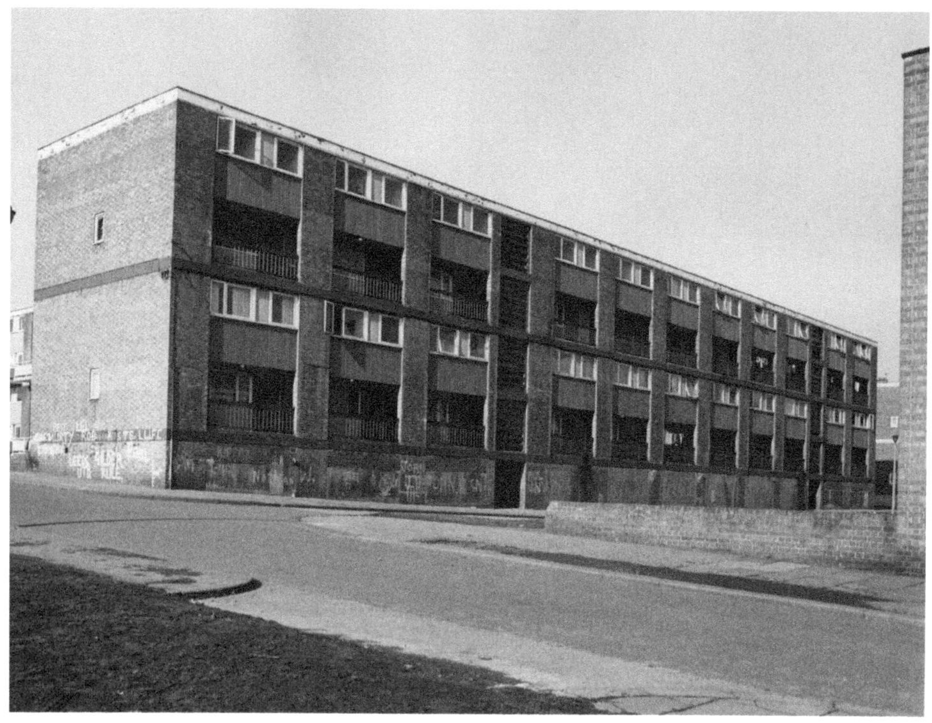

Maisonettes in the St Hilda's area of the town. Built after the Second World War, they did not provide the answer the council wanted to the housing needs of the local population.

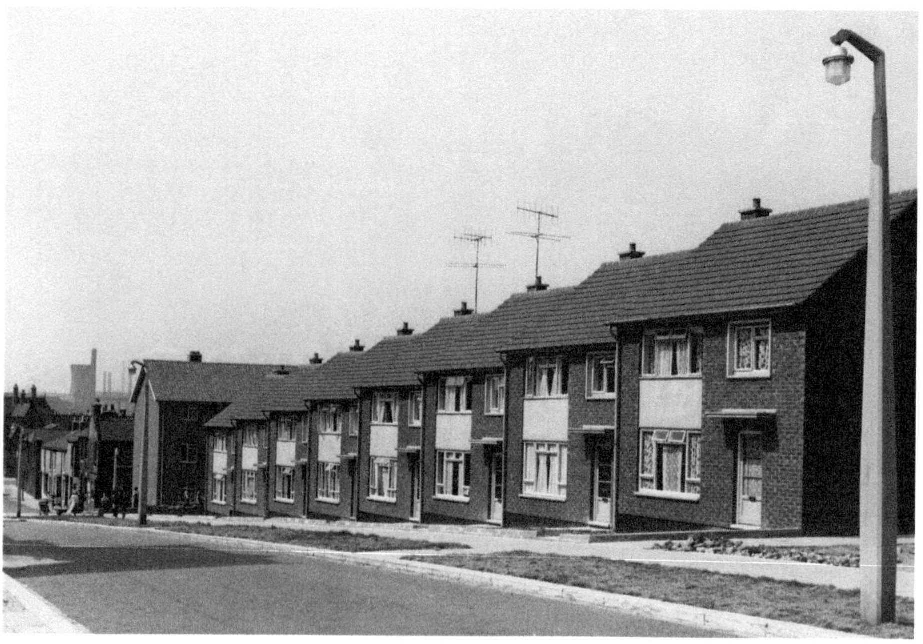

West Street, St Hilda's, as rebuilt in the 1970s after the demolition of the row that included the town's first house.

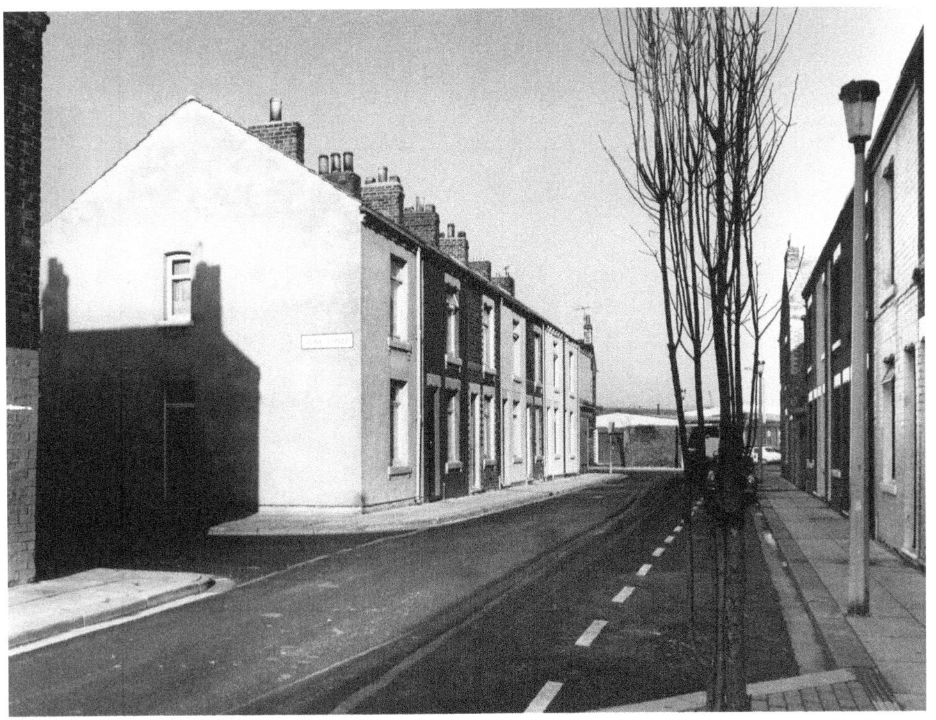

Lune Street, in the former Rivers area of the town. Most of these houses were cleared during the City Challenge and replaced with old-style designed, modern housing called St John's Gate.

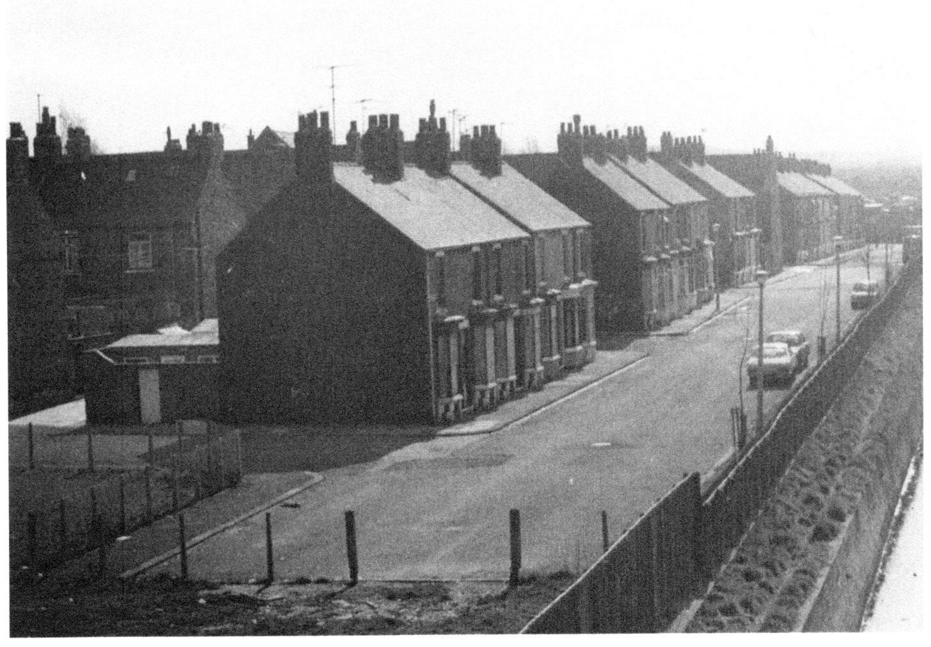

Another typical view of the town's terraced housing.

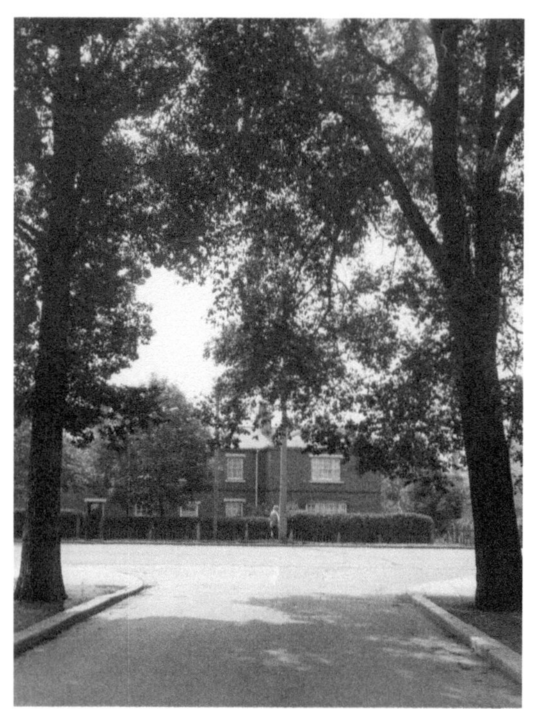

Left: A view to Marton Burn Road, Grove Hill. The council built the houses at Marton Grove, and later Grove Hill, after the First World War, as 'homes fit for heroes'.

Below: Council Houses at Whinney Banks in West Middlesbrough.

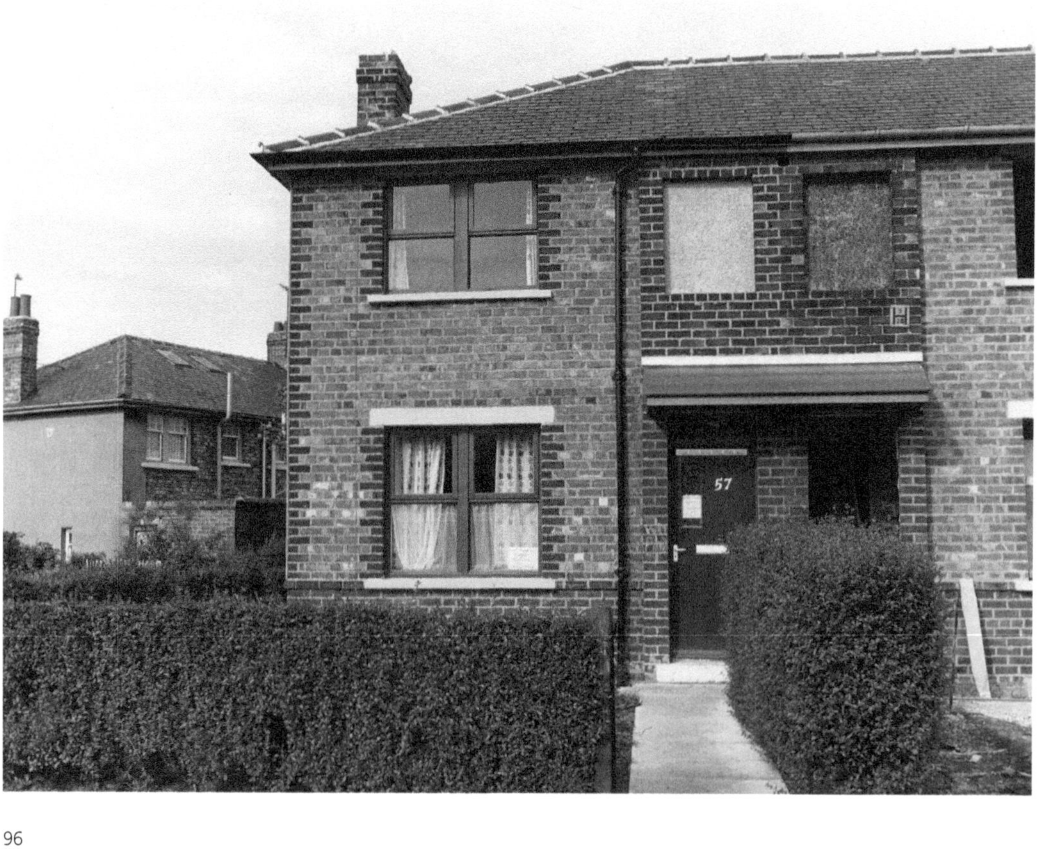

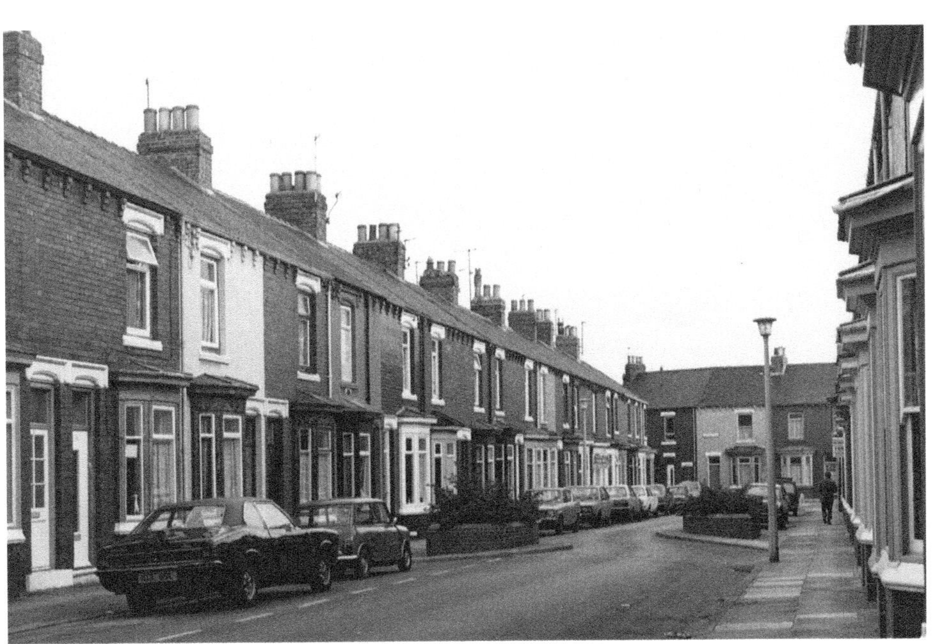

Town centre terraces showing the brick-built planting boxes that were designed to slow traffic, and so make the streets safer for residents with families.

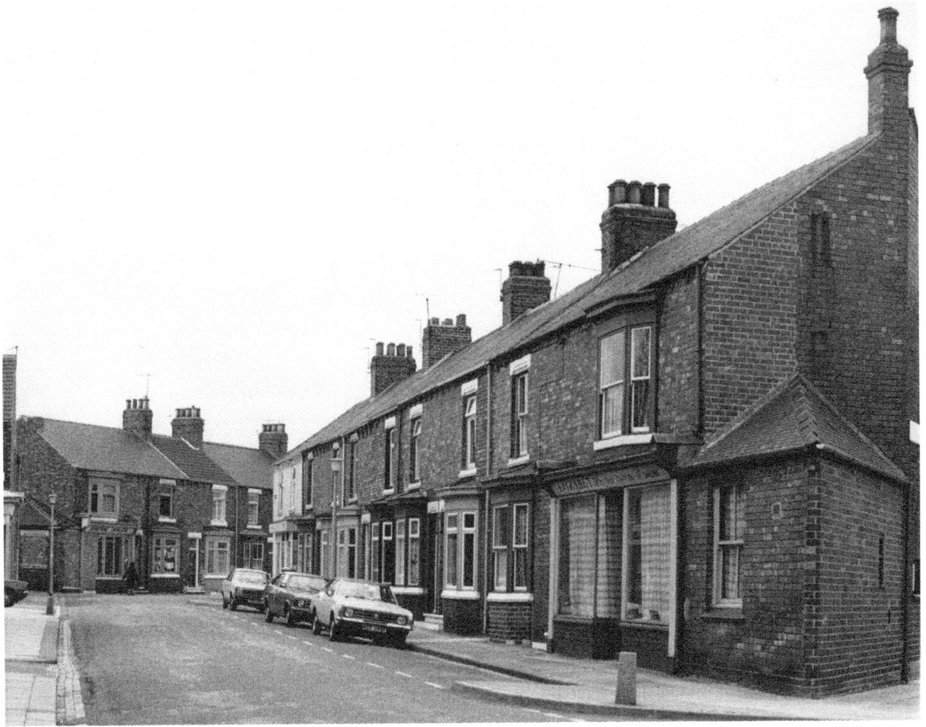

Each area of houses had its own general dealer, as seen here. Elizabeth's hair stylists, with a rather unusual brick side extension to the house, can also be seen.

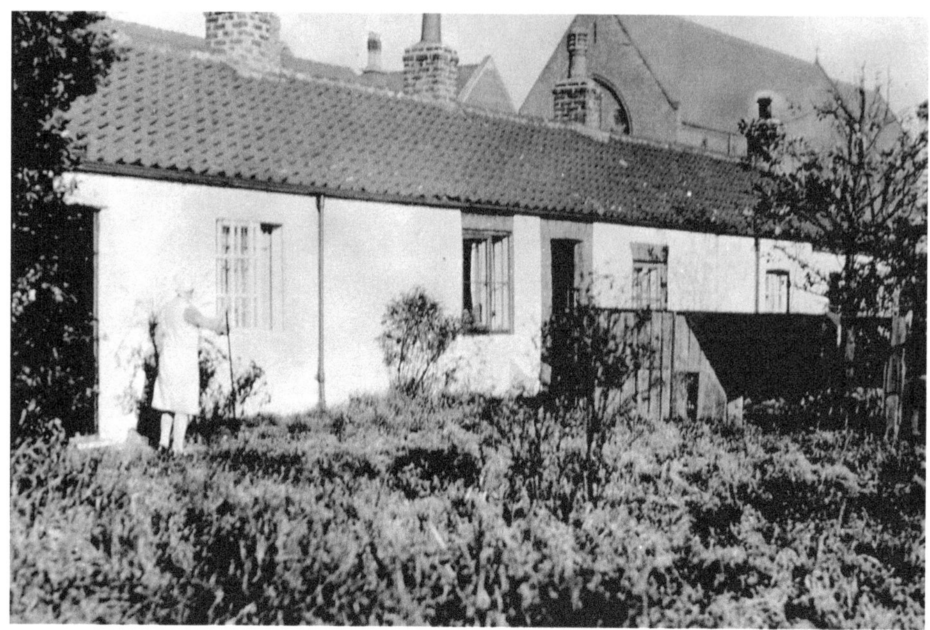

The rear view of the old cottages in St Barnabas Road. Before the building of the church of the same name, which can be seen in the background, this road was called Cemetery Road, because it led to Linthorpe Cemetery. The cottages were still standing into the 1930s but have since been demolished.

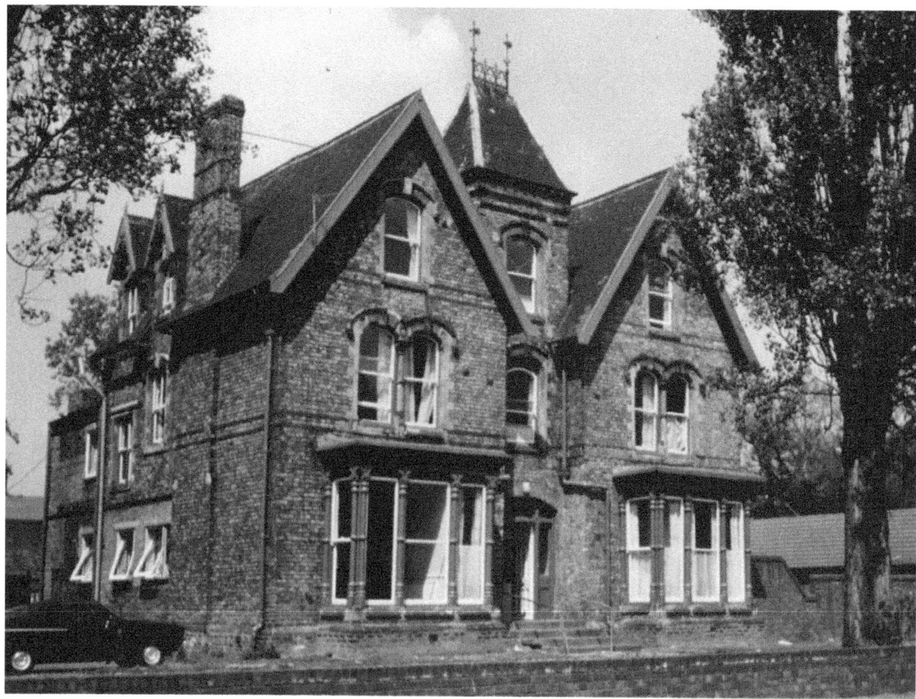

A fine example of a Victorian villa house. This one in Park Road North, overlooking the Albert Park, was built for Alderman William Thomas Keay.

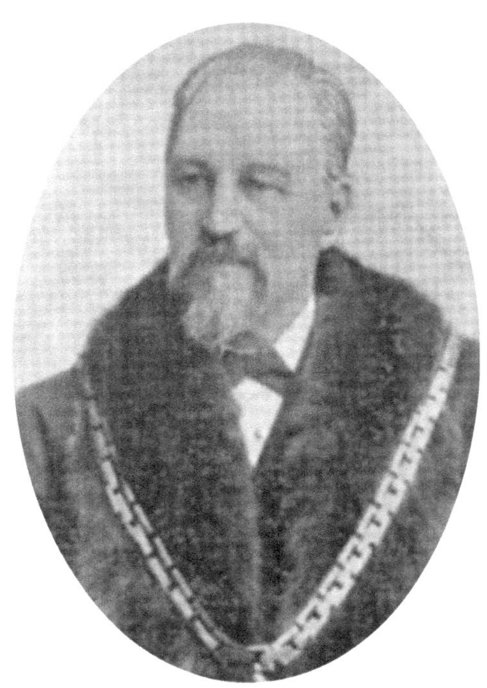

Alderman William Thomas Keay, seen here
while he was mayor in 1898. He died in 1901.

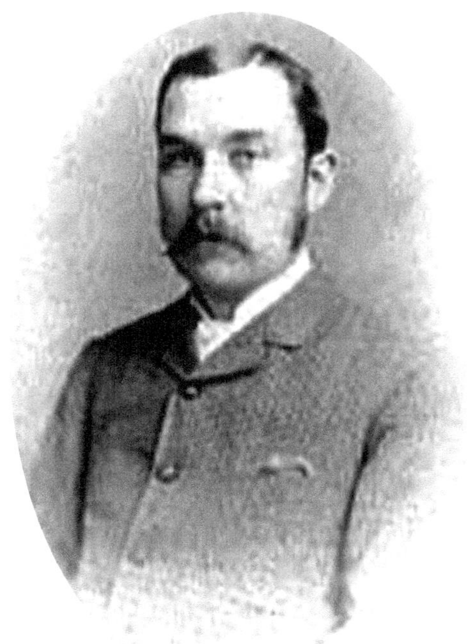

Theodore Hornung, father of E.W. Hornung,
writer and creator of A.J. Raffles, who ran a.
shipping business in Middlesbrough.

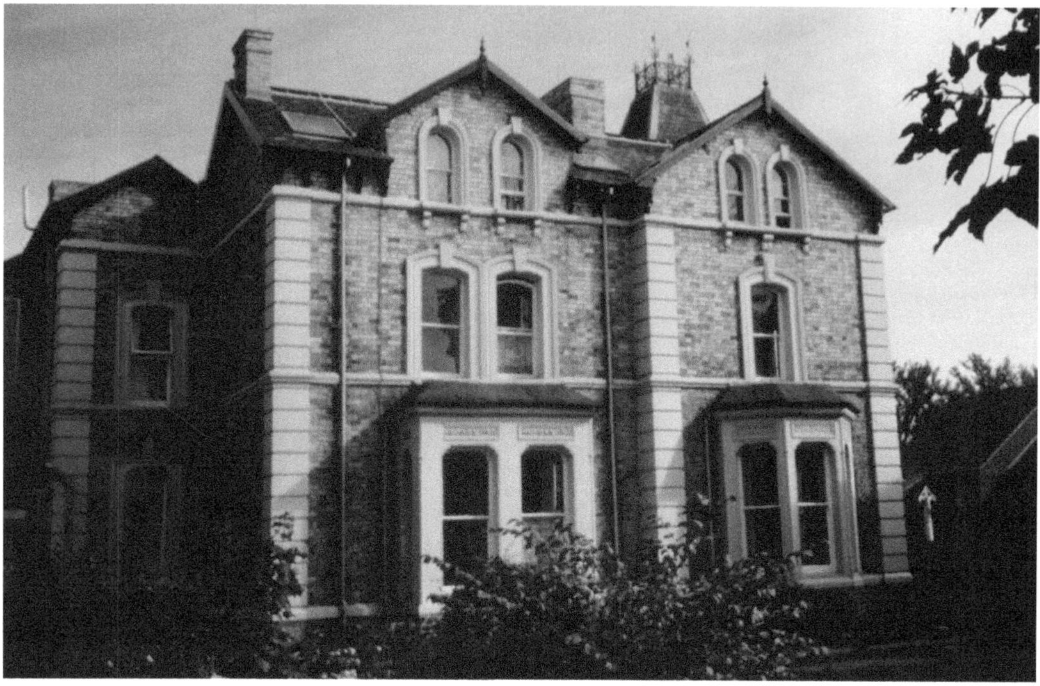

Erdley Villa, Marton Road, Middlesbrough, home of the Hornung family.

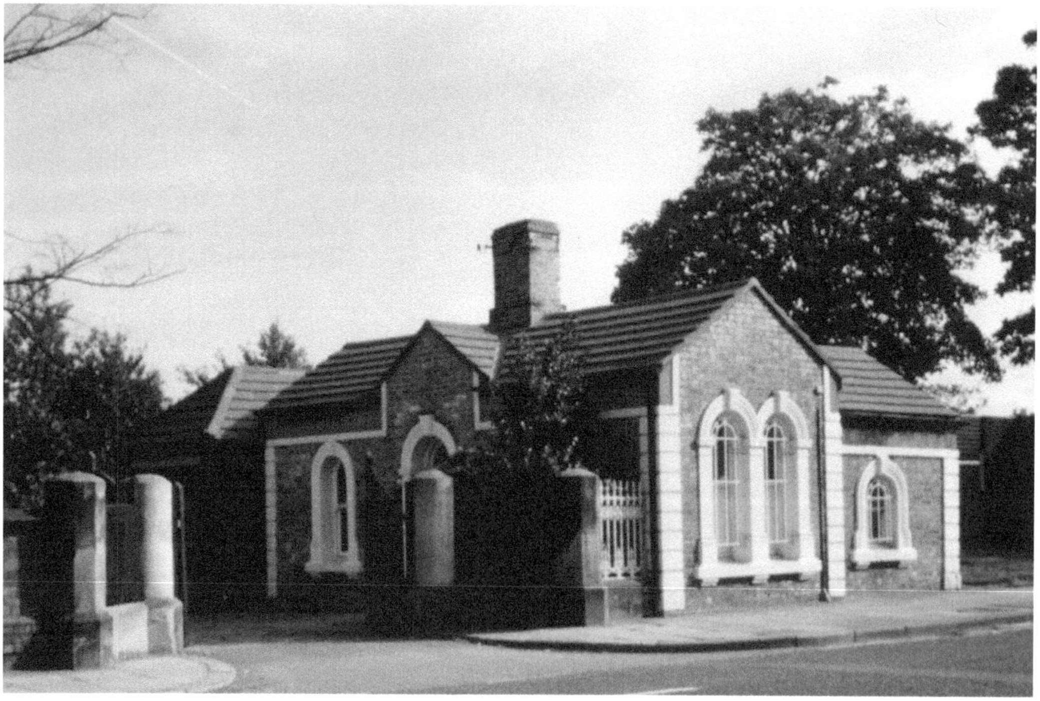

The Gatehouse at Erdley Villa, Marton Road.

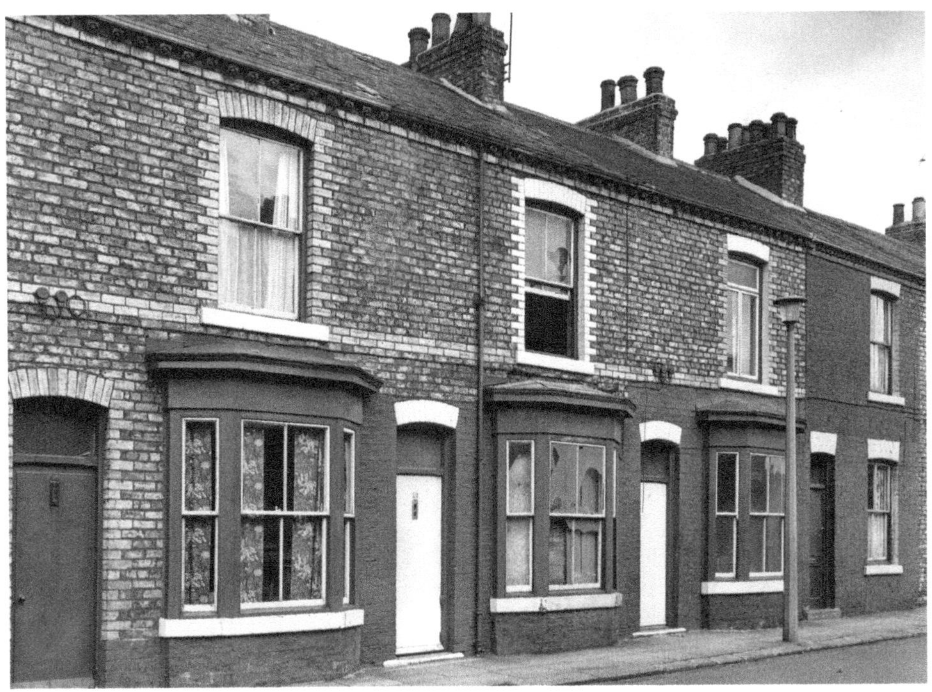

The beginning of the end? A terrace of typical Victorian houses with bay windows awaiting demolition.

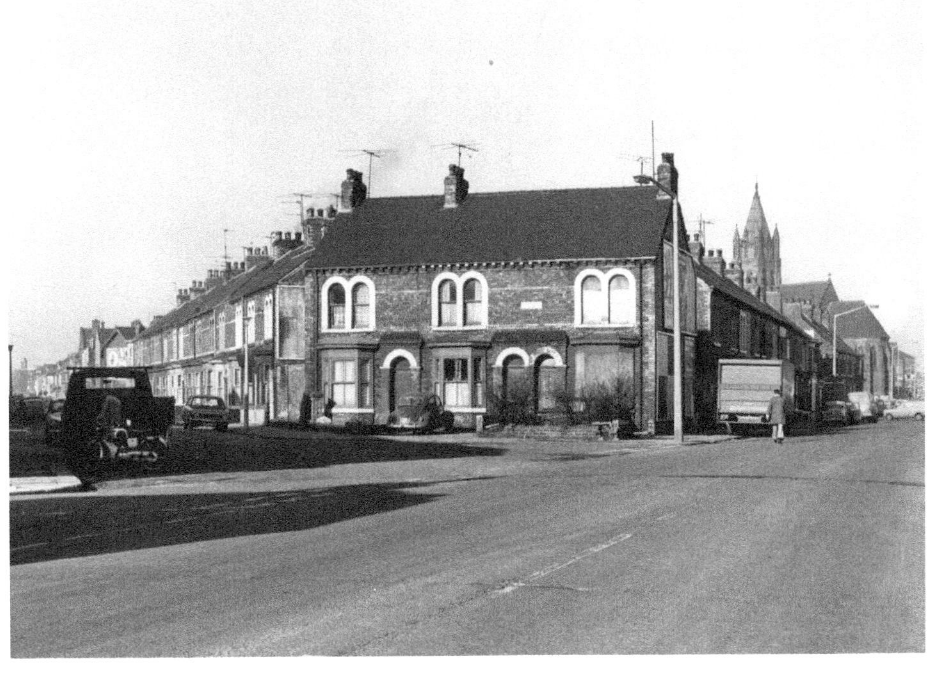

North Ormesby Road, looking towards the town centre. St John the Evangelist's church can be seen in the background. This area has now been redeveloped.

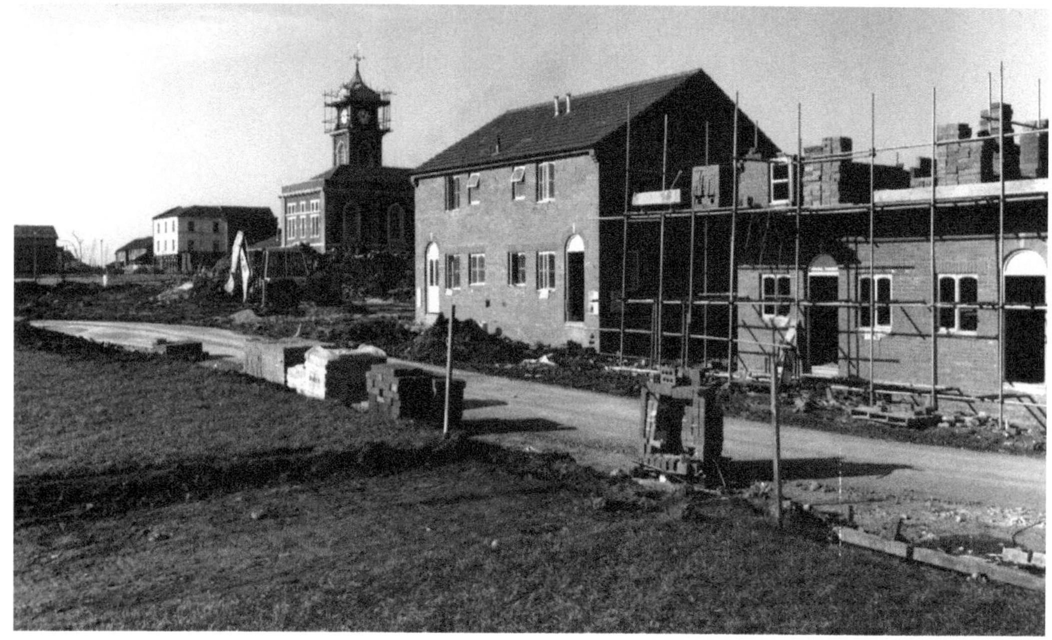

New town houses in Tower Green, St Hilda's. Yuill the builder built 120 houses in association with Middlesbrough Council in the 1980s, surrounding the former town hall and St Hilda's churchyard. As this book is going to print they are scheduled to be demolished as part of the Middlehaven redevelopment project.

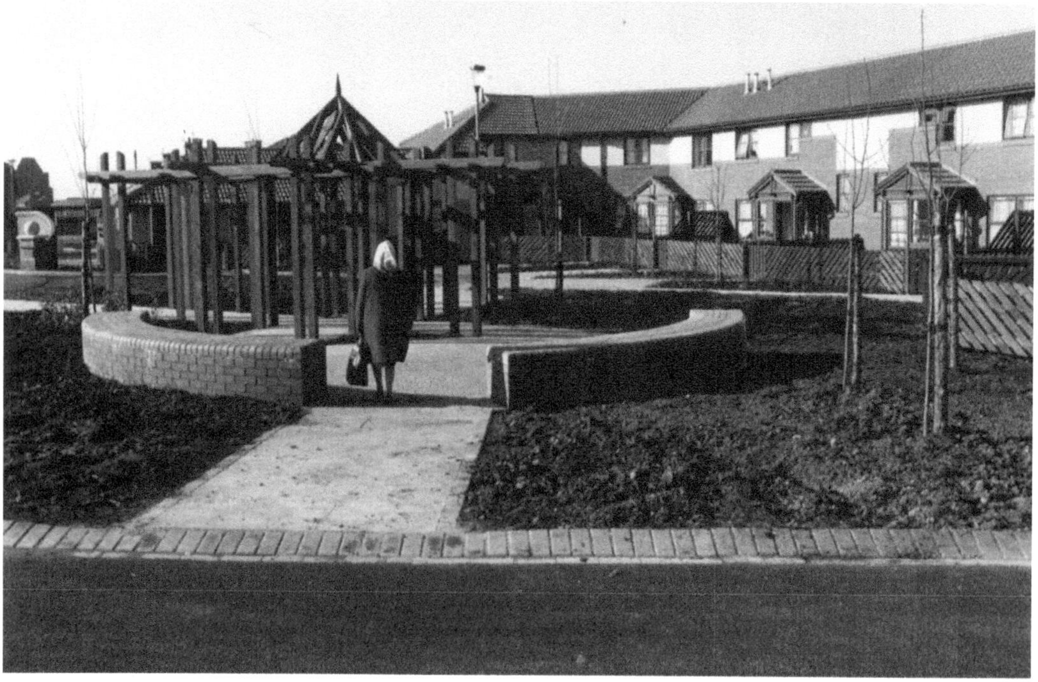

Cathedral Gardens, St Hilda's, semi-sheltered accommodation for older people built by the council in the 1980s, also scheduled for demolition, as is the case with all residential properties north of the railway line.

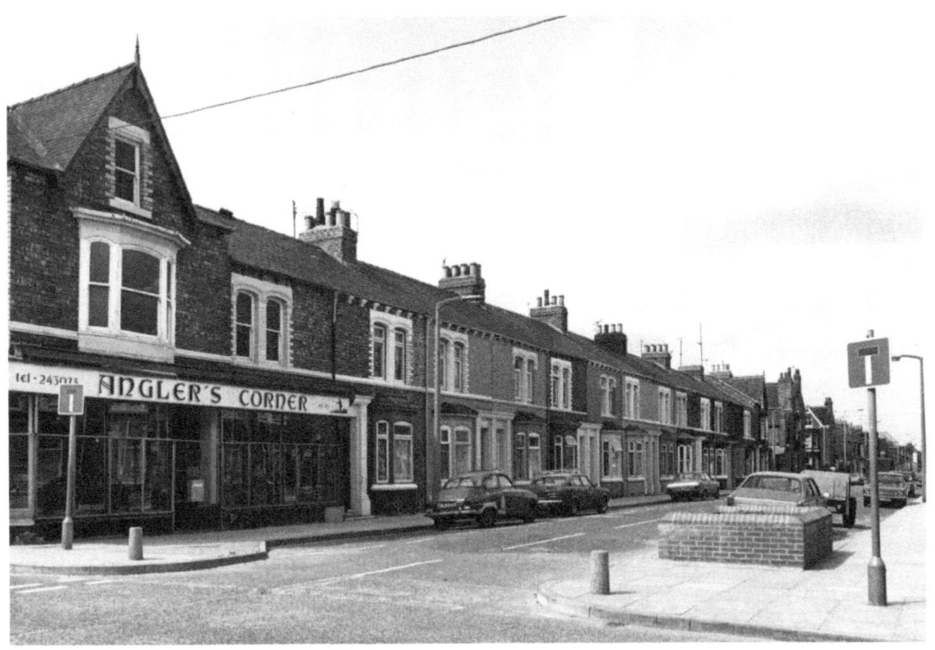

Abingdon Road, Middlesbrough town centre. The Angler's Corner shop is in an interesting location as it is not too far from Albert Park, where fishing is a pastime.

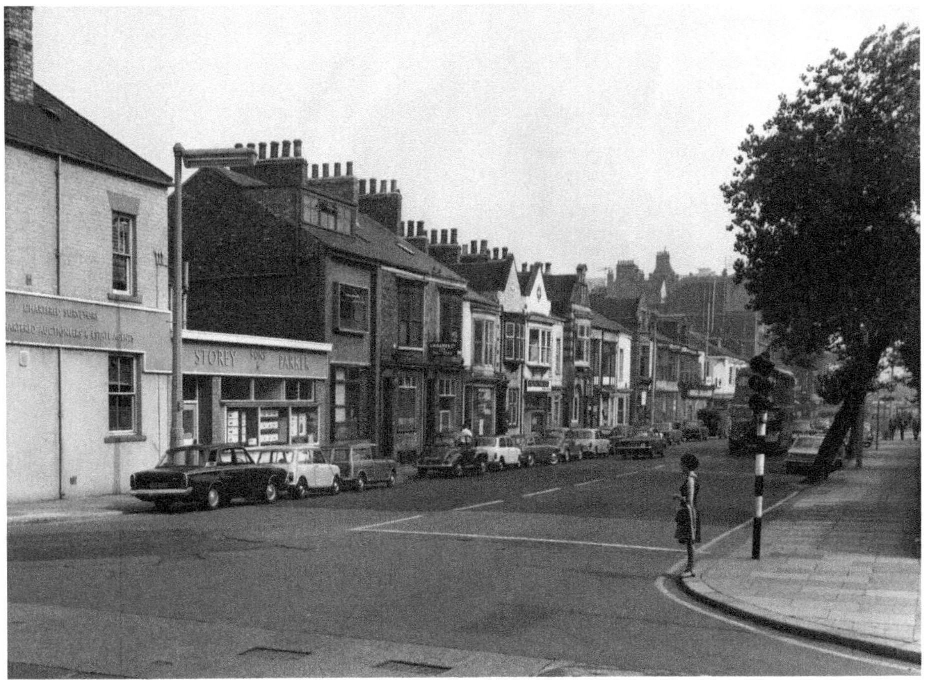

Albert Road looking towards the town hall: this view was taken before the building of the Cleveland Shopping Centre in the 1970s.

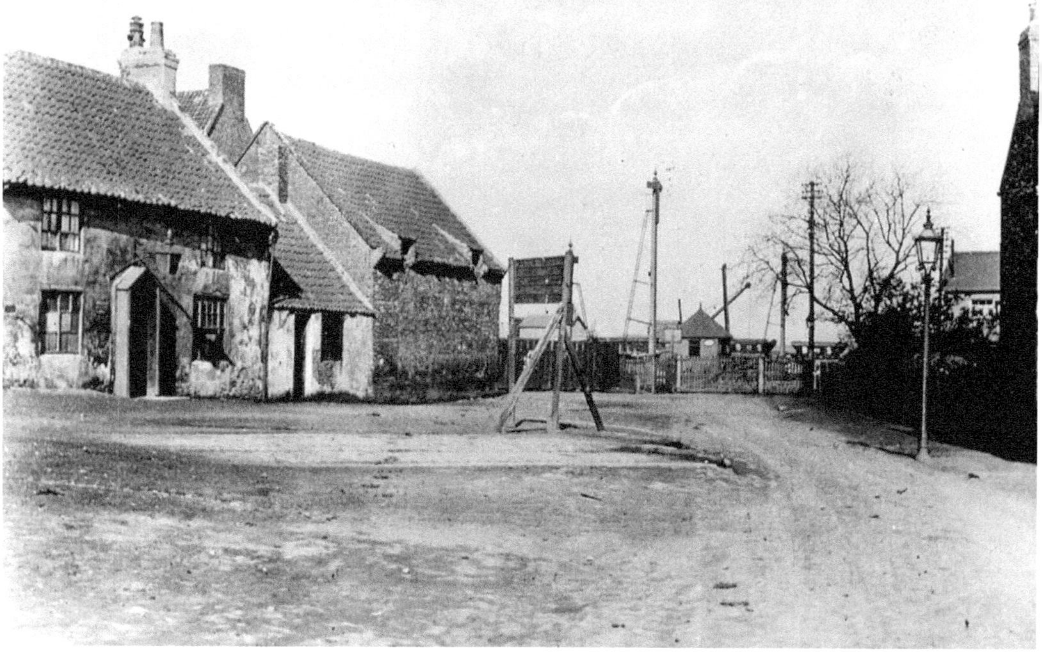

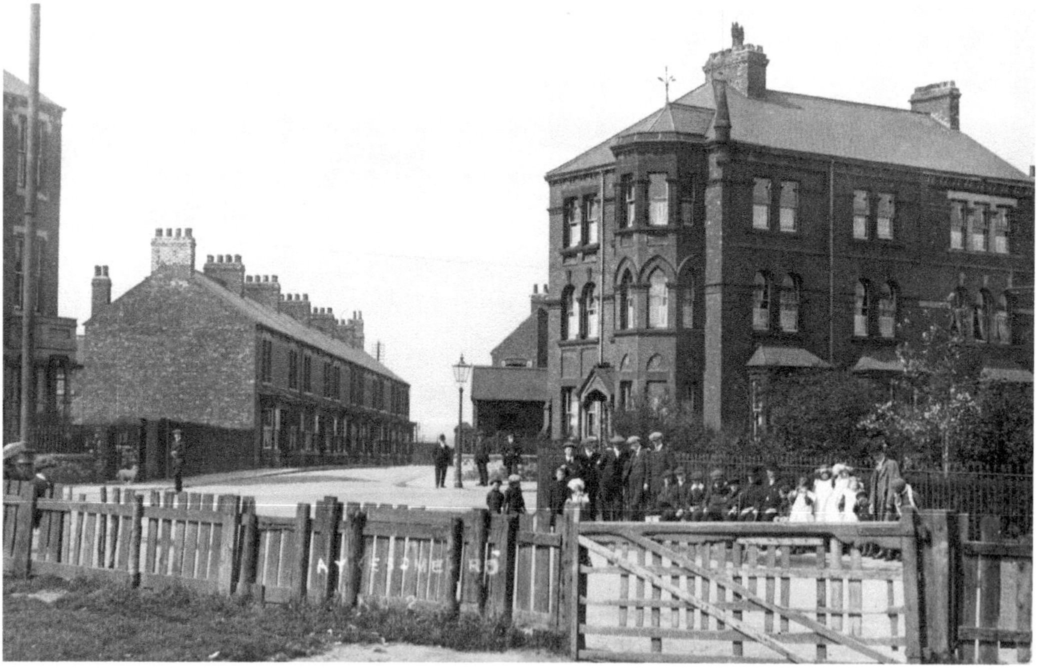

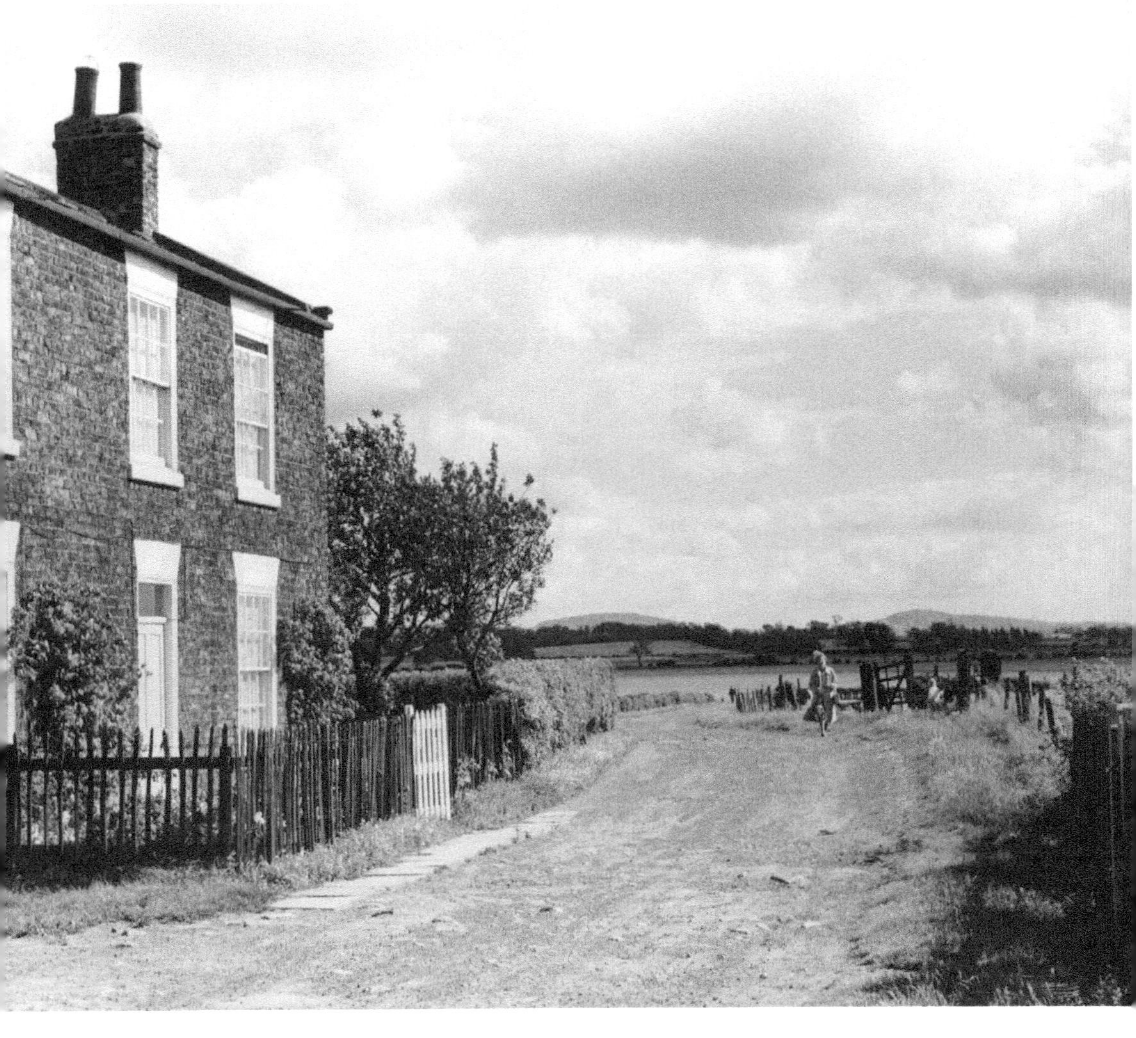

Newham Bridge Farm, Tollesby, Middlesbrough. The land is now occupied by housing and a primary school with the old farm's name. Roseberry Topping can be seen in the background.

Opposite above: Seventeenth-century farm buildings at Newport. This image is taken from a glass negative in the Dorman Museum collection. The railway line that carried wagons to the Ayresome, Dorman Long and Samuelson's Ironworks can be clearly seen, with the wagons bearing the initials B.S., for Bernhard Samuelson.

Opposite below: Newport House, the home of George Carter. The building, along with the other houses seen in this photograph, was demolished to make way for the Newport Bridge in the early 1930s.

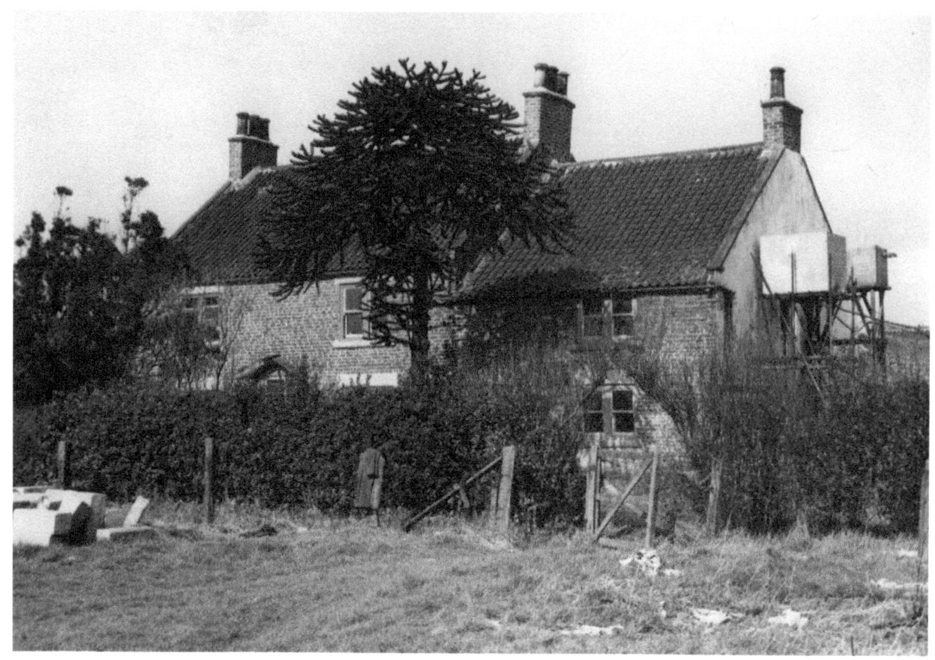

Berwick Hills Farm gave its name to the housing estate that replaced it in the late 1950s.

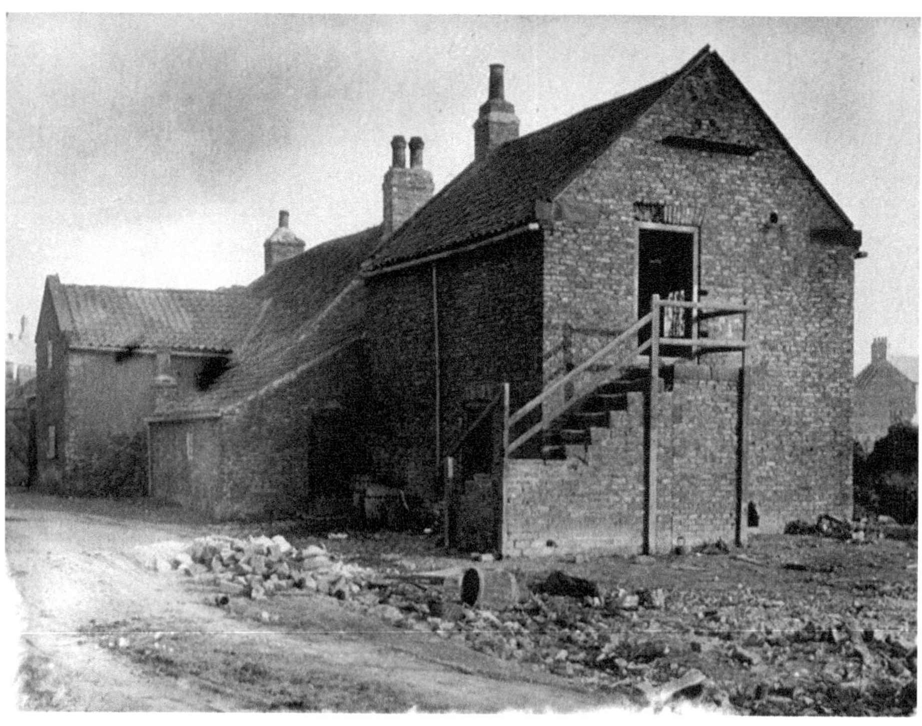

Old Gate Farm, demolished just before the turn of the century, stood on a site now occupied by Kensington Road and Brompton Street, Linthorpe.

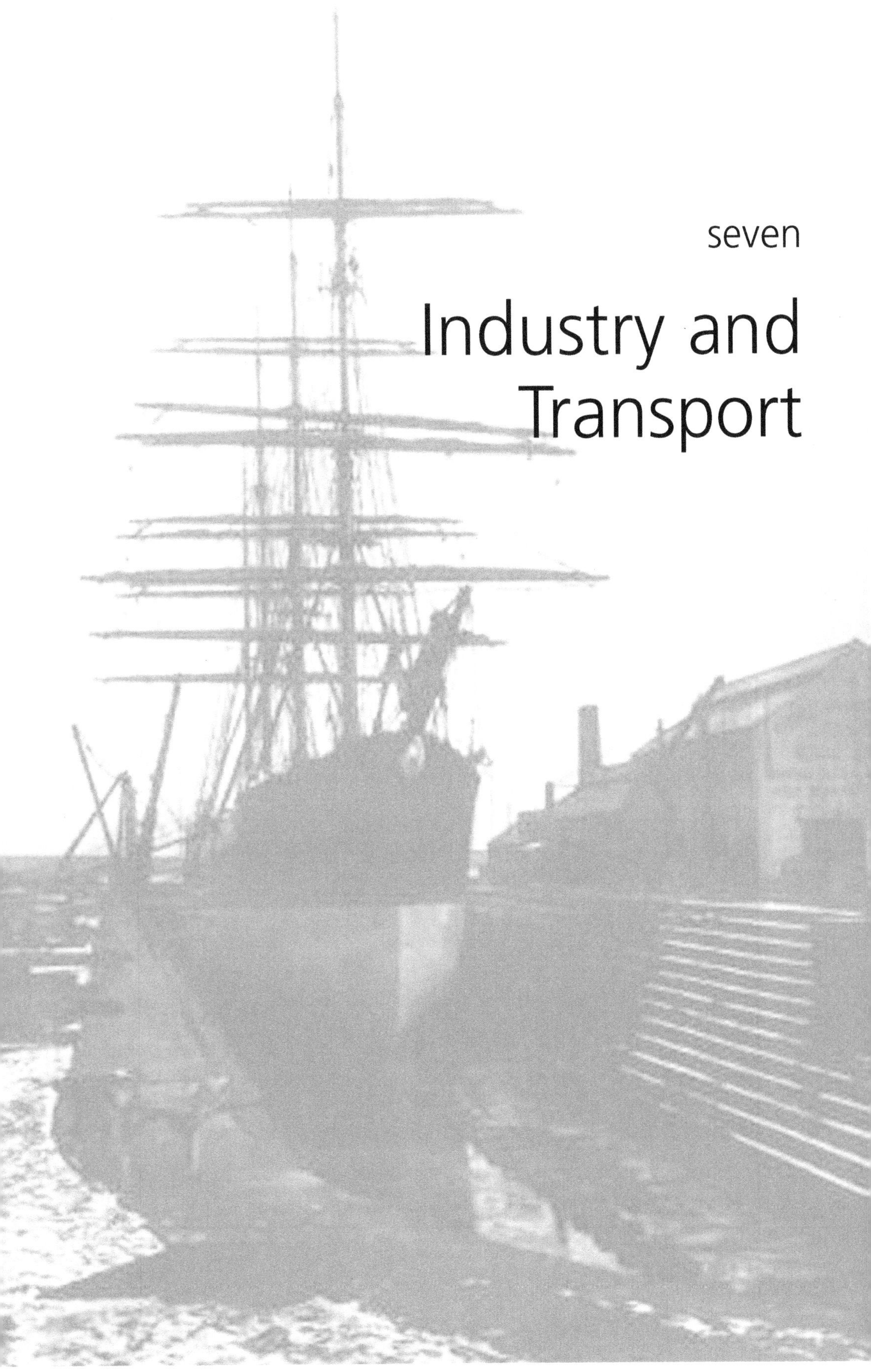

Industry and Transport

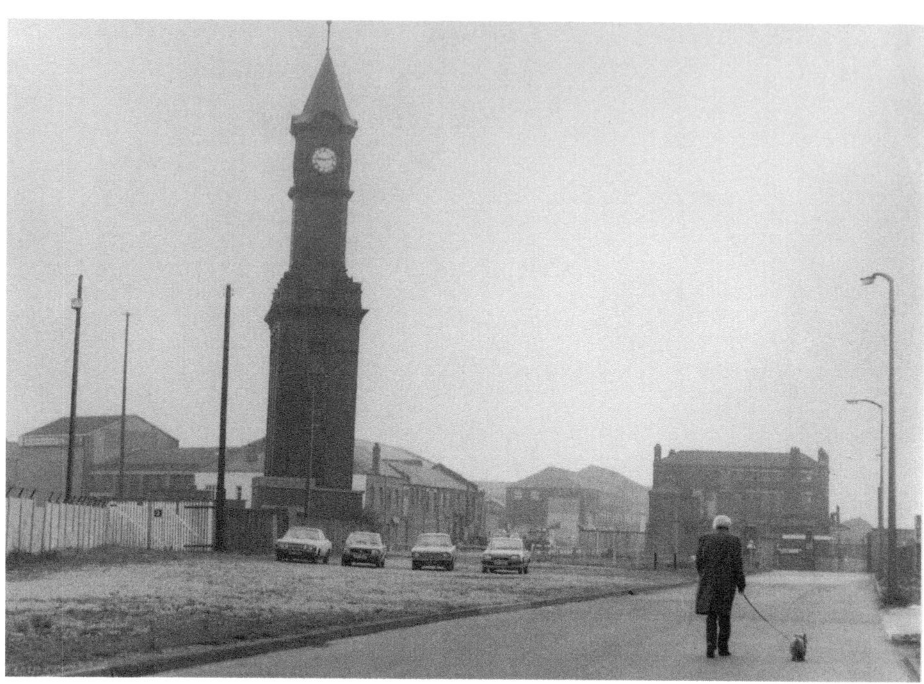

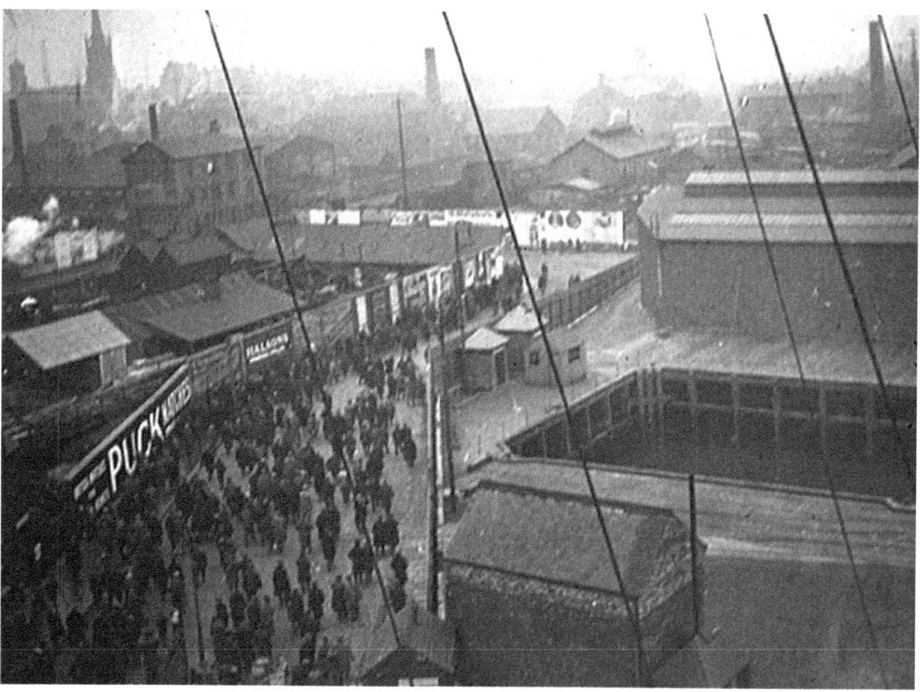

Opposite above: The dock clock, reputedly designed by Philip Webb and seen here in 1980. It was not just a clock when it was originally built, it supplied hydraulic power to operate the dockside cranes and to open and close the dock gates.

Opposite below: Men coming home to Middlesbrough via the Transporter Bridge after a shift at Bell Brothers' Ironworks across the river at Port Clarence.

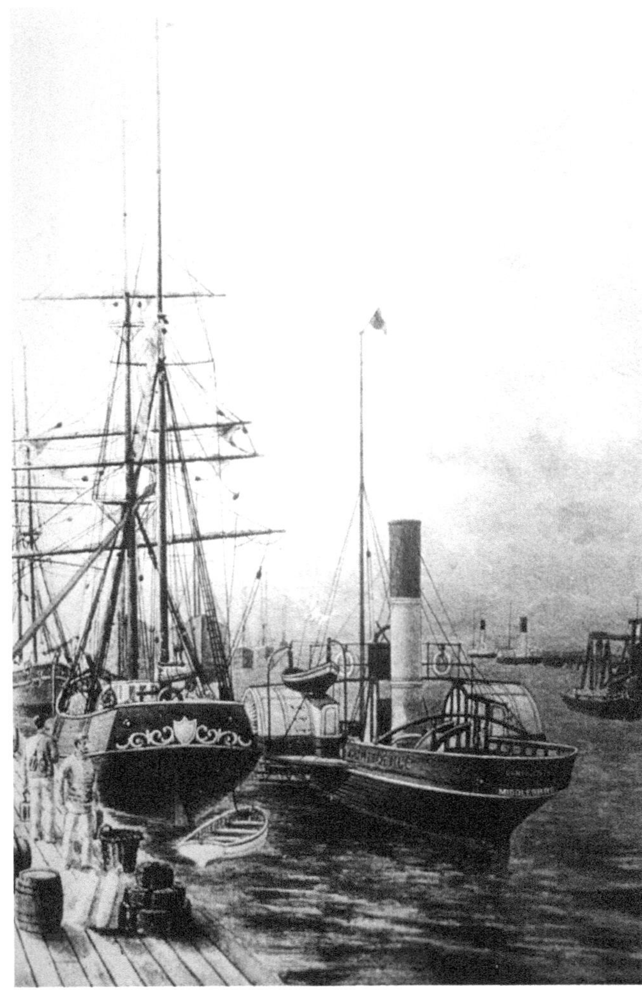

The paddle tug *Confidence* and sailing vessels on the river Tees. *Confidence* was one of the tugs in Gladstone's flotilla when he visited Middlesbrough in 1862 (see page 22).

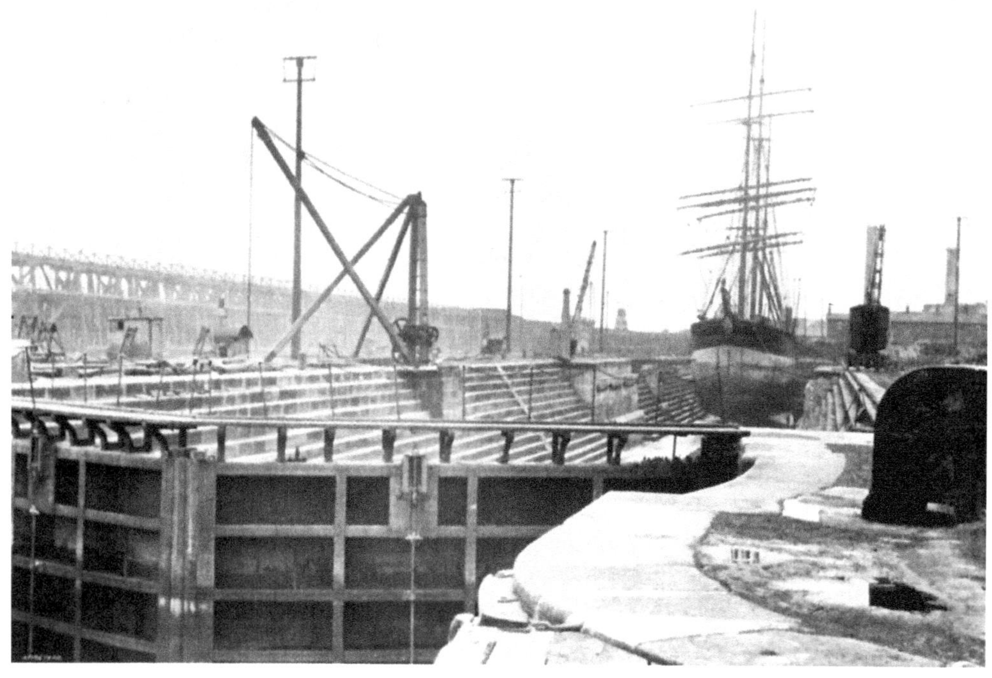

A sailing ship in the graving dock awaiting repairs.

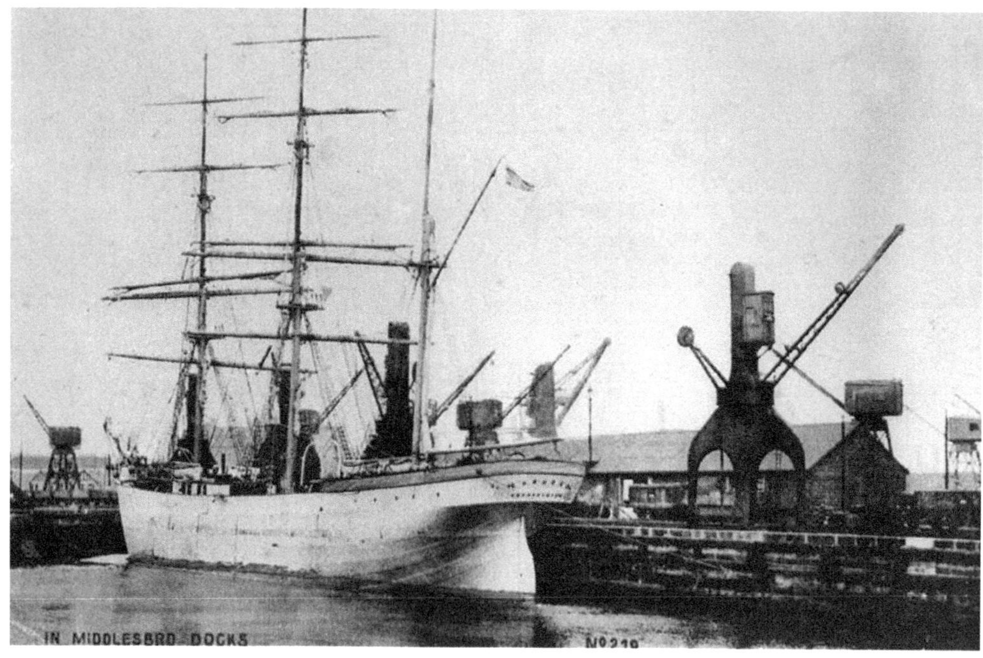

A large sail cargo vessel waiting to unload its cargo at Middlesbrough dock. The dock originally opened for business in 1842, and was enlarged a number of times to accommodate growing trade. Note the huge dockside crane.

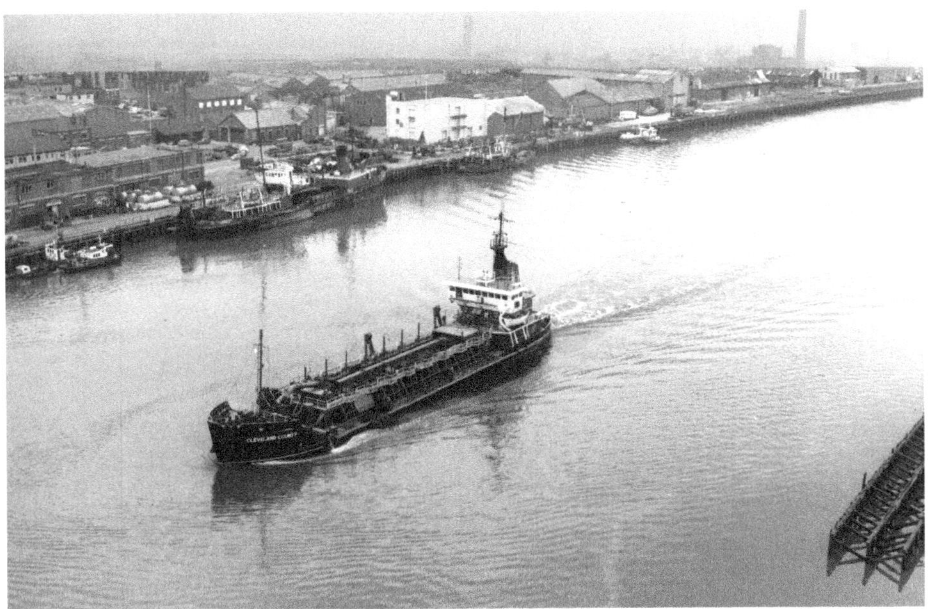

The dredger *Cleveland County*, seen from the top of the Transporter Bridge, making its way downstream and going out to sea to dispose of its cargo. The conservancy work on the river was carried out by The Tees Conservancy Commissioners, later the Tees and Hartlepool Port Authority, now known as P.D. Ports PLC.

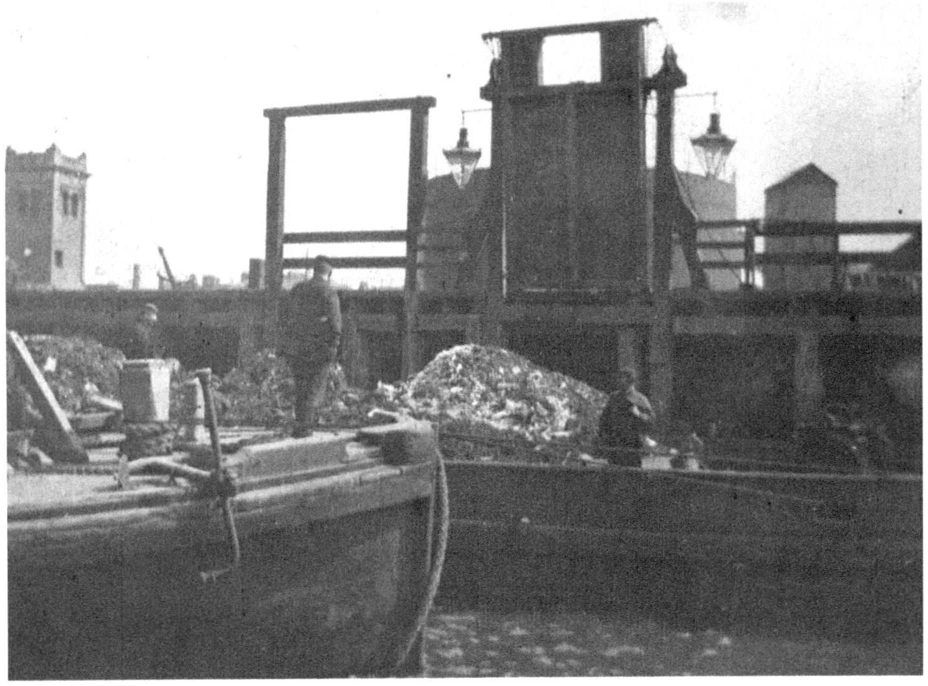

An earlier view of dredgers, seen during building work, possibly during the dock extension work mentioned below.

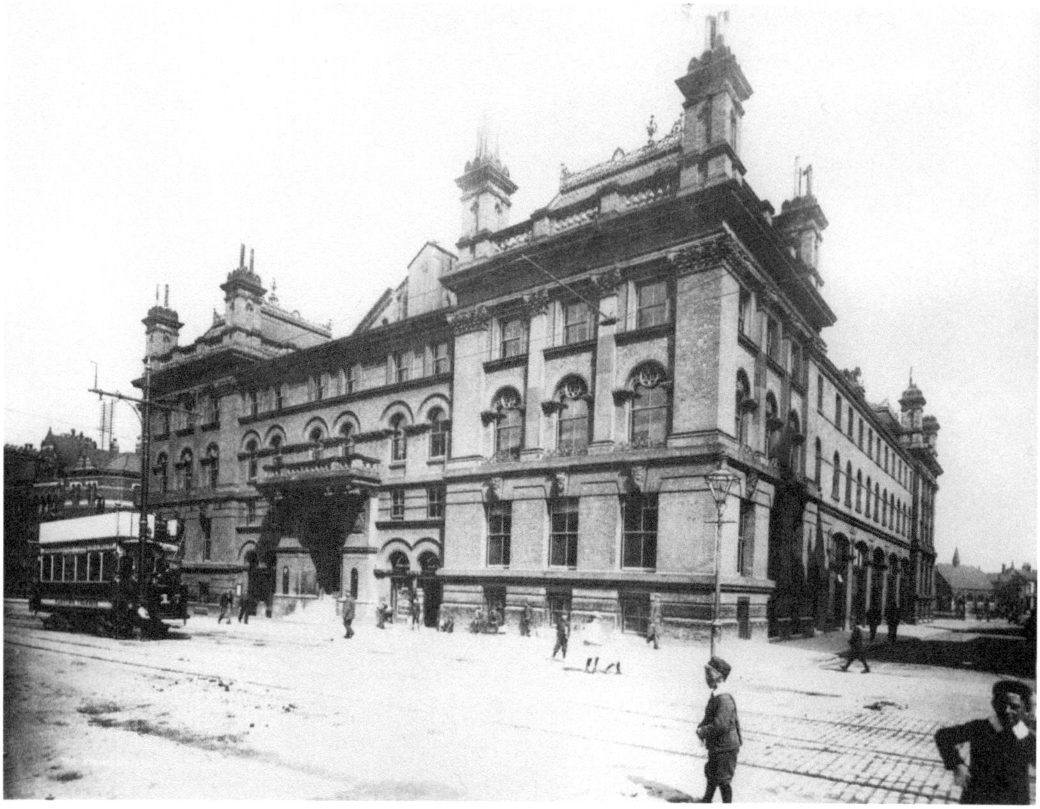

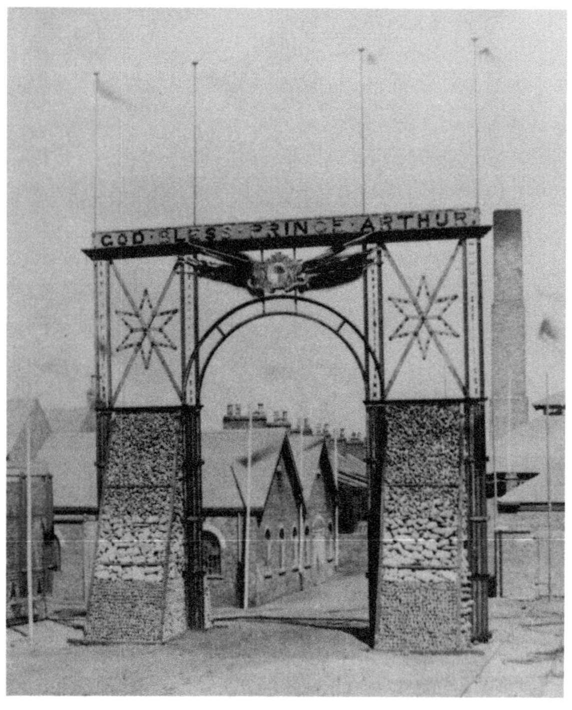

Above: The Royal Exchange. Opened in 1868 by Henry Bolckow, chairman of the Middlesbrough Exchange Co., it was designed by J.C. Adams of Stockton-on-Tees. The building housed a trading floor, meeting rooms, and offices, and was later used by Dorman Long and by British Steel. It was demolished to make way for the A66 northern route.

Left: Ceremonial arch erected at Hopkins Gilkes' Ironworks to commemorate the visit of His Royal Highness Prince Arthur, who came to town in August 1868 to open the Albert Park. The arch is made up on each side of raw materials used in the production of iron.

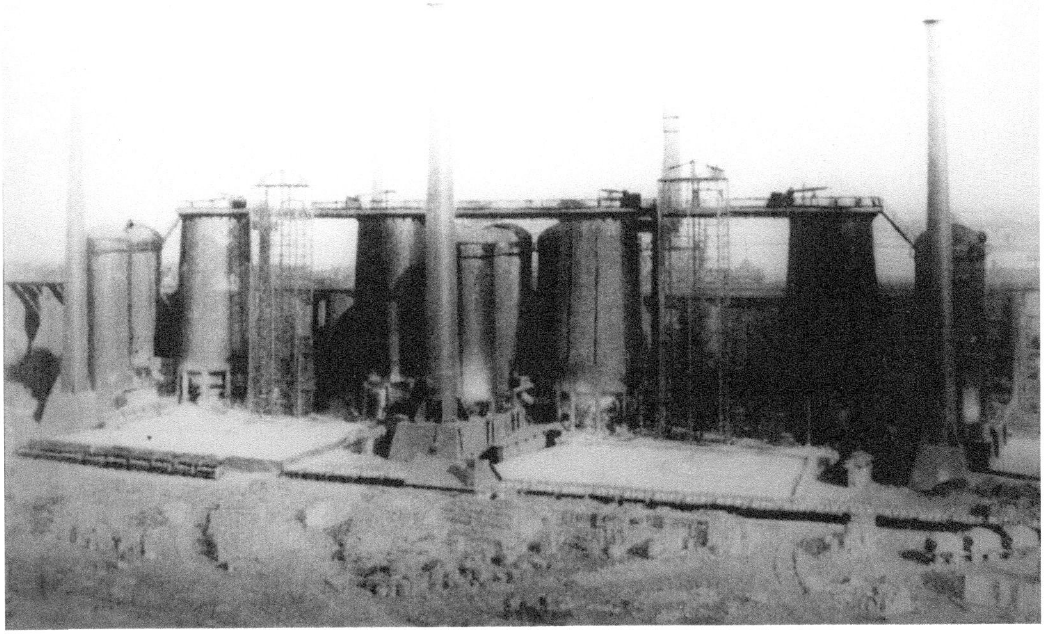

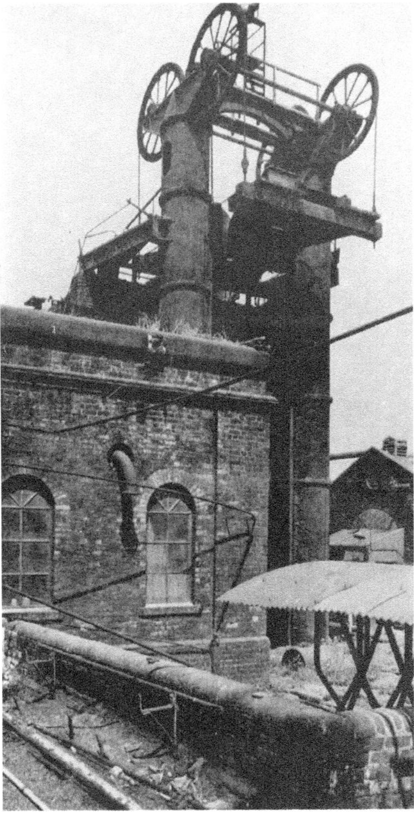

Above: A view of one of the massive range of blast furnaces, once common in the ironmasters' district of town. This area once produced a third of the country's iron output. The area today is home to a heritage trail named after them, with remains of the industrial sites still to be seen.

Right: A scene at Gjers Mills Ayresome Ironworks, showing winding machinery used to power the industrial buildings. This image appeared on an annual report of the Dorman Museum.

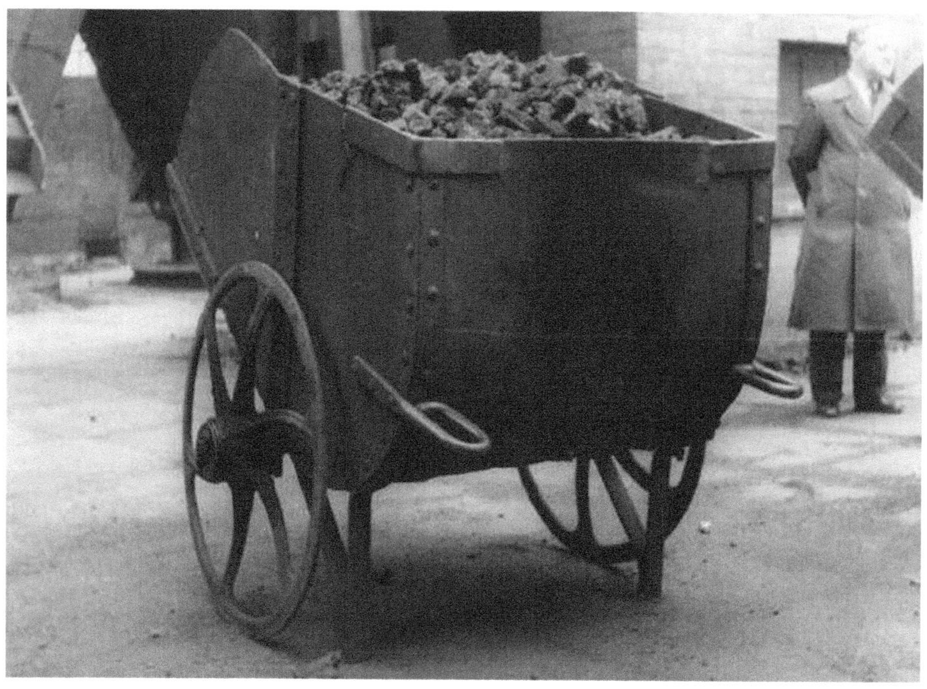

An iron ore barrow. These came in standard sizes and were used to ferry iron ore to be placed in the blast furnace. Originally from Gjers Mills Ayresome Ironworks, it was recovered when the works were demolished and is now on display in the Dorman Museum.

The Subscription List will open on Friday, the 8th November, 1889, at 10 oclock a.m., and will close on the same day at 4 p m., but Country applications will be received by post on the following morning.

DORMAN, LONG & COMPANY,

LIMITED.

MIDDLESBROUGH-ON-TEES.

(Incorporated under the Companies' Acts, 1862 to 1886.)

SHARE CAPITAL - - £350,000,

IN 70,000 SHARES OF £5 EACH,

Of which 23,000 Shares, fully paid, are taken by the Vendors in part payment of the purchase-money,

AND THE REMAINING

47,000 SHARES ARE NOW OFFERED FOR PUBLIC SUBSCRIPTION,

Payable as follows:—	£0	10	0	per Share on Application;
	1	0	0	,, ,, on Allotment;
	1	10	0	,, ,, on 2nd December, 1889.
	2	0	0	,, ,, on 6th January, 1890.
	£5	0	0	

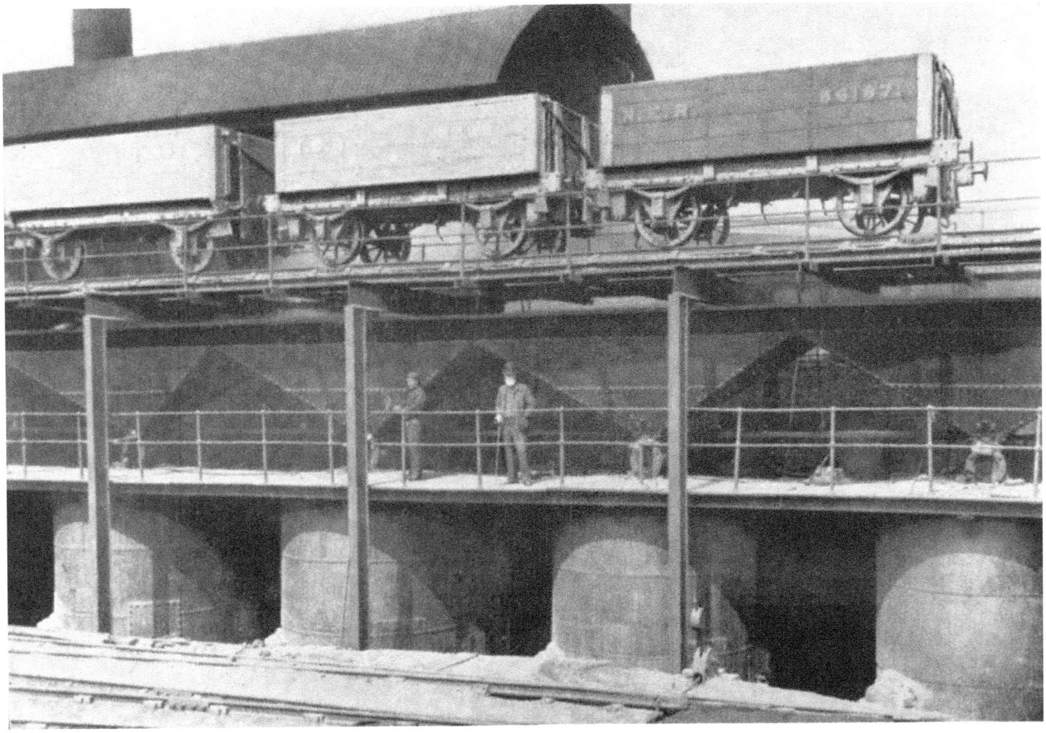

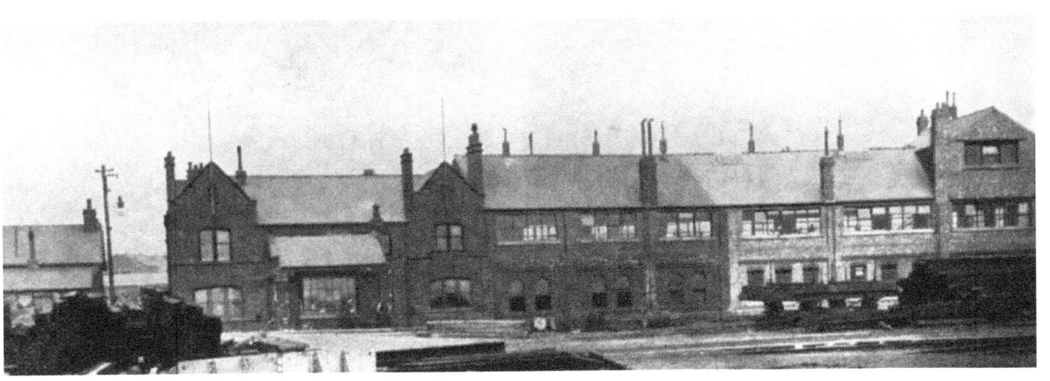

Gas producers at Dorman Long's Britannia works.

The head office buildings at Dorman Long's Britannia Ironworks.

Opposite below: Dorman Long share issue notice, November 1889. Share capital of £350,000 was available in shares of £5 each. The vendors took 23,000 shares in part payment of the purchase money, and 47,000 were available for public subscription.

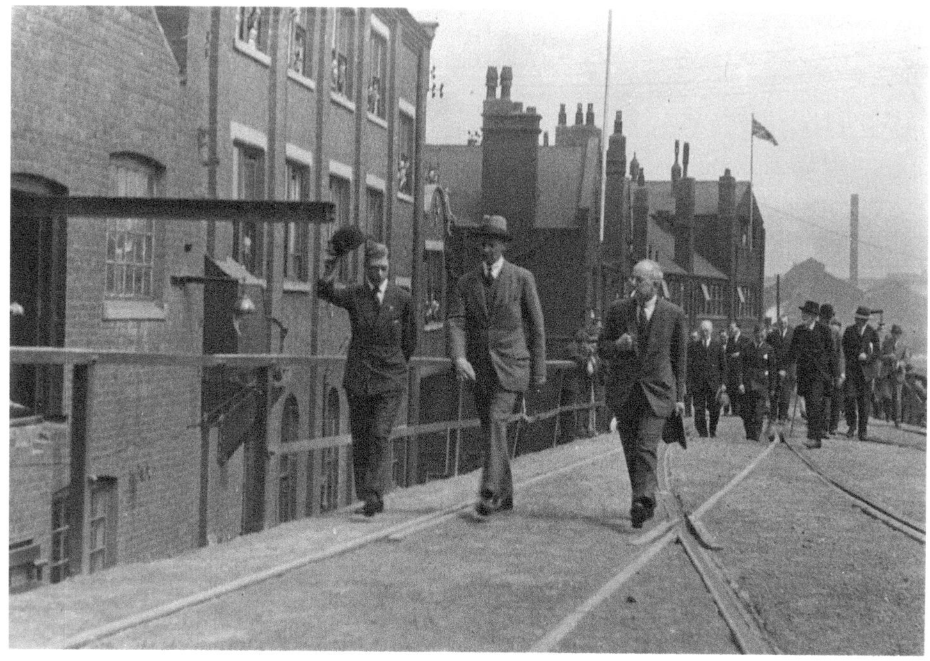

A visit by Edward, Prince of Wales, to the Dorman Long Britannia works in July 1930. The Prince was in town to officially open the Constantine Technical College.

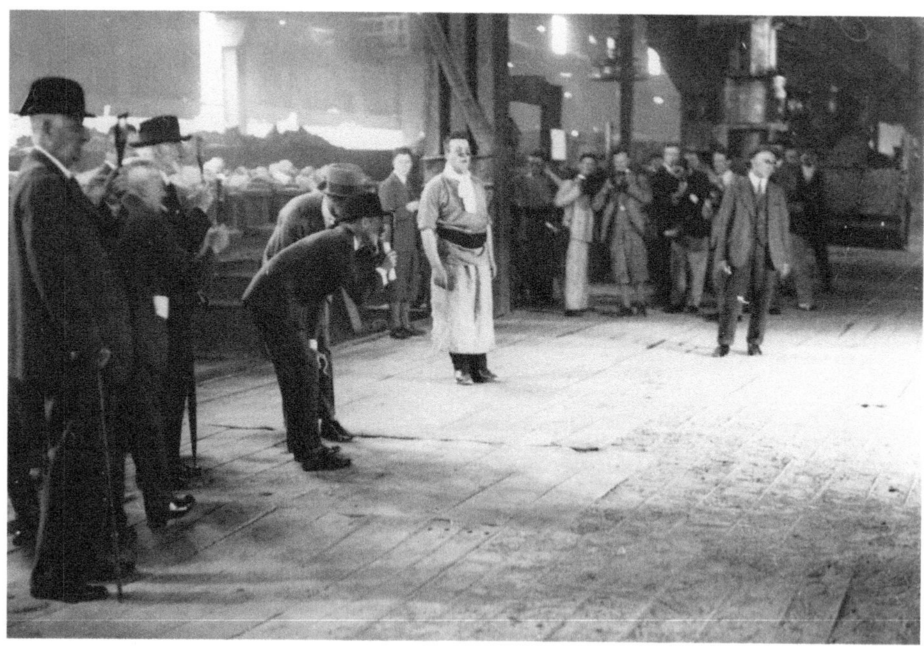

The Prince watching production at Dorman Long. The watchers are using special blue glass filters designed to prevent glare and damage to their eyes. Sir Arthur Dorman is on the extreme left, wearing a bowler hat and third from left, also wearing a hat, is the then Lord Lieutenant of North Yorkshire and joint manager director of Dorman Long, Sir Hugh Bell, Baronet.

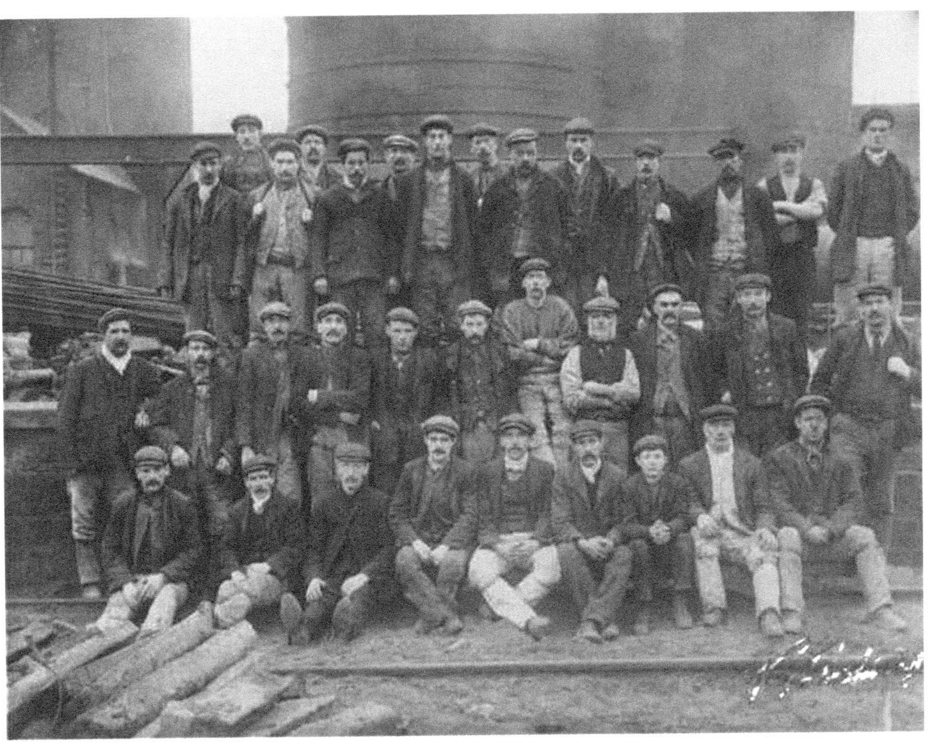

Labourers from the ironworks in the late-nineteenth century.

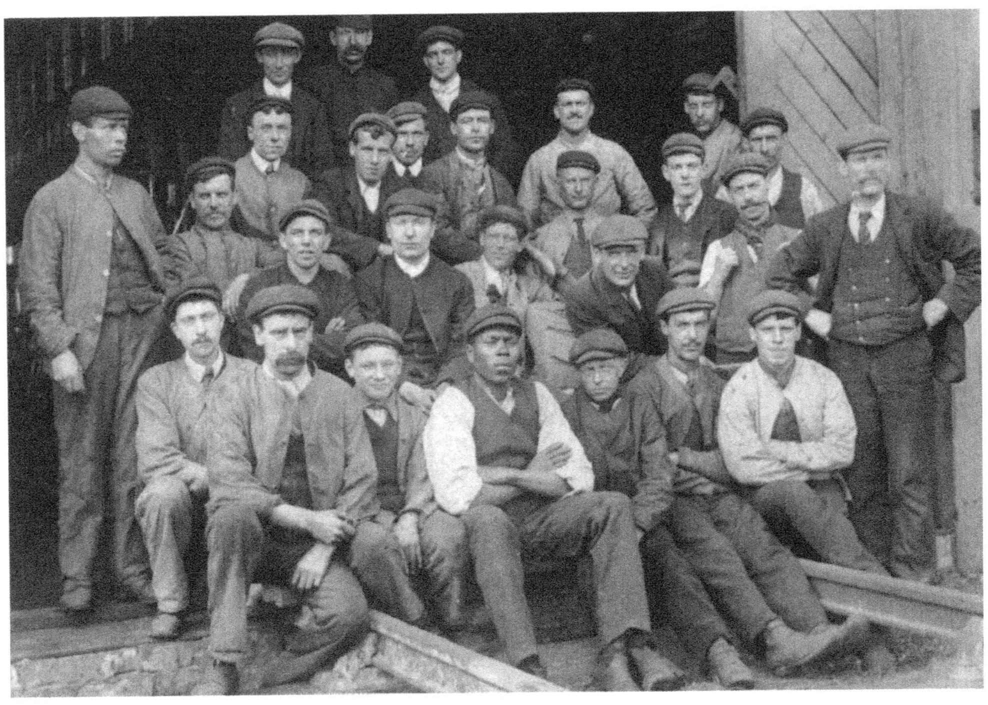

Foundry workers in the late nineteenth century.

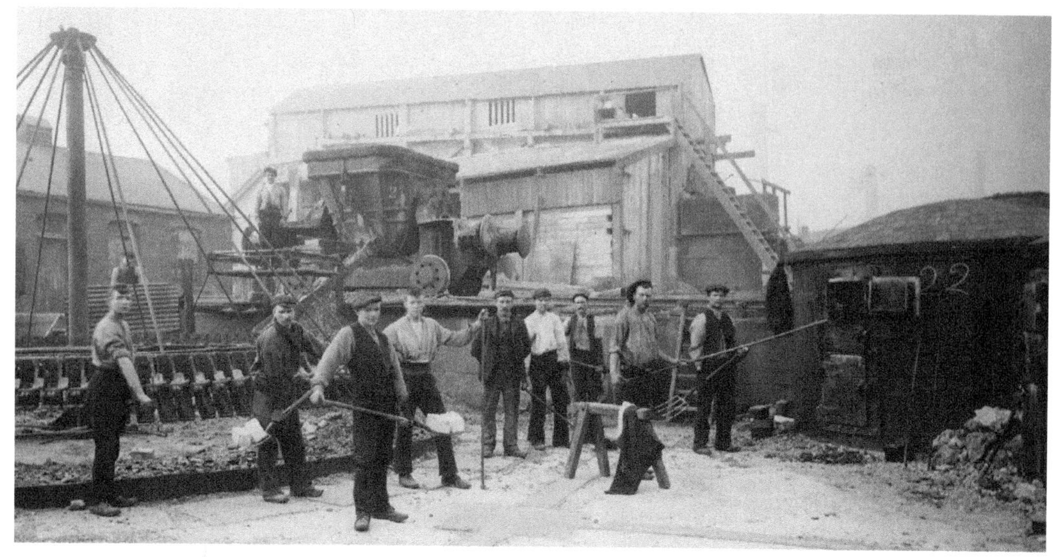

Workers at a brickworks. Clay was abundant in the town and formed the basis of both brickworking and pottery industries in Middlesbrough

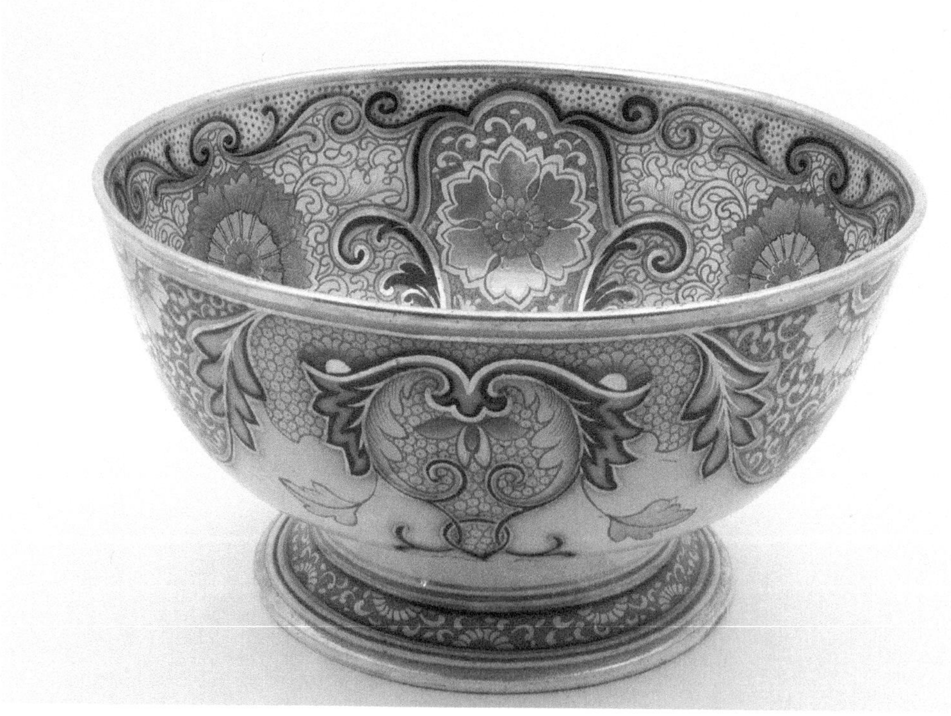

An oriental-inspired design on a rather unique punch bowl made at the Middlesbrough Pottery and to be seen in the Dorman Museum. The Middlesbrough Pottery was the town's first major industrial enterprise.

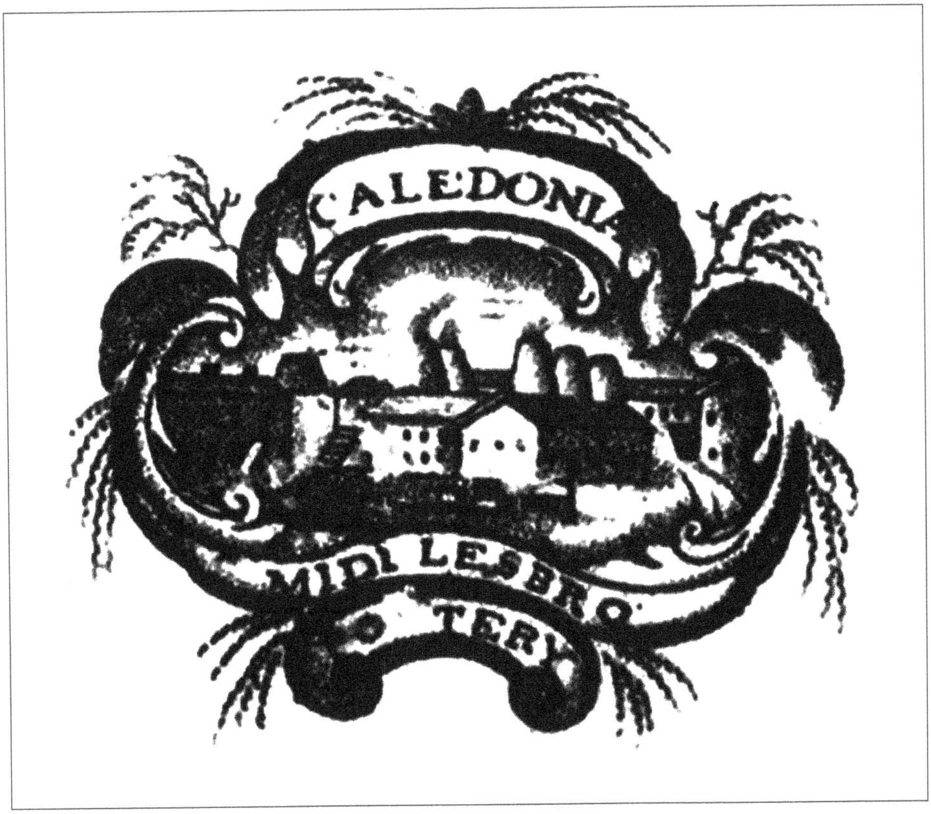

A view of the kilns and other buildings at the Middlesbrough Pottery, taken from a transfer label for the Caledonia design of wares.

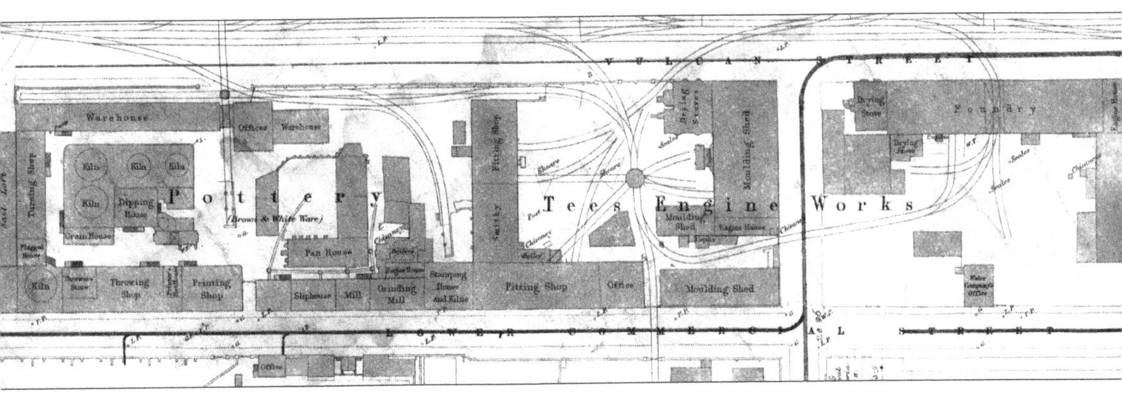

A plan of the Middlesbrough Pottery buildings, Commercial Street, taken from an 1853 map of the town. Note the names on the buildings, denoting their use in the pottery processes.

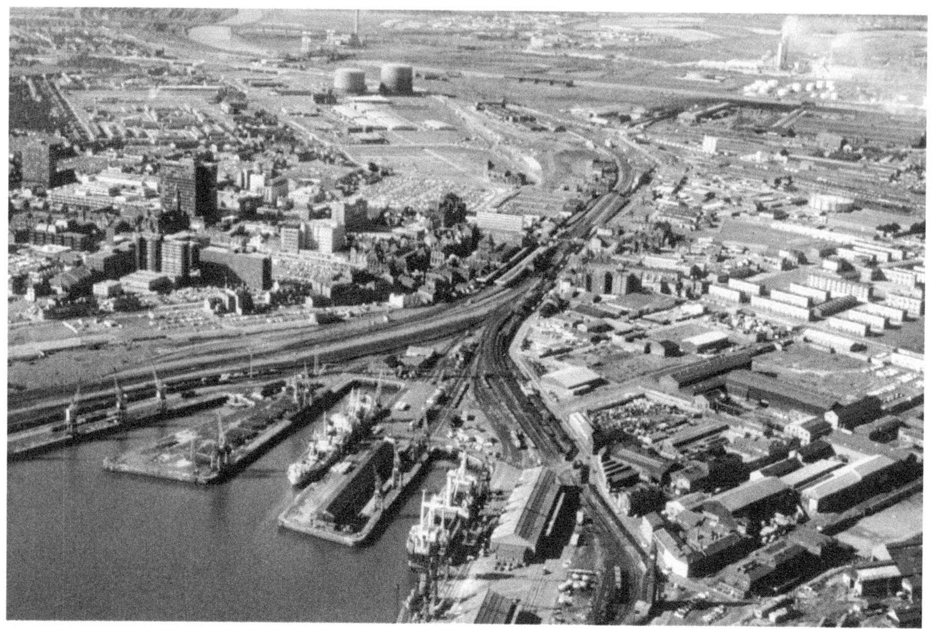

A view of the town centre looking towards the river Tees and showing quite clearly the density of housing in the town centre and the Middlesbrough Dock when in use.

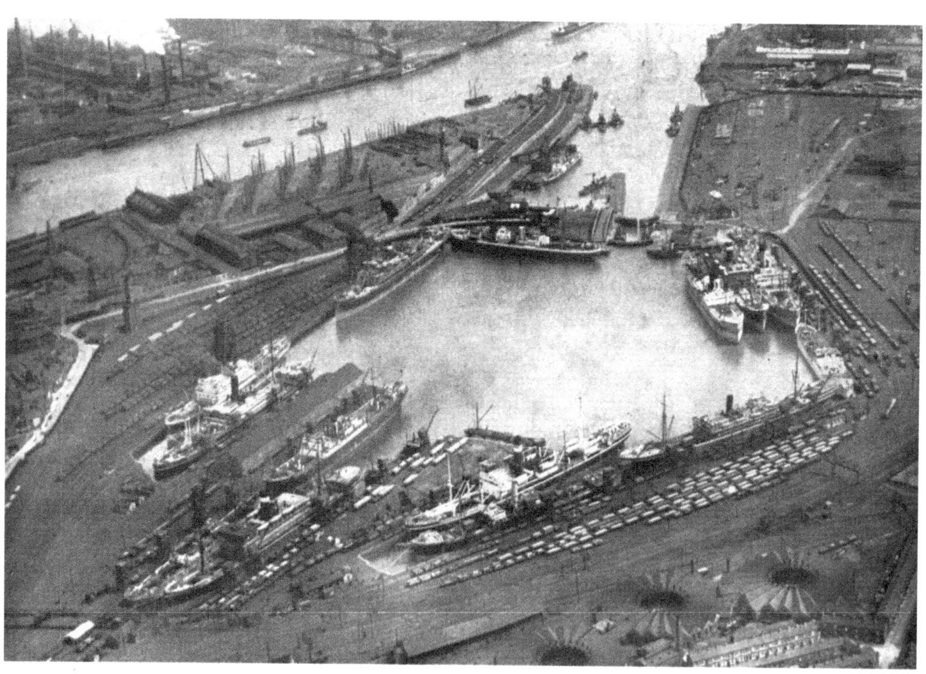

Middlesbrough Dock, seen here working to full capacity unloading a variety of cargo vessels. Note at the bottom right the number of nearby houses and also the engine sheds and turntables of British Railways.

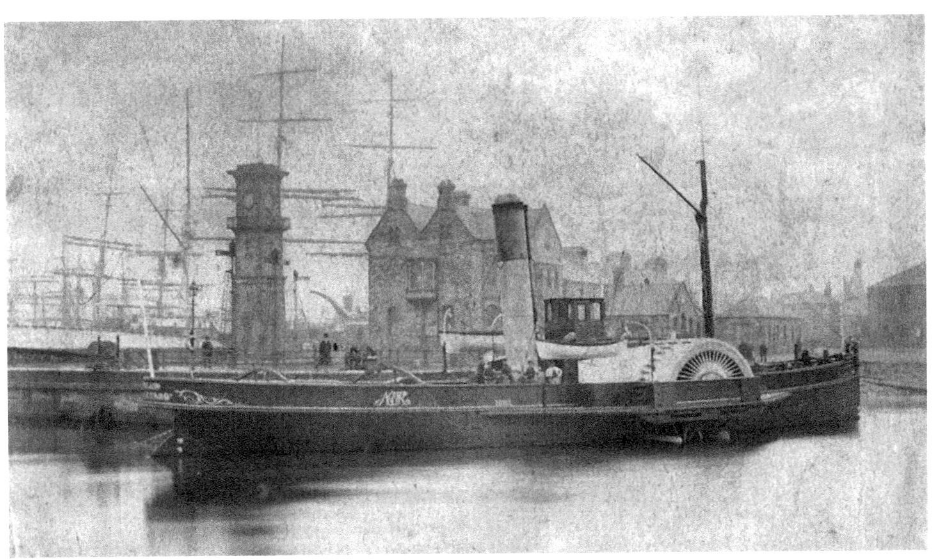

A paddle tug belonging to the North-Eastern Railway, seen in front of the old dock clock and dockside buildings.

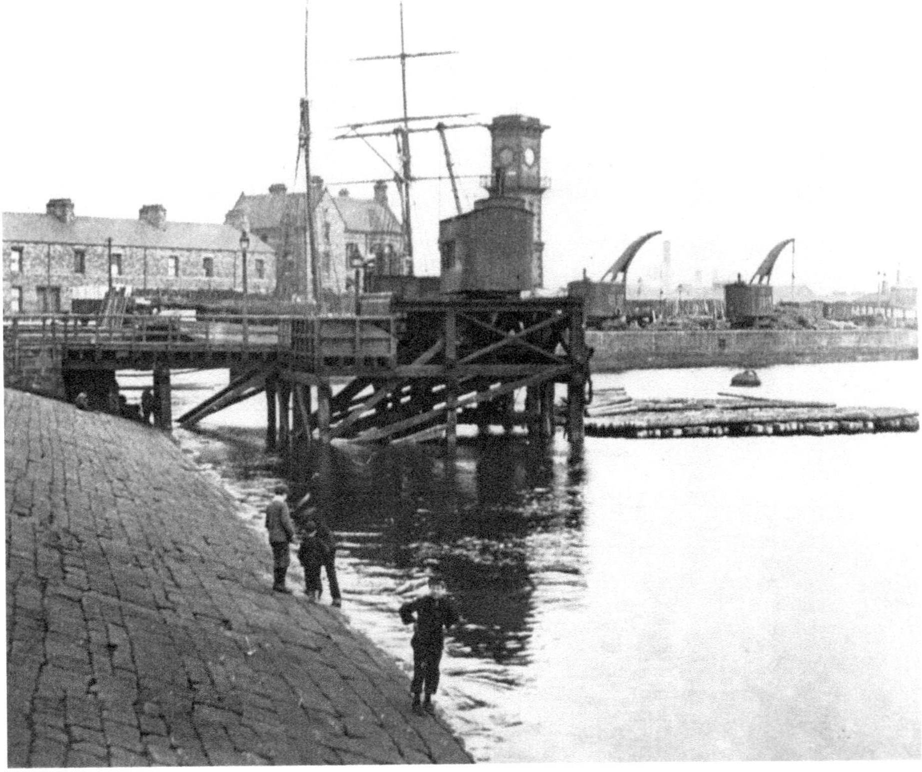

An early view of Middlesbrough Dock. The dock itself was first opened in 1842, and the railway company took control in 1849. It closed in 1980.

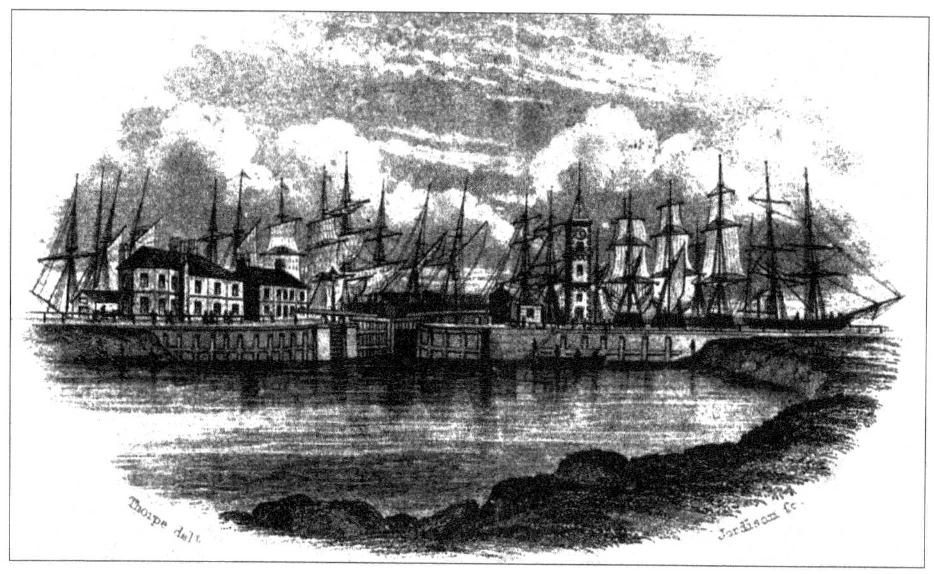

Middlesbrough Dock entrance seen from the river. This early view, by Thorpe, was printed by Middlesbrough printers Jordison. It shows the busy sailing ships and the original dock clock and dock gates.

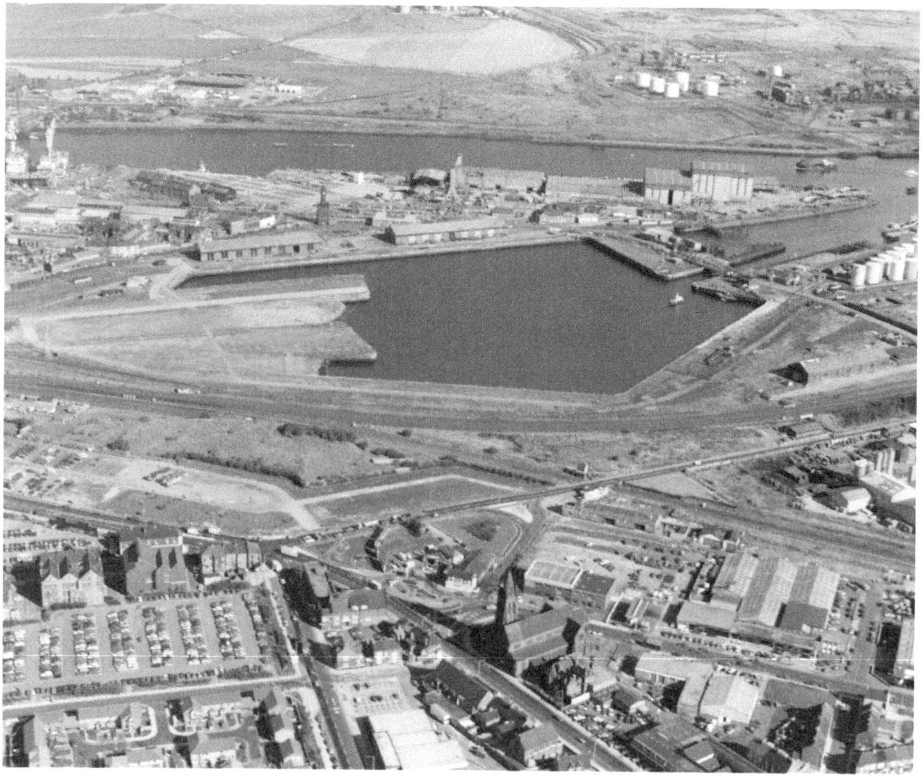

Middlesbrough Dock from the air.

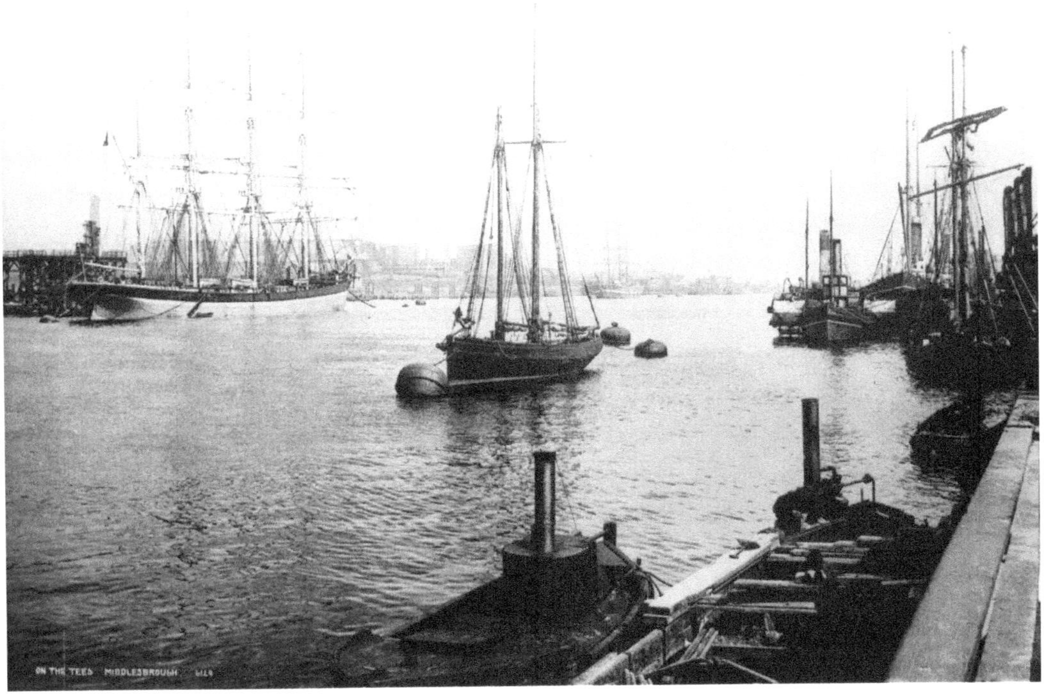

Above: A view of a variety of shipping on the river Tees. Note the sailing ships, the steam tugs, barges and smaller sailing craft.

Right: A delightful atmospheric shot of one of the 'legs' of the Transporter Bridge. Note the workmen climbing the steps. Workmen used to climb across to go to work: it was cheaper than paying to cross by the floating carriage or 'gondola' as it was called. The bridge is now floodlight at night and quite a sight to see.

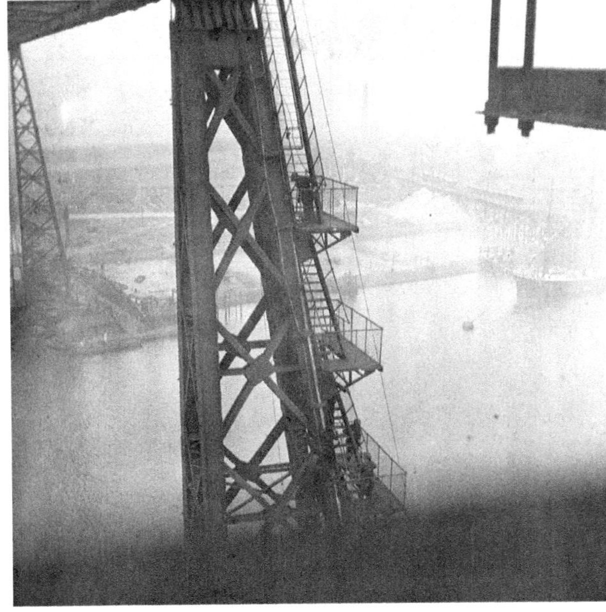

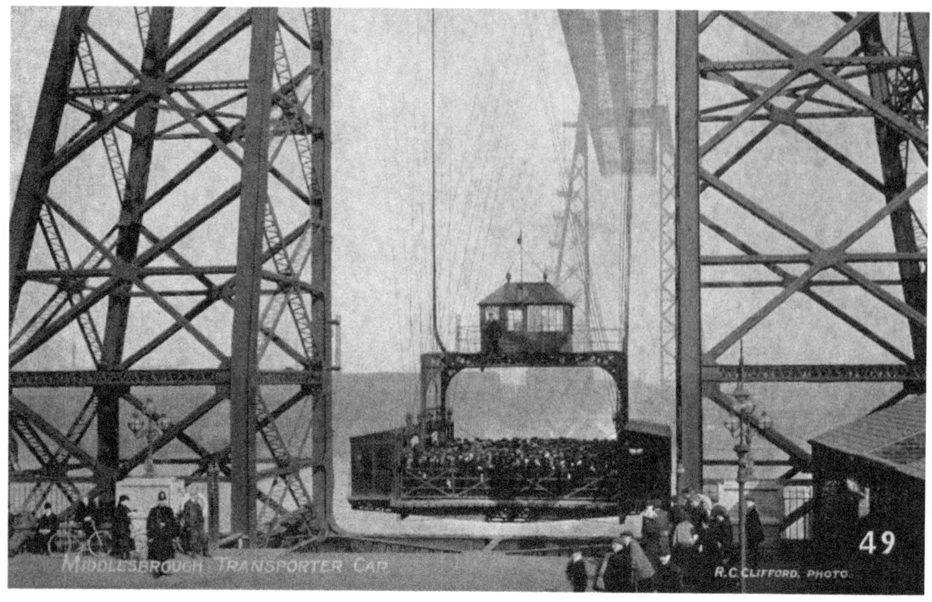

This photograph, by the Middlesbrough photographers Clifford & Co., shows the gondola full of workmen being ferried from Port Clarence. The bridge itself was opened by Prince Arthur of Connaught on 17 October 1911. The bridge was described by Pevsner as 'a European monument, in its daring and finesse surely a delight to see'. A visitor centre at the bridge now relates the history of the bridge and the surrounding area.

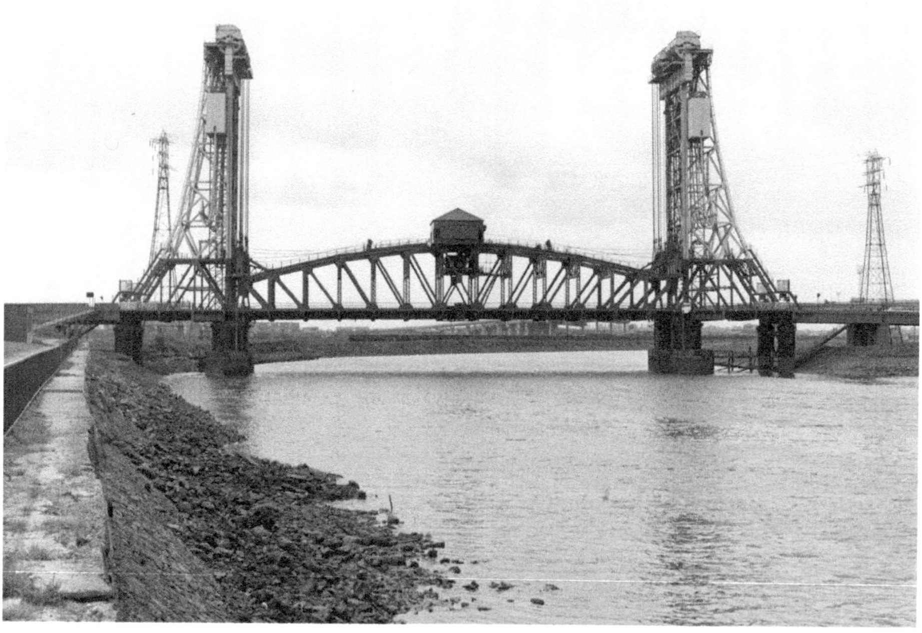

A view of the Tees Newport Bridge, a joint building effort between the Middlesbrough County Borough and Durham County Councils. Designed by Mott Hay and Anderson, it was built by Dorman Long and opened by the Duke and Duchess of York in 1934 (see picture on page 43).

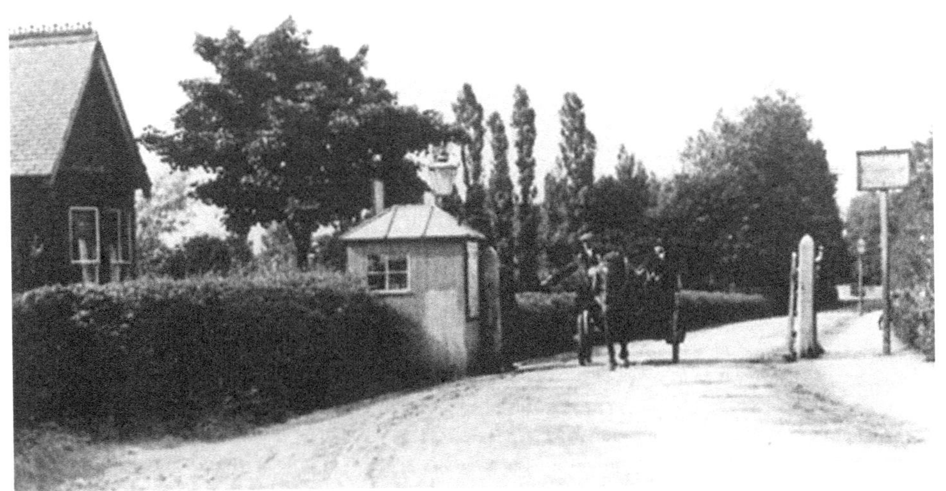

Toll-bar and cabin at Marton road, near to Belle Vue, *c.* 1900. The toll for using the road was paid to the Owners of the Middlesbrough Estate, with revenues contributing towards the upkeep of the roadway. The toll-bars were finally abolished on 31 July 1916.

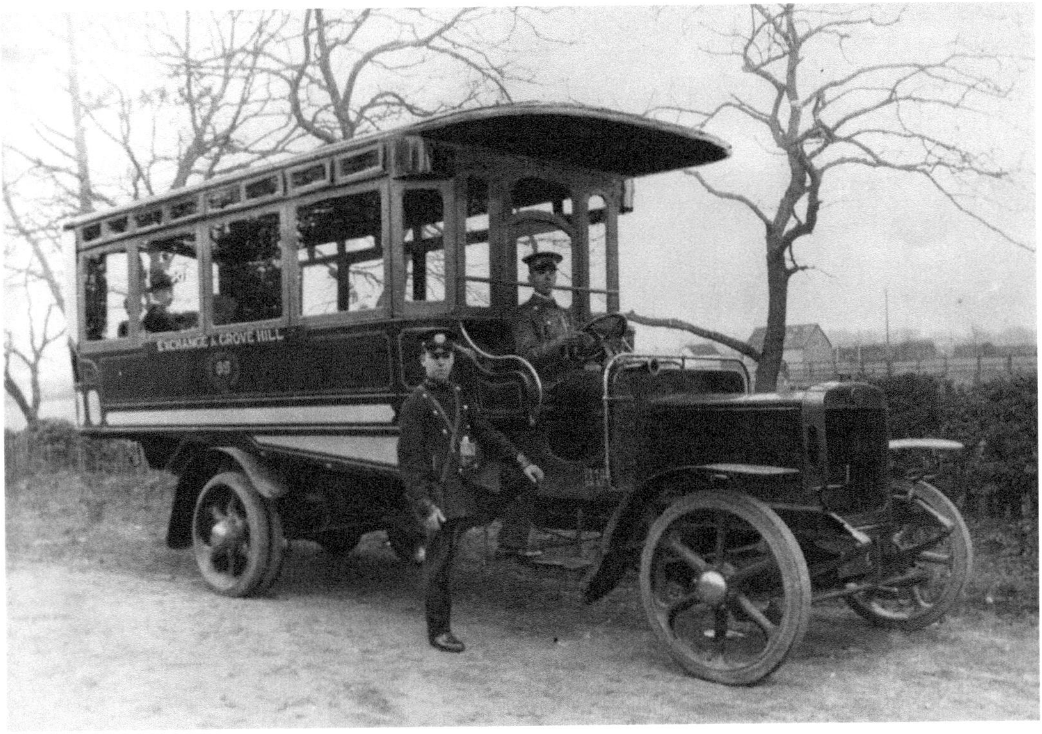

A Middlesbrough Corporation transport motor bus. This one ran between the Royal Exchange, where the bus terminus was situated, and Grove Hill.

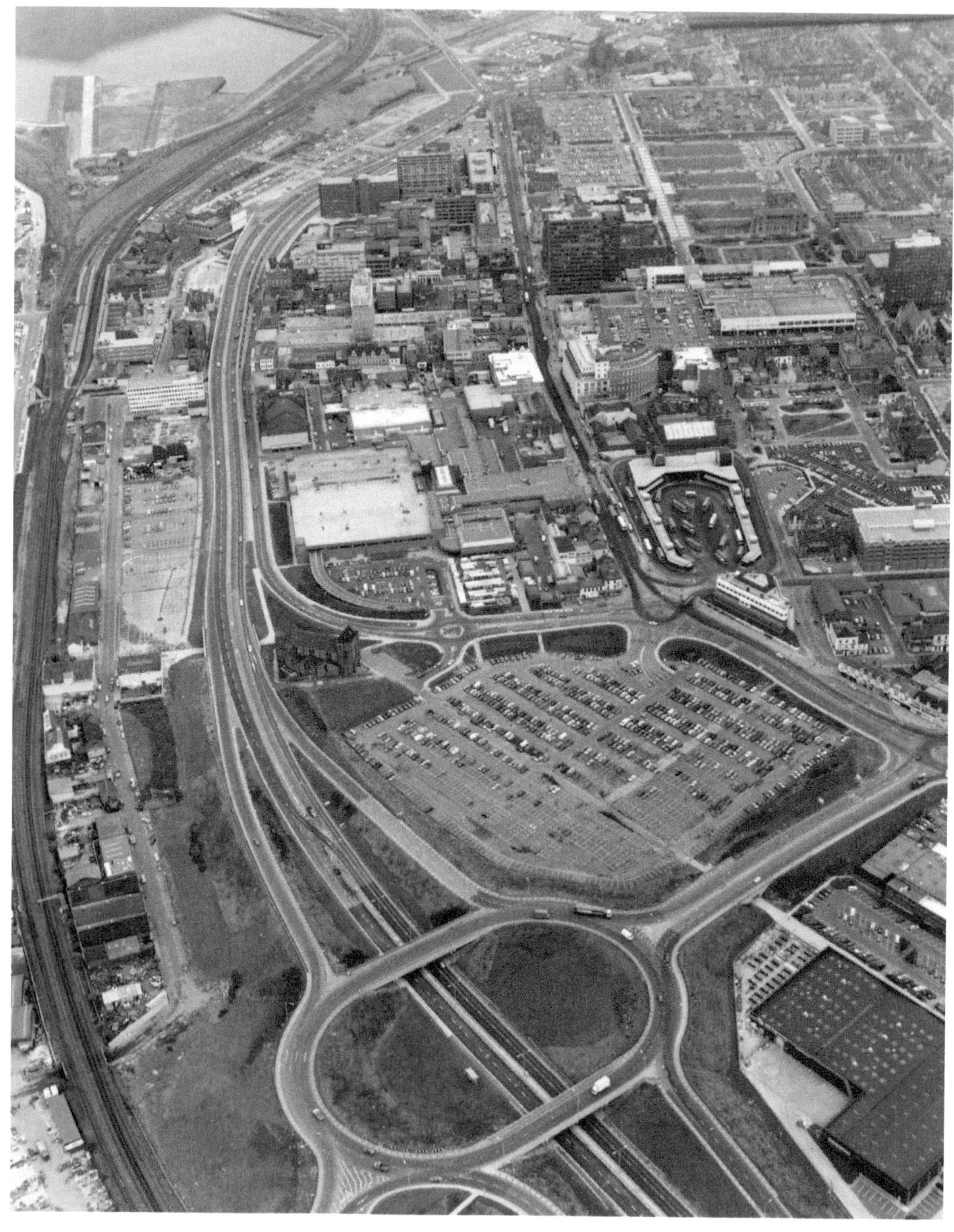

An aerial view of the town in the late 1910s. The railway line can be seen on the left of the picture. At the top of the picture is the river and top right is Middlesbrough Dock.

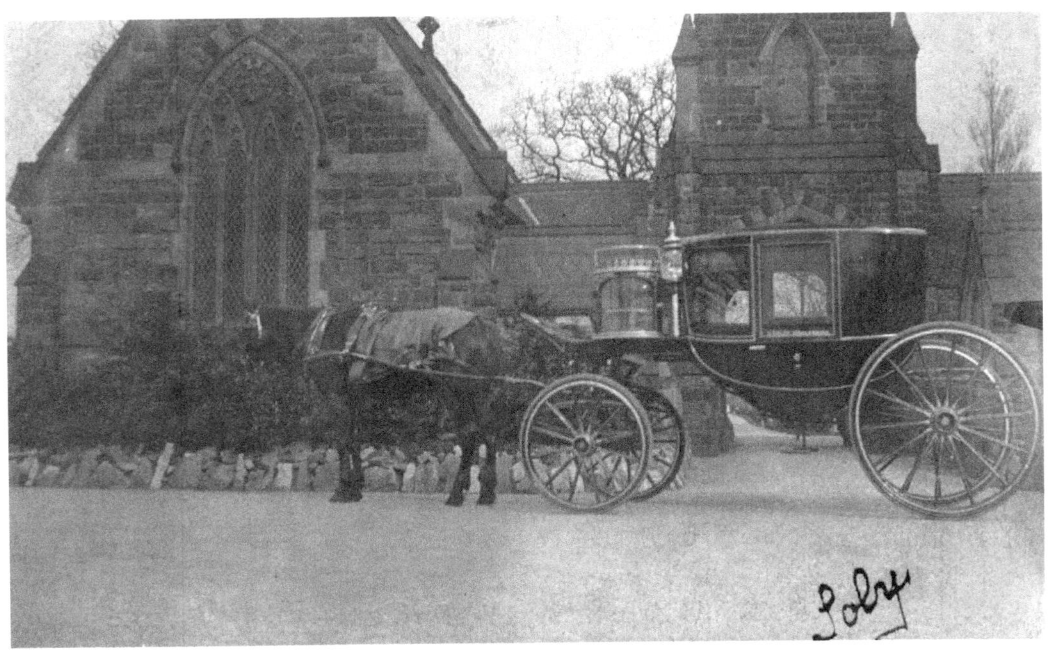

A horse-drawn funeral carriage, belonging to Relph & Co., outside the cemetery chapels at Linthorpe Cemetery.

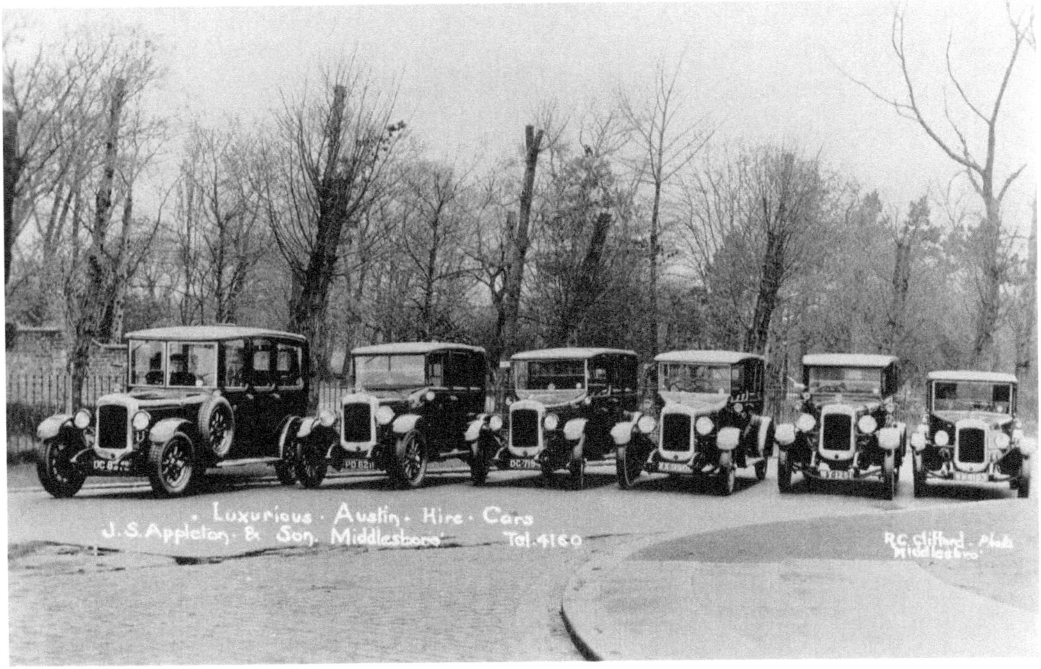

A fleet of luxurious Austin cars: these vehicles were available on hire from J.S. Appleton & Sons. This is another photograph taken by the Middlesbrough photographer R.C. Clifford.

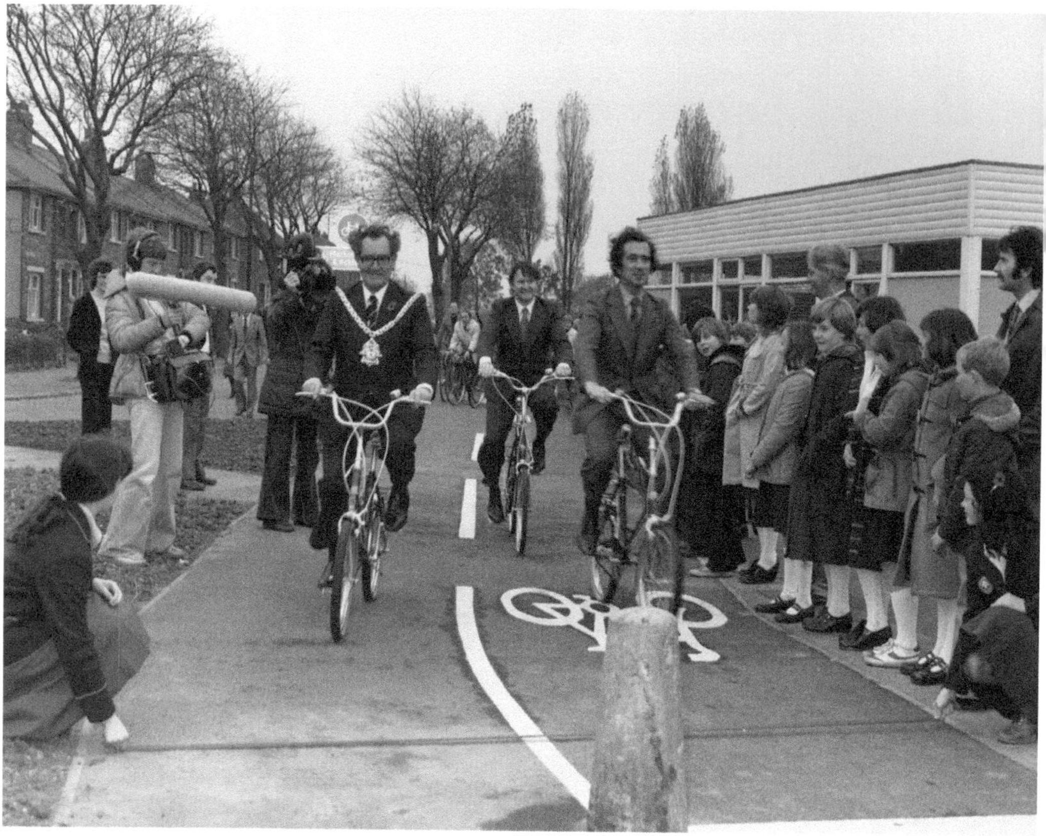

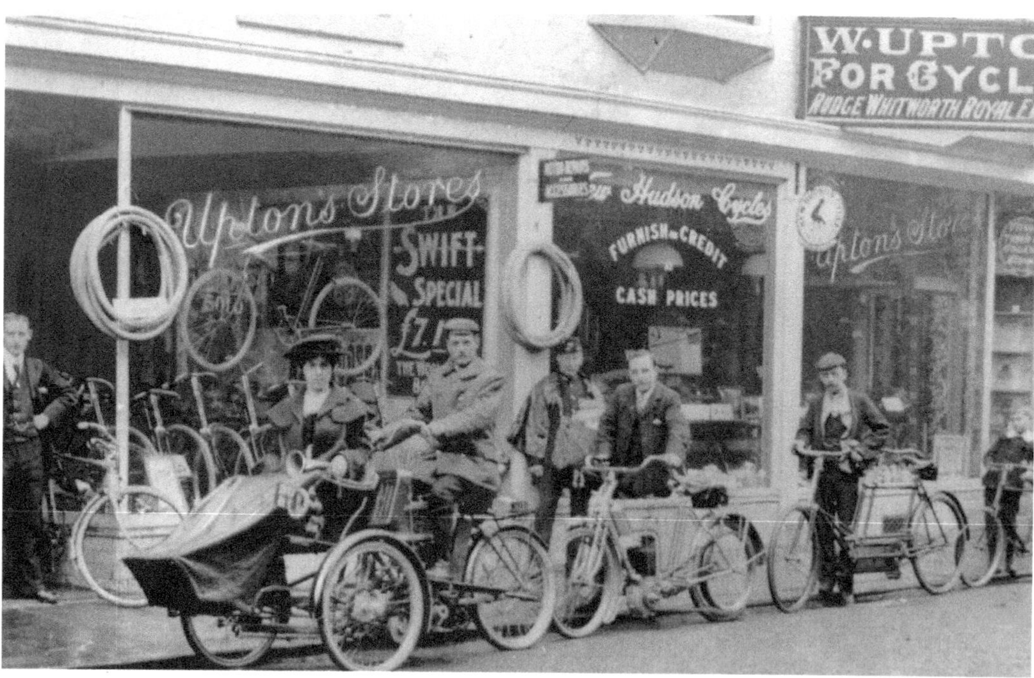

W·UPTO
FOR CYCL
RUDGE WHITWORTH ROYAL F
Upton's Stores
SWIFT
SPECIAL
Hudson Cycles
FURNISH on CREDIT
CASH PRICES
Upton's Stor

NORTH EASTERN RAILWAY

OPENING

OF THE

NEW STATION

AT

MIDDLESBRO'

NOTICE

ON MONDAY, DECEMBER THE 3RD, 1877,

The New Passenger Station at **MIDDLESBRO'** will be Opened for Traffic, and from that date all Passenger Trains will Arrive at and Depart from that Station.

H. TENNANT,

GENERAL MANAGER.

York, November 29th, 1877.

North-Eastern Railway poster advertising the opening of the new Middlesbrough railway station. The new station replaced the former building on the same site. The original railway station was situated in Commercial Street, opposite the Custom House.

Opposite above: A press launch for the cycleway. The mayor of Middlesbrough, Councillor John Stokes, is front left, and front right is William Rodgers MP.

Opposite below: Upton's cycle shop. Mr and Mrs William Upton are seen here, front left, in a rather elegant form of transport from a bygone age.

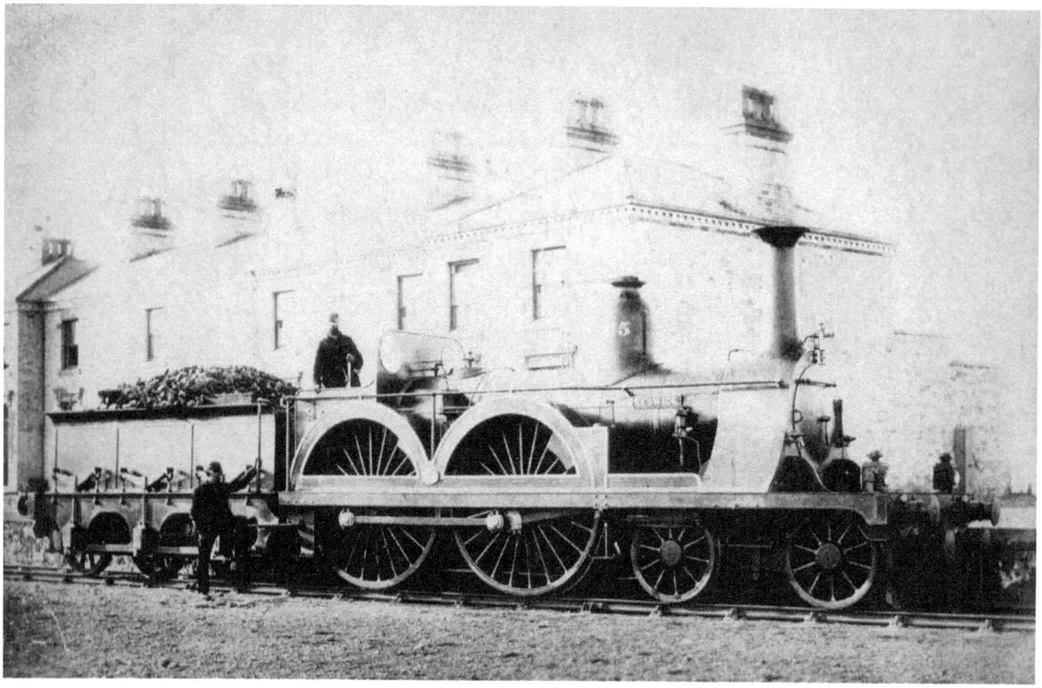

One of the newer styles of steam engines that were used by the North-Eastern Railway. Many of the locomotives were built in Darlington, Doncaster or Newcastle.

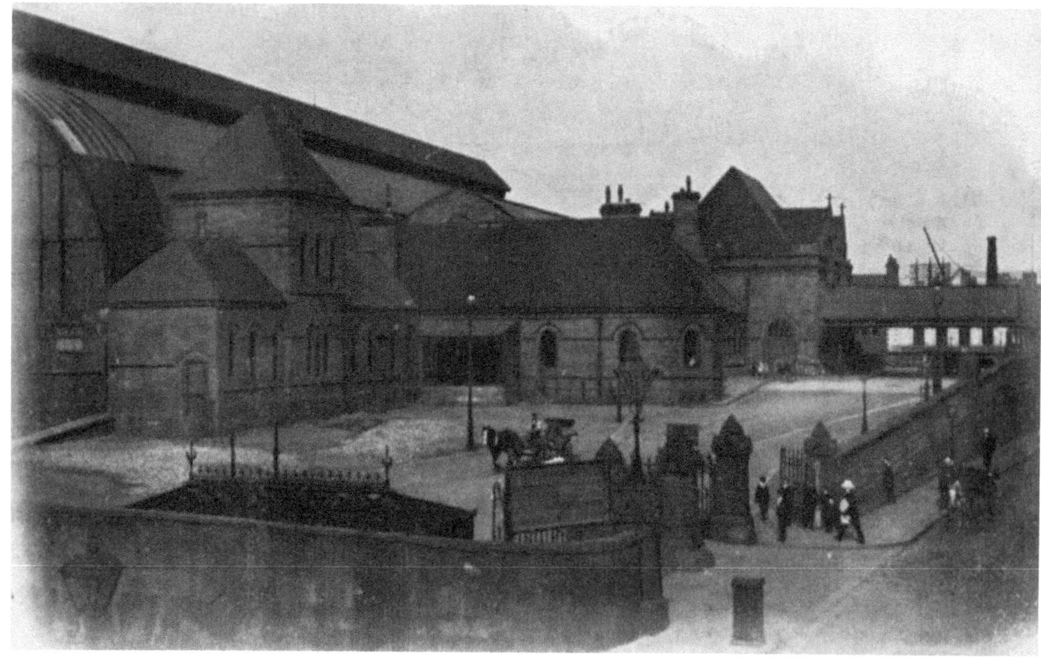

The station forecourt as seen in the early days. This picture shows the carriage entrance and gateway piers in Zetland Road.

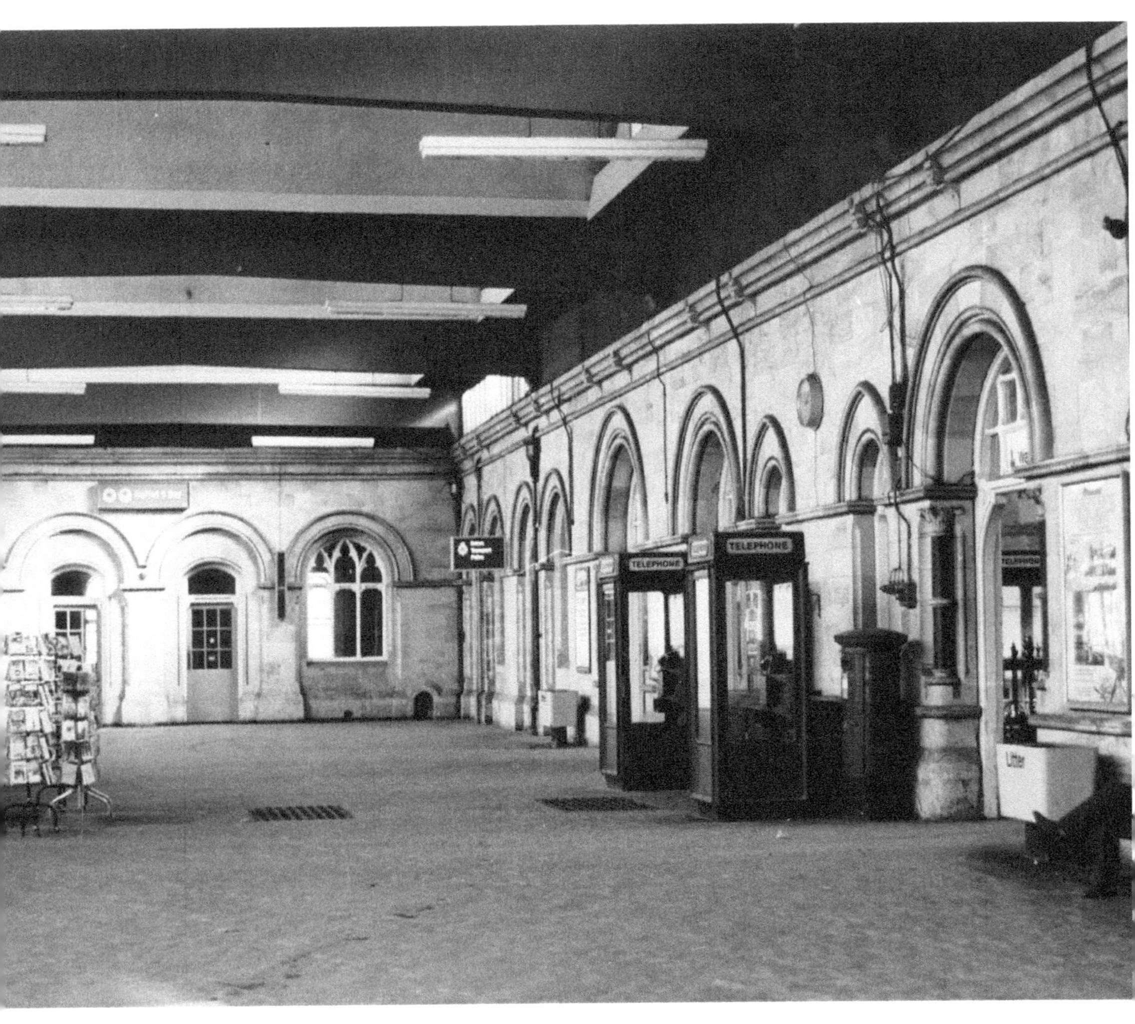

The main platform of the railway station, *c.* 1970. The station was designed by William Peachey and William Cudworth. The station suffered severe bomb damage in a raid in 1942, resulting in the loss of twelve lives. Later the huge glass roof of the train shed had to be demolished.

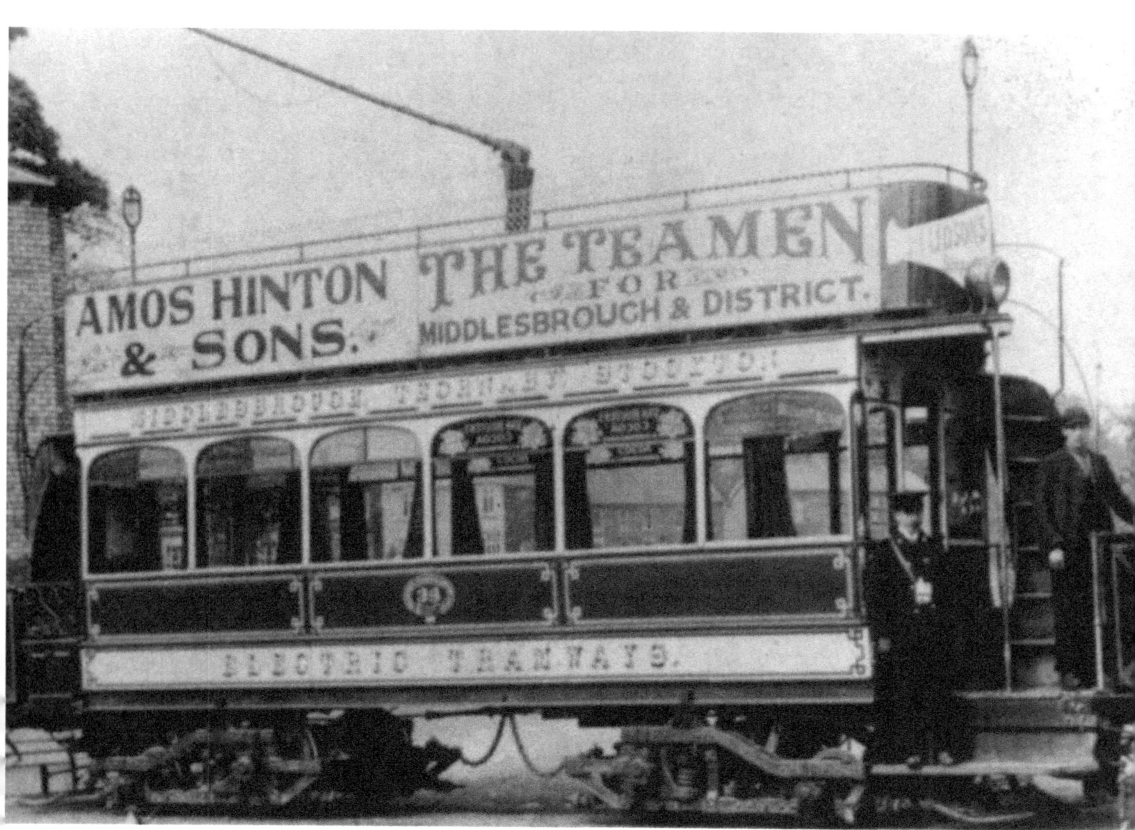

Middlesbrough, Stockton and Thornaby Electric Tramways double-decker tram. This one is advertising Amos Hinton & Sons, the tea men for Middlesbrough and district, and also Hudson's soap at the top of the stairs.

Opposite: Tram number 139, seen here going from Linthorpe to the Transporter. It is pictured on the Avenue in Linthorpe.

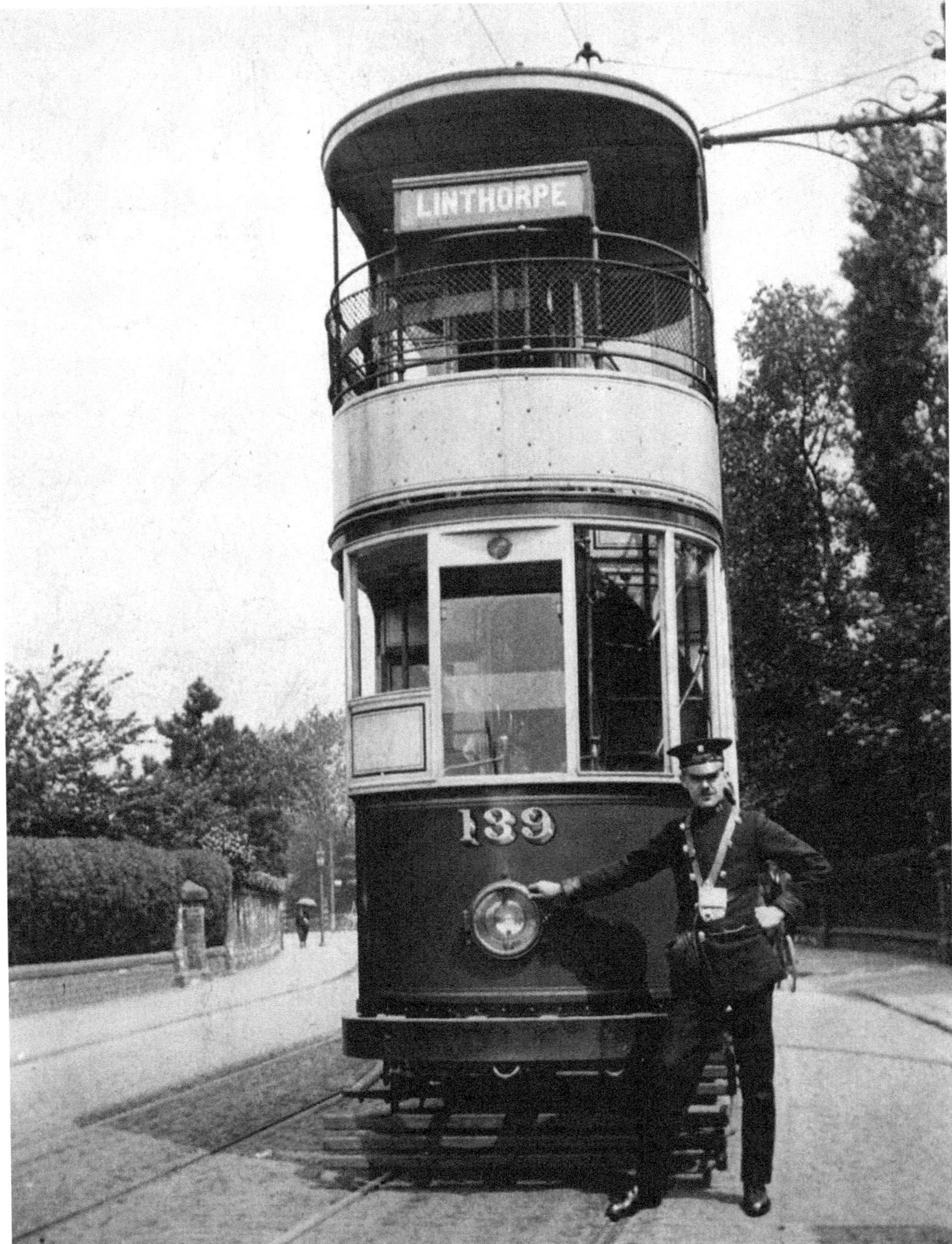

LINTHORPE
139

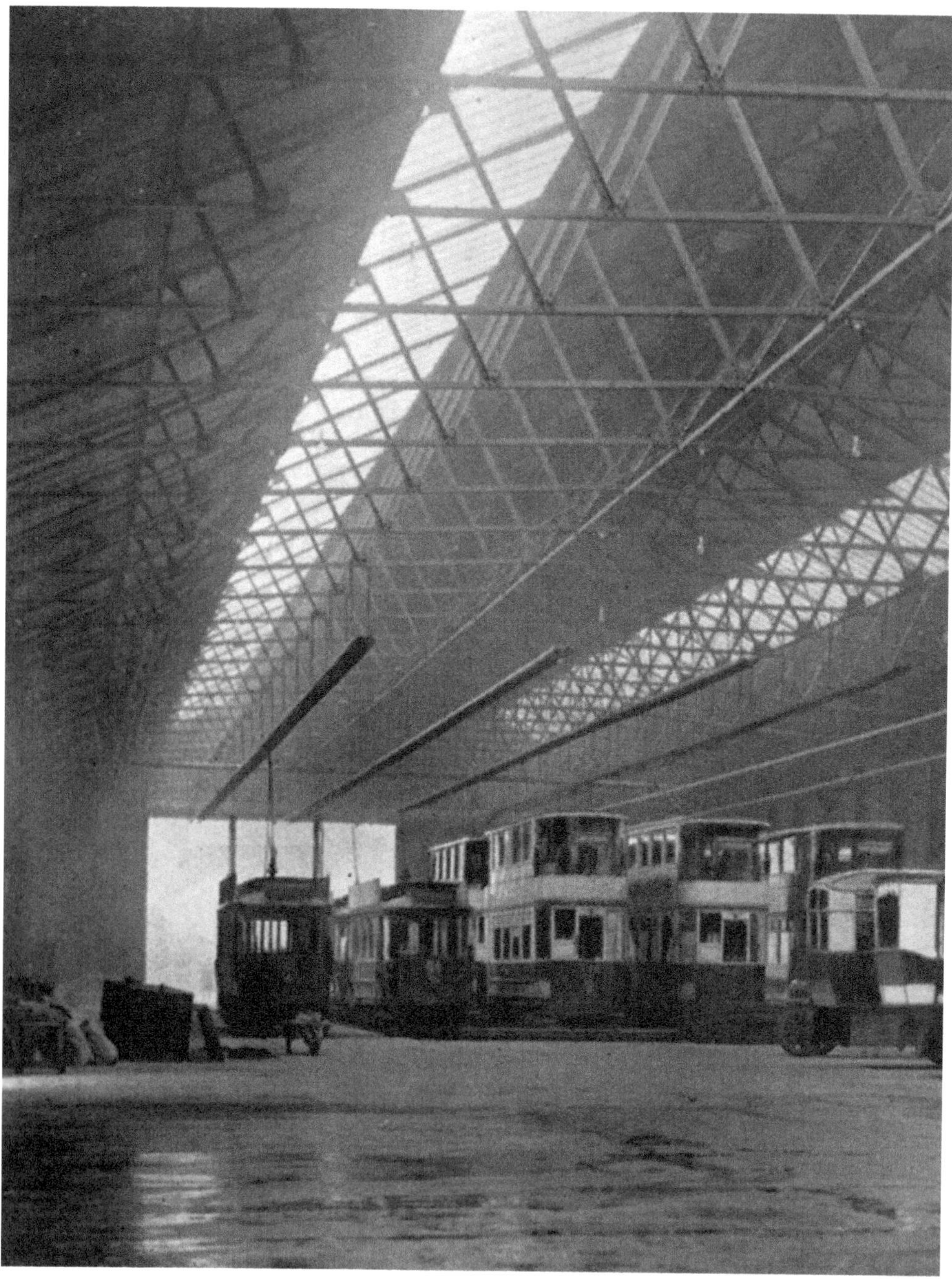

Above: The 'new state of the art' council tramway depot and tram shed.

Opposite above: New double-decker tram on the service to Linthorpe. This tram would have run from the terminus at Linthorpe along Linthorpe Road, then Albert Road, through Queen's Square and down to the Transporter Bridge.

Opposite below: Another view of the new council tramway depot and tram shed.

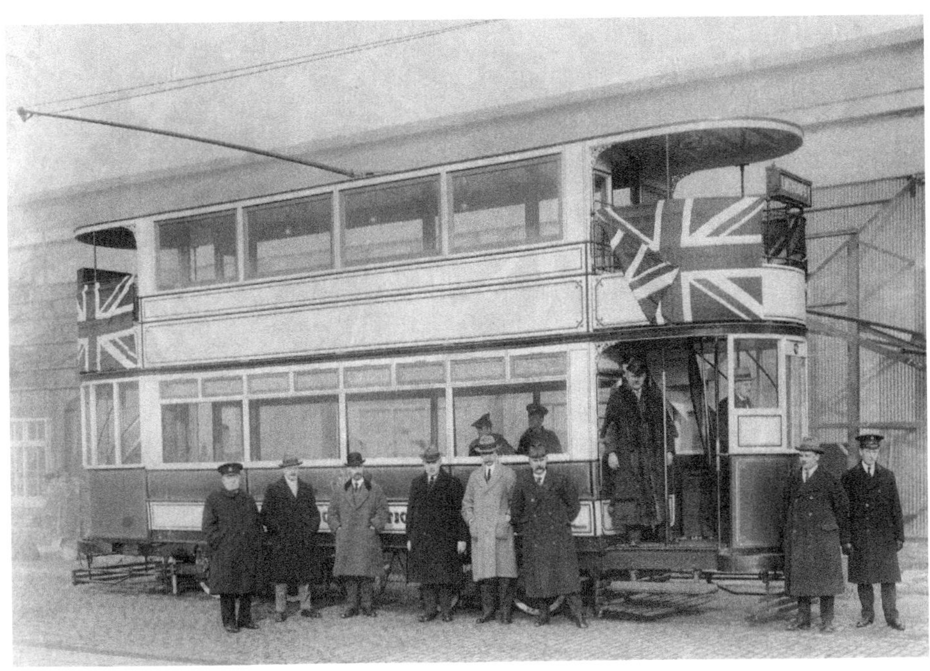

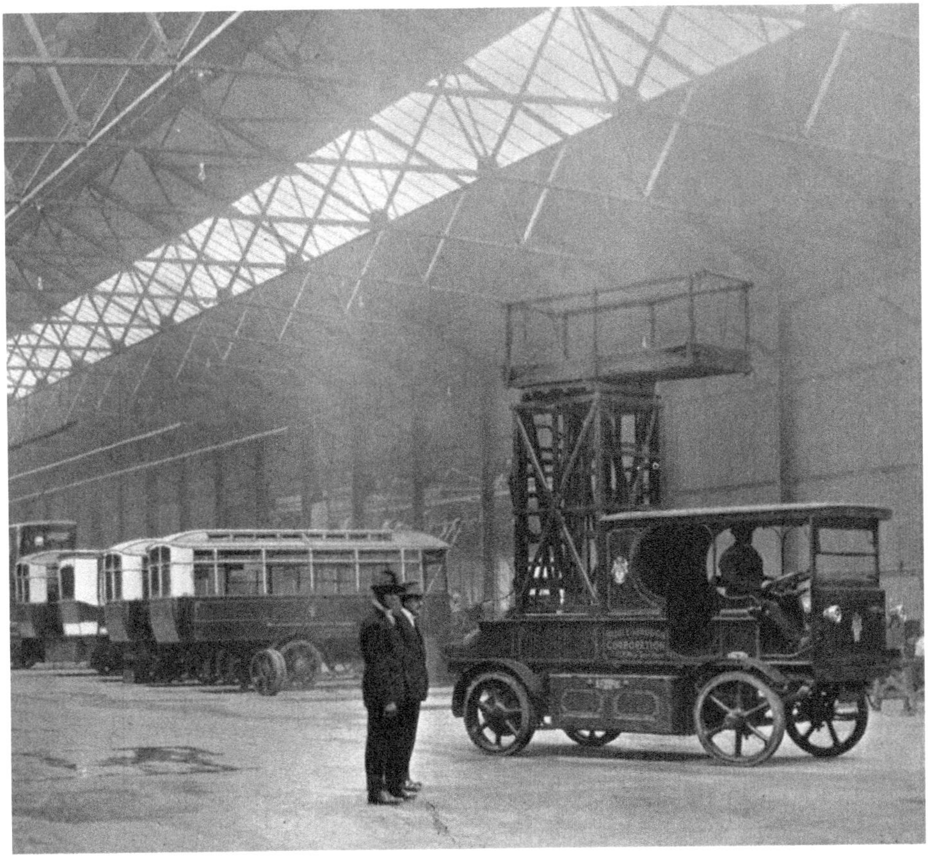

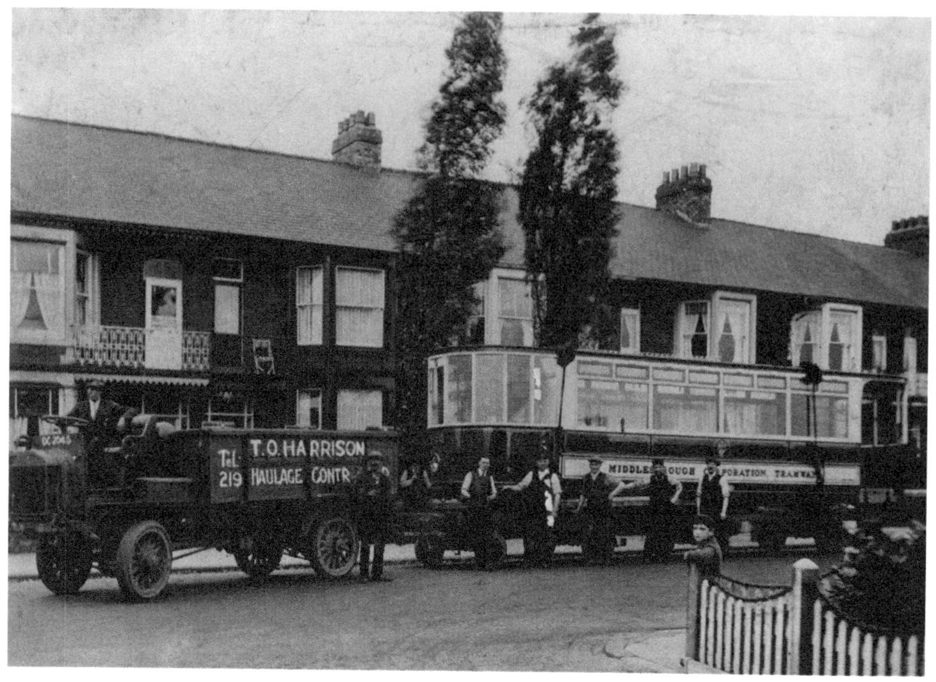

A new Middlesbrough Corporation Tramways tram being delivered by T.O. Harrison, haulage contractor.

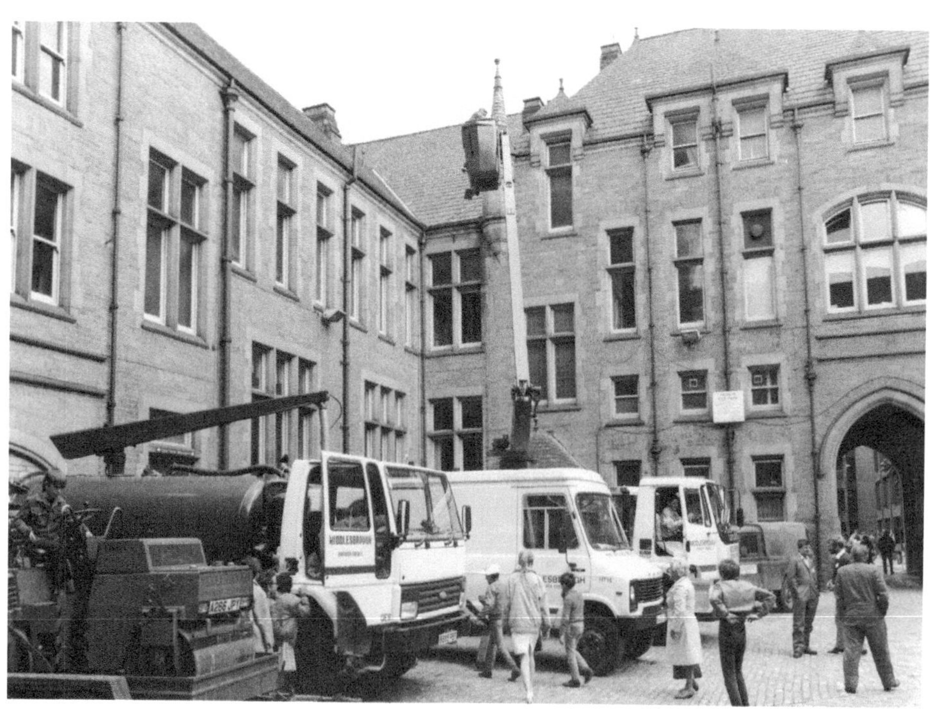

A variety of Middlesbrough Council service vehicles on display to the public in the town hall quadrangle, as part of the Middlesbrough Festival, *c.* 1985.

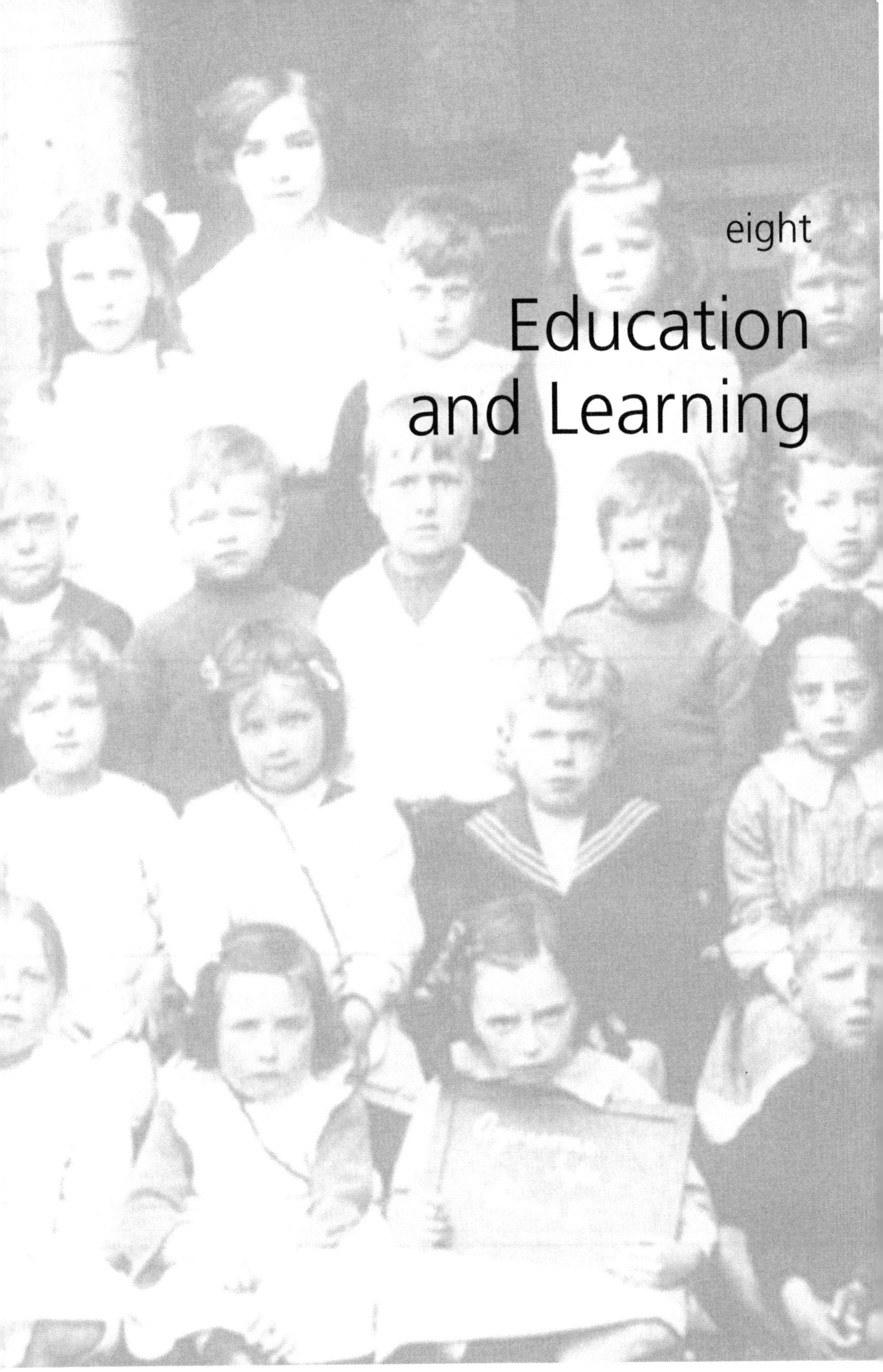

Education and Learning

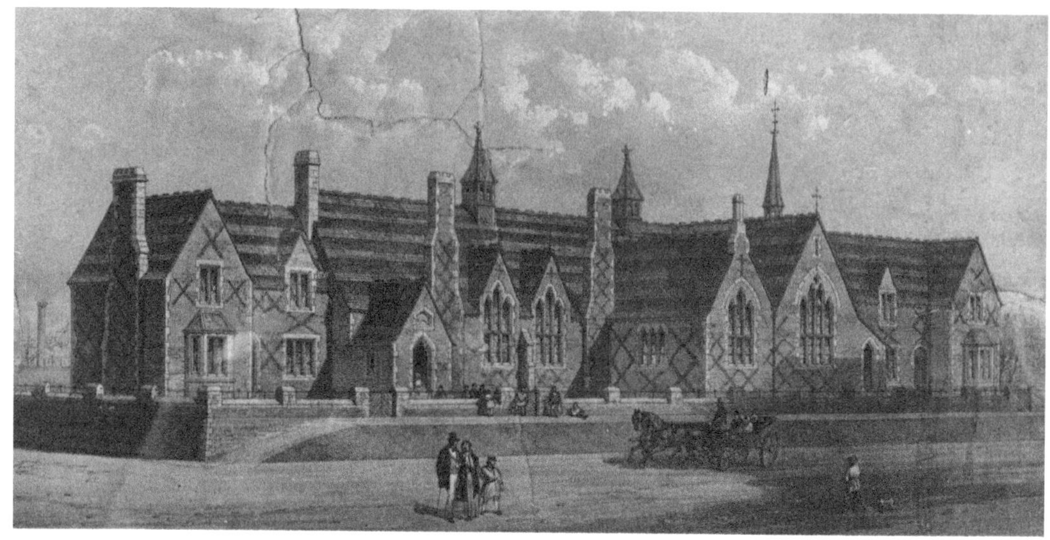

St John's National School at the top of Marton Road, now off Exchange Square. It was opened in 1860 and closed in 1874 before moving to Bright Street.

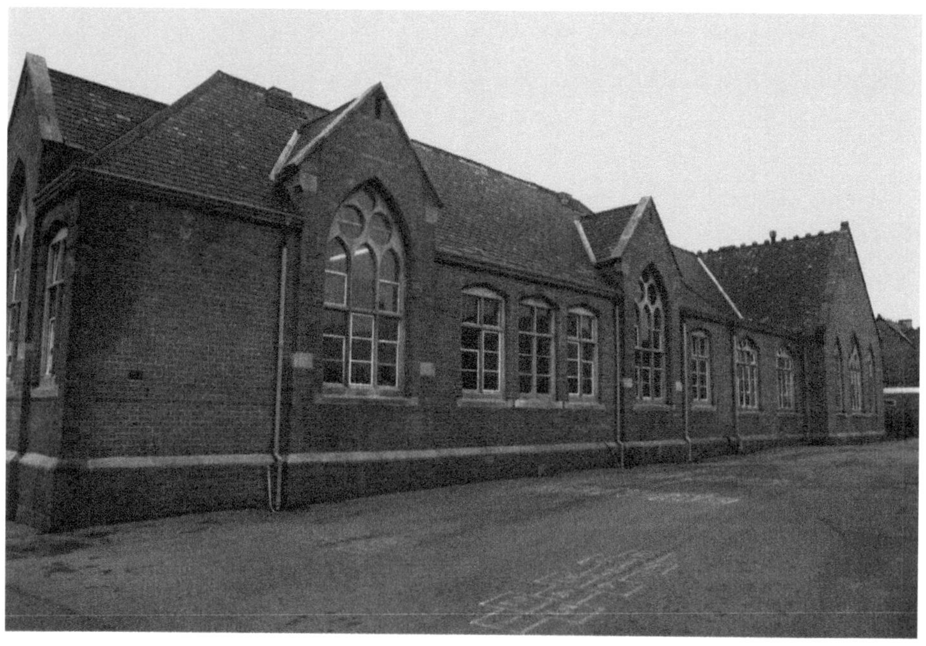

Linthorpe Primary School, Roman Road. The school was opened in 1874 and extended in 1912 when a new wing was built to accommodate the juniors.

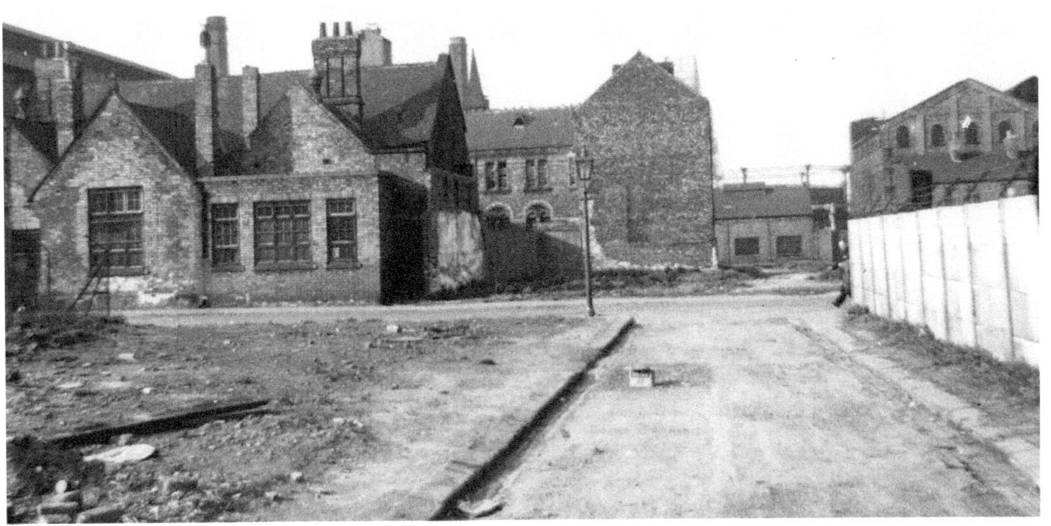

Lower East Street School also opened in 1874. It closed in 1954. At the rear can be seen the Middlesbrough gasworks.

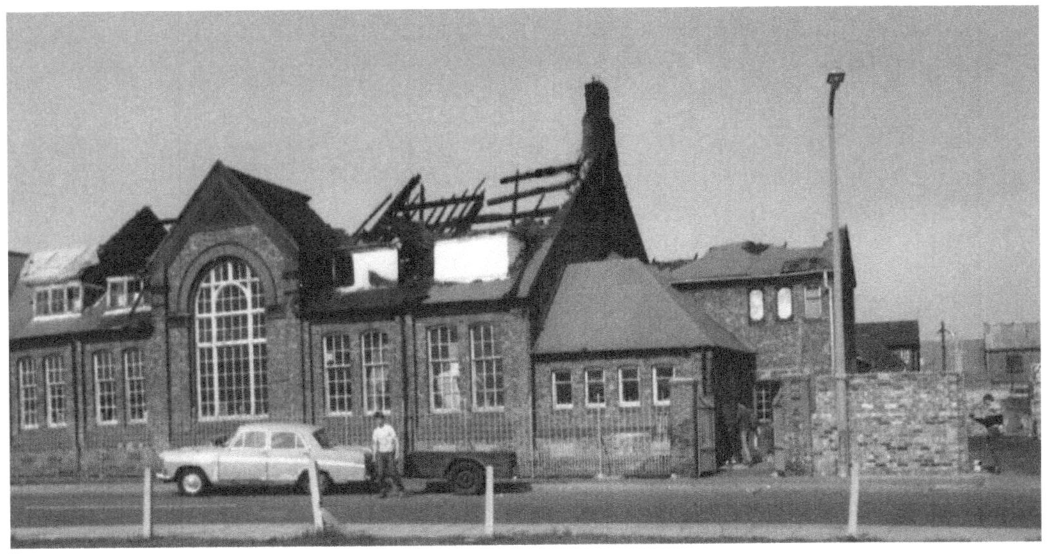

Newport Primary School, Victoria Street, *c.* 1970. It opened in 1885 and was extended in 1900. The building was closed in 1978 before transferring to new premises in St Paul's Road. The school bell is on display in the Dorman Museum.

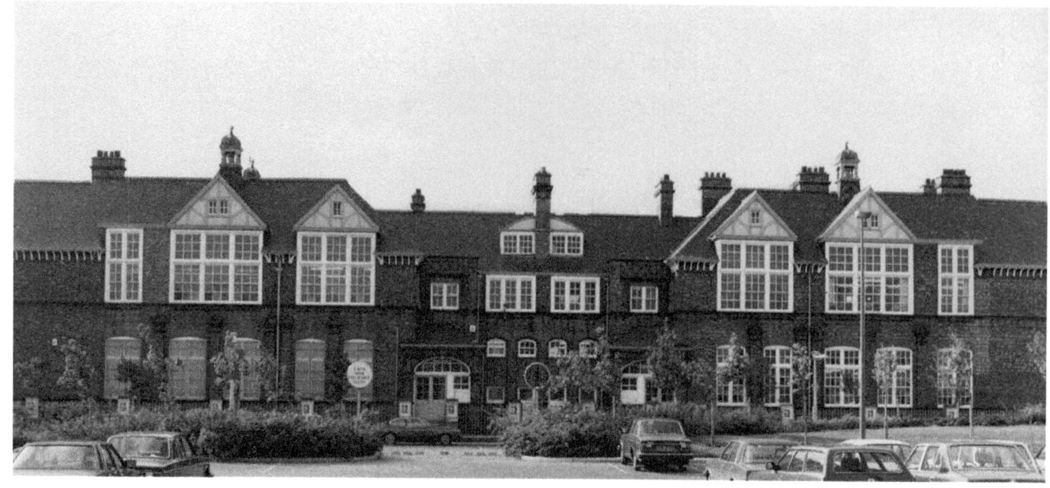

Victoria Road School, opened in 1872. It was closed in 1980/81 and the children were transferred to Abingdon Road. It then served as an art gallery and is now part of the University of Teesside.

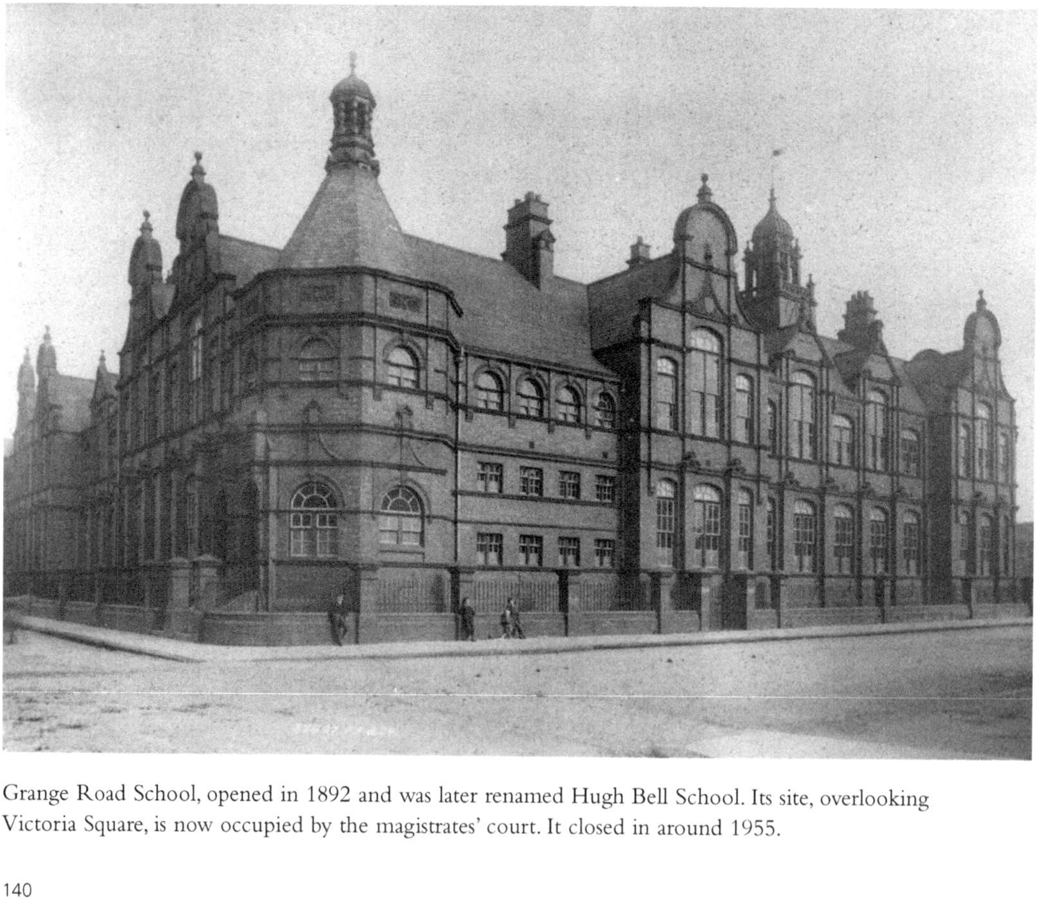

Grange Road School, opened in 1892 and was later renamed Hugh Bell School. Its site, overlooking Victoria Square, is now occupied by the magistrates' court. It closed in around 1955.

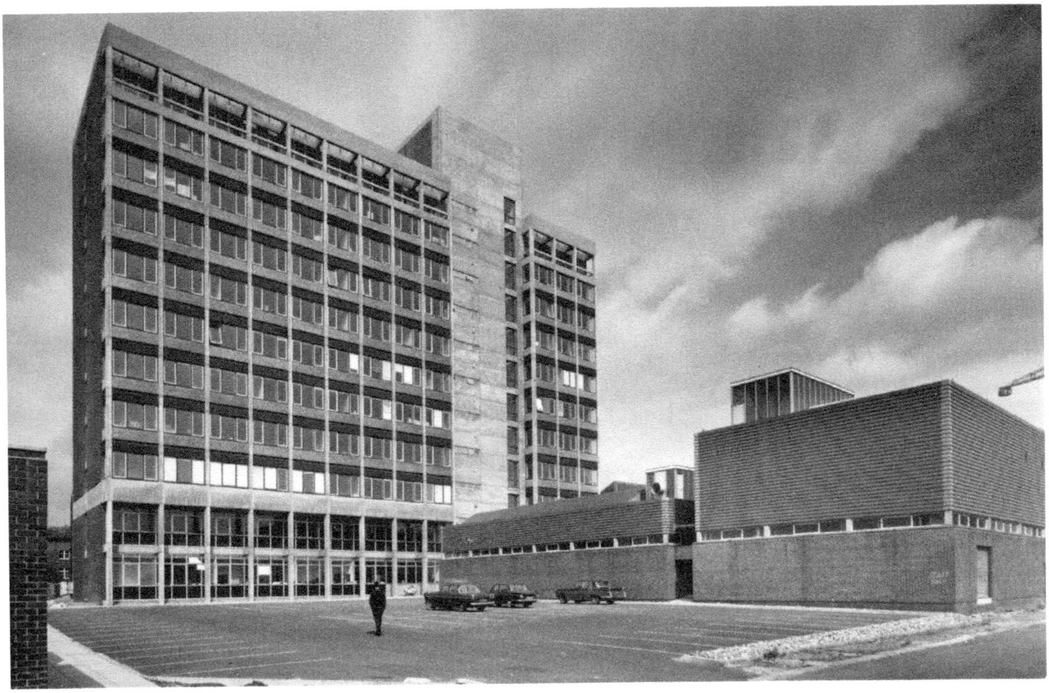

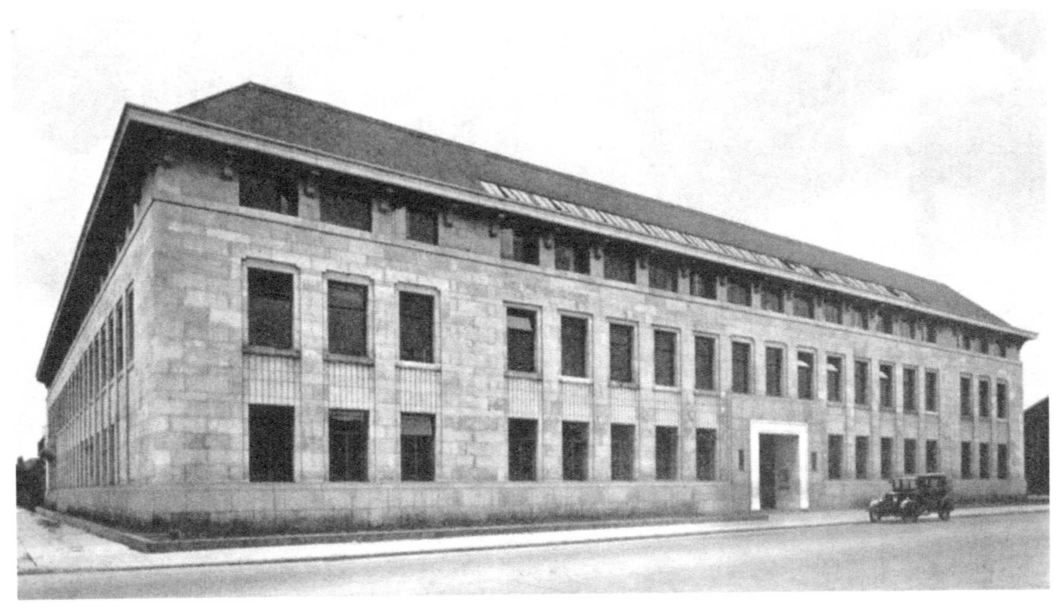

The Middlesbrough Tower at the University of Teesside.

The Constantine Technical College. The Prince of Wales opened the building, a gift of the shipowner Joseph Constantine and his family, in July 1930. It is now part of the University of Teesside.

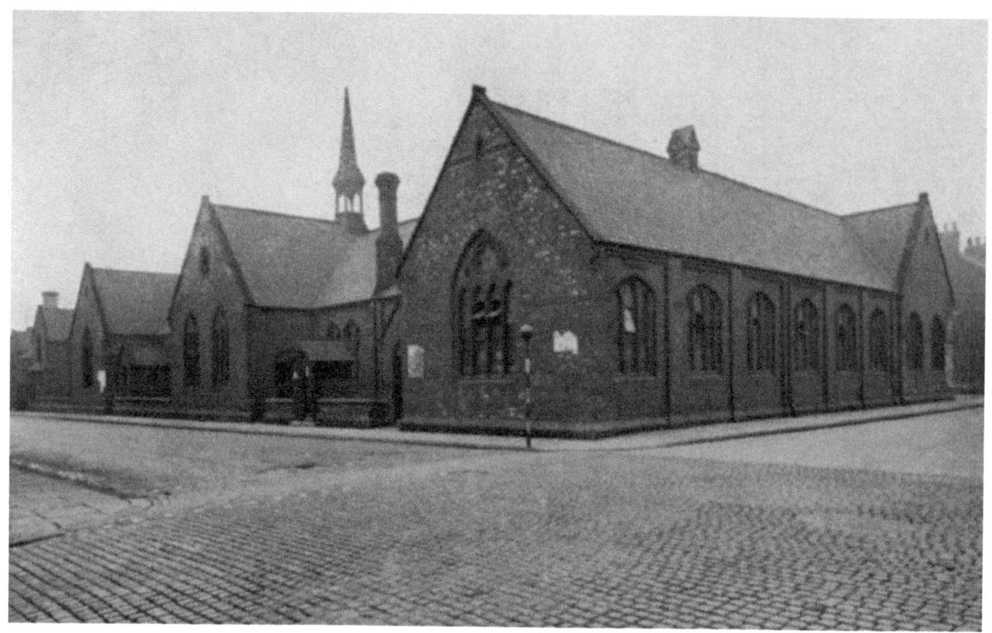

The old Fleetham Street School building. It was opened in 1873, extended in 1881 and 1883, before being demolished in 1937 and a new building erected on the site in 1938. This in turn closed in 1983, although the building continued in use as an annexe to the Art College until 1999.

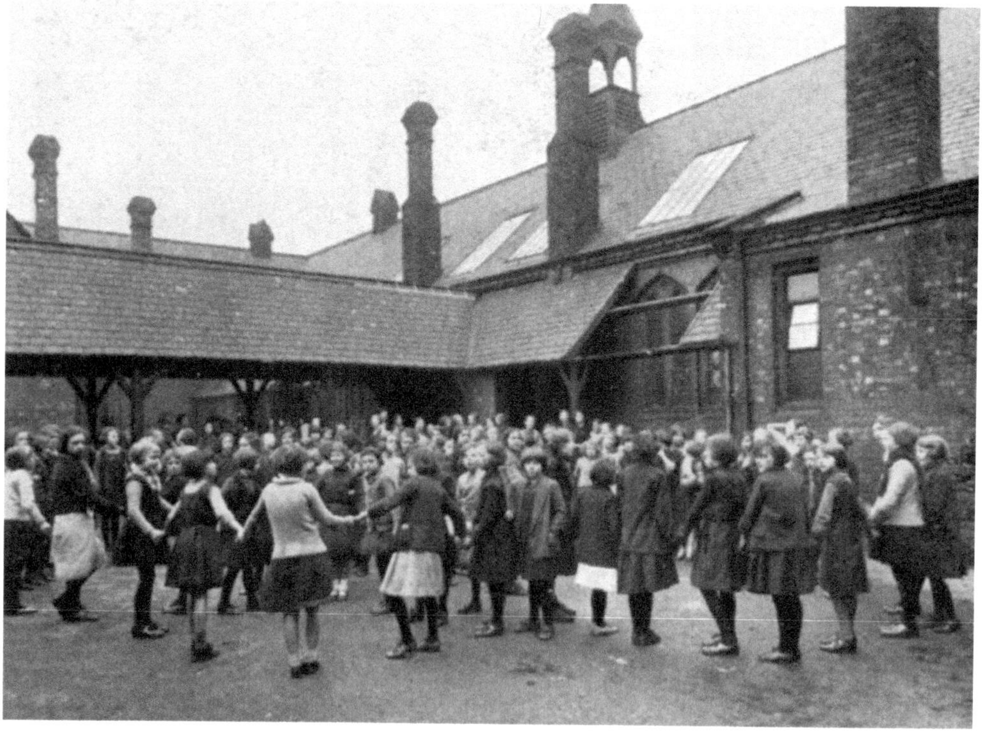

The playground of the old Fleetham Street School, *c.* 1950.

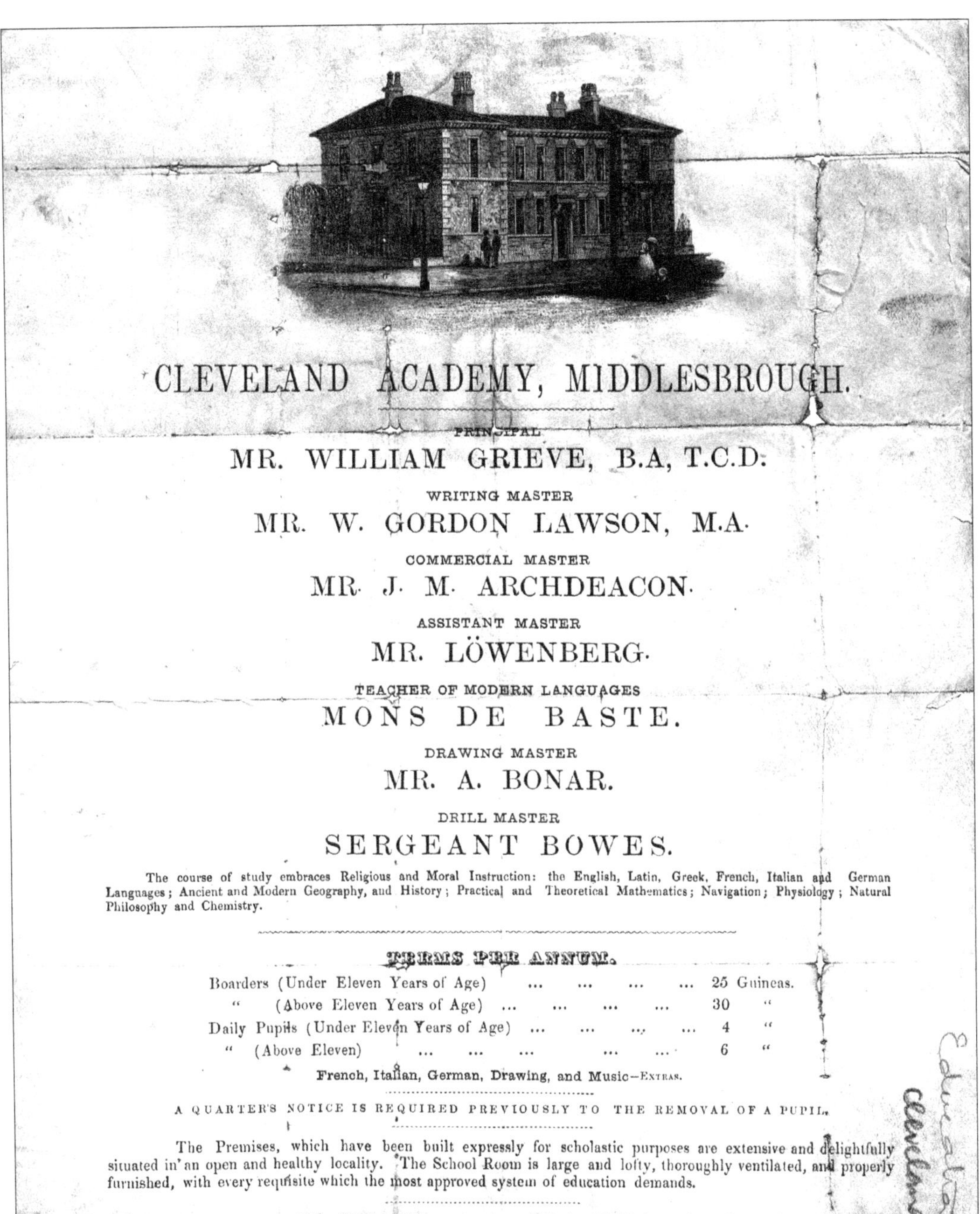

Prospectus for Dr William Grieves' Cleveland Academy, from 1858. This building stood on the site that became Hinton's grocery stores.

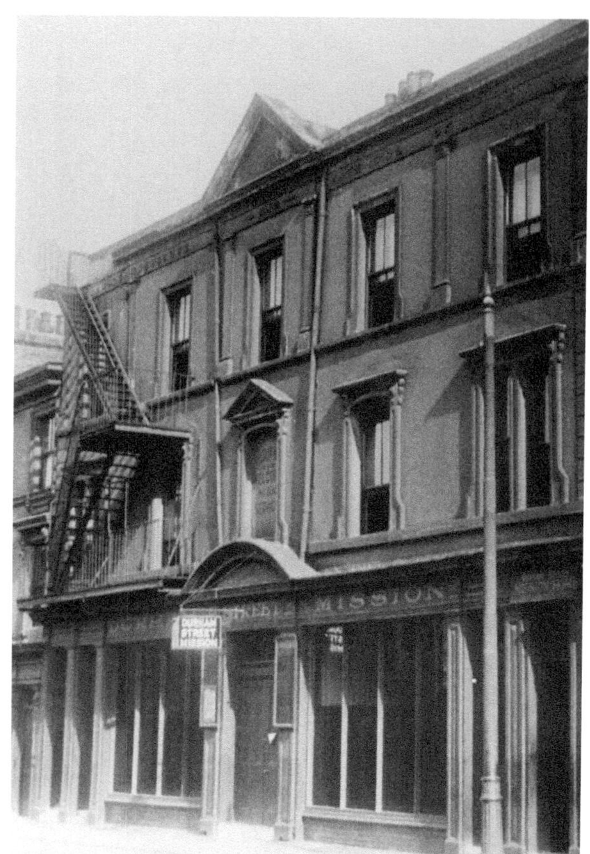

Left: The Mechanics' Institute and School of Art, Durham Street, St Hilda's. It later became the home of the Durham Street Mission.

Below: A class of children from Ayresome Primary School.

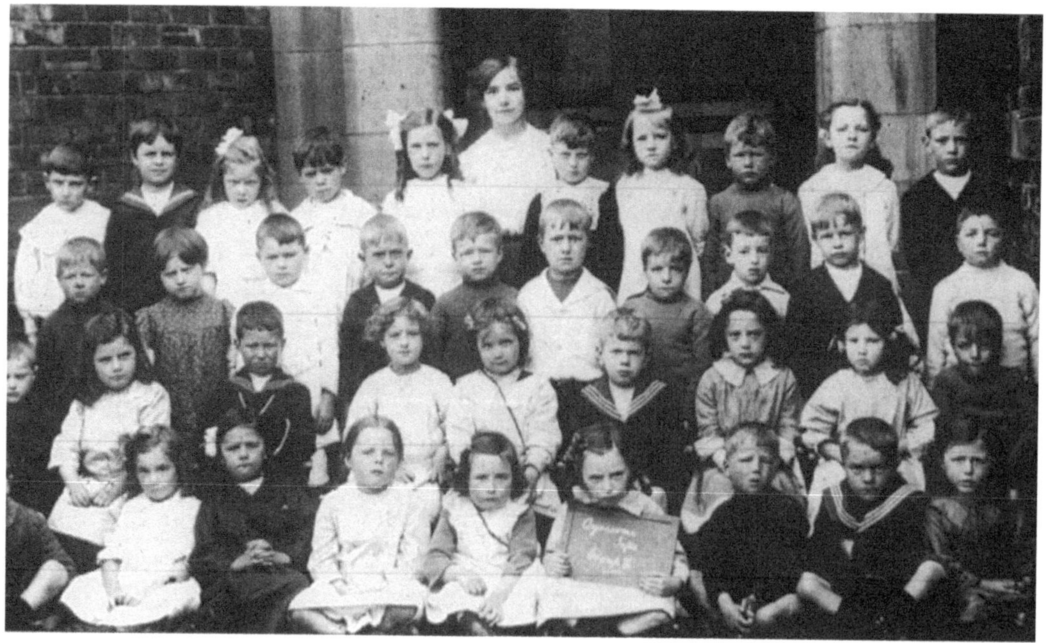

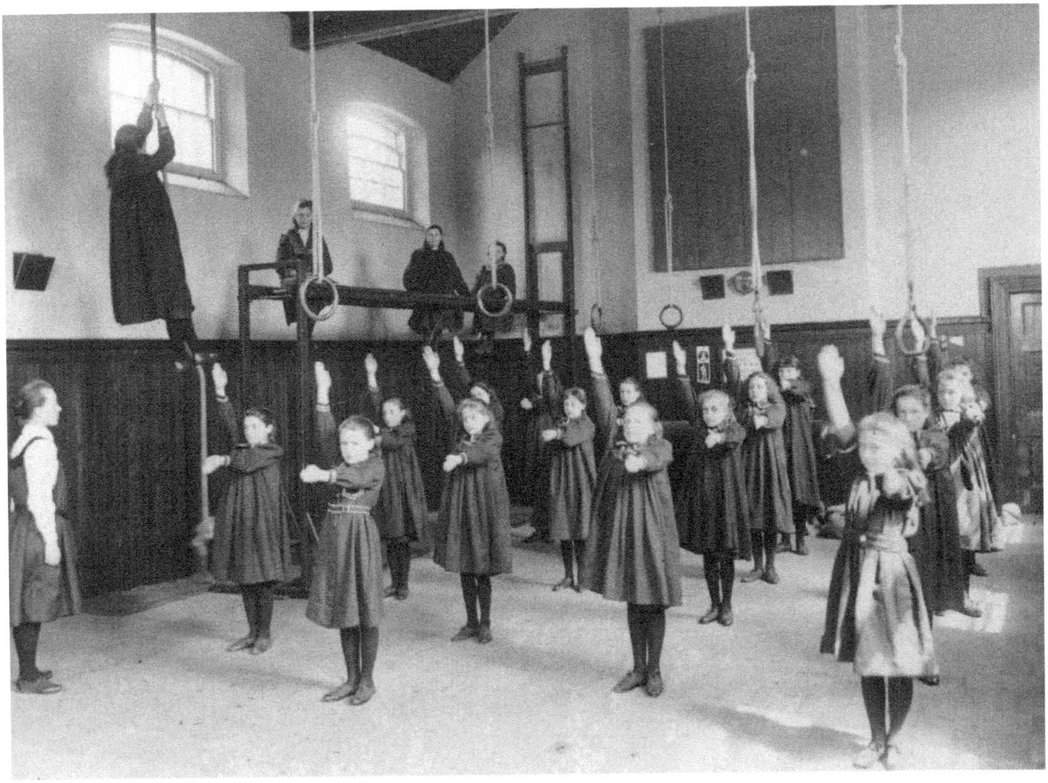

Girls in the gymnasium at Fleetham Street School.

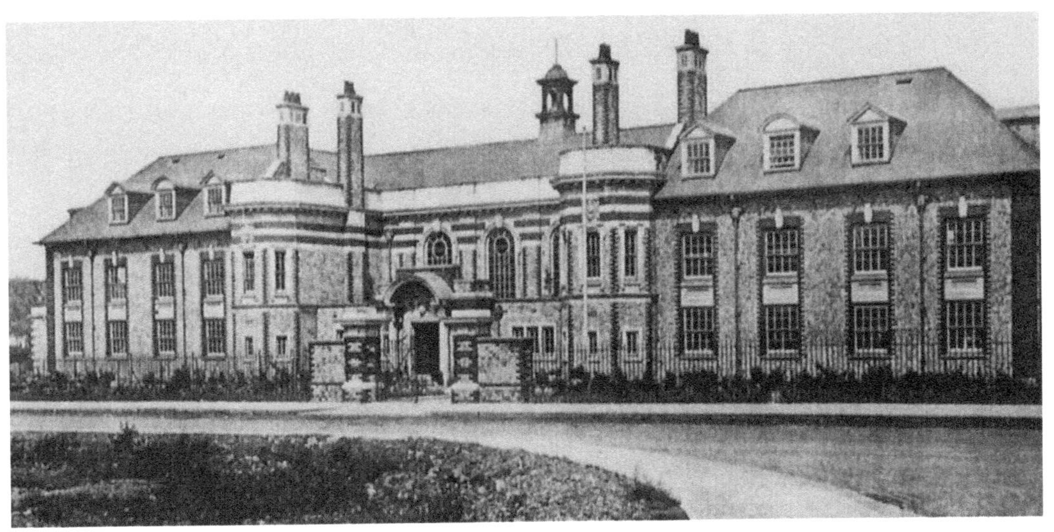

Kirby School for Girls, opened by Prince Arthur Duke of Connaught on 17 October 1911. It later became Kirby College and is now to be converted into apartments.

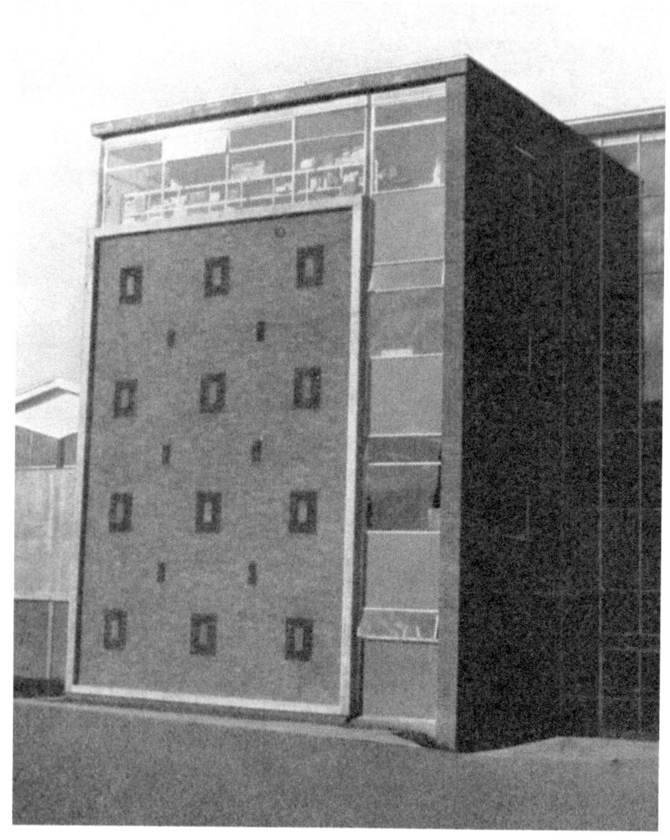

Left: Longlands College, Douglas Street. It was opened in 1958 and merged with Marton Sixth Form College to become Teeside Tertiary College in 1995, later Middlesbrough College.

Below: Cleveland College of Art and Design, Green Lane and Roman Road, Linthorpe, opened in 1960.

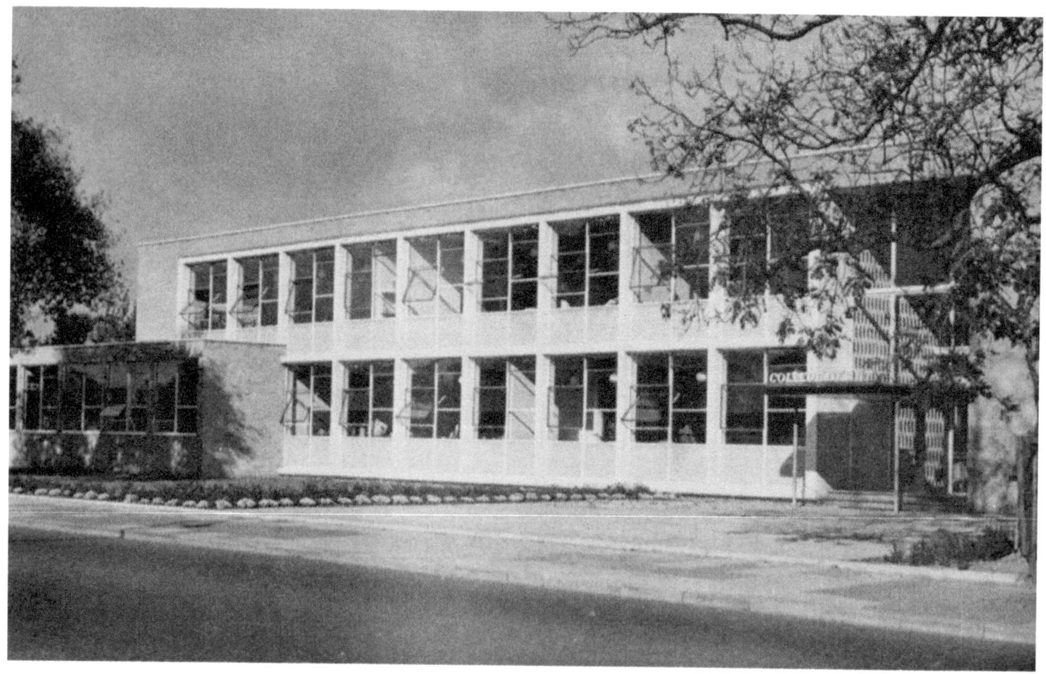

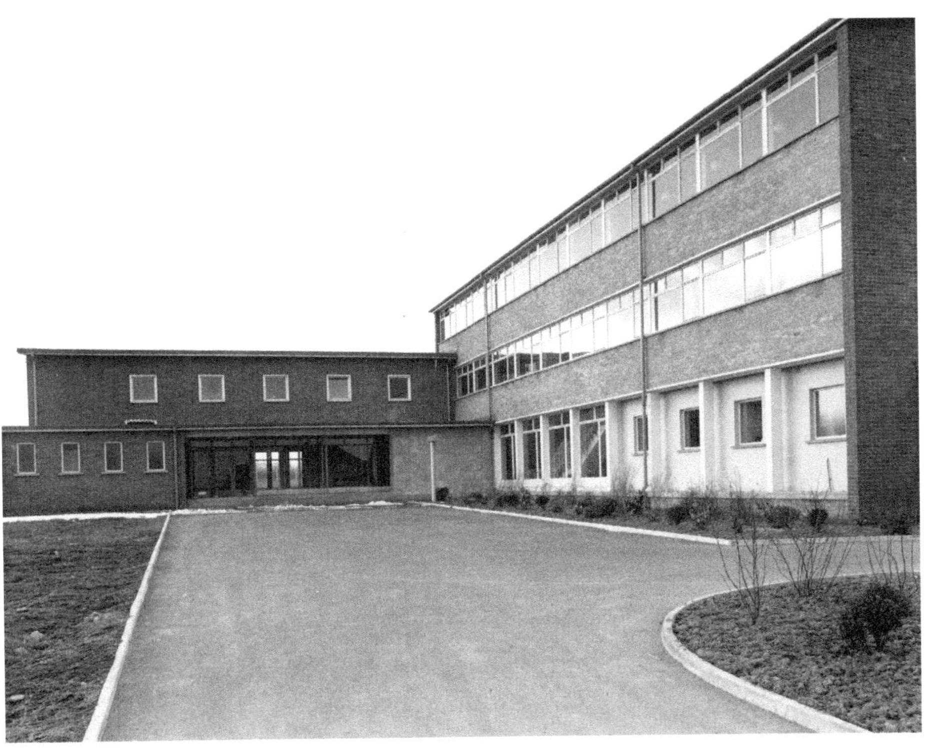

St Anthony's Roman Catholic Secondary School, Cargo Fleet Lane. Built in 1961, it closed in 2002 and is now used as the Middlesbrough Teaching and Learning Centre.

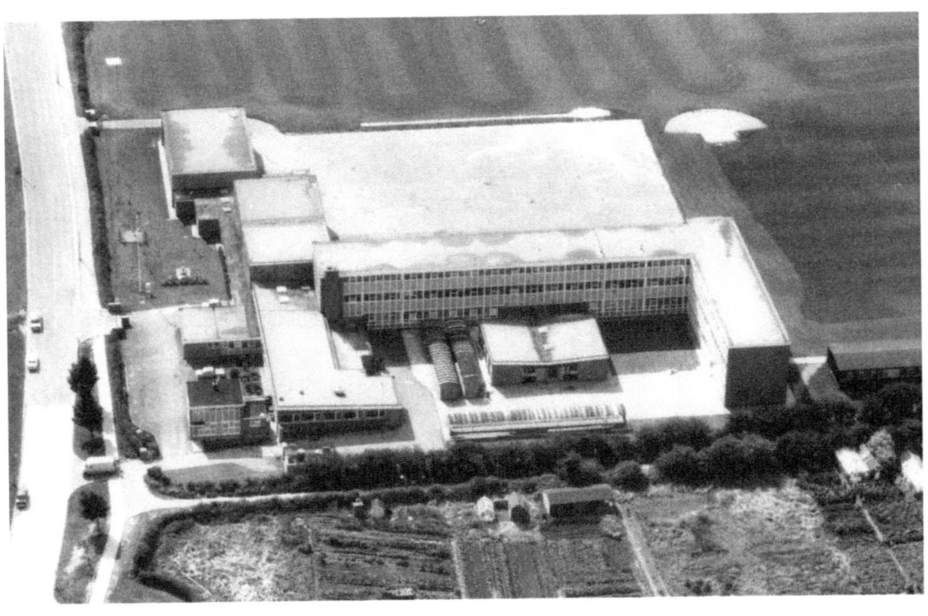

St Mary's Roman Catholic Sixth Form College, Saltersgill Avenue. Originally opened as a secondary school for boys in 1963, it took on its present form in 1974.

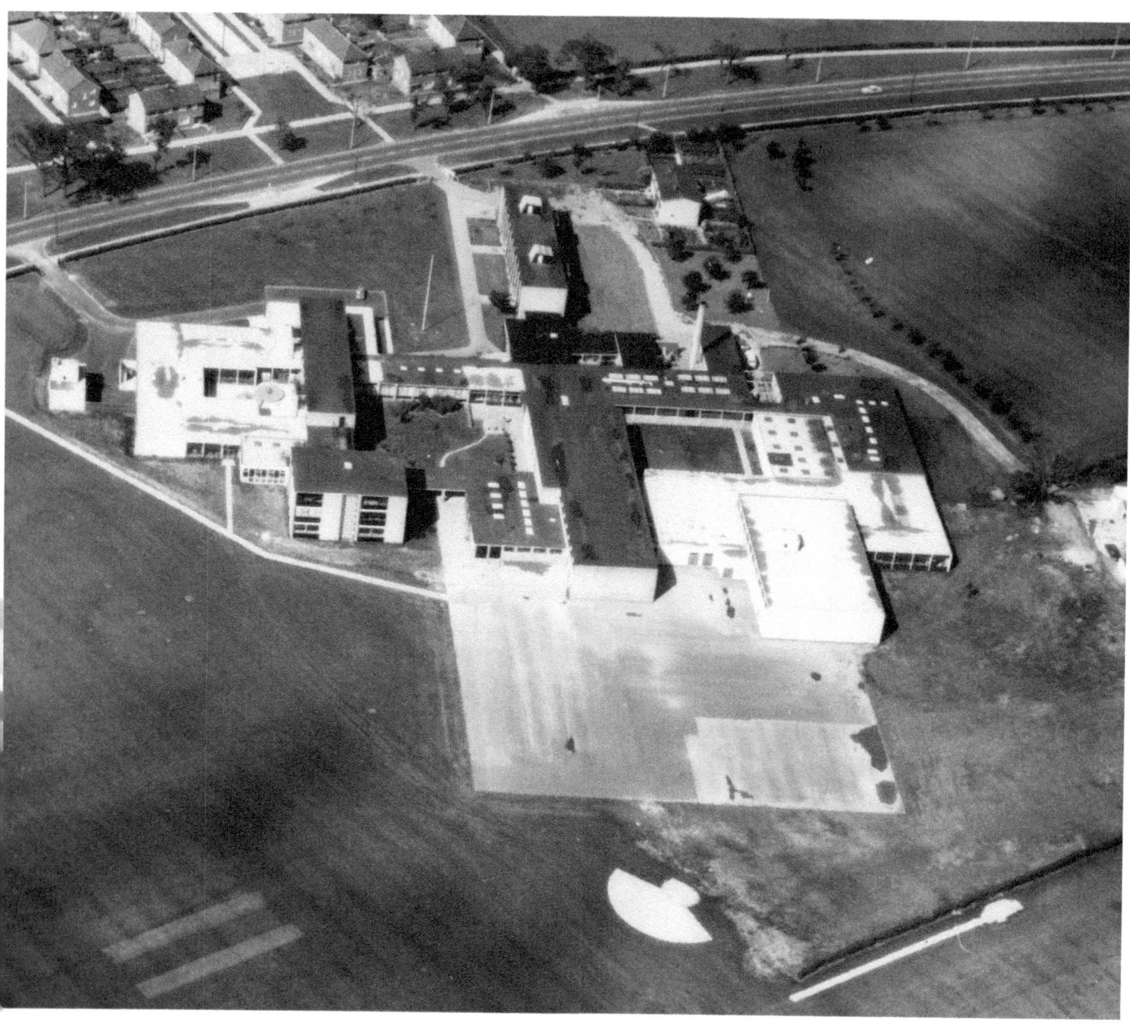

Springfield and Southlands School buildings, Ormesby Road, Middlesbrough. The two schools were amalgamated in 1983.

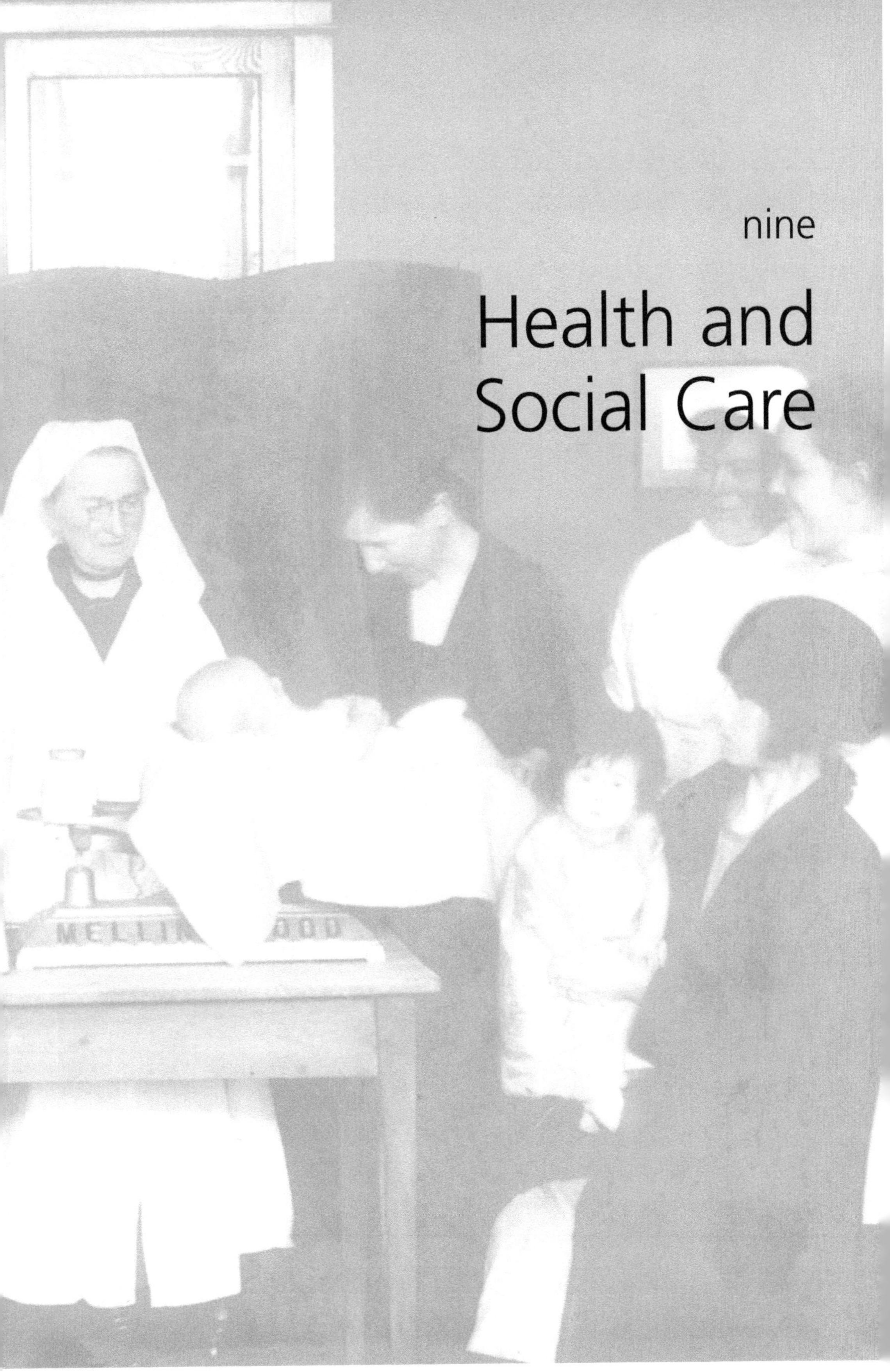

nine

Health and Social Care

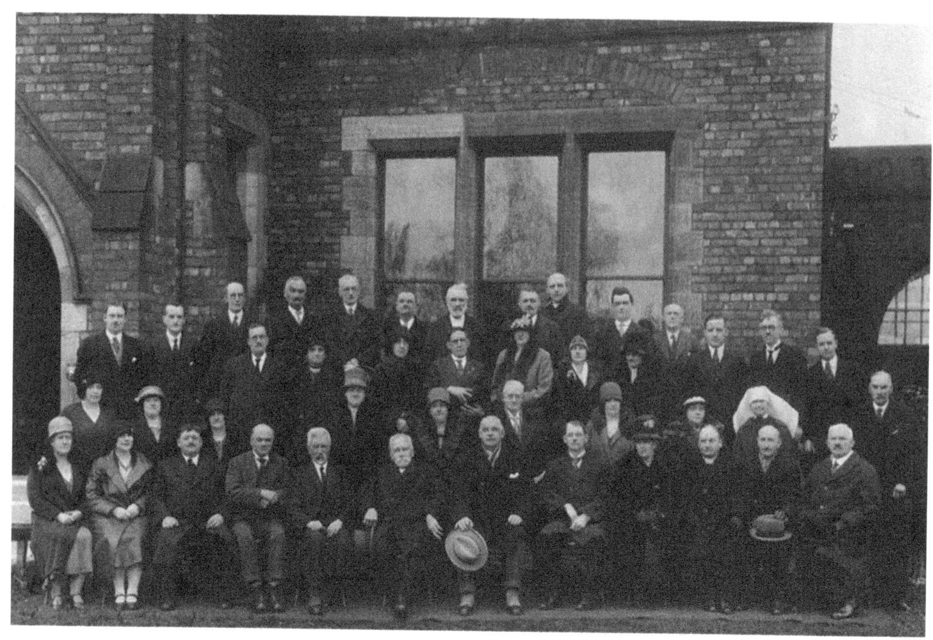

Middlesbrough's Board of Guardians, seen here in front of the workhouse building at Holgate.

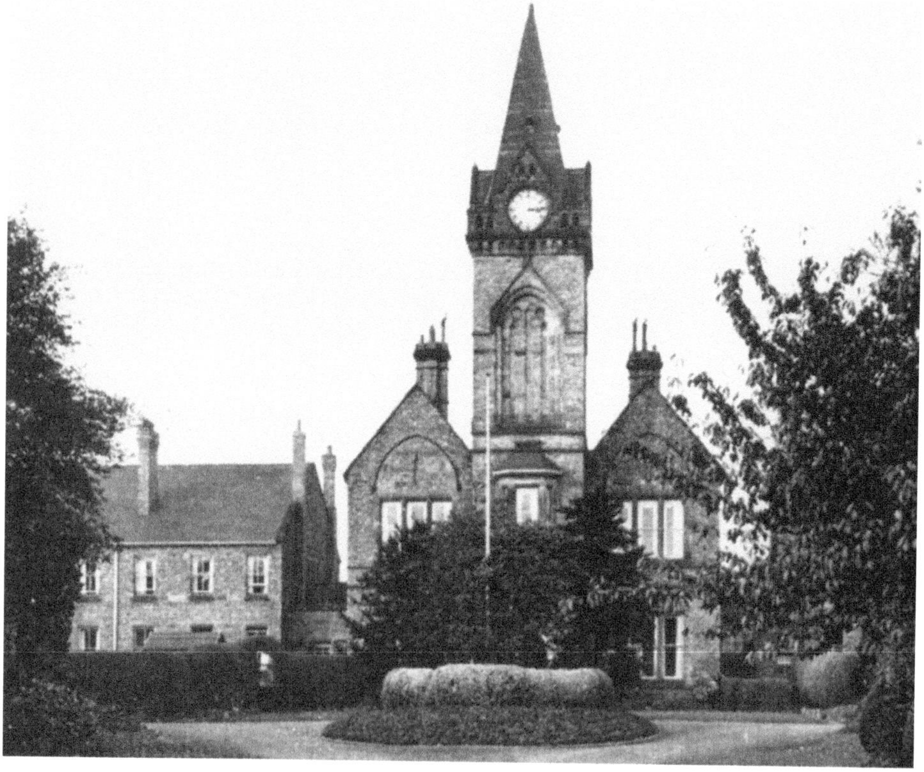

Holgate Tower, the main building of the workhouse complex, built in 1875.

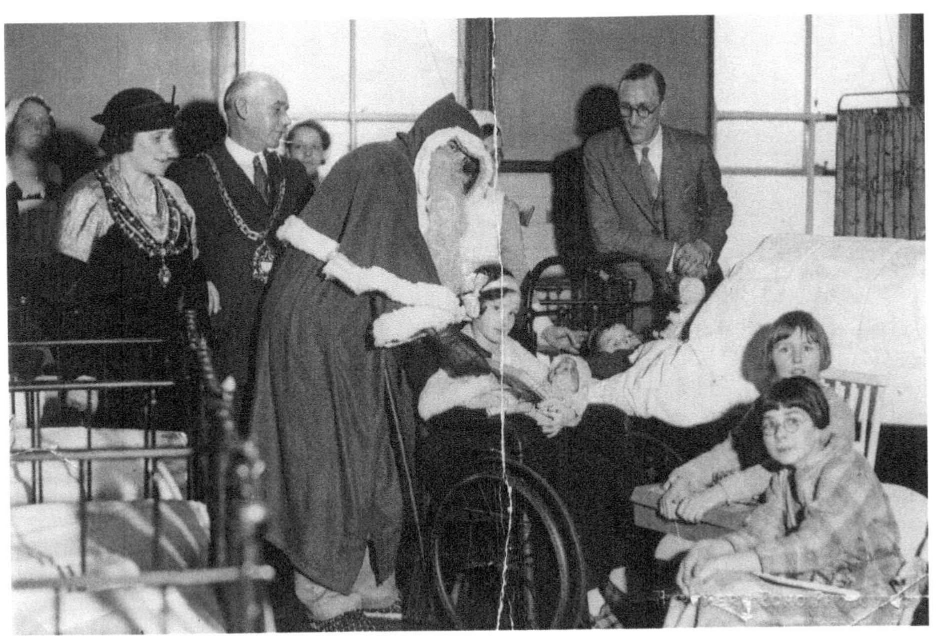

Santa visiting the children's ward with the Mayor and Mayoress of Middlesbrough.

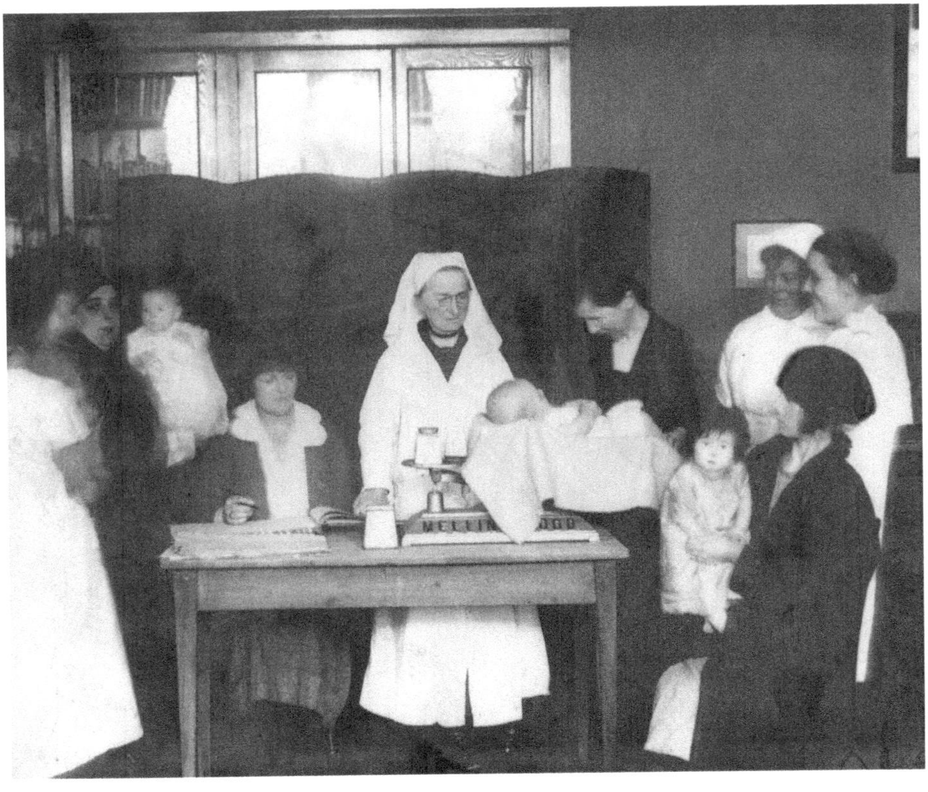

Children being weighed at the baby clinic.

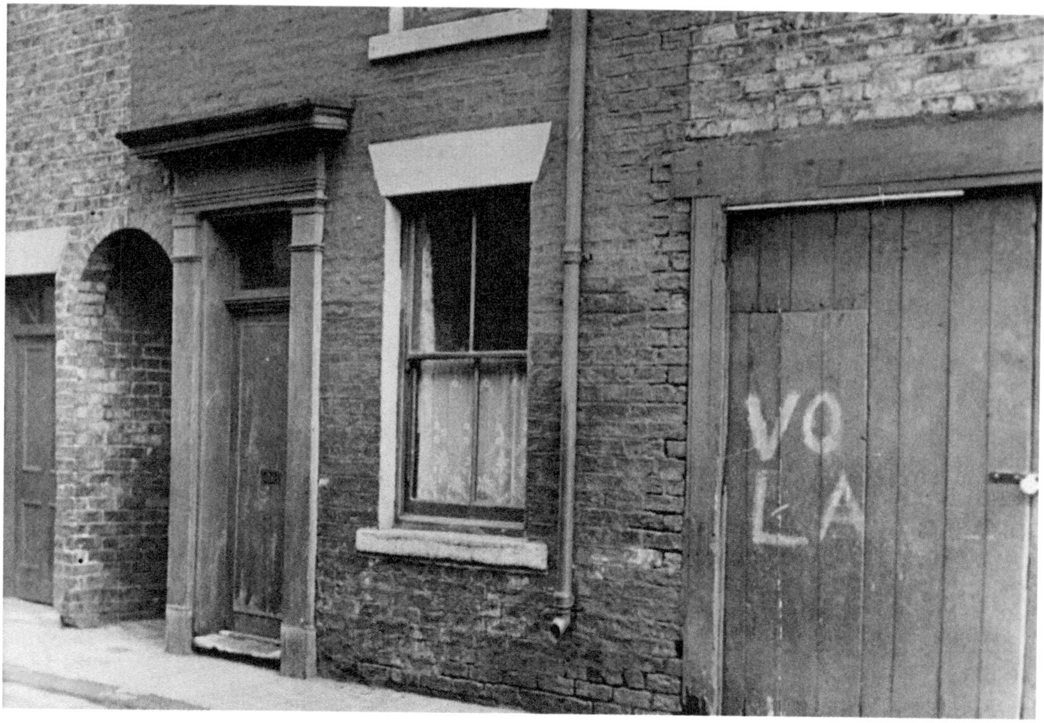

The first hospital in the town had originally been in a couple of houses in Dundas Mews. It transferred to North Ormesby Hospital in 1861.

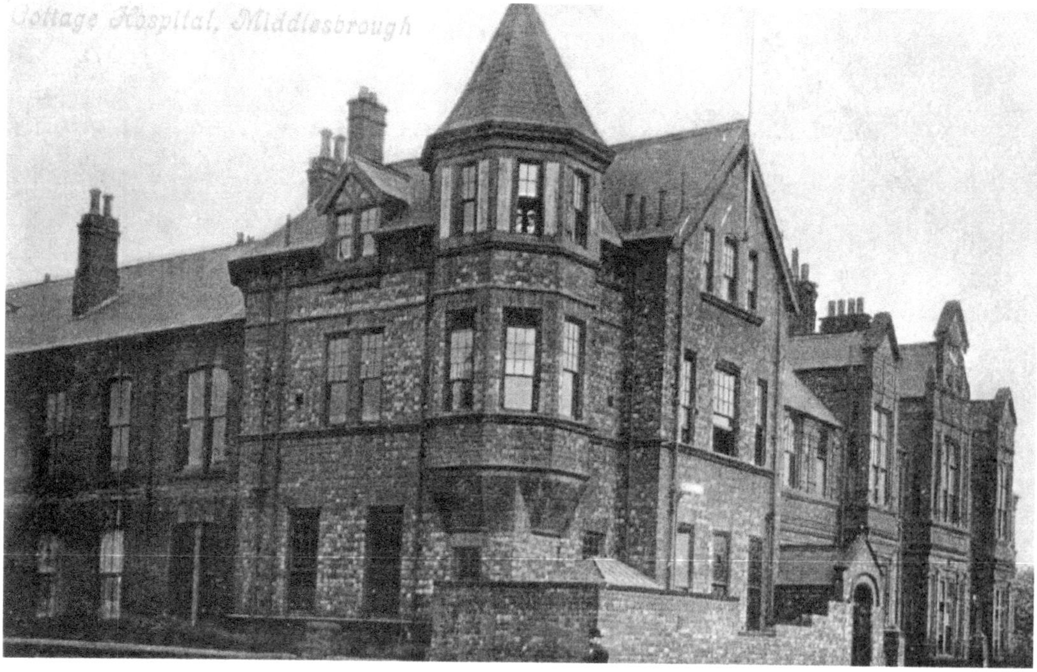

North Ormesby Hospital was built to provide for injured workmen.

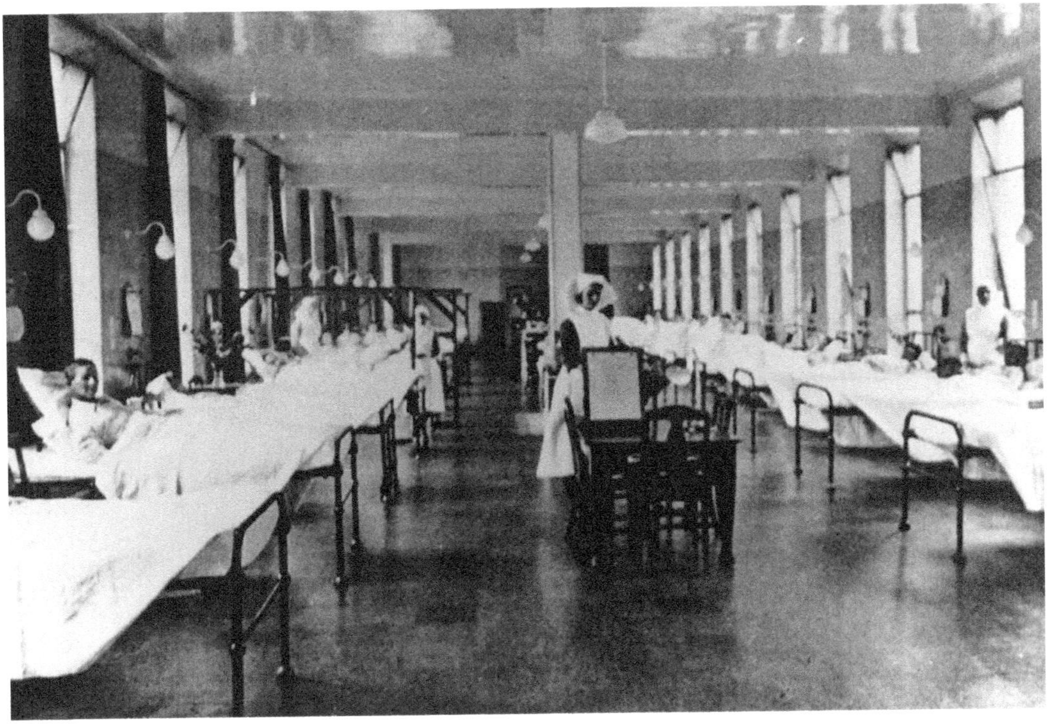

Above: St Cuthbert's Ward, North Ormesby Hospital. A ward for women in the A.B. Cochrane wing which was opened in 1878 and extended in 1924.

Right: An 'iron lung' used in North Ormesby Hospital.

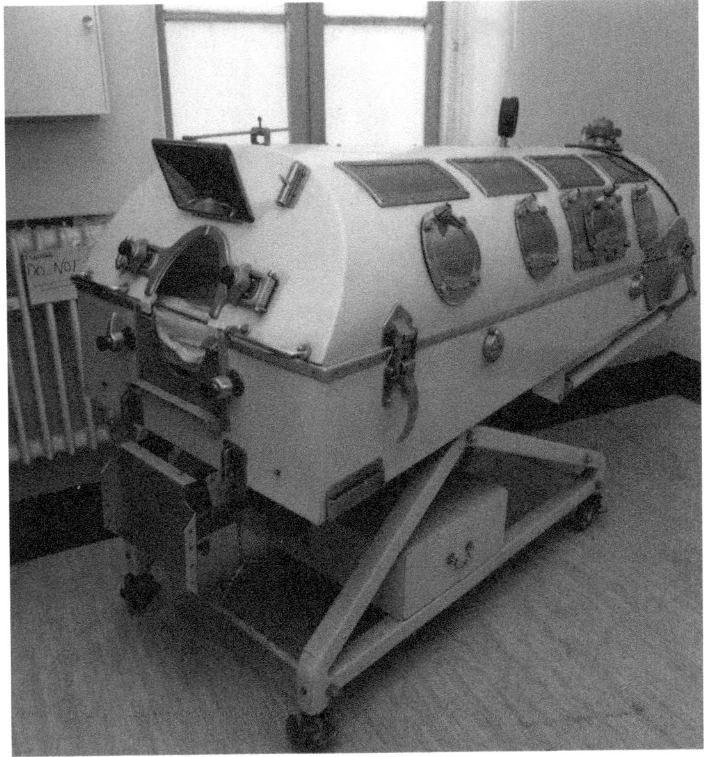

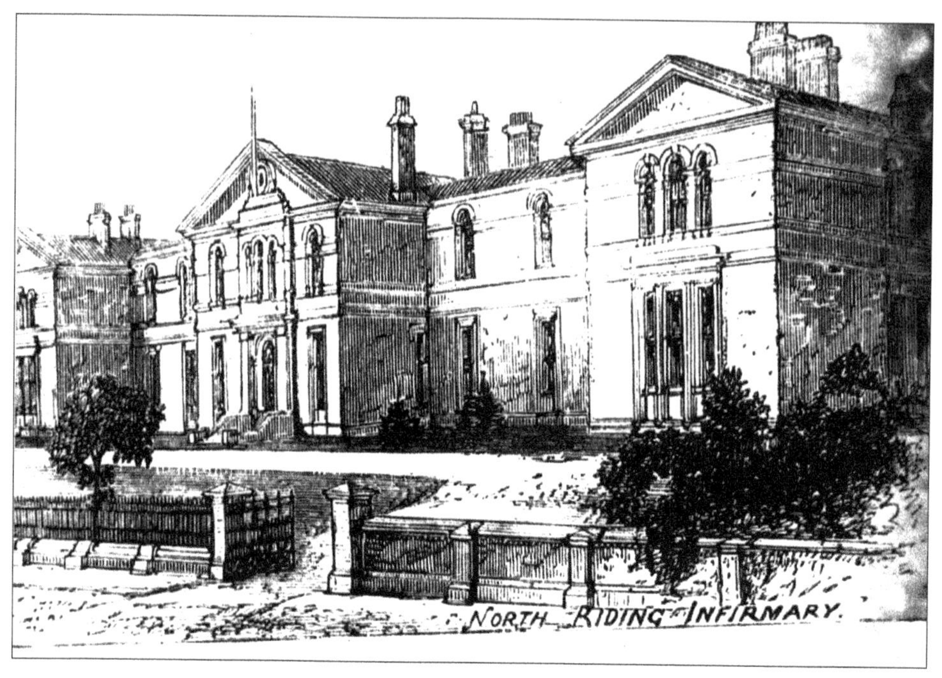

An engraving of the North Riding Infirmary. The building was funded by a number of ironmasters, the main benefactor being Henry Bolckow.

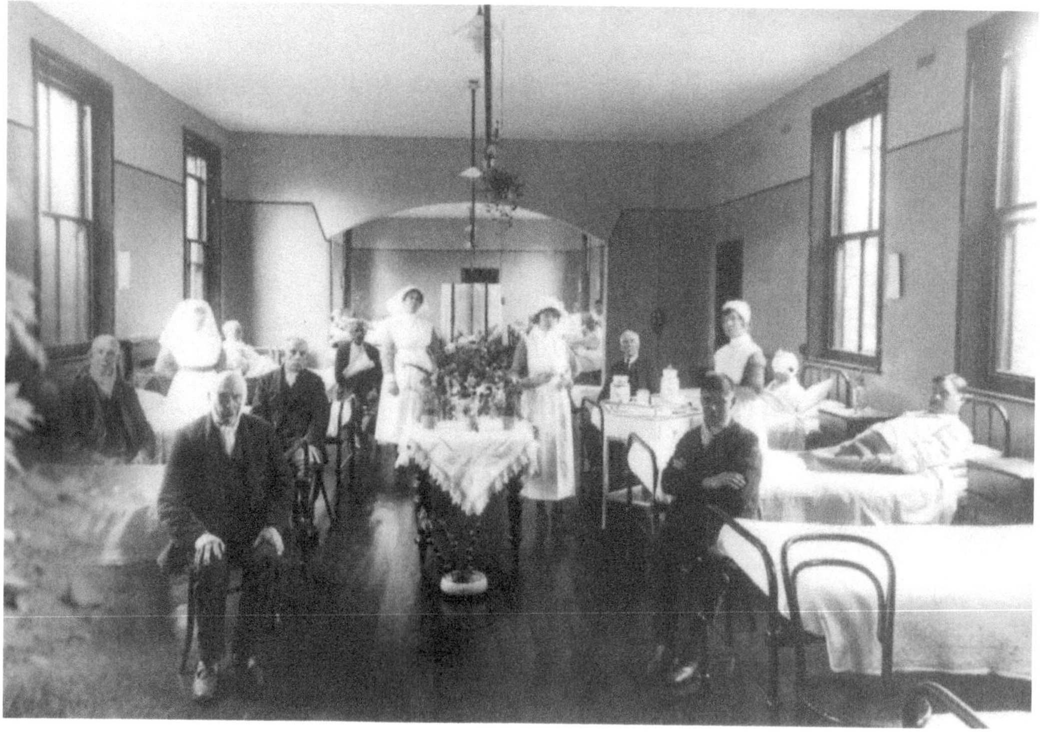

A ward in the infirmary in 1900.

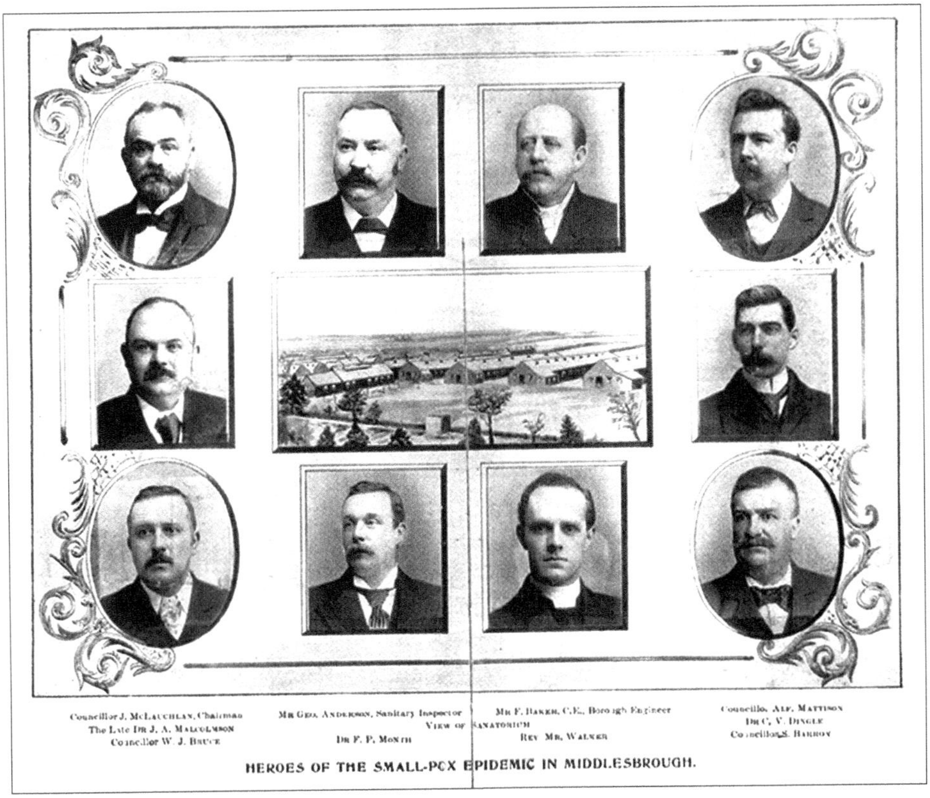

Councillor J. McLauchlan, Chairman   Mr Geo. Anderson, Sanitary Inspector   Mr F. Baker, C.E., Borough Engineer   Councillor Alf. Mattison
The Late Dr J. A. Malcolmson   View of Sanatorium   Dr C. V. Dingle
Councillor W. J. Bruce   Dr F. P. Month   Rev Mr. Walker   Councillor S. Harrow

HEROES OF THE SMALL-POX EPIDEMIC IN MIDDLESBROUGH.

Souvenir print entitled 'Heroes of the Smallpox Epidemic'. A number of councillors and other officials were supportive of the fight to try and stem smallpox outbreak. They included Councillor Mattison, Dr Veitch and a number of others. A major epidemic broke out in Middlesbrough in 1897-1898, with 1,411 notified cases. The existing provision was woefully inadeqaute and new hospital wings had to be built.

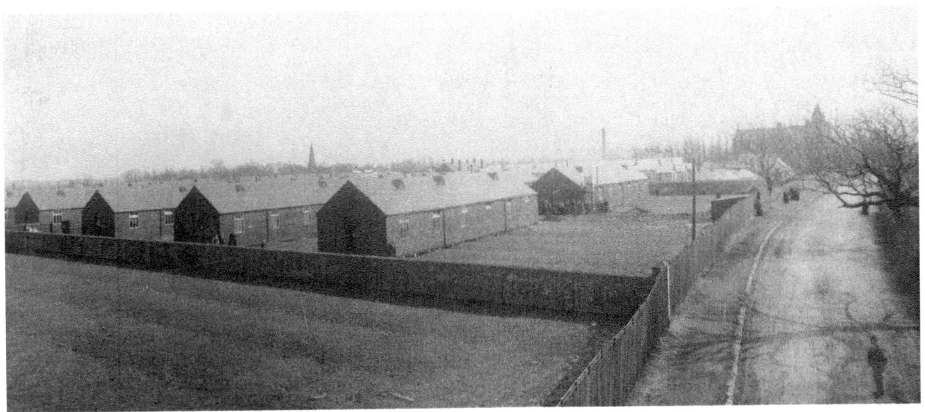

The Fever Hospital, West Lane, Middlesbrough, built to deal with infectious diseases, after extensions in 1900. This hospital opened in 1872, and in 1887 the Matron M.E. Proctor reported that Councillor Hinton had presented fifteen pictures to hang in the wards, and that Mr T.M. Smith, of Wilson Street, had provided a roll of pictures to replace the old prints in frames.

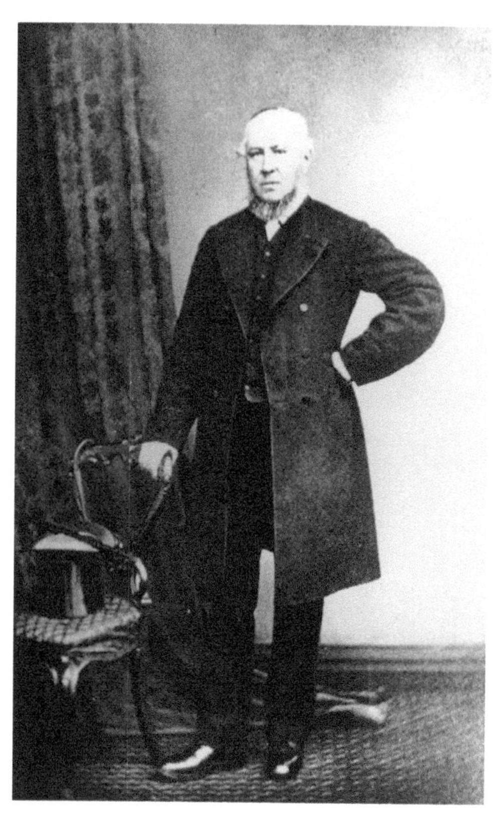

Dr John Richardson MRCS. Honourary surgeon at North Ormesby Hospital from 1859-71.

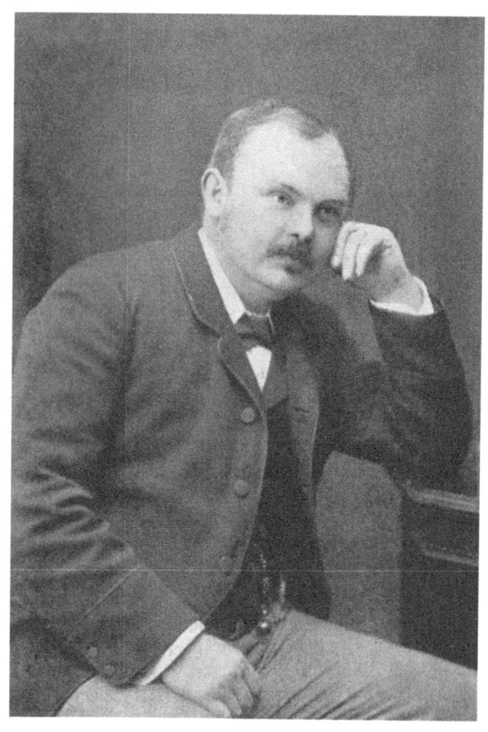

Dr John Andrew Malcolmson, Middlesbrough's Medical Officer of Health from 1873-1898. He died suddenly of apoplexy on 28 February 1898, probably due to stress.

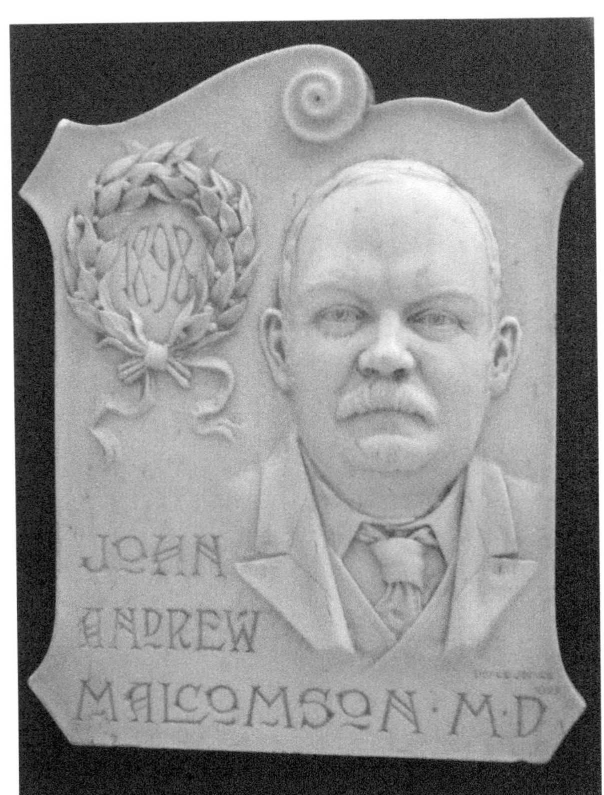

Dr Malcolmson – a 1898 plaque from the North Riding Infirmary erected to express the gratitude of the people of Middlesbrough for his efforts to contain the smallpox outbreak.

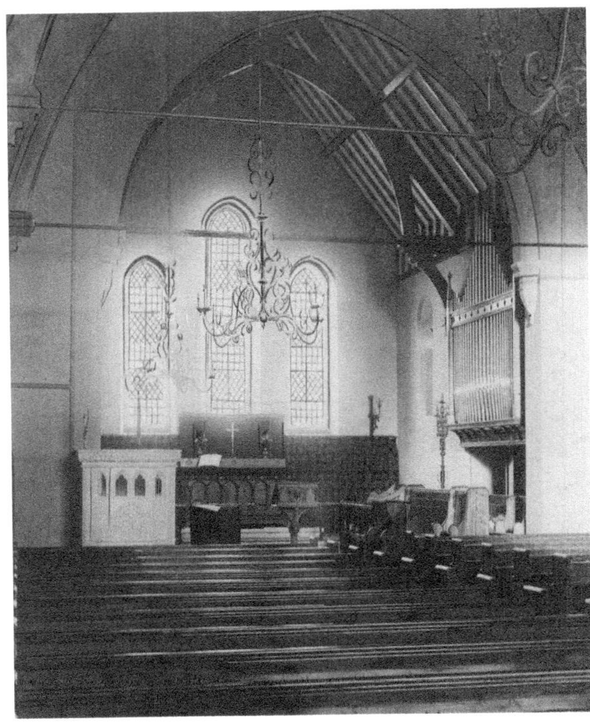

The chapel at St Luke's Hospital in 1899. The first patients were admitted in 1898 to a self-contained community, the Clevelend Asylum. It was renamed St Luke's Hospital in 1924.

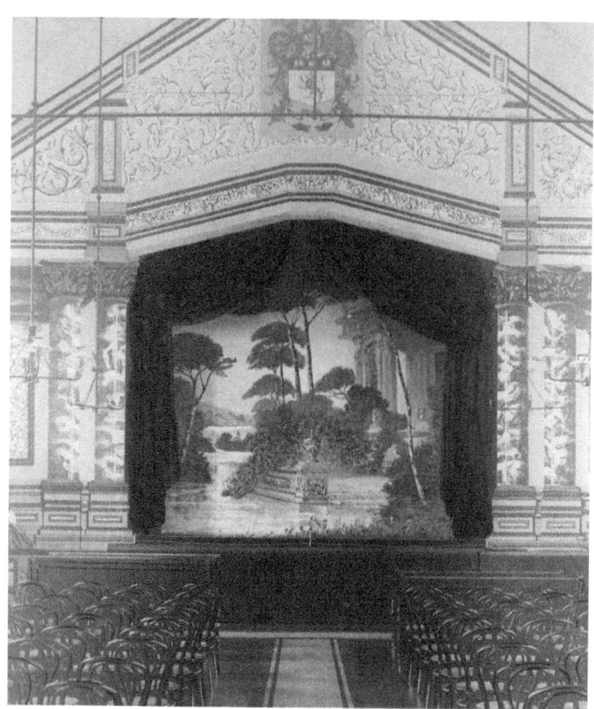

Opposite above: The fire brigade at St Luke's Hospital.

Opposite below: A floating isolation hospital was moored on the river Tees at Eston Jetty from 1895. It had provision for thirty beds and was to prove particularly useful during the smallpox outbreak of the 1890s.

Left: The Recreation Hall stage at St Luke's Hospital.

Below: The dairy at St Luke's Hospital. The man shown here is the bailiff of the farm, Michael Ward.

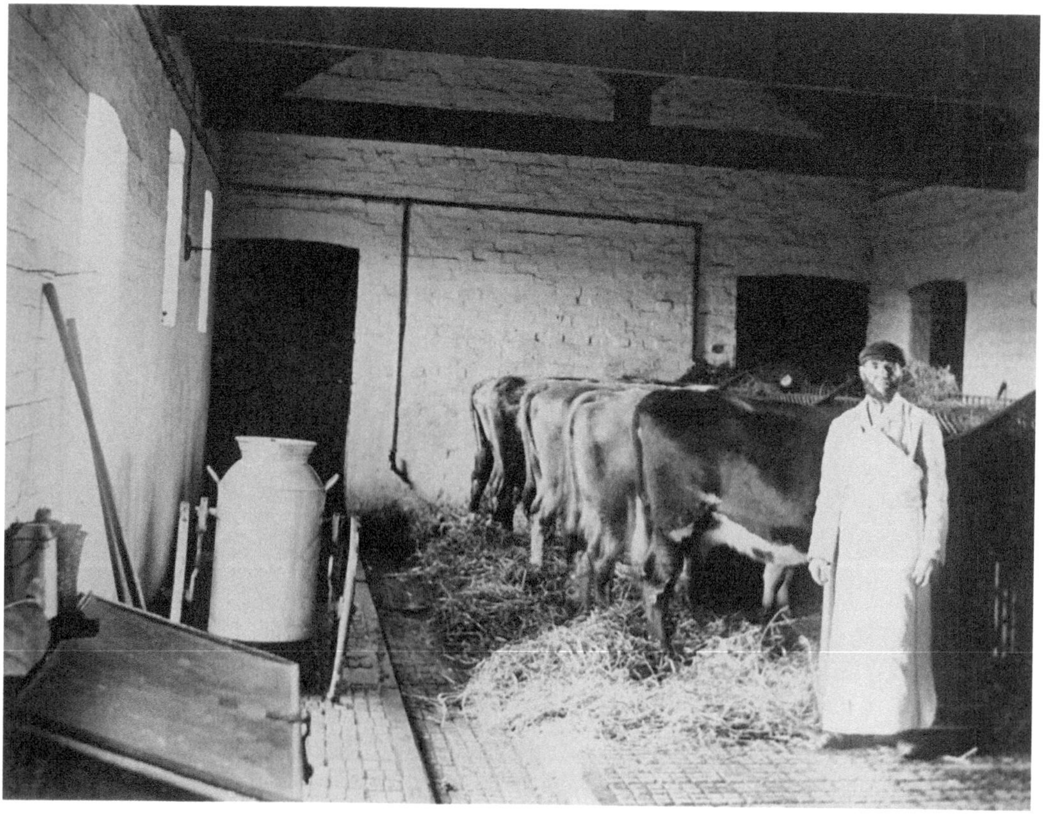

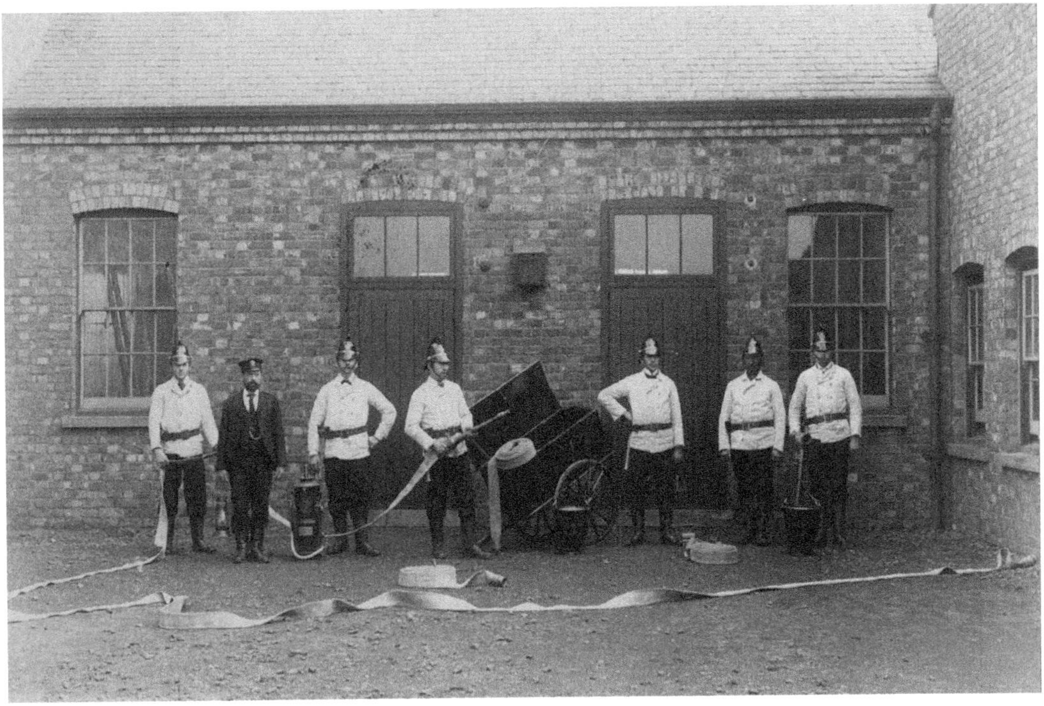

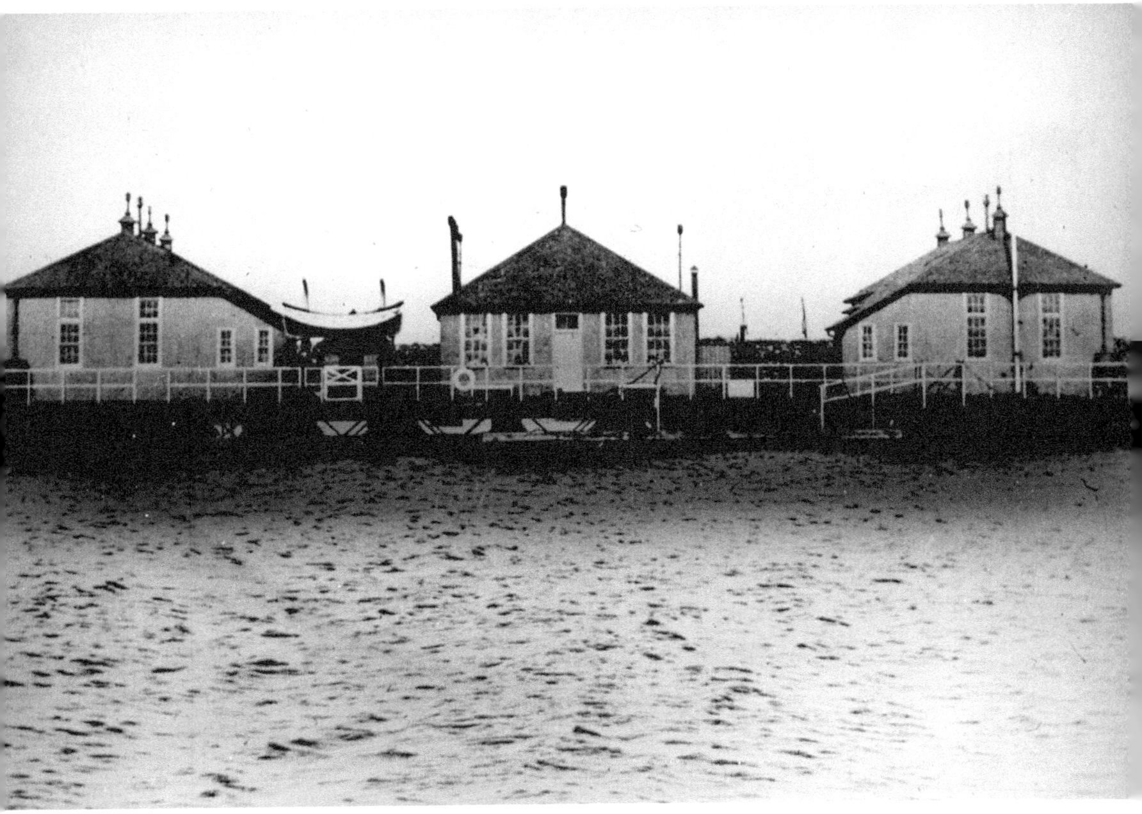

Other local titles published by The History Press

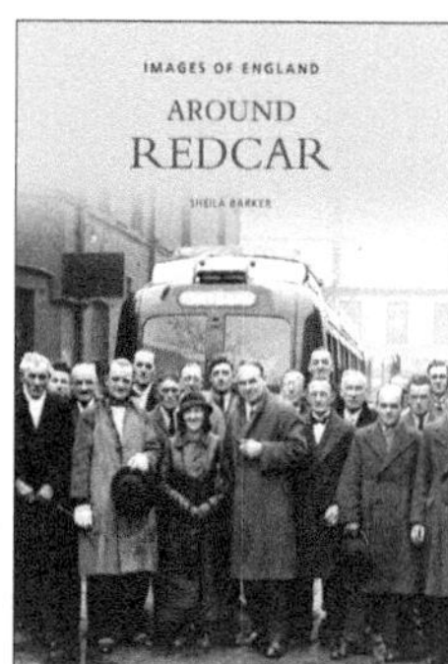

Around Redcar

SHEILA BARKER

This selection of over 220 old photographs illustrates some of the changes and events that have taken place in and around Redcar over the last century. The book also includes old images from the neighbouring communities of Coatham and Warrenby and recalls the life and times of local people at work and play throughout the area.

0 7524 3704 6

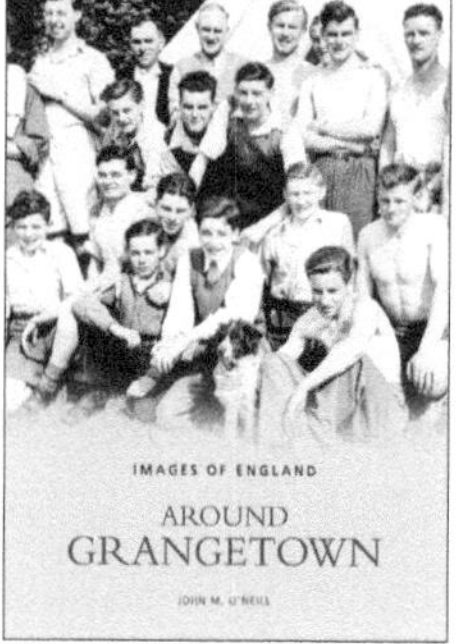

Around Grangetown

JOHN O'NEILL

This selection of over 200 images features some of the important events and developments that have taken place in this industrial town from Victorian times to the 1950s. It describes the impact of the iron and steelworks, which brought housing and employment to the area, and the effects of war on the community, as well as providing a unique pictorial history of aspects of everyday life, from schools and churches, pubs, shops and streets.

0 7524 3282 6

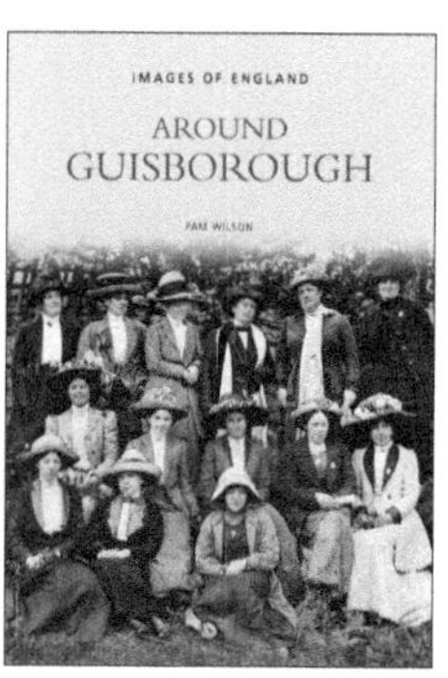

Around Guisborough

PAM WILSON

This collection of over 200 old photographs portrays life in and around the town of Guisborough during the last 150 years. From snapshots of horse-drawn vehicles and charabancs, annual carnivals and motorbike gymkhanas, to views of children playing in fields which now house new generations of Gisborians, each picture reveals the gradual physical change in the buildings and streets, and offers a unique glimpse into Guisborough's past.

0 7524 3075 0

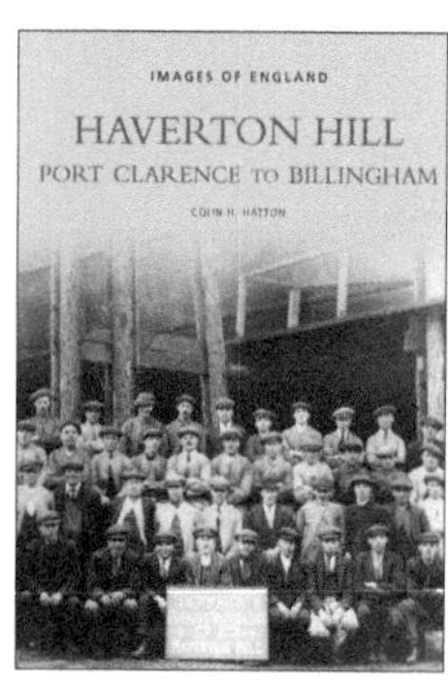

Haverton Hill Port Clarence to Billingham

COLIN HATTON

This nostalgic book of old images with supporting captions tells the story of three rich and varied communities which made up an industrial area covering the north bank of the river Tees. It describes the rise and subsequent decline of the steel and chemical industries and the railways, as well as aspects of everyday life: leisure, churches and chapels, schools, work and sport.

0 7524 3425 X